Flying Tiger

Flying Tiger

International Relations Theory and the Politics of Advanced Weapons

ULRICH KROTZ

OXFORD
UNIVERSITY PRESS

OXFORD
UNIVERSITY PRESS

Oxford University Press, Inc., publishes works that further
Oxford University's objective of excellence
in research, scholarship, and education.

Oxford   New York
Auckland   Cape Town   Dar es Salaam   Hong Kong   Karachi
Kuala Lumpur   Madrid   Melbourne   Mexico City   Nairobi
New Delhi   Shanghai   Taipei   Toronto

With offices in
Argentina   Austria   Brazil   Chile   Czech Republic   France   Greece
Guatemala   Hungary   Italy   Japan   Poland   Portugal   Singapore
South Korea   Switzerland   Thailand   Turkey   Ukraine   Vietnam

Copyright © 2011 by Oxford University Press

Published by Oxford University Press, Inc.
198 Madison Avenue, New York, New York 10016

www.oup.com

Oxford is a registered trademark of Oxford University Press

Library of Congress Cataloging-in-Publication Data
Krotz, Ulrich.
Flying Tiger : international relations theory and the politics of advanced weapons / Ulrich Krotz.
p.   cm.
Includes bibliographical references and index.
ISBN 978-0-19-975993-4 (alk. paper)
1. France—Foreign relations—Germany. 2. Germany—Foreign relations—France.
3. Tiger (Attack helicopter)—Design and construction—Political aspects—France.
4. Tiger (Attack helicopter)—Design and construction—Political aspects—Germany. 5. Defense
industries—Political aspects—France. 6. Defense industries—Political aspects—Germany. I. Title.
DC59.8.G3K76   2011
327.4404309'048—dc22   2010034277

1 3 5 7 9 8 6 4 2
Printed in the United States of America
on acid-free paper

für Peter Katzenstein

CONTENTS

Figure and Tables   ix
Acknowledgments   xi
Abbreviations   xv

1. Political Institutionalization, Social Construction, and Physical Reality   3

2. International Relations and National Interest   28

3. Why Cooperate? (1974–1982)   57

4. Bilateral Will and National Resilience (1982–1984)   84

5. Cost Explosions, Delays, Obstacles, Restoration (1984–1987)   108

6. Becoming Reality (1988–2009)   132

7. Findings, Conclusions, Implications   171

Appendix: Costs, Phases, Names   205
Notes   211
Bibliography   229
Index   247

FIGURE AND TABLES

7.1   Grand Sources of Historical Forces and Specific Factors   191

2.1   Institutionalization and Construction Between States   36
2.2   Historically Rooted Domestic Construction for France and
           Germany (late 1950s-late 1990s)   45
2.3   Interstate Relations and Domestic Construction   46
2.4   Interstate Relations and Domestic Institutional Structures   51
2.5   Sources of National Interest and Policy, and Role of
           Interstate Institutionalization in Selected International
           Relations Perspectives   55
3.1   Case 1: Coming Together (1974–1979):
           Institutionalist-Constructivist Model and
           Empirical Record   75
3.2   Case 1: Alternative Explanations and Possible Outcomes   79
7.1   Summary of Propositions and Outcomes   178
Appendix 1 Phases of Development and Production   207

ACKNOWLEDGMENTS

This book had too long a gestation. Going through my notes and recalling memories now, it strikes me as somewhat unreal at how many different offices, libraries, and archives I have worked on bits and pieces of what is now this book. The manuscript still draws on parts of my Cornell dissertation. Subsequently, while mostly working on other endeavors, the project accompanied me during very enjoyable years at Harvard and as a Jean Monnet Fellow at the European University Institute—my first two waystations after the doctorate. I remember happy days in my office in Oxford, reshaping and revising a first rough draft, while teaching in this university's splendid graduate program in international relations. At Brown, teaching and service in their own ways generated refreshing distance from the developing manuscript and the strange twists and turns that evolved in its historical reconstructions. Again at the European University Institute, this time as an EU Marie Curie Fellow, and then back at Brown, I completed the remaining research and drew together a first full draft that included the twenty-first-century developments. A sabbatical at Princeton as a visiting research scholar provided the time and resources to fully hammer out and polish the manuscript, while again working on other projects. It is time to bring this affair to a close.

A splendid group of scholars has accompanied and supported the development of this research project, and I am pleased to have the opportunity to acknowledge their help and goodwill, whether I have exactly followed their good advice or whether I have slightly (or not so slightly) modified it. Peter Hall, with humbling generosity, offered extensive written and oral comments—although I am not sure how much the present book resembles the project outline that he saw and heard me present too long ago. Andrew Moravcsik has not read or directly commented on this manuscript. But I feel that a series of frequently spirited discussions over the past decade has greatly helped to sharpen and strengthen the project. Helen Wallace, then the director of the Robert Schuman Centre for Advanced Studies, was a truly caring supporter during my second stay at the EUI, and I trust that she knows how much so. Kalypso Nicolaïdis insisted that I begin presentations of this project with a reference to James Bond. I was not fully convinced, but I trusted her. I now know that she was right. David Haglund offered precious and constructive comments on the entire manuscript, sharing his immense knowledge of Franco-German and European affairs in security and defense. John Ikenberry invited me to spend a year at the Princeton Institute for International and Regional Studies (PIIRS), which, while stimulating and refreshing in many ways, proved extremely valuable for this book manuscript, another one, and for other endeavors. At Brown, James Morone, with his indefatigable energy and optimism, has been a model of a senior colleague and supportive department chair. I feel lucky to have worked under his chairmanship during these years. Finally, two anonymous reviewers for Oxford University Press provided valuable comments that helped to prepare the ultimate draft.

Since this book reaches back to some of my dissertation work, it is appropriate to again thank the members of my wonderful dissertation committee at Cornell. Jonas Pontusson was among the very first people with whom I spoke in Ithaca, even before I physically arrived there. He soon became my seminar teacher, colloquium leader, and trusted advisor. While his own research agenda lay elsewhere, his pushing me with ever benevolent skepticism, always engaging, always encouraging, left a lasting impression on me of the power of scholarly integrity and open-mindedness. More than anyone else, Henry Shue taught me to think coherently about the connections between an analytically oriented empirical social science and the ethical dimensions of international relations and policy. The opportunity to observe how this trained analytic philosopher read political science texts remains among the great pleasures and lasting assets of these years. So does the rigor of his thought, his humane intellectualism, and his utmost and noble modesty. Sensing that it might help me in sorting out some of my own thinking, it was Henry who first alerted me to Richard Neustadt's book on the Skybolt affair, originally written as a report for President Kennedy in 1963. Unlike Neustadt, I did not have a letter from the president granting me access to all offices, persons involved, and sources of information. But I took Neustadt's report as a model of lucidity and precision in linking the pursuit of general questions with detailed and analytically important empirical inquiry. Whereas in some ways I ended up attempting to do for a period of almost four decades what Neustadt did for several months, I am not sure whether my own exercise much resembles what Henry might have had in mind. About Peter Katzenstein, the chair of this dissertation committee, I shall say a few words below.

A heterogeneous collection of friends and colleagues in one way or another accompanied me during parts of the journey leading to this book—commenting on parts of the manuscript, contributing the benefit of their own knowledge and expertise, or helping in a variety of other ways. In some cases, they have done so for decades: Rawi Abdelal, Peter Andreas, Jens Beckert, Melani Cammett, Pepper Culpepper, Andreas Daum, Matthew Evangelista, Ted Hopf, Stephan Jirgal,

Jennifer Lawless, Pauline Jones Luong, Damon Lehrer, William Phelan, Daniel Schiffbauer, Adam Segal, Richard Snyder, Nina Tannenwald, Hermann Weinmann, Dariuš Zifonun, and Alan Zuckerman. My childhood friend Sven has never read a single line that I wrote in English. As I left Germany for one kind of career, he embarked on an entirely different one, becoming a chef and a man of distinguished palate. Some decades later, it has become a staple of my life to sit in the cool yard of his restaurant during summer nights, often with books and papers and pencil.

Beyond those named above, the institutions that have hosted me over the years and provided offices, research assistants, and paychecks, and the friends and colleagues already mentioned, I am indebted to a variety of individuals, archives, and libraries in Berlin, Bonn, Frankfurt, Heidelberg, Ludwigsburg, Strasbourg, and Paris, where I collected most of the data for this book. I thank a number of interviewees who, for one reason or another, asked to remain anonymous. I particularly want to thank a few individuals who supplied me with extremely valuable documents for no other reason but their pleasure in supporting a research project.

Special thanks go to the Franco-German Institute (DFI) in Ludwigsburg. Without its library and collections, and its excellent staff, this research would hardly have been possible, and certainly not at this depth and analytically important detail. This research has also benefited from the European Union's MEIF-CT-2003-501292. For valuable research support over this project's long gestation, I thank Joanna Ardizzone, Xavier Froidevaux, Michael Jackson, Alan Johnson, Richard Maher, and Bérénice Manac'h. For superb editorial support over many years, often on short notice and under time pressure, I thank Sarah Tarrow.

The Institute for Qualitative Research Methods (IQRM) proved very helpful for honing this book's research design and solidifying its methodological grounding. Its organizers, not least Colin Elman and Andrew Bennett, among numerous others, merit great applause for establishing and managing this intensive and truly inspiring two-week workshop.

David McBride, my editor at Oxford University Press, deserves praise and respect. Before we began working together I knew only of his superb and impeccable reputation. And as I had suspected, the reputation was well deserved. I am deeply thankful for his support for this book and its ideas, which I felt from very early on, and I am appreciative of his professionalism and sincerity.

During all the years as I was moving around so often, the generosity of my parents, Hildegard and Wolfgang Richard Bernhard Krotz, afforded me the luxury of keeping some permanent quarters, and a reserved destination in which to read and write in seclusion. In addition to apartment, library, and study in the house where I grew up, this rock of permanence comes with a wine cellar, ample supplies of sausage and cheese, access to sports and concert halls, and the pleasures of two nearby spa towns. Without that anchor in southern Germany, at once refuge and home base, my life of the past two decades would not have been possible.

Finally, I am delighted for the opportunity to express my thankfulness to Peter Katzenstein. What I owe to him, in so many ways, remains enormous. It was after reading his work that I applied to Cornell an unsettlingly long time ago. I remember lying on the shores of Lake Constance reading two of his essays, although not among his most widely known works. One was a working paper on the difference it makes to think of the international sphere as structure or as context. The other was a book chapter on the future of international relations theory. After completing the reading and a brief swim in that beautiful lake at the foot of the Alps, I felt sure that where this came from was where I wanted to go to study and learn. I knew little about Cornell or upstate New York. And hardly anything about American graduate school. Peter is a key reason that it all turned out so much more thrilling and rewarding than I could even have imagined then. His teaching, guidance, and stature affected many of us—and surely this student—in profound and lasting ways, far beyond the classroom and academia. Peter was a *Doktorvater* in the ancient German meaning of the term. I often felt that it was not possible to have a better teacher. Then he became a colleague and, may I say, an elder friend. It is a great fortune to receive such gifts, and I shall do my best to pass them on. I dedicate this book to him. In respect, gratitude, and affection.

ABBREVIATIONS

AC3G   (Missile) Anti-Char de Troisième Génération (Third Generation Anti-Tank Missile)

AC3G-LP (Missile) Anti-Char de Troisième Génération à Longue Portée (Long Range Third Generation Anti-Tank Missile)

AGM   Air-to-Ground Missile

ALAT   Aviation Légère de l'Armée de Terre (Light Army Aviation)

ARH   Armed Reconnaissance Helicopter

ARTE   Association Relative à la Télévision Européenne (European Television Association)

BWB   Bundesamt für Wehrtechnik und Beschaffung (Federal Office for Defense Technology and Armament Acquisition)

CDU   Christlich Demokratische Union (Christian Democratic Union)

CFDT   Confédération Française Démocratique du Travail (French Democratic Work Confederation)

CFE   Confédération Française de l'Encadrement (Managers' or Supervisors' Union)

CFTC   Confédération Française des Travailleurs Chrétiens (French Confederation of Christian Workers)

CGC   Confédération Générale des Cadres (General Confederation of Office Workers)

CGT   Confédération Générale du Travail (General Work Confederation)

CNRS   Centre National de la Recherche Scientifique (National Center for Scientific Research)

CSU   Christlich Soziale Union (Christian Social Union)

DASA   Deutsche Aerospace

DGA	Délégation Générale pour l'Armement (General Armament Delegation)
DGA	Délégué Générale pour l'Armement (General Armament Delegate)
DM	Deutsche Mark
DFHB	Deutsch-Französisches Hubschrauberbüro (Franco-German Helicopter Office)
DOM-TOM	Département et Territoires d'Outre-Mer (Overseas Departments and Territories)
DTCA	Direction Technique des Constructions Aéronautique (Technical Direction of Aeronautic Constructions)
EADS	European Aeronautic Defence and Space Company
EC	Eurocopter
EC	European Community
EMU	Economic and Monetary Union
EU	European Union
FAR	Force d'Action Rapide (Rapid Action Force; in English, however, commonly: "Rapid Reaction Force")
FDP	Freie Demokratische Partei (Free Democratic Party)
FF	Franc Français
FO	Force Ouvrière
GIE	Groupement d'Intérêt Économique (Economic Interest Grouping)
GmbH	Gesellschaft mit beschränkter Haftung (Limited Liability Company)
HAC	Hélicoptère Anti-Char (Anti-Tank Helicopter)
HAC-3G	Hélicoptère Anti-Char de Troisième Génération (Antitank Helicopter capable of carrying third generation missiles)
HAP	Hélicoptère d'Appui et de Protection (Support and Protection Helicopter)
HOT	Haut-Subsonique Optiquement Téléguidé d'un Tube (High-Subsonic, Optically Teleguided, Tube-Fired) (Teleguided: Radio or Remote Controlled)
IGM/IG Metall	Industriegewerkschaft Metall (Industrial Union Metal)
ILA	Internationale Luftfahrtausstellung (International Aeronautic Fair, Berlin)
KRK	Krisenreaktionskräfte (Crisis Reaction Forces)
LAH	Light Attack Helicopter
LFK	Lenkflugkörper (Steerable Missile)
MBB	Messerschmitt-Bölkow-Blohm
MoU	Memorandum of Understanding
MTU	Motoren Turbinen Union

NATO	North Atlantic Treaty Organization
OCCAR/Occar	Organisme Conjoint de Coopération en Matière d'Armement (Common Organization for Armament Cooperation)
PAH-1	Panzerabwehrhubschrauber 1 (First Generation Anti-Tank Helicopter)
PAH-2	Panzerabwehrhubschrauber 2 (Second Generation Anti-Tank Helicopter)
PARS 3 LR	Panzerabwehrraketensystem der dritten Generation (Long Range Anti-Tank Missile System of the Third Generation)
PKK	Partiya Karkerên Kurdistan (Kurdistan Workers' Party)
RPR	Rassemblement pour la République (Rally for the Republic)
S.A.	Societé Anonyme (Stock Company)
SNIAS	Societé National Industrielle Aérospatiale
SPD	Sozialdemokratische Partei Deutschlands (German Social Democratic Party)
TADS/PNVS	Target Acquisition and Designation System/Pilot's Night Vision System
TEU	Treaty on European Union ("Maastricht Treaty")
UHU/Uhu/UH	Unterstützungshubschrauber (Support Helicopter)

Flying Tiger

1

Political Institutionalization, Social Construction, and Physical Reality

In the 1995 James Bond blockbuster "Golden Eye," the leading role is played by a helicopter. In the course of the movie, special agent Bond and other characters repeatedly allude to the aircraft's extraordinary capabilities and quality. This is product placement of a particular kind, as this helicopter is not a fantasy creation of the movie industry. The machine is real, the result of the largest, most expensive, and presumably most complicated Franco-German armament program since World War II. Baptized "Tiger," it is the most advanced and most powerful combat helicopter yet—as well as one of the most sophisticated killing machines.

The machine in question is a prototype of a combat helicopter of the second generation, which means several things. Most important, it means that the helicopter is fully equipped to carry and fire self-guiding and self-correcting "fire and forget" missiles. Once fired, these missiles practically find their targets by themselves. In its original design, the helicopter can simultaneously detect four targets—such as tanks, combat helicopters' classic prey—and shoot four "fire and forget" missiles within eight seconds. It can do so from a distance of up to 5,000 meters (about three and a half miles), entirely irrespective of weather conditions or available light. We can easily calculate what that means in terms of military capability: With a fleet of some 200 of these helicopters—as France and Germany each initially envisioned—the two states' armed forces could destroy hundreds and thousands of tanks within a few hours or days of combat.

Such high-tech, high-end, cutting-edge weaponry is fantastically expensive. Indeed, the costs directly or indirectly involved in this program are immense and have steadily risen since the earliest projections and program sketches in the 1970s. Some estimates of the early twenty-first century calculate the costs of the Tigers, excluding the very costly development and production of their arming, at around €7.5 billion (some $11 billion). The weapon system's total costs—including the definition, development, and production of the helicopter itself, its propulsion turbines, the development and production of its variable arming, and various taxes—may figure far into the double-digit-billion-Euro range for each of the two countries.

International relations theory offers explanations and predictions about the processes and outcomes of weapons development and production, allowing us to derive expectations regarding what states want and do in security, defense, and arming. In fact, policy areas that traditionally involve vast economic and industrial resources, significant financial and technological demands, and security stakes of the highest order provide an ideal arena to probe in empirical detail, according to the main theoretical perspectives and intellectual traditions in international relations, critical aspects of world politics and international history.

Underscoring the importance of external security threats in a formally anarchic international system, varying strands of realism emphasize strategic concerns and, at a minimum, the ability for territorial self-defense, along with the desire for defense-technological autonomy, as the key forces driving national interests and state policies. With its emphasis on domestic and transnational society, society-rooted liberalism focuses on the relevant defense industries, on the interests of organized society such as unions or employer associations, or perhaps on the influence of individual industrial leaders in shaping state preferences and public policies. Many of the Tiger dealings are situated in the fairly "institution rich" settings of bilateral Franco-German affairs which, presuming as given some minimal common interests, neoliberal institutionalism stresses as key in facilitating cooperation and formulating mutually beneficial policies. Thus, particularly dangerous, particularly expensive, and rather well institutionalized, armament affairs such as the history and politics of the novel Tiger combat helicopters comprise analytic territory that realist, liberal, and neoliberal perspectives have claimed—albeit for different reasons.

In contrast, the politics of arms production and the political economy of weapons procurement should provide particularly hard cases for social constructivism and historical institutionalism—especially when considering large and costly projects of extreme strategic importance. Matters of arms development and weapons production, thoroughly permeated by state power and national security concerns, the perhaps frequently recondite dealings of the defense industry (or the "military-industrial complex," for some), and the technocratic matters of defense research or details of high-tech weapons technology should prove especially impervious to the autonomous effects of social construction and historical institutionalization.

For these reasons, this book brings together distinct general theoretical views on how the world works, focusing on the particular kind of French-German security and defense history and politics stretching over nearly four decades from Cold War Europe in the 1970s into the early twenty-first century—at the beginning of an entirely new age of global politics. This study argues that specific types of institutionalization and construction between states affect the national interests and security policies of the states involved. This takes place under certain conditions and with certain contingencies. And it does so in time periods and policy areas in which we should least expect this to happen: cutting-edge advanced weapons production involving enormous financial and technological resources, in response to security threats of truly existential dimensions.

This study's findings suggest that—from what we know or can deduce from the most established perspectives in international relations theory—this immensely powerful and tremendously expensive combat helicopter, which James Bond showcases for a global audience of potential buyers, should not even exist, at least not in the shape and time in which it finally appeared. Nor should its history—rocky, fractured, and frequently highly politicized—have evolved as it did. This study offers explanations for the processes and outcomes that drove this history and ultimately brought about this highly advanced machine. The study's considerations and analyses are based on general concepts and propositions on the workings of international relations broadly. The book reconstructs the Tiger's adventurous and fragmented history in empirical detail and investigates it in its proper political context: almost four decades stretching back to the Cold War of the 1970s, when some 35,000 Warsaw Pact tanks behind the Iron Curtain posed a security threat to Western Europe of existential dimensions. Some thirty years after French and German military leaders' first "tactical demands" for a new-generation combat helicopter, the first series-produced Tigers were delivered to the French and German armed forces in the spring of 2005. And in 2009, three French Tigers flew their first military operations in Afghanistan.

Social constructivists in international relations commonly insist that only intersubjective structures of knowledge and understandings can *give meaning to the material world*.[1] In turn, historical institutionalists in both international relations and comparative politics emphasize the importance of historically contingent institutionalization in shaping historical processes and political outcomes.[2] This book draws on both styles of analysis. However, the historical record it presents suggests that historically shaped meanings as well as institutional and organizational configurations also help to *bring about and shape material reality*. Indeed, and strangely enough, they seem to do so in particularly unlikely time slices and policy areas, and in most improbable instances. This book's empirical explorations document how meaning structures and institutional configurations, both domestic and interstate, also helped to *produce* physical reality—in the form of a highly sophisticated weapons system with astonishing capabilities.

There is nothing esoteric about considering how institutionalization, construction, understandings, or meanings—what we think or how we think, individually or collectively—may produce or shape the physical or material world around us. That non-material factors such as aesthetic beliefs or inclinations of taste will literally affect the shape of the physical world surely goes without saying for landscape architects of the past as much as for skyscraper designers of architectural modernity. The same, no doubt, holds true for city and regional planners, sports car engineers, and philosophers of bonsai tree cultivation. With respect to thinking about defense, consider the fortified Italian hilltop villages of the sixteenth century, or Vauban's fortifications a century later. Perhaps tied to political thought more narrowly, less pleasing to the eye, and certainly less romantic from a twenty-or twenty-first century perspective, some kind of socialist political ideology and its concomitant constructions of necessity and appropriateness prompted the physical establishment of the Berlin Wall and the Iron Curtain, and nurtured their prolonged existence. Both edifices provide perhaps idiosyncratic yet certainly telling illustrations of how some kinds of thinking—no matter how absurd or misguided—affected the shape of the physical world.

In all of these instances, nonmaterial factors such as understandings of good or beautiful, constructions of necessity or adequacy, or meanings of rightfulness or appropriateness affected the shape of the material world. In most cases, to be sure, material factors such as financial constraints or matters of technical viability will intertwine with nonmaterial forces. And yet, in each of these instances it is in the first place social construction of a sort, and perhaps political institutionalization in addition, that gives shape to the physical world and helps to produce material reality.

Thus viewed, it is astonishing that international relations scholars have never systematically investigated how major aspects of international politics may shape the physical world in which we live. By focusing on the elements of political institutionalization and social construction that may characterize particular interstate relationships, this book specifically explores how certain kinds of relations between states—by definition central to the subject and discipline of "international relations"—may generate such effects. States may shape the physical world through their goals and actions. If interstate institutionalization and construction affects what states want and do—that is, their (national) interests and policies—the key link for understanding how some aspects of international politics in turn may affect physical reality is the potential (and presumably contingent) impact of such interstate institutionalization or construction on national interests and state actions.

This book particularly scrutinizes the potential impact of the relations between France and Germany on French and German interests and policies over an extended period. But it also operates with general concepts and formulates general theoretical considerations about the workings of international affairs. The ideas, hypotheses, and causal effects that this book explores are not specific to France-Germany (or European international affairs during the period covered, for that matter), but are general considerations to apply to similar sets of relations between states beyond the Franco-German experience. I return to these considerations in the concluding chapter.

After centuries of rivalry between French and German political units, for the some seven decades between the Franco-Prussian War in 1870–1871 and the end of World War II the tensions between France and Germany further escalated. During that period it was common in both countries to refer to the relations between France and Germany as "hereditary enmity," *enmitié héréditaire* and *Erbfeindschaft*. Following World War II, however, France and Germany managed to embark on a period of reconciliation (*réconciliation, Aussöhnung*). This phase of rapprochement—"the cornerstone of all subsequent Western European history"[3]—culminated and found its conclusion in the 1963 Elysée Treaty on Franco-German Cooperation and Friendship. Subsequently, upon and around this treaty the French and Germans installed a dense network of regularized consultation and communication that aimed at connecting the two states on a lasting basis. That network spans policy domains and governmental and administrative levels, comprising an entire host of joint Franco-German councils, commissions, and working groups.

Indeed, it seems that in many instances their tightly institutionalized relationship has affected what France and Germany want and do. However, such effects do not seem uniform. They vary. At times these relations help to bring about similar or compatible interests and policies, while at others there is little or no such impact. Why do their relations seem to affect French and German interests and policies to various degrees in some cases, but not in others? What are the conditions of such effects? What are their limits?

At the same time, these questions are only specific formulations of a general and basic set of questions in international relations, which drives this study and which it equally pursues: What are the conditions under which institutionalized relations between states affect what states want and do? When do such effects come to pass, and when do they not? Why do they appear at some times (although to different degrees), but not at others? The issue, to be sure, is not when states—in general, or more specifically for France-Germany in this book's empirical inquiries—subordinate national interests to joint common projects or undertakings, bilateral or otherwise, but the contingent nature with which institutionalization and construction between states affect the definition of their national interests and their formulation of policy in the first place. Whether posed with respect to two specific countries or more generally, the two sets of questions are congruent. Together, they form the point of departure for this book's considerations and inquiries.

Pursuing this pair of questions requires proper conceptualization of institutionalized interstate relations. Such a conceptualization enables us to connect the possible effects of the relations themselves with other factors of interests and policies, notably from domestic politics. Combining institutionalized relations with domestic factors leads me to formulate a constructivist-institutionalist model of national interest formation and foreign policy formulation. This model integrates domestic and system-level factors and generates a number of testable propositions with respect to this book's initial questions on the seemingly uneven and contingent effects of institutionalized relations on state interests and policies. Thereby this study conceives of institutionalization and construction at the interstate level as a separate causal factor or potential source of national interest and policy, and thus treats them conceptually separately and distinct from domestic factors.

This study's findings show that the inherent logic of the institutionalized relations between France and Germany indeed affected both French and German interests and policies over the almost four decades of history in arming and security affairs covered in this book, and thus indeed helped to bring about a particular kind of material reality in ways not yet researched or documented in international relations or the social sciences at large. Without the autonomous causal effects of the particular institutionalization and construction of their relationship, both French and German national interest definition and policy formulation would have taken very different shapes in many instances. Absent the institutional logic inherent to this specific set of relations, we cannot explain or comprehend either this machine's creation or its timing. Tiger combat helicopters would never have emerged, and the manifold processes and outcomes of these decades of European history and Franco-German armament politics would have been very different in many ways. However, this institutional logic of the interstate relations themselves does not suffice to explain the specific processes and outcomes that together make the Tiger's history. In interplay with the effects of the interstate relationship at the international level, the conditioning impact of both domestic construction and features of the domestic institutional order explain the degree and influence of such institutionalized relations in specific instances. Thus, domestic factors can function as facilitators (or "permittors"), inhibitors, or overrulers of the processes and purposes that these bilateral relations institutionalize.

The intricate, elongated, and multifaceted history of the Tiger combat helicopter provides ideal empirical domains to probe the hypotheses of this book's model of interest formation and policy definition and thus to explore some of the forces that drive international history and politics, shaping the world in which we live. The historical and political settings that situate this book's empirical inquiries should be particularly unlikely to witness autonomous effects of institutionalized relations and should generate especially difficult cases in which to investigate the seemingly variable and contingent effects of institutionalized interstate relationships.

This book reconstructs and dissects a history originating during a time when massive Warsaw Pact tank cohorts posed a fundamental threat to Western Europe's existence in Cold War Europe. Yet it is a political adventure story that stretches across the great 1989 divide and into the twenty-first century when, in quite different political and security environments, the delivery of the first series-produced Tiger combat helicopters to French and German forces in turn opened an era with the Tiger as an international export commodity. This study's analytic endeavors and empirical inquiries aspire to contribute to our knowledge of international relations theory and the general workings of world politics, aspects of arms procurement and state arming, Franco-German affairs, and European international history and politics.

Research Questions and Analytic Tasks

With the 1963 Treaty on Franco-German Cooperation and Friendship, commonly termed the "Elysée Treaty" after the French presidential palace where President de Gaulle and Chancellor Adenauer signed the document, France and Germany established a new foundation for their bilateral relationship. Along with various extensions and additions, and supplemented by a host of symbolic acts and gestures as well as a gamut of state-funded and -organized societal exchanges, the French and Germans developed and increasingly deepened the new foundations of their relations. New institutional framing and consolidating novel construction of Franco-German relations opened an era in which European academics and journalists referred to France and Germany collectively with a vocabulary suggesting that the "Carolingian twins" somehow belonged together as a "tandem," "couple," or "pair." Indeed, in both countries expectations were frequently high that the two would find common denominators or joint positions in foreign policy matters—on the basis of their densely institutionalized relationship. Many Europeans assumed that Franco-German relations did and should affect French and German interests and foreign policies. These expectations frequently seemed fulfilled but were also often disappointed, resulting in a sense of failure and crisis. At the same time, the bilateral Franco-German relationship simultaneously remained characterized by recurrent disagreements and tensions, by deviating interests, positions, and objectives. "The more the two countries approach each other," a *Le Monde* observer once crystallized the matter, "the more their differences, even their misunderstandings, come to light."[4]

Thus, the impact of the institutionalized set of Franco-German relations on French and German "foreign policy will-building processes"[5] is uneven and contingent. Why do these relations seemingly vary in their effects on what the governments of the two states define as French and German national interests, on the basis of which they formulate policies? What is the causal impact of these relations, to which French and Germans have accorded so much importance during the twentieth century's second half? Why do they influence certain difficult foreign policy matters, while in others they do not allow the two states to adjust their interests or find common positions? When do such effects take place and when do they not? Under what conditions and with which limits do they take place? Why do these relations at times have more, less, or no impact on French and German national interests and foreign policies?

These questions only exemplify particular instances of a matching broader and more general set of issues in the study of international relations and foreign policy. They ask, put generally, about the possibility, contingencies, and limits of the potential impact of interstate relations, institutionalized in some way, on the interests and policies of the states involved in them. When do they matter? Why in some instances, but not in others? Sometimes the impact of such relations on the interest definition and policy formulation of the states involved is stronger, at other times weaker, and at yet other times altogether absent. Why do the institutional arrangements—patterns of particular interaction practices and institutionalized social meanings that make up institutionalized interstate relationships—sometimes generate or modify interests and policies among those involved in them to different degrees, and sometimes not at all?

Questions such as these address the bearings on goals and actions endogenous to the relations among states themselves. Such endogenous effects seem to pertain to some sets of interstate relations. But they also seem fragile and highly contingent. Thus viewed, these questions address a core issue in international theory: the possibility and conditions for one kind of international institutionalization to affect the interests and policies of the states in the system—i.e., what they want and do. Through their interests and actions, states in turn may shape the material world or help to bring about physical reality. Whether formulated with respect to France and Germany during the time period under review or put generally, the two sets of questions belong together. They are two sides of the same coin. Together, they represent this book's point of departure.

Pursuing these questions first requires careful conceptualization of the social materials that compose institutionalized interstate relations and the social fabric that constitutes them. Only a firm conceptual grasp of the makeup of such relations enables us to seriously explore their potential effects on those involved in them. The conceptual building blocks and categories crafted to properly capture institutionalized relations between states need to be formulated to enable us to hypothesize generally and systematically about the possible effects of such relations.

In turn, however, generally defined concepts allow us to focus on the particular institutional substance of specific institutionalized relations, and to examine the logic of particular sets of relations—their institutional practices, interaction patterns, and inherent social meaning—during specific and delimited time periods. Chapter 2 defines a number of categories as the conceptual building blocks of institutionalized interstate relations. Within these categories, the chapter then reviews the institutional bedrocks of the relations between France and Germany during the time that most concerns this book's analytic goals and historical inquiries, the period between the mid-1970s and the late 1990s.

The initial questions about the effects of Franco-German relations on French and German interests and policies, and about the effects of institutionalized interstate relations on the interests and policies of those involved in them generally, also direct our attention to other determinants of national interest and foreign policy, notably from domestic politics. Such internal factors by themselves may help shape what states want and do; or they may mediate, condition, or undermine the potential impact of institutionalized external relations on interest formation and policymaking. Variable constellations between the potential effects of the institutional logics of specific interstate relations and other determinants of interest and policy may thus explain why institutionalized interstate relations vary in causal efficacy across time slices and policy areas.

A proper conceptualization of "institutionalized relations" not only enables us to capture and comprehend the institutional logic inherent to certain sets of relations between states but also allows us to connect this ("relational") factor with other putative factors of national interest and foreign policy. In particular, it enables us to juxtapose "institutionalized interstate relations" with domestic factors of interest and policy. Thus, searching for answers to the initial questions, we may think systematically about the interplay between the external impact of institutionalized interstate relations and internal factors from domestic politics broadly.

Some domestic political factors or forces might permit institutionalized interstate relationships to take on causal relevance. Other domestic influences will undermine, neutralize, or override potential "relational" effects on national interests and policies. Are there particular constellations or configurations between domestic-intrinsic and external-relational factors that are more prone to the possible impact of institutionalized external relations? Can we hypothesize about general patterns that particular constellations between internal-domestic and external-relational factors generate regarding the effects of institutionalized relations on the interests and policies of those involved in them?

In chapter 2, this book develops a constructivist-institutionalist model of national interest formation and foreign policy formulation. This model directly connects "institutionalized relations" as a potentially autonomous source of national interest and foreign policy with the two big domestic sources of state interests and policies: domestic construction, and features of the domestic political system (or domestic institutional configurations). The model conceives of interstate institutionalization and construction, domestic construction, and the domestic political system broadly as three separate sources of national interest and policy (although with interrelating or contingent effects), thus treating them as separate concepts. It generates a number of testable propositions with respect to the study's initial questions about the possibility, conditions, and limits of institutionalized interstate relations affecting the national interests and foreign policies of those involved in them.

Focusing on variable constellations between external-relational and internal-domestic influences, this model permits us to hypothesize systematically about the contingent effects of institutionalized relations of national interest formation and foreign policy formulation generally, and of the institutionalized Franco-German relations on French and German interests and policies during the given specific time period in particular. The model sharpens our look at the political processes and outcomes through which state interests and foreign policies take shape, and the role that the institutionalized relations thereby may play.

"National interest," in this book's usage, signifies what states *want* at a given time or time period and policy domain. It comprises their "goals," "desires," "objectives," and "positions," and in this study I consider all of these terms synonymous. This understanding of national interest is fairly common among scholars of diverse theoretical and political provenances, although realists and constructivists tend to employ "interests" while liberals may prefer the terms "preferences" or "state tastes."[6] National interests thus viewed may have different roots and take shape through different internal and external political processes. They may be products of a variety of factors and influences including systemic pressures, international political contexts, various domestic constructions, domestic political culture, party ideologies, domestic economic interests, and societal pressures, as well as the inclinations of single persons in or near the political authority centers. Governments or governmental entities execute the ultimate defining of national interests at a given time and policy issue area. Thus, national interest is historically changeable and is contingent upon variable internal and external political and cultural context.

In this conception, national interests need explanation both as *process* and as *outcome*. Grasping national interest formation as *process* implies explaining and comprehending how one gets there—that is, elucidating which sources, factors, or influences matter when, to what degree, and under what conditions. With respect to process, the task is to explain the mechanisms and conditions under which various sources contribute to the formation of interests; it involves careful "causal process tracing" over time.[7] Thus, national interests form through more or less politicized processes and evolve into more or less contested outcomes.

National interest as *outcome* (content, substance) is what results at the end of a (however delimited) process. This process necessitates explaining what exactly it is that states want at a given time in a certain policy field. Explaining national interests as outcomes involves "structured focused comparisons" of variable constellations among causal factors and outcomes in delimited and delimitable time slices. This may involve both within-case and cross-case analysis.[8]

"Policy" is that which states *do*. Policies are state actions. States act based on what they want—that is, their interests drive policies. Just as they authoritatively define national interests, governments or governmental entities formulate and ultimately adopt policies. How directly or immediately interests translate into policies will also depend on the particular international or domestic political constraints and opportunities in a given policy domain and time or time period. If a state's policy relates to the outside world or is tied to external behavior, as is mostly the case in this study, it is foreign policy. National interests and foreign policies, thus, are historical products of social and political processes. The relevance of construction and institutionalization between states in shaping national interests—which then drive the policies through which states may shape or produce material reality—is at the analytic core of this monograph.

Findings and Arguments in Brief

The institutionalization of interstate relationships implies the establishment of practices, procedures, and social meanings that may endow these relationships with particular intrinsic logics or dynamics. The procedures and meanings inherent to such logics may affect the national interest formation and foreign policy formulation of the states involved in an institutionalized relationship. The potential autonomous effects of interstate relationships, however, are not uniform across time and policy issues. Their impact depends on variable constellations with factors from the domestic political arena of the states involved. This study's constructivist-institutionalist model enables us to hypothesize generally about the uneven and contingent impact of interstate institutionalization and construction on the interests and policies of those involved.

Uneven Effects

It is clear from the historical record of the almost four-decades-long history of the Tiger combat helicopter armament program that the institutionalized relations between France and Germany indeed affected what the two states wanted and how they acted on manifold occasions and in many different historical instances. Without the causal impact of their institutionalized relations on French and German national interest definition and policy formulation, their interests and policies would have taken very different shapes at many important junctures of the Tiger armament history. The overall outcomes of this history would have been very different, and many decisive specific processes would have taken very different directions. In the absence of the pre-configured procedures and social meanings of their institutionalized interstate relationship, France and Germany would not have seriously considered acquiring new tank-killer helicopters as a bilateral cooperation project in the 1970s. Nor would they have recommenced it after several difficulties and failures, or rescued the program from discontinuation on various other occasions during the 1980s. The Tiger helicopter would not have taken the physical and technological shape that it did. In fact, it would never have emerged as the remarkable piece of high-end aeronautic and military technology that eventually resulted.

However, the autonomous effects of the proceedings and meanings inherent to institutionalized interstate relations are not uniform across time and policy issues. Rather, they are uneven and contingent. Importantly, they depend on the modulating impact of factors from the domestic political affairs of the states involved. French and German domestic political affairs, for example, in some instances proved particularly prone to permitting the logic of the Franco-German relations to take effect. In contrast, in other instances domestic politics modified, dampened, or overrode the impact on interests and policies generated by the web of their institutionalized relationship.

Institutionalized Relations Themselves

In order to capture their inherent logics, I differentiate the separate elements that together make up institutionalized interstate relations. Conceptually, I distinguish among three components: (1) regularized intergovernmentalism, that is, regularized, chiefly "business-like" patterns of political-administrative interaction and communication; (2) a host of predominantly symbolic acts and practices by public representatives; and, potentially, (3) a net of parapublic underpinnings that stabilizes the other two elements of institutionalized relations.

Together, these components constitute an institutional reality that incorporates behavioral elements of more or less robustly institutionalized interaction practices as well as social constructions of meaning and purpose. The specific manifestations of institutionalized interaction and meaning may vary across interstate dyads, across policy areas within particular interstate relationships, or across time with respect to both. More important, however, this conceptual breakdown makes it possible to grasp institutionalized relations as a potential factor of national interest formation and policy formulation, and thus to investigate empirically the potential autonomous causal effects that such relations themselves may exert—in very specific situations and policy contexts, with respect to concrete political questions, and at particular points in time or during delimited time periods. The relationships' inherent logics and potential impact, thus, are empirically accessible at very specific times and places, allowing the scrutiny of their observable political implications.

In the Franco-German instance, the first component comprises the dense network of regularized interaction, consultation, and communication, with different interaction densities across policy domains and among governmental and administrative levels of hierarchy. A large part of this Franco-German intergovernmentalism followed from the Elysée Treaty of 1963 and its extensions and additions. It includes the semiannual Franco-German summit meetings, which now resemble joint Franco-German cabinet meetings,[9] and incorporates numerous Franco-German councils and commissions. Further extended and deepened at the turn of the century, a dense net of regularized Franco-German intergovernmentalism encompasses nearly all policy fields and core ministries.[10]

Alongside these regularized intergovernmental "working relations," the Franco-German relationship includes a host of symbolic gestures, rituals, and ceremonies that infuse additional social meaning and purpose into these relations. Such symbolic acts and practices include, among many others, the affectionate gestures by Adenauer and de Gaulle, the memorable image of Kohl and Mitterrand holding hands in joint mourning and recognition of the dead in Verdun, and the parade of Franco-German troops on the Champs-Elysées. Some of these symbolic acts are more or less recurrent events, such as the celebrations at the anniversaries of the Elysée Treaty or the now ceremonial first visit of one country's new head of state or government to the capital of the other. Others, despite being single events, are meaningful as integral parts of the overall fabric. Such predominantly symbolic acts are not directly connected to finding solutions to problems, defining interests, or policies. They are embedded in a wider cultural context comprising Franco-German places of memory of a communal history and "Franco-German couples." Symbolic acts are important and effective because they generate, reproduce, and corroborate meaning, purpose, and direction. They preserve and perpetuate the legitimacy of Franco-German friendship well beyond specific choices, immediate ends, or single cooperation projects.[11]

In addition to regularized intergovernmental contacts and predominantly symbolic practices, institutionalized interstate relations may include what I term "parapublic underpinnings" of international relations. These are publicly funded or organized cross-border interactions that are not intergovernmental, but also do not autonomously originate in the private civil societies of the respective countries. Absent the aegis of the state, its funding and its organizational leadership, such contacts and their institutional effects would not exist. The Franco-German web of parapublic underpinnings consists of three main pillars. The first is a wide range of youth and educational exchanges, crowned by the activities of the Franco-German Youth Office, which has brought together some 7 million young French and Germans since its institution in 1963. Second, there are some 2,000 Franco-German city and regional partnerships (*jumelages*, *Partnerschaften*). The third pillar consists of a host of academic and research institutes, associations, and publications committed to the Franco-German end. Beyond these three pillars, there is a range of parapublic organizations, including the Franco-German television channel ARTE and a long list of Franco-German prizes, commemorations, and other activities. These parapublic underpinnings corroborate and stabilize the public institutionalized contacts between the two states. They supply them with personnel and themes, as well as with social meaning and purpose.[12]

The regularized intergovernmentalism, predominantly symbolic acts and practices, and parapublic underpinnings of the Franco-German relationship generate a specific blend of institutionalized interaction and historically constructed meaning and social purpose. This institutional reality is irreducible to French and

German domestic politics and is separate and distinct from both. Its impact should be empirically accessible in specific policy areas, with respect to specific political questions, and at specific points or delimited periods of time. This study hypothesizes about and explores empirically the causal implications of the overall logic of such institutionalization and construction between states.

Model and Propositions

Proper conceptualization enables us not only to grasp empirically the institutional logic inherent to institutionalized interstate relationships but also to connect institutionalized relations with other putative factors of national interest and foreign policy, most notably from domestic politics. In order to pursue this study's original questions about the possibility, conditions, and limits of the effects of institutionalized (Franco-German) relations on (French and German) national interests and foreign policies, chapter 2 formulates a constructivist-institutionalist model of national interest formation and foreign policy formulation. The model suggests that, first, whether and how strongly institutionalized interstate relations affect state interests and foreign policy formulation depends on the characteristics of the relations themselves, as well as on the direction in which an institutionalized interstate relationship pulls or pushes interest formation and policy formulation in a given time period and with respect to a specific policy question. Second, it depends on the effects of factors from the major domestic sources of interests and policies: domestic construction and domestic institutional structures.

Factors from two different kinds of domestic sources. Among a variety of domestic constructions, I specifically focus on historically rooted elements of collective self-construction. These involve domestically shared views and (self-)understandings regarding the proper and suitable role and purpose of one's own state in the international arena. Internally anchored reference systems, they affect interests and policies. They may complement or be in tension with other factors of interests and policies.

Regarding the domestic institutional features of state and society organization, I focus on domestically rooted aspects of "state strength." State strength is composed of two elements: the degree of centralization with which interests and policies are authoritatively fixed and adopted within the system; and the degree of state autonomy from the influence and pressure of (organized) society. In a strong state, governments define interests at a high level of centralization with a high degree of autonomy from society. The more fragmented and dispersed political authority becomes, and the more society's influence on national interest definition and policy adoption increases, the further state strength diminishes.

Constellations and Observations. By systematically relating factors from institutionalized relations themselves with those of domestic construction and domestic institutional features of the state and state-society relations, we can hypothesize generally about particular constellations among interstate relations logic and the effects stemming from the domestic political arenas of the states involved in such relations. The effects of institutionalized relations should be strongest in the absence of tensions between external relations' effects and domestic construction regarding the proper and suitable role and purpose of one's own state in the international arena. The stronger such tensions, the weaker the institutionalized relations' impact on interests and policies. If the inducements of institutionalized interstate relations directly conflict with interests or policies deriving from historically rooted domestic constructions of either one or both of those involved in such relations, the effects of these relations decline.

Similarly, the causal effects of institutionalized Franco-German relations should generally increase with high degrees of centralization of domestic political authority and high levels of state autonomy from the influence of organized society. On the other hand, fragmentation and dissipation of political authority in the domestic systems and low degrees of state autonomy tend to undermine such effects on national interests and foreign policies.

These general theoretical considerations, hypothesized in chapter 2, function as explanatory guides through the political and historical explorations of chapters 3–6. In those chapters, I test these propositions and their analytic value in explaining *what* interests and policies have formed and *why* they have taken shape in their particular way. These chapters also draw explicit comparisons between the constructivist-institutionalist model's propositions and alternative explanations of French and German interest formation and policy formulation in the respective contexts derived from the major macro-perspectives on international affairs, realism, neoliberalism, and liberalism.

The historical observations presented in this book's empirical chapters document that in some cases institutionalized bilateral processes molded or reconfigured French and German objectives and policies. In other issues, the relations had no effect on interest generation or-modification. In all of these cases, I trace in detail how French and German interests have formed, and how France and Germany acted upon them.

Overall, the general propositions that the constructivist-institutionalist model puts forth proved valuable in shedding light on the study's original questions. In numerous instances, they explained diverse processes and outcomes and the degrees to which the institutionalized Franco-German relationship affected or did not affect French and German interests. In other cases, the model's hypotheses partially captured historical processes and outcomes, and dynamics of national interest and policy definition. In one of the cases that the empirical chapters analyze, altogether different factors and forces outside the constructivist-institutionalist model decisively affected the course and outcomes of an important slice in the Tiger's overall history.

Empirical Inquiries and Presentation

The politics and history of the Tiger combat helicopter program provide ideal empirical domains to pursue this study's research questions. This book slices its almost four decades of armament history into four major periods and then further divides the data into twelve separate case studies. For its empirical inquiries, this book draws on a wide range of primary and secondary sources.

Selection Criteria

Why this program? Why this combat helicopter? Why study the intricate and protracted history of an arms program in great detail? For a variety of reasons, this most comprehensive, expensive, and frequently highly politicized joint Franco-German armament project provides excellent empirical grounds on which to pursue this book's basic questions and test the propositions of its insti-tutionalist-constructivist model. The Tiger armament program's key political episodes also offer ample opportunity for detailed in-case analysis, as well as numerous cross-case comparisons, and to draw comparisons with alternative explanations derived from the major currents of international thought. The various aspects and episodes of this overall history should provide particularly difficult empirical grounds on which to test chapter 2's hypotheses on "who wants and does what, when, and why." The Tiger's history and politics encompass empirical territory and issues for which other theoretical perspectives claim particular analytic relevance or explanatory supremacy.

Realists commonly focus on security threats and their implications. The massive Warsaw Pact tank threat surely constituted a fundamental risk to the territorial survival of the continental Western European states. Because combat helicopters—dubbed "tank killers" by some commentators—are the most effec-tive weapon against tanks, interests and policies in the related policy realms should be driven primarily by realist logic. Neoliberal institutionalists, in con-trast, focus on the efficiency-improving gains that international institutions may provide and allow states to reap. In an "institution-rich" environment such as the Franco-German relationship, and in light of presumable common interests in providing security in the most efficient ways in policy areas that involve great costs, neoliberal institutionalist expectations should particularly apply in affect-ing the processes and outcomes at hand. Domestic politics liberals, in turn, emphasize the importance of domestic economic interests and various pressure groups of organized society. Given the huge material stakes associated with the development and production of cutting-edge weaponry, the factors on which they concentrate should shape the histories and outcomes of major armament projects: Arms programs should be decisively driven by domestic societal actors such as the armament industry, unions, or other organized societal interests. In brief, the empirical domains best suited for this book's analytic endeavors should involve politics in issue areas as dangerous and as expensive as possible. Further, they should allow particular focus on Franco-German political affairs and should reasonably allow us to expect variation among causal factors over time or issues.

To begin with, on the national security side, the empirical inquiries to be selected had to involve very significant security stakes (rather than subsidiary ones). The history of the Tiger concerns core areas of foreign, security, and defense policy. It involves security issues of truly existential dimensions for both France and Germany. Next to the nuclear danger, a massive Warsaw Pact tank attack was the most severe security threat to Cold War Western Europe. In terms of mere numbers, during the 1970s and 1980s the tank ratio of the Warsaw Pact to the North Atlantic Treaty Organization (NATO) ranged from 35,000–45,000 to 10,000–15,000 (the latter figures add France's tanks to NATO's). Combat helicopters were considered the prime anti-tank weapon. The history of the Tiger originates and takes shape as a national security issue of the highest order.

Next, economic stakes, strains on resources, and financial commitments had to be severe (rather than marginal). It was clear from the earliest French and German considerations in the first half of the 1970s that the costs of acquiring new-generation combat helicopters would be enormous.[13] During the first half of the 1970s, the German Ministry of Defense estimated the development costs at only about a quarter billion deutsche marks (for Germany alone). By January 1986, estimates had arrived at FF 4,317 million for France and FF 3,963 million for Germany, with additional acquisition costs calculated at between DM 3 and DM 4 billion for each country. In the new century, various official sources estimate the total program costs (still apparently excluding the development and production of the helicopters' turbines as well as the development and production of the arming) at €7.5 billion or more.

The Tiger's ultimate overall costs are still difficult to calculate and involve some secrecy. Its final total costs, evidently, will also depend on how many Tigers France and Germany eventually acquire. It is now highly unlikely that the French and German forces will receive 215 and 212 machines respectively, as initially envisaged and still confirmed in 1999. As of 2008, France projects ultimately obtaining 120 Tigers, and Germany at least 80. Depending on the version and exact finishing, in the early twenty-first century the Tiger's unit costs are expected to figure between approximately €24 and €30 million apiece or more (and likely to rise). Including definition, development, and production of the helicopter as well as its propulsion turbines; the development and production of the Tiger's variable arming (commonly excluded from cost figures), particularly the costly third-generation "fire and forget" missiles; and various taxes, the Tigers' overall costs for France and Germany may figure deep into the double-digit-billion-Euro range. The Tiger's incipient career as an international export article will further contribute to making Tiger matters a multi-billion-Euro affair.

Further, the empirical materials had to concern primarily the bilateral relations between France and Germany. Since I wanted to learn specifically about the
Franco-German relationship's impact on French and German interests and policies, I sought to study political matters in which the potentially disturbing effects
of the two states' other institutionalized relations could be kept constant or as low
as possible (*ceteris paribus*). The history of the Tiger program broadly, for the most
part a Franco-German one, minimizes the possible effects of other institutionalized bi-or multilateral relations, particularly those in the European Community/
European Union (EC/EU) and NATO contexts.[14]

Finally, the empirical material should provide as much variation as possible in
constellations between interstate logic and domestic factors that this study's institutionalist-constructivist model generated in hypothesizing on the contingent
effects of institutionalized interstate relations. A perfunctory glance at the combat helicopter's history suggested that there would be wide variation in the factors
and constellations that I had defined.

History and Cases

Chapters 3–6 reconstruct some four decades of French, German, Franco-
German, and European security, defense, and armament politics with respect to
the Tiger's history broadly. This history begins in the early 1970s, after the French
and German armies had formulated their initial demands for new helicopters. In
1975, the French and German Defense Ministers first exchanged notes regarding
the possibility of the joint development of a Franco-German combat helicopter.
The period from the late 1970s to the mid-1990s, frequently politically turbulent,
more than once saw the potential Franco-German helicopter program practically
defunct or on the verge of being aborted; it decisively shaped the Tiger as a
cutting-edge weapon and piece of physical reality. In 1999, France and Germany
ultimately ordered the first batch of eighty series-produced helicopters, which,
after many difficulties and much politicking, they had designed and developed
together. The first of these Tigers were delivered to the French and German armed
forces in the early twenty-first century, with other states' Tigers to follow soon. In
August and September 2009, three French Tigers flew initial combat missions in
the fight against the Taliban in Afghanistan—far from the targets originally envisioned for this advanced weapons system some thirty-five years before. During
these decades, four French presidents have led the country and four chancellors
headed the German government, a dozen or so prime ministers of various French
governments and many more French and German ministers have come and gone,
a superpower collapsed and a Cold War ended, and France and Germany each
won the world championship in soccer.

These four chapters also dissect this history. I have first disaggregated
the time period from 1974 to 2009 into four main temporal sequences, each

beginning or ending with a major signpost, contract, or governmental agreement of the overall process: 1974–1982, 1982–1984, 1984–1987, and 1988–2009.[15] Each of the empirical chapters covers one of these main periods. I then further cut these four main slices into numerous temporal episodes or topical slices as units of investigation.[16] This yields twelve rather different cases at different times regarding very disparate and concrete political issues from the overall empirical investigation.[17]

These cases range from such diverse matters as the basic issues—such as why cooperate in the first place, and on what terms—to strategic and tactical issues related to the development of a new-generation helicopter at an early stage. They also concern very specific technical matters such as the helicopter's weight, arming, military performance requirements, the origins of major components, and matters of financing and scheduling the project. From the late 1980s on, I examine general political questions associated with the project such as export policy, as well as the organizational and industrial implementation of this arms procurement program.

Although all connected to the overall program, many of these cases are little related to one another. Obviously, for instance, the financial difficulties of the 1990s would not have pertained to the common helicopter project if France and Germany had not "come together" and started the program in the late 1970s and early 1980s. They are temporally contingent. On the other hand, many of the political issues around the helicopter program that I discuss as cases in their respective time slots are so little related that one can consider them as independent in their historical substance. The case of the potential Tiger export to Turkey, for example, is an empirical case independent from, say, the just as political issue of which targeting and night vision system to include in the helicopter's physical configuration. Many of the twelve cases are time dependent on each other; but they concern a large number of processes and outcomes in diverse political contexts over more than three and a half decades.

What is it that qualifies each of these episodes as a case or case study? What makes these case studies comparable, what unifies them?[18] To begin with, the political and historical relevance for the overall history and program gives each of the twelve cases its significance and justifies the particular attention that presentation as a case warrants. Together, these major decisions, intermediary outcomes, or most significant signposts decisively compose and shape the overall history that chapters 3–6 reconstruct: Each case analyzes a distinct and distinguishable outcome (or set of outcomes) that is important both on its own terms and for this book's historical explorations.

Second, and equally important, the book's general analytic purposes bring these cases together and make them comparable: Each case is distinct and separate enough to offer a discrete opportunity to test chapter 2's hypotheses with respect to the general constellations between interstate relations and domestic construction on the one hand, or interstate relations and domestic structures on the other, as well as various alternative explanations derived from the main perspectives in international relations theory.[19]

Thus, the cases of chapters 3–6 at once allow us to scrutinize all important issues broadly and inclusively associated with the politics and political economy of this history of Franco-German arms development and production, and to examine a number of big, general theoretical ideas of how the world works in very specific settings and in great empirical detail. Frequently, this involves investigating political interaction, government choices, and courses of events—sometimes politically highly charged and at other times involving regularized routine politics—in almost daily detail. These cases' empirical relevance serves the purpose of reconstructing the main aspects of the almost forty years' history taken on by chapters 3–6; their theoretical relevance allows us to pursue this study's analytic goals and to probe some general theoretical propositions. The combination of both qualifies and unifies them.[20]

Each of the chapters 3–6 starts out with two or more purely empirical sections. These sections reconstruct the course of historical events related to Franco-German armament politics broadly and depict how French and German interests and policies evolved in these areas, both chronologically and by topic. These sections, historical narratives, serve to lay out the course of events and are followed by two analytic and explanatory sections whereby I distinguish between "processes" and "outcomes."

The analytic sections on "processes" particularly consider the social context and the reference frame of historical institutionalization and social construction informing the armament history and politics under review. They are geared to clarifying and comprehending the historical forces and social meanings and purposes underlying and driving the political processes covered in each of these chapters. These sections focus on the particular historical and institutional settings affecting how French and German interests have formed, and how France and Germany act upon them in each historical slice.

The sections on "outcomes" specifically focus on explaining the respective (intermediate) French and German interests and policy outcomes in the given temporal slices and particular political issues. Thereby, I review the usefulness and appropriateness of the theoretical propositions that I derived from chapter 2's institutionalist-constructivist model. With respect to the particular outcomes in each chapter, these sections also comparatively evaluate alternative explanations stemming from the major macro-perspectives on international relations. These sections specifically offer within-case analyses of each chapter's outcomes. Where appropriate and illuminating, chapters 3–6 employ counterfactuals or counterfactual reasoning. Chapter 7 provides some cross-case comparisons involving all of the study's twelve cases.[21]

Origin of Data

In researching this book's various empirical parts, I have drawn from a wide range of sources.[22] To begin, I drew from a broad variety of archival materials, including governmental and parliamentary documents, various governmental reports, official statements and publications, press conferences, and a variety of speeches. Many of these stem from French and German governmental or other public sources, or from entities of the Franco-German interaction net itself. I fleshed out these data with several thousand newspaper and magazine articles and other press materials. As is common practice, I often do not indicate when I rely on press materials as background, or when I use them in conjunction with data from other sources, for example official publications or specialized journals on defense technology. However, I do cite these when I quote directly (either a passage or a certain formulation), when it is appropriate to make traceable the origin of the information, or—most commonly—when a substantive article that reveals the author's name puts forth a distinct argument or analysis of the issue at hand. This is often the case in the leading nationwide publications such as *Frankfurter Allgemeine Zeitung, Süddeutsche Zeitung, Die Zeit, Der Spiegel, Le Monde, Le Monde Diplomatique,* and *Le Figaro.* These and other publications often have specialists on certain policy domains whose articles or commentaries are of great analytic value. Some, such as *Le Monde* or the *Frankfurter Allgemeine Zeitung,* have frequently had such excellent information channels to their governments, or at least to some ministries, that their news coverage often comes close to being quasi-official. Overall, about 60 percent of the press materials used stem from German sources. The rest is mostly of French origin, or comes from British, American, Swiss, or other sources.[23]

Further, I have drawn from a very broad variety of secondary literatures, including the tremendous number of publications on all aspects of Franco-German relations, French and German foreign and security policy, and numerous related issues on France and Germany. A number of interviews with a diverse range of personalities complete and supplement the collection of empirical data. Interviews provided background information, verified empirical presentations and conclusions, and, occasionally, filled in specific data that could not have been obtained otherwise.

Combat Helicopters

What are combat helicopters of the second generation? What is it that makes such helicopters, especially together with missiles of the third generation, such an extraordinary arms system? Given the prominent role this weapon plays in the book's empirical chapters, it is appropriate to take a brief look at second-generation helicopters as machines, and at their remarkable military and technological capabilities. Since the history and politics around this arms program between the mid-1970s and the end of the century holds the most import for this study's more general analytic objectives, it is especially important to comprehend the significance of the anti-tank versions of such helicopters for defense (or defense-planning) against tanks, and to grasp the strategic and tactical options they provide in projected anti-tank combat.[24]

A long list of technological advancements, integrated in the new weapons system, distinguishes combat helicopters of the second generation from their first-generation predecessors. The core feature is that they are fully capable of combat at night and in all weather conditions—unlike first-generation helicopters, which can fly and fight only during the day and in favorable weather. Further, second-generation helicopters were designed to be fully equipped with missiles of the third generation, ultimately of a long range of more than 4,000 or 5,000 meters. These capabilities rest on the second-generation machines' decisive technological component, the "night vision and targeting system" (TADS/PNVS).

A combination of newly developed optical and electronic devices, involving sensors, cameras, lasers, and infrared technologies, allow both "night vision" and (nocturnal) "target acquisition." Both pilot and gunner are equipped with a fully helmet-integrated vision system that provides electronically reproduced images of their near and distant surroundings, of the battlefield, or of potential targets. Aided by infrared cameras, pilot and gunner can identify and aim at targets at distances between 4,000 and 5,000 meters. In sum, the TADS/PNVS, together with the parallel arming improvements, enables a second-generation helicopter to be fully operational around the clock and to detect targets extremely quickly and at a great distance: it can identify four targets simultaneously and fire missiles at each one in less than eight seconds.

Other characteristics that distinguish second- from first-generation helicopters include a more resistant overall structure and mission durations of more than two and a half hours. Although not invincible, second-generation helicopters have a significantly higher degree of "survivability" that they owe to several features, including increased armoring and resistance to enemy fire, and the ability to combat from a greater distance. All of the new generation helicopter's major components such as cell, turbines, rotors, avionics, diverse functional equipment, and software are new developments and often use new materials. Overall, a combat helicopter of the second generation differs dramatically in technical specification, capability, performance, and potential arming from a first-generation combat helicopter. This ensemble of technological advancements makes it a helicopter of a new generation, not the update of an older one. Complex arms with an extended life cycle, these helicopters are expected to remain in service for some three decades or more.

Combat helicopters of the second generation can be fully equipped to carry optimally and fire missiles of the third generation, ultimately of a long range. Not quite a single arms system, second-generation helicopters and third-generation missiles relate in several ways. "Night vision," the ability to quickly designate several targets simultaneously at great distance, and the potential to fire third-generation missiles all connect to the TADS/PNVS technology. Journalists and defense experts often refer to third-generation missiles as "fire and forget" missiles. Once aimed and fired, they find their targets by themselves. Thanks to an advanced infra-red sensor technology in the missile's head that reacts to heat, third-generation missiles "recognize" their targets and "know" what they are supposed to hit. After firing, they may self-correct their flight in order to hit their designated mark.

This, roughly, is the difference among missiles of different generations: missiles of the first generation are aimed and fired; once fired, they either will hit their targets, or they will not. Missiles of the second generation can be corrected after having been fired. As the missiles proceed, the gunner can guide their flight in order to improve the chances to hit the targets. For that purpose and during that time, however, the helicopter from which they were fired remains without shelter and cannot hide. Missiles of the third generation, in contrast, "know" their target at the moment of launching. They will "find" their target by themselves: That is what "fire and forget" means. Thus, immediately after firing from a distance of up to three miles or more, second-generation helicopters can hide or leave the battlefield, enormously increasing their "survivability."

Given the sum of its characteristics, the capability of an army's fully functional fleet of more than 200 highly mobile second-generation helicopters, as France and Germany each initially expected to acquire, is easy to calculate: within a few hours or days of combat, it is able to destroy hundreds and thousands of enemy tanks. It is the most advanced and most efficient anti-tank weapon.

In addition to carrying third-generation missiles, Tiger combat helicopters will be armed in a range of mixes, comprising cannons, small unguided missiles, and air-to-air and air-to-surface missiles of various first-and second-generation types and ranges. The Tigers will take on a wide range of helicopter missions including armed reconnaissance and monitoring; anti-tank combat; ground troop support; and escort and protection for transport and other helicopter operations. Capable of multiple fighting tasks, they will operate day and night, in all weather conditions, and perhaps even in nuclear, biological, or chemically contaminated areas.[25]

Areas of Study and Contributions

This book's research questions and analytic objectives, theoretical and conceptual explorations, and empirical inquiries contribute to the study of world politics and international relations theory in general, and to security studies and arms procurement more specifically; European integration and European international history and politics; and French and German foreign and security affairs, as well as Franco-German relations.

With respect to international relations theory and the general working of world politics, this study investigates the possibilities, contingencies, and limits with which institutionalization and construction between states—types of interactions and meanings—may affect the definition of national interests and formulation of policies. Through affecting interests and policies, political insti-tutionalization and social construction not only give meaning to the material world, but help to shape and bring about physical reality at times and policy areas in which we should least expect. Thereby, this study connects factors from different levels of analysis that are commonly employed separately, and mingles historical institutionalist and social constructivist styles of analysis in new and fruitful ways.[26] The study highlights the importance of spatially more differen-tiated and historically more nuanced institutionalization and construction in the international sphere than the system- or world-region-wide institutionali-zations or constructions on which various brands of systemic constructivism, the "English School," or sociological institutionalism have commonly focused.[27] Through its historical and empirical investigations, furthermore, this study uncovers new causes and mechanisms of state arming and arms procurement that have not been identified in the relevant literature in security studies.[28] Quite generally and broadly perhaps, this book's conceptualizations and theo-retical approach point to a comprehensive and conceptually robustly grounded perspective on the grand sources or reservoirs of the forces that shape interna-tional history and world politics. This perspective offers new and creative ways of connecting causal factors of varying types and origins, and enables us to pose novel questions regarding the workings of international affairs.

Moreover, this book reconstructs an important kind of European international politics and history that seems to have been obscured or neglected by the com-mon focus on European Cold War history on the one hand, and Brussels-centered multilateral European integration on the other. This piece of history has its origins in the shadow of the Cold War during a period of existential menace. Yet, it did not recede into history along with the Warsaw Pact, the Soviet Union, the Iron Cur-tain, and the Cold War's East-West confrontation. The Tiger's history and politics unfolded in its own logic, occasionally intertwined, but often rather detached from Cold War affairs and stretching across the great 1989 divide and into the twenty-first century. Thus, this book's empirical reconstructions show important aspects of European international political history that span the post-war and post-Cold War periods, and that, while reducible to neither, are part of both.

In the same vein, Franco-German relations are neither just a subset of, nor reducible to, wider European integration. There is an important reality of Euro-pean international affairs outside and beyond the multilateral EU framework—especially in the domains of the traditional "high politics" of foreign policy, security, and defense, where EU integration had long remained the weakest and least developed. Bilateral relations such as those of France-Germany have their own life and relevance and in their own ways exemplify European integration of a different sort, which unfolded outside the multilateral EU framework of integration. In many respects and instances, in fact, the Franco-German connection underlay and perhaps functioned as a catalyst for the multilateral EC or EU frame. Through much of the post-war period, EC or EU integration arguably depended significantly more on a certain kind of Franco-German relationship than vice versa.

Finally, this book also contributes to the substantive literatures on French and German foreign relations and especially on Franco-German affairs. Given the plethora of writings on Franco-German matters, especially in Europe, and in light of Franco-German relations' elevated political importance within European political affairs, it is surprising that the question of the effects of the relations between these two states on their respective national interests and foreign policies has never been explicitly posed or systematically studied—even more so, as there is circumstantial and anecdotal evidence to indicate the existence of such causal connections and pathways.[29] This book offers a fresh look that brings empirical detail and historical precision to important aspects of almost four decades of Franco-German interaction. Rather than contending idiographic idiosyncrasy, however, this perspective is based on general concepts and is deeply wedded to an analytically oriented social science. Chapter 7 will return to the various theoretical and empirical strands of research and scholarship to which this book's questions, conceptualizations, and inquiries relate and contribute.

International Relations and
National Interest

La conduite des États ou des unités politiques militairement
indépendantes, même si on la suppose rationelle, ne se réfère pas à un
seul objectif. Dire que les États agissent en fonction de leur intérêt
national, c'est ne rien dire tant qu'on n'a pas défini le contenu de cet
intérêt.

Raymond Aron[1]

Je schärfer aber die Bedeutsamkeit einer Kulturerscheinung zum klaren
Bewußtsein gebracht werden soll, desto unabweislicher wird das Bedür-
fnis, mit klaren und nicht nur partikulär, sondern allseitig bestimmten
Begriffen zu arbeiten.

Max Weber[2]

This chapter develops a constructivist-institutionalist model of national interest
formation and foreign policy formulation. Focusing on variable constellations
between the logic of institutionalization and construction at the interstate level
on the one hand and domestic factors on the other, this model offers a number of
general hypotheses about the potential, contingent, and uneven impact of institutionalized interstate relations on states' interests and policies. The chapter
first distinguishes among three main components of interstate institutionalization and construction: regularized intergovernmentalism, predominantly symbolic acts and practices, and parapublic underpinnings of interstate relations.
Institutionalized relations between states, thus conceived, are sets of regularized intergovernmental interactions that include elements of shared meanings
and social purpose. Proper conceptualization allows us to empirically capture
the distinctive effects that such interstate institutionalization and construction

may generate. It also enables us to connect interstate relations thus conceived to other presumed factors of state interests and foreign policy, notably from domestic politics. Thereby, this chapter generates a total of six empirically testable propositions regarding the potential and variable impact of interstate institutionalization on national interests and policymaking. This book's theoretical explorations thus consider interstate institutionalization and construction, domestic construction, and domestic political structures broadly as separate sources of national interest and foreign policy, treating them conceptually separately. Depending on different constellations between interstate logic, the domestic constructions of one or both of the states involved, or their domestic structures broadly, this chapter's model hypothesizes, the impact of an interstate relationship on the national interests and policies of the states involved may be strong, moderate, or absent. Three contrasting views drawn from the most established general theoretical perspectives in international relations theory offer potentially competing approaches to the origins of national interests and foreign policies and to how interstate institutionalization may or may not affect state goals and policymaking.

Institutionalization and Construction Between States

Empirically examining and analytically capturing the causal implications of the relations between states first requires careful conceptualization of what it is that makes up such relationships. In so doing, I distinguish among three building blocks or categories of interaction that together constitute interstate institutionalization and construction: regularized intergovernmentalism; largely symbolic acts and practices; and (possibly) a variety of parapublic underpinnings. Together, these sets of political practices, in their particular historical manifestations, define particular relationships between states in given periods. This conceptualization allows us to investigate the specific, overall impact of such relations on the interests and policies of those involved in them. The institutionalization and construction of Franco-German relations in the post-war period have been both wide ranging and dense, as well as distinctive.

Regularized Intergovernmentalism

Regularized intergovernmentalism consists of reiterated patterns of interaction and communication among governmental and administrative officials who act as representatives of their states or state entities. Such connections broadly include interstate institutionalization of all kinds and at a variety of levels. Regularized intergovernmentalism in given time periods may have particular rhythms and organizational shape.

Such regularized intergovernmentalism helps to define "business as usual" among two or more states. In framing normal ways of handling things, it may channel why and how to solve problems and formulate policies in a wide range of policy domains. It keeps issues on the agenda that concern those states involved in the relationship. It may "bind personnel"—that is, groups of people who deal with one another professionally on a regular basis—whether in friendly or adversarial fashion. It makes states "keep in touch" regarding certain issues. Especially if the relations are constructive, regularized intergovernmentalism may generate pressures "to come up with something" or "something new."

Regularized intergovernmentalism in particular pre-structures proceedings and contributes to standardizing the conduct between the states involved. Thereby it may generate routines and common codes of conduct. Thus, in all of these ways, regularized intergovernmentalism helps to shape standards of normality and normal expectations. The interaction and communication patterns that it implies may help to make some courses of action intuitive while making others implausible. They may help to legitimize some possible routes of policy and delegitimize others.[3]

Franco-German regularized intergovernmentalism between the 1960s and the early twenty-first century has been wide-ranging, dense, and distinctive.[4] At its core, the Elysée Treaty (or "Franco-German Treaty," or "Treaty"), with its various extensions and additions, has constituted the main framework of the robust Franco-German bilateralism. The Treaty defined semiannual Franco-German summit meetings as regularized procedures. Initially, these meetings involved the German chancellor, the French president and prime minister, a handful of ministers from the key ministries, and their staff. Frequently they stretched over two days, to be concluded by joint press conferences on what had been achieved and what remained on the agenda ahead.

These summit meetings grew quickly and massively after the Treaty's conclusion in 1963, expanding to include more ministers and increasingly larger delegations from the two states' ministerial bureaucracies. By the 1980s, the "summits" comprised all major foreign and security as well as domestic policy areas, often stretching across all levels of governmental and administrative hierarchies. Furthermore, through the addition of a number of protocols to the Treaty, France and Germany further increased the frequency and intensity of their bilateral regularized intergovernmentalism. Following the 1982 creation of the Franco-German Security and Defense Commission, for example, in 1988 they instituted the Franco-German Defense and Security Council that further bound together the two states in these policy areas.

In order to prevent political misunderstandings, exchange opinions and background information, and bind yet closer especially policy- and decision-making proceedings, in 2001 France and Germany decided to increase the frequency of consultations on the highest political levels. Named after the Alsatian town in which the scheme was conceived, the "Blaesheim process" meant that the two states' foreign ministers or heads of state and government would hold informal and discreet talks every six to eight weeks. Since 2003, following the fortieth anniversary of the Elysée Treaty's conclusion, the semiannual Franco-German meetings took on the title "joint Ministerial Councils." Yet again expanded, they now include the two governments' entire cabinets as well as delegations from all or almost all of the two states' ministerial bureaucracies.

The Franco-German regularized intergovernmentalism has developed a dynamic of its own, contributing significantly to the establishment of a particular kind of institutional fabric between these states. For almost half a century since its inception, this robust bilateral intergovernmentalism has helped to keep France and Germany hanging together in spite of a wide range of forces that might have promoted drift or rift. Potential domestic factors of rupture or instability have included, among others, changes of governments, presidents, prime ministers, chancellors, or other key personnel on one or both sides of the Rhine; the "chemistry" among French and German political leaders and the personal proclivities of the individuals in key positions in the French and German states; ideological differences among the political parties in power in Bonn or Berlin and Paris; changing and diverse coalition governments in Germany; and the rise of *cohabitation* in France.[5] And potentially disruptive international factors have prominently included the end of the Cold War, the rise (and apparent decline) of American unipolarity, German unification, various rounds of European Union enlargement, and expanding and intensifying globalization.

Navigating through times of such significant internal change and external transformations has not been without bouts of friction or crises between the two states. But France-Germany did not break. The regularization of their intergovernmentalism has helped them to hang together for almost half a century in a particular way that survived the great 1989 divide in Europe, and that has proven both resilient and adaptable during the frequently turbulent years of the post-Cold War era and early twenty-first-century world politics. During these decades of internal and external change, Franco-German bilateral intergovernmentalism has standardized Franco-German intergovernmental affairs, created routines, and outlined normal ways of handling things; it has bound together and, over time, helped to socialize cohorts of diplomatic and other governmental personnel; and, in a variety of ways, it has generated and perpetuated social meaning.[6]

The fabric and patterns of this bilateral intergovernmentalism with its manifold communication channels and regularized contacts have lastingly connected heads of states and governments, ministers, and ministries from both countries and compelled them to streamline and coordinate their policy- and decision-making schedules. In particular, the semiannual summit meetings, with the preparations preceding and the agenda following them, have engendered their own rhythms. They have often taken on difficult issues not satisfactorily resolved on lower hierarchical levels, or set agendas for issues to be dealt with and resolved in the future. Frequently, they set up working groups with specific tasks to report back to the high and highest bilateral levels in a subsequent summit. Thus, even if only tenuously, they have intertwined processes of French and German national interest formation and policymaking. At the core of this bilateral regularized intergovernmentalism, "the Franco-German Treaty," noted long-time French Minister of Foreign Affairs and Prime Minister de Murville at the Treaty's twentieth anniversary, "has over time . . . become an essential part of the life of our peoples"—"a basic element of the foreign policies of our two countries."[7] The Franco-German regularized intergovernmentalism has become part of a bilateral polity that helped to define a particular international regional system.

Symbolic Acts

Predominantly symbolic acts and practices are gestures, rituals, and ceremonies that do not directly aim at solving problems, formulating interests and positions, or making policies. Typically, such acts refer to a larger historical and cultural context that reaches beyond the time horizon of immediate daily politics. Symbolic acts are a distinct category of international political practices with their own tradition and reality. Such symbolic acts and practices are not primarily about cooperation in specific instances. Rather, more generally, they denote what it *means* to act together. They lend significance to a relationship, indicating what is "at stake," or what it is "all about." Representing a deeper and more general social purpose underlying specific instances of cooperation or difference, they are about the value and intrinsic importance that social relations incorporate. Typically, predominantly symbolic acts and practices are embedded in a broader historical and cultural context.[8]

Symbolic acts and practices generate, corroborate, and perpetuate meaning and purpose in the relations between states. They help to construct the standards of normality that shape expectations, conduct, and levels of harmony and conflict, contributing to predictability. Symbolic practices further provide relationships with reference points for success and failure of single actions or sets of policies, which may entail the success or failure of inimical policies in weakening the position of adversaries, as much as in cooperation with allies and friends. Finally, meaning and purpose created by symbols contribute to the shaping of collective identities at the international level: who belongs to whom, for what reason, and for what purpose. Conversely, they also make clear who does not belong together, who are "the others," adversaries or enemies. They legitimize some goals and actions and delegitimize others. Symbolic acts and practices construct social meaning and purpose well beyond the immediate ends of the short term. Such meaning and purpose cannot be reduced to other types of international activity or aspects of institutionalized interstate relations, such as regularized intergovernmentalism or others. They help to shape the stage on which much of daily politics unfolds.

The dominant Franco-German post-war meaning originates in a string of symbolic acts between 1958 and 1963. During this period, in a series of often stirring gestures, ceremonies, and speeches, French President Charles de Gaulle and German Chancellor Konrad Adenauer generated and instituted new, transformed meaning and social purpose for an incipient era of Franco-German affiliation and proximity. These symbolic acts included their demonstrative private meetings, joint travels through the two countries, participation in the first joint parade of Franco-German troops, kneeling and praying next to each other in Reims, a list of speeches, and their hug and fraternal kiss after the signing of the Elysée Treaty.

A host of chiefly symbolic acts and practices has since reproduced, perpetuated, and corroborated the meaning and purpose of the Franco-German relationship that these two men instituted. Some of these practices are more or less regularized and recurrent, with dates marked on the calendar. Among many others, they have included the commemorations and celebrations of the signing of the Elysée Treaty and the custom of first visits or first receptions of new personnel after changes in key public positions. A new French president or German chancellor, for example, traditionally takes his or her first trip abroad to the other's capital very soon after resumption of office. Outstanding among the single events in this category is Kohl and Mitterrand's 1984 standing hand in hand over the graves of French and German soldiers in Verdun, as well as de Gaulle and Adenauer's kneeling next to each other in Reims in 1962. But there are many more, including a joint troop parade in Paris on France's national holiday on July 14, 1994, and President Chirac's reception as the first foreigner to speak before the German Bundestag after the German parliament had returned to Berlin post-unification. As single events, these are meaningful integral threads of an overall fabric. Singular, they are part of a whole.[9]

The dominant Franco-German purpose of the past five decades has its characteristic normative justifications or explanations in the two countries' political discourses. For the most part, the appeals are historical, referring to the necessity to overcome a long history of anguish and suffering; allude to cultural affinity; or hint at the Franco-German role in providing stability or consolidation in European affairs. In the Franco-German example, symbolic acts endow this bilateral relationship with specific meaning and specific purpose. They help to institutionalize Franco-German relations as a value and, often, as an end in themselves.

Parapublic Underpinnings

Parapublic underpinnings of international relations are cross-border interactions by individuals or collective actors belonging neither to the public world of states nor to the private world of societies. They escape the common binary distinctions of state-society or public-private, representing a third kind of international interaction that is "parapublic." Parapublic practices are not forms of public interaction among states, because participants do not relate to each other as representatives of their states or governments. Yet, these practices are also inadequately conceptualized as transnational links among private individual or collective actors, because they do not autonomously originate in private society and, critically, because they are largely state financed or organized. Without state funding or public organizational support, such activities would barely exist. Parapublic practices are a distinct and substantial type of international activity that underpins relations between or among specific states.

A proper conceptual grasp of the parapublic underpinnings of international relations enables us to comprehend how a multitude of diverse interactions and processes relate to one another and how they, in their entirety, constitute a particular type of international institutional structure. Parapublic institutionalization may best be characterized as "transpolity." It underpins and connects to interstate institutionalization and construction.[10]

The public funding or organization of international parapublic activity comes with the institutionalization of social purpose. For example, the Franco-German television channel ARTE presents world news and even weather from a "Franco-German" perspective. Publicly funded or publicly organized youth activities across borders virtually always embody social purpose. Parapublic underpinnings of interstate relations are normatively charged. They are not neutral or value free. Accordingly, those between France and Germany have helped to define a particular Franco-German meaning and social purpose.

Parapublic practices have at least three specific kinds of partially overlapping effects, which together construct international social purpose: First, they provide a great variety of resources for joint undertakings most broadly conceived. Second, through transpolity educational and training programs that are frequently part of the parapublic weave, they socialize their participants, thus cultivating a certain kind of personnel to later practice international affairs by staffing public (and private) offices. Thus parapublic institutionalization helps to produce and re-produce personnel immersed in the frame of value, signification, and social purpose of the particular interstate relationship that they underpin. And, finally, parapublic institutionalization generates and perpetuates social meaning by shaping standards of normal expectations, helping to define political success and failure, defining legitimate political ends, and contributing to the formation of the rudiments of international collective identity. In all of these ways, parapublic underpinnings can stabilize public interstate institutionalization and construction, and supply interstate relations with themes, meaning, and personnel. Parapublic underpinnings may perpetuate and strengthen value and legitimate public goals. They may contribute to creating and maintaining a certain atmosphere.

Franco-German institutionalization and construction consists of much more than the relations between two states. It also comprises an encompassing variety of parapublic connections among the French and the Germans, which the governments of the neighboring states have helped to fund and organize, but which have evolved into something more. At the same time, at least the parapublic underpinnings of the Franco-German relationship face considerable limitations: Their impact is very indirect, as effects do not emerge mechanically and are not altogether assured. And in the Franco-German case, they have hardly brought about a true cross-border Franco-German public sphere, nor have they removed the enduring domestic cultural and social dissimilarities that often separate French and Germans.

The parapublic underpinnings of Franco-German relations comprise three main pillars:

1. Extensive youth and educational exchanges, with the Franco-German Youth Office alone involving some 7 million participants since 1963. This pillar further includes more than 100 fully integrated study programs between French and German universities, enrolling thousands of French and German students. They are fully trained in both languages and receive university degrees from both countries.
2. More than 2,000 "twinships" between French and German towns and between various regional entities such as *départements* or *régions* and *Landkreise* or *Länder*. Although ranging widely in intensity of contact and exchange, such twinships have institutionalized massive Franco-German transpolity interaction through a great variety of programs and activities.
3. A host of institutes and associations concerned with Franco-German matters and committed to Franco-German affairs.

A variety of additional parapublic elements, including publicly supported mass media institutions and a multitude of prizes accorded for advancing Franco-German matters, complement these three main staples.

In their entirety, these parapublic interactions compose distinct historical formations. They are part of a bilateral institutional order. They have undergirded the "special" relationship between France and Germany over the past half century and have helped to endow it with a particular value, meaning, and purpose.[11]

Table 2.1 **Institutionalization and Construction Between States**

components	*manifestation in Franco-German affairs*	*overall effects*
regularized inter-governmentalism	• Elysée Treaty w/extensions and additions across policy areas; • semiannual summits w/preparations and homework • reg. intergovt. below and beyond the Elysée Treaty	• *standardize conduct of states involved;* pre-structure proceedings; shape standards of normality as well as deviation from normality; construct normal expectations, from cooperation to conflict • *generate and perpetuate social meanings and purpose:* legitimize and make intuitive some course of action, . . .

Table 2.1 Institutionalization and Construction Between States (*Continued*)

components	manifestation in Franco-German affairs	overall effects
		... delegitimize and make implausible others; provide reasons to want and to do some things, and not to do others—alone or with others
predominantly symbolic acts and practices	• originating in de Gaulle-Adenauer's symbolic acts: Colombey, Reims, travels, etc. • recurrent symbolic practices: Treaty anniversaries; tradition of "symbolic firsts" • single events as part of a whole: Verdun 1984; parades (Champs-Elysées 1994 etc.); and many more	• *engender rudiments of collective identity* or co-define otherness; stabilize order in international affairs, understood not as absence of conflict, but as regularization
(potentially) parapublic underpinnings	• massive youth exchanges (7 million participants) • some 2000 city and regional partnerships • host of institutes and associations • other parapublic elements (media; prizes)	

Institutional Logics

Thus conceived, institutionalized relations between states are sets of regularized interaction, meaning, and social purpose. They may imply elements of interstate and (as in the case of parapublic connections) transpolity institutionalization and construction. Their institutionalization of patterns of interaction and meaning gives them their historical significance and political relevance. Relations change when interaction patterns and the meaning that they incorporate are reproduced differently over time. A fundamental change of their interactions and meaning will transform them. Rupture will terminate them.

Each of the components of institutionalized interstate relations—regularized intergovernmentalism, symbolic acts and practices, and parapublic underpinnings—contributes distinct aspects to the relationship between states. Each may exert separate influences on the states involved. However, this book explores the total impact of interstate institutionalization and construction on national interests and foreign policy, looking at the combined influence of these relations between states. Thus chapters 3–6 scrutinize the overall effects of the particular relations between France and Germany rather than testing for the separate causal effects of the single components that together make up the relationship.[12] In combination, the components of interstate institutionalization and construction generate a variety of general effects: (1) Institutionalized relations standardize conduct. They pre-structure proceedings and help to shape normalities and normal expectations. (2) They generate and perpetuate social meanings and purpose. Thereby they legitimize and make intuitive some courses of action, delegitimize and make implausible others. They also provide reasons to want and to do some things, and not to do others—alone or with others. (3) They may engender rudiments of collective identity or co-define otherness. By doing so, in a broad sense, they help to stabilize order in international affairs—not understood as the absence of conflict but as regularization. These political effects and causal implications may overlap and are not necessarily mutually exclusive.

This conceptualization allows us to empirically research the possible autonomous impact of such relations as a whole on the interests and actions of the state-actors involved. It should further enable us to connect "interstate institutionalization and construction" with other potential factors of national interest and foreign policy and to theorize generally about the formation of interests and policy. The conceptualization should also allow us to pursue specific hypotheses on the contingent, apparently variable impact of interstate institutionalization and construction on state interests and policies in particular political settings, historical periods, or points in time. If particular kinds of interstate relations indeed affect the state-actors involved, this conceptualization should make their empirical implications observable and accessible in both specific political processes and historical outcomes. It thus should lay the groundwork for within-case process tracing and explanation as well as cross-case analysis.[13]

Interstate Relations and Domestic Construction: Propositions 1–3

Historically rooted domestic construction refers to national historical experiences and to dominant interpretations of their meaning and implications. Central elements of such domestic-level construction can vary widely across otherwise similar states. Core components of French and German domestic construction have differed significantly between the late 1950s and the mid-1990s. Generally, connecting external interstate institutionalization with internal historically rooted domestic construction generates empirically testable hypotheses as to why institutionalized interstate relations apparently vary in their impact on what states want and do.

Domestic Construction

Historically rooted domestic constructions are internally shared views and understandings regarding the proper and suitable role and purpose of one's own state as a social collectivity in the international arena. Here, they refer specifically to self-views of a country's proper place and role in the world, including foreign and security policy. They are products of history, memory, and interpretation. They may be broken down into a few core components, centrally defining such self-views and their implications. They typically come with characteristic vocabulary that both reflects and substantiates these core elements of domestic construction. Their main historical reference points are rooted in national historical experiences.

Such domestic role constructions cannot be reduced to the interests or ideologies of dominant groups, parties, or single persons in or near power, or to organizational features of state and society. Nor is such domestic construction merely the sum or the overlapping consensus of individual or group interests. As an analytic concept, historically rooted domestic construction encapsulates "what we want and what we do as a result of who we think we are, want to be, and should be," in light of national historical experiences and dominant interpretations of their meaning. As internal reference systems, such domestic constructions affect national interests and foreign policies.[14]

At a minimum, these historically rooted domestic constructions are shared among the national political and administrative elites, across a variety of publicly organizational units of the state, and among the relevant foreign policy community, which includes advisors and researchers as well as academic and journalistic commentators and observers. A strong elite consensus and wider public appreciation of the core elements of such domestic construction will increase the concept's analytic leverage.

Such domestic role constructions are internally anchored historical creations. They may be contested, but they tend to endure. They are neither invariably fixed nor necessarily immutable across time. They appear, develop, and become dominant during one period of time; change, decay, or recede into history during another. Yet, neither are they purely transient phenomena. Often they display astounding temporal tenacity. As factors of interest and policy, they can be captured by empirically extracting their core elements and the characteristic set of prevailing vocabulary at a given time and place.[15]

Domestic constructions of self and proper role and purpose in the international arena are a major source of influence on what state governments define as national interests and cast into policy.[16] Their varying causal effects on national interests and policy may complement the effects of other sources of national interests (such as interstate institutionalization and construction, or the impact of domestic interest groups), or they may be in various degrees of tension with them. Domestic constructions affect national interests and foreign policies in different ways: They both *pre*scribe and *pro*scribe. They prescribe in that they induce interests and policies. They may motivate certain wills, goals, and actions, and they may make plausible and intuitive certain objectives but not others. Yet domestic constructions also proscribe in that they rule out or subdue options. They make some interests and policy options intuitively implausible, categorically exclude them as wrong or unacceptable, or make them unthinkable by putting them outside realistic consideration.[17] Frequently, interests and policies that derive from historically rooted domestic construction are viewed as normal, right, and intuitively plausible and appropriate within the respective country.

France and Germany

Between the late 1950s and the second half of the 1990s, central elements of French and German historically rooted domestic construction differed sharply. Sets of French and German vocabulary, terminology, and notions associated with such elements of domestic construction both express and substantiate these differences. Delineating domestic construction elements comparatively also brings to light more clearly what a particular role and purpose is *not*. Germany's and France's domestic constructions of role and purpose, like any country's, are also the sum of momentous absences.[18]

Legal Framing, Rule of Law, Regularized Conduct ("Verrechtlichng"; "Verregelung")

The first core element of the German self-cultivated self-view encompasses the propensity that it befits Germany to promote and consolidate an increasingly precise legal framing of international affairs; to support broadening the legitimacy of the international order; and generally to advance the international rule of law, legally codified procedures, and regularized conduct.[19] Substantively and processually, this component encourages formulating one's wants and policies in conformity with already existing international rules. It promotes the advancement, deepening, and consolidation of international law and rule as a general policy goal in itself. It also channels interests toward specific international policy issue areas such as human rights and the environment.

"Never-On-Our-Own"

A second main German domestic construction component comprises a general dislike for "going alone" or "doing it alone": unilateralism as unsuitable for oneself, especially in security affairs. "[T]ogether with our friends and partners" is one standard way to state the matter—"[o]nly together with our partners, not against them, can we win the future," as then Foreign Minister Klaus Kinkel elaborated programmatically. It suits Germany, in the words of then Federal President Richard von Weizsäcker, to "avoid any type of 'showing off' and any unnecessary 'going alone.'"[20]

Military Force as Last Resort Toward Non-Selfish Ends

The third German role element incorporates great skepticism and a very restrictive attitude toward the use of force. The self-view consensus strongly embraces non-military instruments as both normal and fundamentally preferable for achieving one's goals.[21] A peculiar mix of ends, functions, and implementation characterizes Germany's acceptance of the potential use of military power only as a last resort. Self-defense aside, the ends cannot be narrowly national-selfish, and a broad international consensus must justify them. The function of force is to (re)channel conflict into non-military forms as quickly as possible. Its implementation must be legitimized by broadly supported international decisions and realized by a broad international coalition, ideally under the aegis of an international organization.

These elements of domestic construction come with a set of characteristic vocabulary that reflects and underscores their meaning. Key German notions notably comprise responsibility, stability, and predictability (*Verantwortung, Stabilität, Berechenbarkeit*), as well as reliability, calculability, accountability, and continuity. Standard formulas establish that Germany, "due to its history," has a "special (co-)responsibility," or that Germany must be a predictable partner in the quest for regional and global stability. Frequently, role and purpose terms come as compounds or in combinations—"responsibility politics/policies" (*Verantwortungspolitik*) or Germany as a "reliable friend and partner as anchor for stability and peace."[22] During the period covered here, Germany's domestic construction discourse was characteristic and bounded.[23]

The substance of France's domestic construction elements differs in kind from Germany's, with vocabulary and notions mirroring these differences. Similarly, the historical roots of constructions of France's proper role in the world differ radically.

Independence

This chief French role-component implies a view of self as standing alone, able to act in as many foreign policy fields as possible "on one's own terms and without endangering a dependent relationship with any other country." This role element encompasses France's "full foreign policy independence in the world of states." It includes a "dogged interest in maintaining . . . national separateness," and the "ideal of autonomy of decisions." "[I]nsisting on independence and autonomy has remained a firm dogma of French parties: communists, socialists, and Gaullists alike."[24] Some consider "'independence' the leading notion" of the Fifth Republic's foreign policy.[25]

Activism

This second French role component refers to shaping world politics and participating in the management of international affairs—including the use of military force. Charles de Gaulle crystallized the activism element succinctly in rehearsing what he considered France's appropriate role and purpose in all world regions and key international institutions: "In each of these areas, I want France to play an active part"—elaborating that "it is essential that that which we say and do be independent of others."[26] Some four decades later, Foreign Minister Hubert Védrine, long-time diplomatic advisor and Elysée secretary general under President François Mitterrand, describes a "French will to will."[27] Together, "independence" and "activism" lead to an "interest in participating in the international community but on one's own terms and without endangering a dependent relationship with any other country."[28]

(Potential) Presence

"France, the only West European nuclear power along with Great Britain, present on five oceans and four continents," the 1990–1993 *Loi de Programmation Militaire* prototypically formulates, "has chosen to ensure her security by herself to guarantee her independence and maintain her identity." "France has always understood itself as a globally acting middle power." It intends to pursue "an active foreign policy in every part of the world and every sphere of international life."[29] France's overseas *départements* (DOM), integral parts of the "motherland," and its other territorial holdings of varying political-administrative status (TOM) corroborate this (potential) presence role component.[30] "Confetti of the empire," they are leftovers of another institutional time.[31] Yet, it is not the material tenure of these quite costly territorial splinters that matters but the role conception to which they contribute. "The French continue to produce their history as the accomplishment of a universal mission."[32]

France's domestic construction terminology, too, relates intimately to a historically shaped and domestically anchored conception of self in international affairs. Yet it diverges sharply from Germany's. It is the vocabulary of another normality. Standard French role terms include "greatness," "rank," and "glory" (*grandeur, rang, gloire*), and a few related terms like "dignity," "prestige," and "pride." *Grandeur* is perhaps the key term denoting historically shaped French self-views.[33] The notion of *rang* typically comes in such formulations as: France has to "take its rank," live up to its rank, or "keep its rank"; France must occupy "a place in the front rank," "its traditional place in Europe and the world as a nation"; the "impossibility of being satisfied with a second role for France."[34] In a passage that became part of a national canon, de Gaulle delineates a conceptual abstract that is in its own way a condensation of a national self-categorization and role: "France cannot really be herself but in the first rank. . . . France cannot be France without greatness."[35]

Origins: Historical Raw Materials, Reference Points, and Dominant Interpretations

Crucial elements of proper national role and purpose in the world evolve domestically, in relation to or against one's own collective past and interpretations of its meaning and implications. The emergence and consolidation of such historically rooted construction seems to involve three key components: a broad and typically amorphous set of historical raw materials; a selective focus on a number of central historical reference points; and some dominant, more or less widely shared interpretations of the meaning and political implications of these reference points for one's role and purpose in the international arena. The histories of France and Germany surely provided the two countries with quite different assortments of historical raw materials after World War II. And indeed, the French and the Germans chose markedly dissimilar historical reference points, which they endowed with distinct meanings and political significance, and to which they referred when thinking about themselves and their foreign policy roles. After the dust of the war had settled, by the late 1950s, their respective historical reference points had fully crystallized and the key meanings and implications they associated with them had consolidated.[36]

In the German case, the historical legacies of World War II and the Holocaust, with the conception of a democratic Germany as a counterdesign to the barbaric Third Reich regime, are constitutive.[37] Dominant interpretations of the meaning and implications of "no more war" and "never again Holocaust" are at the core of Germany's historically shaped domestic constructions of the country's proper international role and foreign policy in the post-war decades. It may be trivial to state that two disastrous world wars, the moral devastation of the Holocaust, scorched earth, mass slaughtering, and miles of barbed wire have left their traces on Germany's collective psyche in the decades to follow. It is also true.

The historical reference points of French domestic construction differ fundamentally from Germany's. Here, it is the indivisible model-republic, the first nation with a *grande armée*, conquering and ordering Europe via a civil code and Cartesian clarity. It is a self-view of a collectivity always at the forefront of political, social, scientific, technical, cultural, and moral progress. De Gaulle succeeded in fusing an assortment of basic orientations into a more or less coherent self-view of a social collectivity, providing "links between . . . the nation's inner life, its *essence* as France, and its place in the politics of nations." He "set the terms of discourse about French foreign policy in ways that have persisted"[38]—"both for public perceptions of France's proper role in the world and for the working of policy-making processes at elite level."[39]

But the General did not invent a new French self-view. Similar themes have stretched from before to after his tenure. Already during the World War II, for example, the national council of the *Résistance* defined "defending the nation's political independence, restoring France to its power and greatness and its universal mission" as proper French purpose, post-liberation. Some of the materials and motives from which de Gaulle drew long predate him, with deep roots in French history and from deep layers of historical time. For instance, traces of "the striving for national independence" as "a quasi-natural law like maxim for all foreign and security political action," today an "untouchable component of French reason of state," reach back a thousand years. This Capetian heritage has been handed over to Richelieu, Louis XIV, the Jacobins, and Napoleon Bonaparte, finally arriving at Mitterrand.[40]

Hypotheses 1–3

Whether and how strongly interstate institutionalization and construction will affect state interests and policies in specific political contexts or situations, we may now hypothesize, will depend on constellations between the effects of institutionalized interstate relations and those of historically rooted domestic construction. One can think of three basic constellations between these two sets of effects: There can be no conflict between them; there can be tension; and they can directly clash. If there is no conflict, the effects from these two sources will be additive. Unencumbered by the influence of domestic construction, in this constellation the effects of institutionalized relations should be strong. This is the first hypothesis that I derive from the model.

The stronger the tension between the effects of externally institutionalized relations and internal domestic construction becomes, the weaker I expect the

**Table 2.2 Historically Rooted Domestic Construction for France and Germany
(late 1950s-late 1990s)**

	Germany	France
core components	• "never on our own" • legal framing, rule of law, regularized conduct (*Verrechtlichung, Verregelung*) • military force as last resort toward non-selfish ends	• independence (standing alone, proud, independently) • activism ("will to will") • (potential) presence (universal mission; *rayonnement*)
representative terminology	responsibility, stability; reliability, predictability calculability, accountability; continuity	greatness, rank, glory; dignity, pride, prestige
historical reference points	World War II; Holocaust	indivisible model-republic; *grande armée*; as collectivity at forefront of political, social, scientific, and cultural progress and sophistication

impact of institutionalized relations on interests and policies to be. To be sure, in a bilateral relationship, for example, tension may stem from the domestic construction of either one or both of the states involved and the logic of their institutionalized relationship (the hypothesis here is not about possible tensions between the two countries' domestic constructions themselves). In the Franco-German case, for example, for very different reasons, either domestic construction (or both) may not fit together well with the logic of their institutionalized bilateral relationship. The second hypothesis that I suggest thus holds that if the effects of institutionalized relations and domestic construction are in tension, the impact of the institutionalized relationship will be weaker. Institutionalized relations might still be effective, but their effects will be encumbered.

This is the third hypothesis: If the effects on national interests and foreign policies induced by institutionalized relations directly clash with effects originating from core components of domestic construction, then the impact of interstate institutionalization and construction on national interests and foreign policies will decline. In this constellation, I hypothesize, domestic construction effects will generally be preponderant, trumping the interstate institutionalization effects. The latter effects will be feeble or recede.[41]

Thus viewed, depending on the constellation, domestic construction may function as facilitator (or permittor), inhibitor, or overrider of the effects of institutionalized interstate relations.

Table 2.3 **Interstate Relations and Domestic Construction**

		effects of institutionalized relations and domestic construction on national interest and foreign policy
effects of institutionalized relations vs. domestic construction-effects	no conflict	**additive** effects of institutionalized relations strong (**H 1**)
	tension	**mixed** effects of institutionalized relations weaker (**H 2**)
	clash	**domestic construction-effects preponderant** effects of institutionalized relations decline (**H 3**)

Interstate Relations and Domestic Institutional Structures: Propositions 4–6

"Domestic institutional structures" are historically grown or politically negotiated features of domestic institutional orders. They comprise aspects of the political system, organized society, and state-society relations. Domestic structures are a grand reservoir for investigating the formation of national interest and the shaping of public policies.[42] For analytic purposes here, however, this study focuses on two confined features that characterize national polities: (1) the centralization of political authority to define interests and formulate policies in the domestic political system and (2) the degree of state autonomy from the influence of the particularistic interests of organized society. Both authority centralization and state autonomy may vary overall across states and their political systems. But both features also vary across policy domains and potentially over time within domestic political systems. Within the French and German political systems, degrees of both political authority centralization and state autonomy vary and are empirically identifiable in given policy contexts and periods or points in time. Hypothesizing about variable constellations between the logic of institutionalized interstate relationships and authority centralization or state autonomy at the domestic level generates three more propositions regarding the variable impact of interstate institutionalization and construction on the interests and policies of the states involved.

Authority Centralization and State Autonomy

Political authority centralization and state autonomy affect how states define interests and formulate policies. Together, they condition the likelihood that single state or governmental entities have enough leverage to affect or to block national or public interest definition and policy formulation—either from their own positions in the political system or as agents of societal groups.

The *degree of political authority (or power) centralization* determines the hierarchic level at which interests are authoritatively defined, policies fixed, and decisions taken for the entire social collectivity in a given political system. The higher the hierarchic level at which this takes place, and the less consideration that must be given to the voices or demands of other public entities of equal or subsidiary rank, the more centralized the organization of a political system. Political authority centralization decreases as single governmental or state entities (*staatliche Teileinheiten*)—such as military leaderships, parliamentary committees, or subfederal territorial units like *régions* or *Länder*—become more important with their respective "particularistic interests" in the overall formation of interests and policies.

The strength or weakness of a coalition government composed of two or more parties—whether government is streamlined or, for example, cohabitation-divided, or whether executive and legislative branches of government competitively check and balance each other with fragmentary effects and authority dispersion—also contributes to the degree of authority centralization in a system. The more units contributing to the formulation of positions, the more political authority or power is dispersed in the system. Fragmentation and dispersion are not only the result of the number of entities participating in or constructively co-formulating interests and policies. They also relate to the number of government or state entities that can block or veto such decisions. Thus, high degrees of authority centralization can also mean few "veto points" to block or undermine state or governmental position fixation and policy formulation.[43] Degrees of authority centralization help to determine the difficulty of arriving at positions and policies and the number of different entities of state governments that contribute to the formulation of interests and policies, as well as how many entities are capable of "vetoing" positions or policies.

A high degree of *state autonomy* means that a government may develop and fix interests and policies with little or no influence from the particularistic interests of domestic or transnational organized society. The easier the access of organized society to the political power centers where public positions are authoritatively fixed, and the greater the influence of certain groups on what the government or administration adopts in a given policy issue area and time, the lower the degree of state autonomy. State autonomy shapes the role and influence of organized domestic or transnational society in determining national interests and foreign policies. It conditions whether, where, and how organized society can access the political process that brings about interests and policies.

Degrees of political authority centralization, along with degrees of state autonomy from society's influence and pressure, together define "state strength." High degrees of authority centralization and state autonomy give rise to high degrees of state strength. In a strong state, governments define interests on a high level of centralization with a high degree of autonomy from society. In reverse, fragmentation or dissipation of political authority among state and governmental entities and little autonomy from the influence of private societal interests mean low degrees of state strength.

France and Germany

Overall, during the time period relevant for this study, the French state is stronger than the German state: It is more centralized and has, in many policy domains, more autonomy from its society. However, degrees of centralization and autonomy vary significantly across policy domains and contexts for both France and Germany.

Labeled *"monarchie républicaine"*[44] and "the institutionalization of leadership,"[45] Fifth Republic France has frequently been cited as close to the ideal type of a strong state: a system with a strong president and a government and administration highly centralized in many fields.[46] During much of the Fifth Republic, the French state has enjoyed high degrees of autonomy from organized society in many policy domains—sometimes actively taking control of aspects of French society. For example, the state has controlled economic activity in many industrial sectors. In many areas of production, far into the 1990s, the French state has cultivated one or two national champions that it has owned or controlled in various legal forms. In industrial areas of concern to national security, not only has the state been autonomous from industry, but it has more or less run it. Both centralization of political authority and state autonomy are very high in arenas such as foreign affairs and defense, even in times of *cohabitation*.

However, with the arrival of *cohabitation*, political authority has, in a number of policy areas, been split among president, prime minister, and government. In sectors such as agriculture, education, and transport, the French state has proven quite vulnerable to the pressures of a sometimes seemingly anarchic society. Features that determine the strength of the French state in a particular policy area and time period include whether or not France is *cohabitation*-ruled, and if so how the respective policy area is divided among president, prime minister, and government; how much influence the national assembly can exert; how much impact the French *régions* have; and how much pressure society is able to mobilize.

In democratic Germany, as a counterdesign to the *Führerstaat* of the Third Reich, political authority has generally been decentralized. This includes horizontal features of decentralization as well as vertical ones among federal and *Länder* levels. At the federal level, the executive branch of government shares political power with an influential judiciary branch, including a fully independent and often very influential supreme court. Political authority of the federal executive is intricately intertwined with a comparatively powerful *Bundestag* as federal legislature. Within the federal executive, single ministries frequently enjoy considerable independence from the chancellor and his or her office. This is often pronounced, because at the federal level Germany is typically ruled by coalition governments composed of different parties. Federal coalitions, in turn, must work out positions and policies with *Länder* governments of various partisan compositions in many policy areas. For good reasons, Germany has been described as "the grand coalition state."[47] In addition, and with further authority-decentralizing effects, numerous public tasks performed by the state in other systems have been transferred to domestic "parapublic institutions."[48] The autonomy of the German state is constricted in many policy domains by an efficiently organized society.[49]

However, in some policy areas—notably foreign relations and defense—political authority is much more centralized at the federal level than in others (e.g., education). In several domains, again including those having to do with foreign affairs, the German state also enjoys comparatively higher levels of autonomy. In these policy areas, centralization of political authority may be high when a strong chancellor is in charge of his coalition and in control of his party, with a sufficient majority in the *Bundestag* and its committees. This situation, in combination with elevated degrees of state autonomy, can lead to high degrees of state strength regarding the "political will-building process *(politischer Willensbildungsprozess)*." Other features affecting degree of political authority centralization and state autonomy include the allocation of authority among federal and sub-federal levels; the number of ministries involved; the relations among those ministries; the role of the chancellor's office; the distribution of power within the respective coalition government (the strength of the chancellor and the majorities in the Bundestag and its committees); the strength of domestic parapublic institutions; and the organizational mode of societal interests and their access to the power centers.

Hypotheses 4–6

Connecting interstate institutionalization and construction with features of the domestic institutional structures of the states involved generates three more testable propositions to answer the questions presented here. It appears plausible that variable constellations between "state strength"—the degree of authority centralization in the political system and state autonomy from organized society—and institutionalized interstate relations help to determine whether and how strongly the latter affects interests and policies. Generally, I expect that the higher the degrees of authority centralization and state autonomy, the more likely it is that institutionalized relations will have powerful influence.

The fourth hypothesis proposes that high degrees of both authority centralization and state autonomy are most conducive to institutionalized relations taking effect upon national interests and foreign policies. High degrees of state strength will increase the likelihood that institutionalized relations will matter. In this constellation, domestic structures are an underlying permissive cause, allowing institutionalized external relations to become most effective. The fewer governmental or state entities with the power either to influence or to block potential effects of external relations, the more likely it is that the latter will have influence. The fewer veto points, the less likely it is that potential effects of institutionalized external relations will get "swallowed," or vetoed, from within the polity. In other words, fewer domestic cooks make it more likely that the pot will be (at least partially) internationally prepared. Institutionalized external relations may still have effects upon interests and policies even in the presence of veto points, if the institutionalized external relations' effects do not collide with the goals of those entities with veto power, perhaps under the influence of societal pressure. But if there are fewer veto points, the veto likelihood is lower.

Fifth, I hypothesize that "medium" degrees of state strength will tend to negatively affect the relevance of institutionalized external interstate relations. Fragmentation and dissipation of authority in the domestic system and lower levels of state autonomy will generally undermine their potential effects. If state strength is declining, either because authority centralization or state autonomy or both are decreasing, the "particularistic interests" of single governmental units (such as military leaderships, parliamentary committees, or sub-federal territorial units) or the particularistic interests of organized society will become more relevant for the substantive formation of the national interest or policy in a given policy area and time period. That shift, in turn, will increase the likelihood of incompatibilities or frictions with effects on interests and policies as induced by institutionalized external relations. Lower degrees of autonomy might not *necessarily* oppose the effects of institutionalized relations, if domestic societal interests happen to pull in the same causal direction as their state's institutionalized relations with other states. But the likelihood that subsidiary governmental entities and particularistic societal interests *can* undermine will increase.

The sixth and last hypothesis holds that decentralization and dissipation of political authority in the system, as well as low state autonomy, will undermine the relevance of institutionalized relations as a factor of national interest and policy. The weaker the state, the more domestic societal interests and "particularistic interests" of single, often subsidiary governmental entities will affect interests

Table 2.4 **Interstate Relations and Domestic Institutional Structures (here: authority centralization and state autonomy)**

		effects of institutionalized relations on national interest and foreign policy
authority centralization and state autonomy	high	**effects of institutionalized relations potentially strong** domestic structures most permissive (**H 4**)
	medium	**institutionalized relations weaker yet still effective (H 5)**
	low	**effects of institutionalized relations generally decline (H 6)**

and policies. Consequently and concomitantly, in this constellation the interaction and meaning of interstate institutionalization and construction will matter the least.

Other Perspectives and Competing Views

This section presents three theoretical perspectives that contrast with the constructivist-institutionalist explanation developed so far. Each of these views offers a different position on the origins of national interests and foreign policies, implying different answers to explain the varying impact of interstate institutionalization on interests and policies. I focus on three of the most established perspectives in international relations: realism (which I present in two versions with slightly different yet compatible emphases); neoliberal institutionalism (stressing efficiency yet sharing several assumptions with neorealism); and a society-rooted domestic politics version of liberalism. These general international relations perspectives differ significantly in their intellectual core tenets and main assumptions as well as on most of these issues that this study raises. Each of them offers a distinct view of the particular historical context that situates this book's empirical inquiries, and each entails empirically identifiable implications in specific political contexts and situations. On the one hand, the factors and forces emphasized by each perspective—together with those put forth by the constructivist-institutionalist model—may be complementary in achieving the fullest explanation possible of the processes and outcomes that chapters 3–6 scrutinize. On the other hand, these perspectives as well as the constructivist-institutionalist view may be competitive in their relative merit in explaining these

outcomes and in illuminating whether and to what degree interstate institutionalization may have played a role in the shaping of interests and policies.

Realism

Realist views on the origins of national interests closely intertwine with central
realist tenets on the nature of international affairs and the defining features of the
international condition. Realists stress the importance and underlying implications of formal anarchy of the international system—that is, the absence of
regional or world governmental structures with credible means of enforcement
beyond the state, making the international system a self-help system. States, frequently presumed unitary and instrumentally rational in realist thinking, are the
key actors in world politics. They seek security and influence. The global or
regional distribution of power and threat—including the capacity to harm or
influence others—are the key historical variable features driving world politics.
Core national interests derive from the enduring and variable features of the
external security context thus defined. States desire to safeguard their security,
political independence, and decision-making autonomy, and to defend their overall position in the system; armament policies tie in closely to these objectives.
States arm in response to security pressures, power imbalances, and military
threats. They arm in order to secure their capacity to defend their territorial integrity, their national independence, and their political autonomy.[50]

Political realism is no uniform theoretical monolith but comprises various currents and versions. How much emphasis is put on structural imperatives and how
much room there may be for other sources of national interests will depend on the
specific version of realism and the historical context.[51] However, the characterization above formulates an overlap among the major contemporary versions of realism on the key sources of national interests as bases for policy. In this book's
historical investigations in chapters 3–6, I usually focus on the strategic-security
orientation of realism that dwells on external security contexts and security pressures broadly. However, whenever appropriate, I include the expectations of a
political economy version of realism, mercantilism or economic nationalism,
which further emphasizes striving for national economic strength, independence
in strategic industries, and industrial developmentalism especially in key strategic and defense industries as sources of state interests that guide policymaking.[52]

Interstate institutionalization has not been a key focus of realist analyses of
world politics, and realists have questioned the relevance of international institutionalization for the most important questions in that realm.[53] International institutionalization, in general realist terms, means tools to further the preconfigured
interests of the powerful states in the system. Alliances, for example, are temporary
associations among atomized state-actors for specific instrumental purposes
such as the balancing of power or threat.[54] Realists will not expect that such

institutionalization would autonomously affect, modify, or reconstitute the interests of those states involved. The most important forces to shape French and German national interests, during the time period and geostrategic situation of this study's empirical inquiries, should be rooted primarily in the Cold War security context, implying truly existential threats to the physical survival of both countries. French and German security and armament policies should be formulated in response to it. In reverse, the structural rupture of 1989–1991 should have significant and identifiable implications for French and German security and arms policies.

Neoliberalism

Neoliberal (rationalist microeconomic) institutionalism, in contrast, places great emphasis on the role of international institutions.[55] Such institutions, in this view, are "persistent and connected sets of formal and informal behavioral rules that constrain activity, shape expectations, and prescribe roles."[56] They may take the form of formal organizations, regimes, or informal conventions. While stressing the role of institutionalization, neoliberal institutionalism shares many of its precepts with realism: States are the key actors; they are assumed to be unitary and instrumentally rational; they interact in a formally anarchic system; and their interests are exogenous to interaction and institutionalization. International institutions are arrangements motivated by national self-interest.

In the neoliberal view, international institutions allow states to realize gains that they otherwise could not. International institutionalization thus affects state policymaking but not the underlying state interests. In fact, rationalist institutionalists view minimally mutual or overlapping state interests as a fundamental precondition for the endurance and viability of international institutions. For states working through them, these institutions must imply the promise of otherwise unattainable gains.[57] Thereby, however, neoliberal institutionalism does not imply specific views on the origins of national interests, which are exogenous to analysis and presumed as given or described in given political contexts. They may have a great variety of sources, including those stressed by realists; but they may also originate in domestic politics, domestic construction, or elsewhere.

International institutions thus perform functions that are beneficial for states with preconfigured interests. They allow states to overcome coordination problems and provide fora for repeated interaction. "Rationalist theories of institutions view institutions as affecting patterns of costs. Specifically, institutions reduce certain forms of uncertainty and alter transaction costs: that is, the costs of specifying and enforcing the contracts that underlie exchange. Even in the absence of hierarchical authority institutions provide information (through monitoring) and stabilize expectations. They also make decentralized enforcement feasible, for example by creating conditions under which reciprocity can operate."[58] Along the same lines, international institutions help to monitor compliance; inhibit cheating and free riding; resolve distribution problems; provide or collect information; make commitments more credible; and establish focal points of coordination. Since rationalist institutionalists consider transaction costs in international affairs to be high and world politics to be characterized by high degrees of uncertainty, in the neoliberal view, these functions matter a great deal.[59] Thus the institutionalization of the Franco-German relationship, on the basis of some preconfigured separate yet overlapping national interests or preferences of the two states, should above all help France and Germany to realize gains that they were unable to obtain in its absence. Institutionalized Franco-German relations are a means to increase efficiency.

Liberalism

Both as a political ideology and a perspective of social analysis, liberal approaches represent a major tradition of thinking about world politics. As a generic outlook and unified approach to international affairs and foreign policy, society-rooted liberal "inside-out" explanations have recently enjoyed systematization and integration.[60] Rather than focusing on the state as the single most important actor in world politics, liberals consider a multiplicity of actors. They particularly prioritize domestic and transnational societal groups, assumed to be instrumentally rational, as the primordial units of social and political life. These include a great variety of interest groups, domestic and multinational corporations, unions, political parties, national and international nongovernmental organizations, social movements and other coalitions, foundations, and various others. Such "voluntary associations with autonomous interests . . . are the most fundamental actors in politics,"[61] made up of private utility-maximizing individuals. And rather than assuming states as unitary actors, liberals view states as arenas for politicking, interest representation, and coalition building. Governments are responsive to societal interests and pressures; ultimately, they represent conglomerates of coalitions and interests of groups and individuals. The most fundamental (although note single) forces driving history, and the ultimate causes of state behavior, liberals believe, derive from social pressures.

Society-rooted inside-out liberalism offers a crystalline perspective on the formation of national interests or state preferences. They derive, most importantly, from coalitions of powerful domestic and transnational social actors. Domestic politics means translating private group interests into "state preferences." State goals stem from domestic societal pressures, notably from organized group interests, whereby the economic interests of societal actors are primary.[62] They "reflect the objectives of those domestic groups which influence the state apparatus."[63] While societal groups articulate preferences, governments aggregate them and represent them in a principal-agent relationship. Thus, national interests result from domestic interests that governments bring to international negotiations.

"The prospect for international agreement will depend almost entirely on the configuration of societal preferences; in negotiations, governments have little flexibility in making concessions, proposing linkages, managing adjustment or otherwise settling on the 'lowest common denominator.' International agreement requires that the interests of dominant domestic groups in different countries converge; where they diverge, coordination is precluded." Thus, "[t]he configuration of domestically determined national preferences defines a 'bargaining space' of potentially viable agreements."[64]

Interstate institutionalization and construction is not central to society-rooted inside-out liberal approaches. However, governments may set up, nourish, or work through interstate institutionalization if it suits and furthers dominant societal interests. International institutionalization and its political relevance, in this view, should be tied to the preferences of domestic and transnational actors. According to liberal expectations, thus, Franco-German relations should rest upon and be driven by French and German domestic societal interests. Franco-German security and armament affairs, in particular, should reflect material domestic or transnational French and German group interests.

Table 2.5 **Sources of National Interest and Policy, and Role of Interstate Institutionalization in Selected International Relations Perspectives**

	realism: strategic-security orientations	*realism: mercantilism and economic nationalism*	*neoliberal institutionalism*	*liberalism*
sources of national interest as basis of policy	external security context; external threats; security pressures; power imbalances	national economic strength; independence in strategic industries; developmentalism	various (presumed or inferred; no explicit theory)	domestic and transnational societal group interests
role of interstate institutionalization and construction	subsidiary or irrelevant	subsidiary or irrelevant	important for policy making, if otherwise unattainable gains realizable	secondary, yet potentially relevant if furthering societal interests

Summary

Investigating interstate institutionalization's potential causal relevance for the shaping of national interests and foreign policies first requires careful conceptualization. Such conceptualization allows us to empirically capture the possible effects of certain relations between states. It also enables us to hypothesize about variable constellations between the logic of interstate institutionalization and construction and other presumed factors shaping national interests and policy-making, notably from domestic politics. This book's constructivist-institutionalist model integrates the three major sources of national interests and foreign policy—the external relations of states at the level of the international system; domestic constructions of self, role, and purpose in the world; and domestic features of the political system broadly, along with state-society relations. The model offers empirically testable hypotheses (or theoretical propositions) regarding the possibility, contingency, and limits with which interstate institutionalization may affect those involved. Other established perspectives in international relations offer diverse and potentially competing views on the origins of national interests as the bases on which states formulate policies, as well as on the role of interstate institutionalization and construction in shaping national interests and foreign policies. These views, too, imply empirically observable implications in specific political contexts and historical situations.

3

Why Cooperate? (1974–1982)

Processes of national interest definition and policy formulation are at times smooth and expeditious affairs. Yet, they also can be protracted, contested, and highly politicized. The formation and definition of French and German interests and policies regarding the acquisition, development, (physical) configuration, arming, production, and potential export of a new combat helicopter has occupied the governments and administrations of the two states for almost four decades. Stretching from ideas to develop such a new weapons system in the early 1970s, exchange of letters between France and Germany's defense ministers regarding the matter in 1975, through frequently stormy political times during the 1980s and 1990s, to the first definite orders of the high-end weapons product in 1999 and the ultimate delivery of the first series-produced machines to the French and German armed forces in March and April 2005, these processes culminated with the Tiger's first military deployment in the late summer of 2009.

At times, French and German officials at varying hierarchical levels and representing various governmental and administrative entities have interacted to produce new common interests and positions, or to modify existing ones. At other times, sharp disagreements have surfaced. In various contexts and political constellations, individually or collectively, France and Germany developed, reviewed, molded, or sometimes staunchly defended pre-existing French and German interests, positions, and goals. Ultimately, this long, complicated, and at times fragmented history led to the advent of a technically highly advanced, militarily eminently high-performance and financially exceedingly costly Franco-German combat helicopter *Tiger* or *Tigre*.

Chapters 3 through 6 reconstruct this history and explore the French and German interests, positions, and goals—"state tastes"—as the basis on which France and Germany formulated policies with respect to the combat helicopter arming issues from the 1970s into the new century. In particular, these chapters aim at explaining and understanding the seemingly variable and contingent effects of the institutionalized Franco-German relationship on French and German interests and policies. These four chapters' historical reconstructions provide ample empirical grounds for testing the hypotheses derived from chapter 2's institutionalist-constructivist model of national interest formation and policy formation. On the same empirical grounds, these chapters also probe other explanations, derived from the main currents of international thought, of *what* states want and do, what they do not want and do not do, and *why* they want and do what they want and do.

Overall, chapters 3–6 hold that this book's constructivist-institutionalist model illuminates and answers these questions better than alternative hypotheses and explanations derived from the various other macro-perspectives in international relations theory. In order to understand and explain French and German interests and policies over the decades covered here, one needs to comprehend the origins of interests as bases for policies. Chapter 2's institutionalist-constructivist model helps us to understand aspects of French and German interests and policies that originate in the logic of the Franco-German interstate relationship itself. The model's hypotheses also explain the variable degrees with which the institutional logic of this bilateral relationship affected what France and Germany wanted and how they acted. At times, however, factors and forces outside the reach of this model were also significant. Explanations derived from other main perspectives on international relations and foreign policy capture them to different degrees.

This chapter investigates the early years of French, German, and Franco-German second-generation combat helicopter politics. It begins with French and German defense planners' demands for new anti-tank combat helicopters in the first half of the 1970s. It then proceeds to analyze the two main outcomes of these years: France and Germany's initial "coming together" in combat helicopter matters between 1974 and 1979—even though their interests were fundamentally different—and their subsequent inability to truly collaborate in launching the program from 1979 on, faltering with the failed joint helicopter definition phase by 1982. As a case or observation, the first of these outcomes shows how the Franco-German institutionalized relations and the two states' historically rooted domestic constructions of self-understanding and roles in the world additively affected French and German interests and policies. During the five years that this first case encompasses, tensions between the factors of interest and policy do not yet become manifest. The analysis of the second main outcome of these years shows that in the subsequent Franco-German interaction, diverging French and German interests, informed in important ways by their respective domestic constructions of French and German role and purpose in the world, led to the stalling of cooperation during the first joint helicopter definition phase at the lower governmental and administrative levels. Both the logic of their institutionalized relations and their respective domestic constructions decisively drove the processes of French and German interest formation and policy formulation processes over the eight years covered in this chapter.

Coming Together (1974–1979)

At approximately the same time in the first half of the 1970s, the French and German military leaderships separately expressed the need for combat helicopters of a new generation. Most important, these helicopters were to match the existential security threat to Western Europe posed by overwhelming Warsaw Pact tank cohorts on the other side of the Iron Curtain. Subsequently, the French and German governments initiated a political process relating to combat helicopter matters that, one way or another, would occupy the two states for decades to come. However, formulating their goals independently and in isolation from one another, the two states' military leaderships based their demands on quite dissimilar defense scenarios and threat definitions (and, as shall be seen, upon other considerations, in the French case).

I take these military demands as points of departure for this book's empirical analyses and as entry points and baselines for the pre-configured interests of administrative-governmental entities affecting the overall national interest definition. The arms procurement case became politicized, reached higher political levels, and entered the force field of Franco-German interaction and meaning late in 1975, when the two states began to consider jointly defining and developing anti-tank helicopters of a new generation. The historical reconstructions to follow begin with the respective German and French threat analyses and the analyses of the military situation, then moving to other considerations and factors relevant to defining the characteristics of the helicopter. I then summarize the consequences of these factors for the helicopter-to-be regarding (1) schedule of development, production, and delivery; (2) physical configuration and performance; and (3) arming.[1] After outlining these different demands, I examine the respective French and German views regarding how to obtain the desired equipment, and then discuss how France and Germany first came together on combat helicopter issues.

What the *Bundeswehr* Wanted

The demands of the German *Bundeswehr* in terms of physical configuration, performance requirements, arming, and delivery schedule for a new-generation combat helicopter resulted largely from the North Atlantic Treaty Organization's (NATO's) conventional defense planning and the German armed forces' role within the integrated NATO command in Europe. Based on a 1974 threat analysis and projections of future military scenarios along the Iron Curtain, and considering the German forces' part within NATO's doctrine of "forward defense" along the German-German border, West German military leaders expressed an urgent need for the acquisition of anti-tank helicopters of the second generation. Facing legions of Warsaw Pact tanks overwhelmingly numerically superior, and realizing that this quantitative imbalance would persist in the years and decades to come, German defense planners considered their lack of an adequate weapons system a very serious equipment deficiency. The army leadership wanted to be in possession of this efficient key weapon against advancing tanks *as soon as possible*—specifically, by the second half of the 1980s.[2]

In December 1975, a decision was made on the *Staatssekretär* level, hierarchically located immediately below the minister, to supply the German forces with 212 anti-tank helicopters of the first generation (PAH-1) between 1979 and 1984. This was from the very beginning considered only a temporary measure—a provisional solution to the problem as defined. This first-generation anti-tank helicopter, BO 105, was a militarized derivative of a civil MBB helicopter, and German defense planners considered it inadequate even before it went into service. Its inability to fight at night was only its most dramatic shortcoming. As the helicopter could not be equipped with a night vision system, even adverse weather conditions could gravely restrict its usability. Further deficiencies included its low top speed of only 210 km/h; its limited autonomy (*i.e.*, the length of time it could remain airborne) of just one and a half hours; and its ability to carry only six second-generation HOT missiles. On top, it lacked commensurate self-protection capacities, one major reason for its insufficient "survivability." Seeing the PAH-1 as no more than a temporary measure to bridge no more than five to eight years, German military planners in 1974 vigorously voiced the pressing need for an adequately high-performance second-generation helicopter to fill the gap.[3]

In line with NATO's doctrine of forward defense, German military and arms procurement planners expected that, in the case of a Warsaw Pact attack, allied forces would quickly assume dominance and control of the airspace above the projected battlefield (*Luftüberlegenheit*). In this scenario, the alliance's anti-tank helicopters could fully concentrate on fighting enemy tanks, without major interference from Warsaw Pact helicopters, slow planes, or other anti-helicopter forces. Furthermore, in this scenario the new helicopters would operate above allied troops, being endangered only secondarily by the opponent's ground forces.[4] Correspondingly, the desired helicopter should be a "polyvalent" weapon system primarily designed to combat adversarial tanks. Yet, it should also have some self-defense capability against other helicopters, even if that was of subsidiary priority. Thus, the helicopter should be powerfully armed with both air-to-air and air-to-surface missiles.

As specified by the group of German army officers in the Defense Ministry assigned to issues of defense against tank units, the helicopter ultimately was to carry at least eight anti-tank missiles of the third generation, with a range of 4,000 meters ("long range") or above.[5] However, German defense planners expected that the development and production of such missiles, under way as a British-French-German cooperative venture, would not be completed until several years after the delivery of the new helicopters to the German army. Until then, Franco-German HOT missiles would equip the next-generation helicopters. Later, depending on the combat situation, combinations of second-and third-generation missiles should also be options. For the purposes of self-defense, the German army leadership further intended to arm the helicopter with four American air-to-air Stinger missiles.[6] The helicopter would be in the five-ton class.[7]

Other desired performance specifications included a high "survivability," provided by additional self-defense missiles against other helicopters, a substantially extended flight autonomy of two and a half hours, and an increased speed (of about 270 km/h). Whereas they considered these specifications to be imperative, leading German army officers underscored that the "essential characteristic of a new helicopter had to be the full capability for night-combat."[8] This was the core of the Defense Ministry's "tactical demand" of April 1974.[9] According to the "military-technical goal specification" of May 1978, the ministry fixed an order for 212 machines to be delivered beginning in 1986.[10]

What the French General Staff Wanted

French defense planners, too, indicated the need for a new combat helicopter during the first half of the 1970s. They also predicated their interest on their threat definition, defense doctrine, and deployment contingency planning—all of an entirely different sort from those of their German colleagues. However, in defining the shape of the desired new equipment, they also had wider political and political-economic motives related to the role of the French state in the economy and a certain French self-understanding. Such diverse motivations of different origins were intricately interwoven. The helicopters that French defense analysts wanted differed radically along all dimensions (schedule, physical configuration and performance, arming) from the German army leaders' specifications.

The French general staff's threat definition rested upon entirely different premises and doctrinal bases from that of the German military planners. According to French defense planning at the time, the French military would intervene in the "European theater" only after NATO's forward defense along the German-German border had already collapsed and Warsaw Pact troops had already substantially advanced or even reached French territory. In this "two battles scenario," the menace with which the French army would be confronted, and for which its combat helicopters had to be adapted, thoroughly differed from the one the German military planners prepared for within the NATO frame: It was characterized by the massive arrival of enemy tanks, protected by surface-to-air weapons, and, additionally, supported by armed helicopters and slow aircraft.[11]

Predicated on this scenario (and in combination with other motives to be discussed shortly), the French general staff essentially wanted not one but two different helicopters. One helicopter type should *exclusively* serve to combat tanks (and thus be armed solely with third-generation anti-tank missiles, still in the process of being developed). A second type would support the first and protect it from adversarial helicopters and other air defense systems. For these purposes, this second helicopter should, among other differences, have a higher top speed of around 300 km/h, and be armed entirely differently.

However, next to matching threat definition and military contingency planning, at least two other important factors drove French helicopter procurement interests and policies. Both factors induced further Franco-German differences in equipment matters: the French interest in arms export for budgetary industrial-developmental reasons in a state-led national economy and the "independence motive." The export motive strongly underscored the advantage of two different helicopters, each lighter and with a lower unit price than a "polyvalent" multifunctional helicopter. Lighter and cheaper helicopters could be merchandised much more easily in the international marketplace than heavier and more expensive ones. Furthermore, splitting up the functions the two helicopters had to fulfill would make at least one of the French models also marketable to customers whose first priority was not to prepare for massive tank attacks but rather to acquire cutting-edge combat helicopters for other purposes. The export motive also implied various differences in technical specifications. "For French purposes," a veteran observer of Franco-German affairs remarks, tongue only half in cheek, "the helicopter needs to withstand sandstorms, whereas along the Elbe such climatic calamities need not to be expected."[12] The motive of (symbolic, technical, or other) "independence," finally, expresses and promotes a core element of France's historically rooted domestic views of France and its role in the world. "Armament production," a think tank analyst puts it, "is a function of the policy of independence."[13]

These various reasons and motives induced preferences that differed along all dimensions from the German ones. First, since their military functions would be split, regarding the basic physical configuration, France wanted helicopters that would be lighter and cheaper than the German multifunctional "polyvalent" one. This basic difference affected core technical features of the helicopter's design and construction. For example, in the French conception the helicopter should be motorized with only one turbine, whereas the German military planners' design foresaw two separate turbines.

Another difference was the seating of the pilot and gunner. At first glance a matter of subsidiary relevance, France wanted the pilot and gunner to sit next to each other, an arrangement expected to allow the construction of a lighter helicopter than would "tandem seating"—where the two crew members would instead sit one behind the other. Given their military contingency planning, the Germans preferred the latter.[14]

A third distinct difference between the French and German conceptions was the issue of the *origin* of the target acquisition and night vision system (TADS/PNVS)—together with the arming with the new-generation missiles, the central feature of the second helicopter. Germany wanted to buy or produce under license a readily available American system, while France preferred to develop its own.

A fourth key difference related to the physical configuration of the desired helicopter, which quickly became apparent, was the question of whether the TADS/PNVS should be installed in the mast, on the roof, or on the nose of the helicopter. The French general staff, technical experts, and the responsible civil servants in the respective ministries felt strongly about incorporating the vision system in the mast of the helicopter rather than in its nose (where it is installed in the American Apache helicopter). French military planners expected such an installation to better enable the helicopter to hide behind houses, trees, and hills while in combat. Furthermore, such an installation would represent "considerable technological progress"; they viewed the mast installation as technologically more challenging, prestigious, and distinct from the American solution.[15] These were only the central physical configuration differences between the French and German sketches for new machines; there were numerous others, including speed requirements.

Finally, the French general staff wanted to arm its two helicopters not only differently from one another but also wholly differently from the Germans' "polyvalent" combat helicopter. The anti-tank-only helicopter should be armed exclusively with anti-tank missiles of the third generation, without any self-protective arming. The principal arming of the support and protection helicopter would be a thirty-millimeter cannon of a short range of 1,200 meters.[16] To equip either of the two French helicopters with American missiles (as the Germans presumed for their helicopter as a matter of course) was not even considered in Paris.

On top of everything, the preferred French and German schedules for the delivery of the desired new helicopter differed widely. Unlike the German military planners, the French general staff was in no hurry to acquire the new machines. The French army's Gazelle SA 342 helicopter could already deliver HOT missiles, flying at a maximum speed of 250 km/h for two and a half hours without interruption. Its military leadership considered this equipment satisfactory until the mid-1990s or the end of the century.[17] Receiving the new helicopters roughly together with the long-range third-generation missiles (AC 3G "Trigat," LFK) around the end of the old or the beginning of the new century was about soon enough for the French military. In other words, some ten or fifteen years after the desired delivery date for a new German helicopter would, for the French *armée de terre*, be just in time.[18]

In sum, what the army leaders and military planners of the two states wanted differed radically in terms of physical configuration, performance specifications, arming, and delivery schedule. There was congruence on the most fundamental level: both wanted a second-generation helicopter capable of combat at night and in all weather conditions, which could carry, once available, long-range third-generation missiles. There, congruence ended. Put differently: what the French and German defense planners wanted were different machines, at different times, with not much in common but the name: "combat helicopter of the second generation."

How to Obtain Combat Helicopters?

In addition to collaborating with France, Germany entertained, in the second half of the 1970s, two other possibilities for obtaining new-generation helicopters. One was buying the American Apache AH 64. The Apache helicopter was not a brand-new product but was considered to have proven its qualities, including in the Vietnam War. The Apache was about the weight desired by the German military planners, and it could be equipped with the American-made Martin-Marietta night vision and targeting system. Further, it could have been armed with the desired combination of air-to-air and air-to-surface missiles. Finally, one critical advantage was that it would have been readily available. Several of the German military planners preferred the acquisition of Apache AH 64 helicopters as early as the 1970s. Buying this helicopter would remain an alternative that would be evoked by German defense managers more than once as a quick, feasible, and desirable solution to the established military needs in the two or so decades to come.

Second, Germany considered developing and producing a new combat helicopter with Italy. The years 1973–1974 saw short-lived contacts on lower military and administrative levels to assess the possibility of a joint German-Italian project involving the companies MBB and Agusta.[19] These contacts were discontinued in 1974.[20] Following the orders of its government, the Italian helicopter company Agusta then went on alone to develop and produce a new helicopter. The A-129 ("Mangusta") would become a helicopter of 3.7 tons. The first of these helicopters were ready for delivery during the 1980s. Dissatisfied with the progress and specifications of the Franco-German helicopter in the years to come, the German army leadership would consider the acquisition of Mangusta helicopters (next to American Apaches) as possible alternatives to the continuation of the Tiger project.

There is no indication whatsoever that the French government ever contemplated alternatives to co-developing and co-producing such helicopters with Germany, or developing and producing them on their own. Neither the general staff, the military planners in the ministries involved, nor the administrations of the prime minister or president in the *Hôtel Matignon* or *Elysée* palace, respectively, ever gave a thought to the possibility of buying the American Apache. In addition, there is no data to suggest that the French defense planners had contemplated co-developing with the Italian army, government, and industry.

"[T]he idea to carry out the helicopter projects together was born on a political level between Germany and France in 1975."[21] In November 1975 and again in January 1976, the French and German Ministers of Defense, Yvon Bourges and Georg Leber, for the first time exchanged letters stating the common need for an anti-tank helicopter capable of fighting during day and night.[22]

The two states began systematic investigations of the possibility of defining common military requirements in order to co-develop and construct a combat helicopter in the course of 1976. Representatives of the French Technical Direction of Aeronautic Constructions and their German counterparts, in a number of common gatherings in October and November 1976, established a list that comprised the various studies that would have to be jointly undertaken during an initial preparation phase.[23] Parallel to the predominantly technical issues discussed in these meetings, the French and German military leaderships convened for a number of talks on the same matter. In these two series of meetings, France and Germany decided to embark on a "preparation phase," which began in November of the same year, and to set up three working groups concerning, respectively, the operational, technical, and administrative matters of the envisioned helicopter project.[24]

By the end of 1977, these groups had worked out a number of common military specifications leading toward the rough establishment of a common Franco-German military requirement.[25] At the same time, during these negotiations and preparatory working sessions, German and French experts and military officers encountered severe difficulties in arriving at identical or even compatible positions on various issues central to the potential project, key among them those listed above.

After this preparation phase and governmental consultations, the two states initiated and entered a "conception phase" that lasted from April to June 1978.[26] At that point the two states' experts converged on the motorization, agreeing to equip the envisioned helicopter with two engines to be developed specially. The timetable developed during this conception phase projected the common development and testing of the helicopter between 1980 and 1986, so that the delivery of the new-generation combat helicopters to the German and French armed forces could begin in 1986 and 1987, respectively.[27] However, during this conception phase, France and Germany's fundamental disagreement on the targeting and vision system fully surfaced, as German army and defense officials expressed their strong preference for acquiring or producing under license Martin-Marietta's proven and readily available TADS/PNVS.

Germany's preference for this solution had two main rationales. The first were financial considerations. Developing one's own navigation and firing system was likely to be more expensive than acquiring the Martin-Marietta product and risked unpredictable cost increases. The second reason related to scheduling. An independent development program bore the risk of delays that would affect the overall program and that were difficult to assess at this early stage of planning. Given Germany's strong interest in having the powerful second-generation helicopters as fast as possible, it was unwilling to bear that risk. In brief, an independent development would most likely cost more money and more time. In sharp contrast to German views, France fervently favored the development of a "European" night and bad weather visioning and targeting system, irrespective of the probable cost increases and likely delays that such a development process—basically from scratch—would cause. The disagreement would accompany the cooperators for years to come.

Falling Apart (1979–1982)

In spite of a variety of unresolved disagreements, in April 1979, France and Germany began embarking upon a "definition phase" (*phase de définition, Definitionsphase*) that would last until April 1981 and was supposed to pave the way toward a joint Franco-German combat helicopter. However, by October 1980, the fundamental discrepancies and incompatibilities between the goals of the two states' military planners lay fully bare. After this definition phase had ended without the joint definition of technical, military, financial, and temporal requirements, various French and German governmental units attempted to save the helicopter program as a joint undertaking between mid-1981 and March 1982. After all efforts to initiate cooperation had failed, there remained hope for collaboration in spite of the divergent military demands.

Jointly Defining and Admitting Failure

On April 19, 1979, after two days of consultations between French and German delegations headed by Defense Ministers Yvon Bourges and Georg Leber's successor Hans Apel, Bourges announced in Bonn that with the preliminary studies "practically completed," the construction of a common anti-tank helicopter could be decided upon before the end of the year.[28] France and Germany, as the leading French and German newspapers unanimously reported in their commentaries on the announcement and the preceding diplomatic activities, "are determined to reinforce their cooperation in the armament sector."[29]

Two months later, the French air and space company *Société National Industrielle Aérospatiale* (SNIAS) announced during the Aéro Salon air fair in Paris that it wished to apply its "in many defense technological areas successful cooperation" with Munich's MBB to the development and construction of an anti-tank helicopter of the second generation.[30] The two companies had well-established contacts and a productive history of collaboration in technology and defense development dating back to the 1960s.[31]

After concluding an intergovernmental framework "agreement on the principles" on October 16, 1979, France and Germany embarked on an eighteen-month definition phase scheduled to last until April 1981.[32] During that time, joint working groups were to define the helicopter's basic physical features, establish its technical performance, and sketch timetables for the program's various sequences as well as a calculation of its costs.

However, by October 1980, it became clear that it was impossible to bring the utterly disparate French and German operational and technical demands in accordance with the financial frame that the two governments had sketched out for the project. During the definition phase, new "mixes" of the helicopter's technical, military, and financial elements had to be tailored. Both sides agreed that the projected costs needed to be decreased, requiring modifications to all of the elements. Yet, on a few decisive questions, the working groups were unable to arrive at common or sufficiently similar positions. The French army representatives and technicians were willing to reduce their initial operational requirements, achieving cost reductions by trading in performance. The Germans, on the other hand, were less willing to modify their military requirements. Instead, they endeavored to save costs by reducing the prices of some of the helicopter's component parts. In particular, they continued to insist on their preference for Martin-Marietta's night vision and targeting system.

The definition phase ended in April 1981, according to schedule. However, it closed with a common Franco-German statement of failure, after the two states' technical experts, military representatives, and defense planners were unable to formulate the design and development of a Franco-German helicopter. Although they could develop common positions along several lines, major differences remained too broad. Still, neither the French and German governmental top levels nor the subsidiary levels of defense and armament planning implied that the failure of the definition phase automatically meant burying the plan of co-developing and producing a Franco-German helicopter.

Rescue Attempts

The months after the definition phase failure saw two major attempts to save the cooperation project. In September 1981, the French national armament delegate (DGA) and the German defense ministry's arms procurement *Staatssekretär* together asked the prospective main contractors, Aérospatiale and MBB, to collaborate in creating a helicopter project that would "fulfill the minimal technical specifications" as demanded by the French and German defense planners, and, at the same time, remain within the budgetary frame that the French and German governments could accept.[33] By November 1981, the two contractors had worked out a joint proposal, which they presented to the French and German governments. This plan was more responsive to prior French military wishes. German defense and military representatives, however, were not satisfied with the performance definition and considered insufficient the possibilities of further developing the helicopter for the demands of the German army. Particularly irritating for some German representatives was the proposal's failure to envisage the inclusion of the American TADS/PNVS—thus trading in potential performance improvements for the costs of a night vision and targeting system that had yet to be developed. Consequently, German military planners and defense ministry officials turned down the Aérospatiale-MBB proposal.

In order to escape blame for undermining the viability of Franco-German armament cooperation, and still hoping to make the program possible, in March 1982 the German armament secretary in the defense ministry made a counterproposal for a different configuration for a Franco-German helicopter. This proposal corresponded in many respects with the initial wishes of the French general staff and defense ministry's military planners. Most notably, it re-adopted the one-engine propulsion, which would allow for an overall lighter helicopter, deviating from the German army leadership's initial specifications. Yet, the proposal delineated the inclusion of the Martin-Marietta TADS/PNVS. Including this core component of American origin into a ("European") Franco-German combat helicopter, however, was not an option and would remain entirely unacceptable for Germany's partners across the Rhine. That doing so would most likely save costs and almost certainly save time were arguments that French officials could not prioritize. Consequently, they turned down this latest German suggestion. Political scientist Stephen Kocs thus succinctly and— from a "practical" point of view—correctly summarizes the state of Franco-German helicopter affairs in March 1982: "For all practical purposes, the project was dead."[34]

After Failure

One afterglow of Franco-German activities regarding the putatively dead project was a July 1982 demonstration of arms technology that included the night firing of HOT missiles—a Franco-German arms technological show-and-tell achievement. This display of defense technological capability was intended to illustrate the maturity of the "European technology in visionics."[35] However, the French documentation of technological potency remained, as the Neo-Gaullist RPR deputy to the National Assembly Louet somewhat bitterly remarked, without "a favorable echo in the Federal Republic."[36]

Parallel to such bilateral activities, the French and German armies and subsidiary planning units in the French and German Defense Ministries entertained alternatives to the Franco-German co-development of combat helicopters during 1982. Parts of the German defense administration again toyed with the idea of buying helicopters from outside producers. In particular, parts of the military leadership continued to consider the American Apache as well as, by the early 1980s, Italy's all modern A-129 Mangusta.[37] After the contacts between Germany and Italy had evaporated some eight years ago, Italy and Agusta had in the meantime made major progress with a national helicopter development. The A-129 Mangusta (at 3.7 tons, including maximum load, significantly lighter than the expected Franco-German helicopter) was to be available very shortly at a price most likely below the cost of a Franco-German helicopter that had yet to be developed.[38] Some French planners, on the other hand, undertook preliminary studies on the possibility of a purely national French development of new combat helicopters.[39] Neither of these considerations, however, led to palpable results, and they would be buried forever later that same year.

In a talk at the "German-French Society" in Munich in late September 1982, General Jacques Mitterrand, brother of French President François Mitterrand, former inspector of the *armée de l'air*, then president of the state-owned air and space company SNIAS/Aérospatiale, expressed the hope that the French and German governments would "decide upon the joint construction of a helicopter *in spite of* the differing demands of the forces of the two states, so that the two countries could realize a common military project pointing toward the future (*Zukunftsprojekt*)."[40] The talk must have sounded strange to military planners and strategic thinkers tinkering with their projects and projections, disconnected from a world of social interaction and meaning. But it sounded normal to the audience concerned with visibly good and tight relations between France and Germany that had gathered in Munich to listen to the prominent French visitor. In retrospect, General Mitterrand's words sound like a foreshadowing of much that would happen in the twenty months after his talk.

Understanding Process (1974–1982)

Many of the themes that characterize Franco-German armament cooperation can already be identified during these early years when the quantitative interaction density in Franco-German helicopter affairs was still low, or, as during the stalled definition phase, located at subsidiary hierarchical levels among technical experts and military planners. The institutionalized Franco-German relationship and the dissimilar respective domestic constructions of French and German role and purpose in the world substantially guided French and German interest formation and policymaking, and drove the political processes helping to bring about actions and outcomes. In this specific time period and area of defense politics, they make comprehensible the apparent paradox of why Franco-German cooperation finds promotion and is intuitively plausible in spite of the different goals—and why such cooperation, once under way, then turns out to be so difficult.

Franco-German "coming together" was fueled by and came about because of the interaction, meaning, and social purpose inherent to the relations between France and Germany at the time. Their respective domestic constructions of self-view and role delimited the number of possible avenues by which combat helicopters could have been acquired, and their interstate relationship did the rest. It made a bilateral cooperation intuitively plausible and immediately desirable—notwithstanding the tremendous discrepancy between the machines actually desired by each party. With the partial exception of Germany's brief considerations of cooperating with Italy or buying American, neither of the two countries seriously pursued obtaining the desired weapons system other than by a joint development program. But once they had entered the common definition phase, the diametric effects of the dissimilar domestic role constructions on their interests and policies made a smooth cooperation difficult.

Disagreement arose on seemingly secondary technical details, including seating order and one- or two-turbine propulsion. Yet, many of these conflicting wants are not minor differences in taste but represent interests and preferences rooted in fundamentally disparate domestic self-images—even if the latter's effects are sometimes indirect. These are prime examples of how the recurrent difficulties of joint conceptual Franco-German defense planning resulted from fundamentally different assumptions regarding security, defense, and arming. The specific interaction and meaning of their bilateral dealings at the interstate level pulled France and Germany together. Their dissimilar domestic constructions pushed them apart. Both interstate logic and domestic construction already underlay their bilateral political processes in armament between 1974 and 1982. Without these two sources of national interest and foreign policy, neither the repeated attempts at Franco-German armament cooperation in those years nor their resurfacing difficulties can be properly understood.

Already during the 1979–1981 definition phase, but also thereafter, the intuitive Franco-German answer to discrepancies was "changing the requirements" and "finding new mixes" that included all of the technical, military, and financial elements, in an attempt to make the cooperation viable. The immediately intuitive answer was *not* to drop the still only potential joint venture, fulfilling the individual requirements before trying to collaborate within the financial confines and mismatching time schedules. Put differently, both countries not only embarked on a bilateral cooperation program that would very likely be more expensive than shopping abroad or developing alone but chose to reconsider their performance requirements, and, very relevant for Germany, their scheduling requirements, over simply dropping the project. Although they succeeded in some respects, by April 1981 there remained too many disparate positions in too many important matters.

After the definition phase had ended in April 1981 without establishing the frame specifications of a joint helicopter, it was evident that other alternatives would allow the satisfaction of the initial goals more suitably. That was especially true on the German side, where buying American Apache helicopters (or cooperating again with Italy) would not only equip the German army with the so strongly desired helicopters much more rapidly but also be much less demanding of resources. For France, financial efficiency considerations were never at the heart of the matter, and, as discussed, there was much less time pressure, as France desired the helicopters only some ten or fifteen years later anyway. But within France too, those who evoked efficiency arguments did so in opposition to the potential common program.

Their historically shaped domestic constructions again strongly conditioned what the two states conceived of as alternatives in the early 1980s. For France, there is no evidence during this period that, next to joint venturing with Germany, anything but proceeding entirely alone would have been considered in any governmental or administrative unit. Domestic construction of self-image prohibitively ruled out buying American or even incorporating key American components (such as the night vision system). For Germany, with no such domestic construction effect at play, buying American (or co-developing with Italy) remained options—although momentum and meaning of Franco-German affairs pulled it away from realizing them. Yet, both France and Germany felt propelled to "save" the program, even though there was really nothing to be saved—except a confirmation of the institutionalized relationship itself.

These years also already illustrate particular constructions of meaning and failure in Franco-German relations. Policymakers and observers alike considered the Franco-German inability to define common requirements, financing, and scheduling a failure, assuming that something must have gone wrong. Consequently, France and Germany launched two major rescue attempts in order to somehow save the apparently hapless project in the months after the common definition phase had ended. In the process, they tried a typical remedy used when Franco-German matters get stuck: changing the hierarchy level on which interaction takes place. In September 1981, that meant moving helicopter issues up to the French national armament delegate and the German Defense Ministry's *Staatssekretär*, responsible for arming and armament procurement. The two quickly agreed to return the task to the two helicopter companies Aérospatiale and MBB, demanding that they work out joint requirements that would "fulfill the minimal technical specifications" as originally set out by French and German defense planners.[41]

Within a year and a half, the common goals regarding the helicopter had been shifted from cooperating (for whatever reasons) in order to fulfill demands as defined by defense planners and accepted by the defense ministries, to finding "new mixes" as during the definition phase, to designing a common helicopter that would fulfill the prior "minimal technical specifications"! That there was a shared sentiment of failure in April 1981—just as after March 1982—and that France and Germany felt that they had something to save is remarkable enough. After all, nothing had happened yet, the investments had still been very limited, and development work or other expensive and comprehensive research had not yet been undertaken. Note how value-charged such rescue attempts were: There was already something that deserved to be rescued from being dropped or overrun by "national shortsightedness." What deserved saving had already acquired a value.

Many European observers on Franco-German relations do not pose the question, as in this chapter's title, why cooperate? They routinely operate on the tacit and normatively highly charged assumption that Franco-German cooperation is a value that goes without saying in a taken-for-granted reality. Especially those close to the daily business of policymaking enter the scene asking "why" questions only when things, according to their value frame, go wrong.

American neoliberal institutionalists also rarely pose the questions that this chapter has tried to answer. From a rationalist perspective, atomized actors with fixed preferences cooperate in order to maximize efficiency: to reap benefits or gains that they otherwise could not attain. In the present case, by April 1981 it had become thoroughly evident that there was not enough overlap in interests to maximize efficiency or reap common gains. In a rationalist world, the actors should then part ways and maximize otherwise. As far as shared sentiments of failure or of falling short of some standard, there should be none. Neoliberal institutionalists are quick to assume that efficiency gains must be realized in the process of international cooperation—otherwise the phenomenon should not take place. In reverse, they seem to assume that the absence of cooperation must be due to lack of common interests or of efficiency gains to be realized. Both assumptions, the historical inquiries so far indicate, may not necessarily be warranted. Other forces may either generate interstate cooperation or undermine it.

Explaining Outcomes

Two counterintuitive outcomes between 1974 and 1982 need explanation: Why did France and Germany enter armament cooperation in combat helicopters in spite of their widely divergent interests? Once they began working together, why were they then unable to get the program under way? These years' two main outcomes constitute this book's first two cases or observations: "getting together" (1974–1979) and then being unable to cooperate (1979–1982).

Case 1: Getting Together in Spite of Nothing in Common (1974–1979)...

Why did France and Germany "get together" at the outset in the second half of the 1970s, although the demands that the army leaderships had formulated were so disparate in almost all respects from the very beginning? Given that Italy, too, wanted a new-generation combat helicopter in that period, and given that U.S. Apache helicopters were readily available, why, for example, did France not co-develop and co-produce with Italy, and Germany buy American? The logic inherent to Franco-German relations, institutionalization and construction at the interstate level, and French and German historically shaped constructions at the domestic levels together explain why France and Germany developed an interest in entering the cooperation.

Once the militarily defined demands had been generally accepted by the governments around 1975, France and Germany, along with Italy, wanted new-generation helicopters. French and German interests and policies could have shaped themselves in ways that led to several different historical results. There were a number of possible combinations that could have led to attaining the desired material, all of which could have been historical outcomes: First, France, Germany, and Italy could have obtained new helicopters by developing and producing the demanding and expensive material together. Any two of the three (France-Germany; Germany-Italy; France-Italy) could have cooperated, with the third either developing by itself or buying American. Or all three could have bought from an external supplier. All of these combinations of mutually exclusive outcomes (read: would-be realities) could have become history. Some of them were actively entertained by the French and German governments. One of these historical possibilities emerged, while several conceivable others did not.

Regarding its *prescriptive* effects, this is a case in which the German domestic construction guided the German interest formation process rather than deterministically pushing it to one single solution. Internally anchored German self-understandings of proper role and purpose made it quite natural either to cooperate with or to buy from close allies. It also went without saying for the Germans to buy suitable arming of the helicopter from states with which it held close ties, if they could offer what fell within the range of what was considered militarily useful (such as the American Apache AH 64).

The *proscriptive* effects of French domestic construction, however, ruled out buying this prestigious and (together with the third-generation missiles) potent arms system abroad (and especially in the United States). France found it suitable from the very beginning to produce all of the cutting-edge technological components that would make up the core of the machine. It was determined to develop and posses the technology for this high-end weapons technology (especially with respect to the TADS/PNVS, the core element of the new-generation helicopter). That France would buy the American Apache (or any other, for that matter) was not even considered in Paris. Regarding the arming, only an all French-made, or at least French co-made, system was an option.

Considering only the effects of the factors "French and German domestic construction," the number of possible historical outcomes was already greatly reduced. For France, two options that were considered feasible in Paris remained: Going alone or with Germany. For Germany, there remained three: Cooperating with France, cooperating with Italy, or buying American.[42] The causal impact of the inherent logic of Franco-German relations—bilateral institutionalization and construction at the level of the international system—did the remaining work to bring about the state of things by 1979, a temporary equilibrium outcome. This bilateral institutionalization and construction made cooperation on a helicopter program in a demanding arms system immediately and intuitively desirable for both France and Germany.

In his detailed report on the Franco-German helicopter project to the French National Assembly's Commission of Defense and Armed Forces, RPR deputy Louet notes that from the beginning, the project was driven by overarching "political reasons"—as opposed to economic or other possible factors which he discusses as well.[43] "The necessity to constantly deepen the friendship between the two countries," as he describes and clarifies the shared understanding driving the process, "can only be reinforced through all cooperation programs that have succeeded. Conversely, a failure as the one of the cooperation on a Franco-German combat tank or a European fighting air plane, brings to light the impossibility of agreeing on the fabrication of common equipment, always causes sore feelings (*est toujours mal resenti*), and so weakens the friendship between the two nations."[44] Strikingly, the Neo-Gaullist deputy, who, in his report for the French National Assembly at times sharply criticizes the planning and organization of the program, dryly lists the demands of "deepening of the friendship" as one element that contributes to France's interest formulations in arms procurement. More strikingly yet, apparently a matter of course, it is, for him, off the target screen of criticism.

On the German side, the Social Scientific Study Group SALSS, in a report to the board of Germany's Social Democratic Party (SPD) on the *Bundeswehr's* military and armament planning, identifies the shared expectations and demands of the Franco-German relationship as an important reason why Germany neither went ahead in its discussions on a joint project with Italy nor bought the readily available American helicopter. Aware of the extra costs implied by cooperation with France, SALSS summarizes in a perhaps not entirely appropriate tone: "The so terribly important friendship with France has been brought a financial sacrifice."[45] Already at that early stage, there was a clear sense that if Germany were to develop and construct a combat helicopter, a potential cooperation with France had to be given priority. The discontinuation of a potential Italian-German helicopter program, political observer Wolfgang Hoffman points out, was also affected by "consideration for the Franco-German alliance."[46]

That by 1979 France and Germany were ready to jointly enter a combat helicopter definition phase is particularly counterintuitive, as the machines requested for the respective defense contingency plans fundamentally differed in almost all technical and military specifications as well as other wider political objectives (such as the French export and prestige goals). The desired machines shared the name—they could all be labeled "combat helicopters"—but there the similarities ended. The many differences were already clear in the years before 1979. Aware of the frictions to follow from the different operational wishes as laid out by the military leaderships, and arguing from a practical military point of view, Louet later wrote in his national assembly report: "If the needs were very different, it would have been wiser to respect that and to abstain" (from developing and constructing together).[47] The social forces at work, however, led France and Germany *not* to abstain but instead to value engagement.

In short, the respective French and German domestic constructions significantly reduced the number of feasible options regarding obtaining the desired weapons system. The relationship's institutionalized interaction and meaning did the rest. It led the two states' governments to prefer Franco-German cooperation as intuitively plausible and self-evidently desirable, beginning with the first exchange of letters between the French and German defense ministers. From the third source of interests, features of the domestic political systems (as spelled out in chapter 2's institutionalist-constructivist model), there was not yet measurable impact on French and German national interest formation in the matter. However, one might view as permissive the absence of domestic collective societal actors undermining the emergent cooperation.

In decisive ways, their institutionalized relationship and their respective historically shaped self-understandings at the domestic level guided French and German political wills during these first years of the dawning cooperation. In that early stage of the Franco-German combat helicopter project, Franco-German institutionalization might be viewed as a pre-existing magnetic field attracting single (potential) projects and helping to shape how to pursue them, thus informing the formation of French and German political interests on the bases of which they formulated policies. The quantitative interaction density regarding the matter was still low. The qualitative element of the legitimacy to the other position before the interaction was strong. And the institutionalized meaning, here, was very strong, and clearly significant as social purpose. Table 3.1 summarizes the institutionalist-constructivist model's proposition, together with case 1's empirical record.

Table 3.1 **Case 1: Coming Together (1974–1979): Institutionalist-Constructivist Model and Empirical Record**

	buy American (Apache)	*co-develop and produce w/Italy*	*all national program*	*bilateral Franco-German program*
Germany	considered; undermined by effects of inst. F-G relationship (pulling G away from "buying American")	considered; yet: against logic of institutionalized F-G relations	not considered; some proscriptive domestic construction effects ("mistrust and national narrow-mindedness")	induced by logic of inst. interstate relationship; no tension w/ domestic construction: effects of inst. relations strong
France	not considered; strong proscriptive domestic construction effects ruled out option from the beginning	not considered	considered; only alternative to bilateral F-G program seriously entertained	as for Germany

A variety of alternative explanations derived from the main perspectives in international relations theory offers various expectations or predictions with respect to the possible outcomes of case 1, and, to different degrees, sheds light on aspects of its history and politics. Overall, expectations derived from rationalist and materialist perspectives on international relations, because of their difficulty capturing historical institutionalization and construction of meaning, either at the systemic or domestic levels, have difficulty dealing with the question: Why did Germany and France "come together" in pursuing the development of a new combat helicopter in the first place?

Realist perspectives will dwell on the external power or threat imbalances as the initial stimulus for both French and German interests in new-generation helicopters. Indeed, the initial impetus for French and German desires for a massive fleet of high-performance anti-tank helicopters sprang from a particular historical situation in the mid-1970s. (Leave aside for the moment whether the Cold War could be best understood as a bipolar material structure, a structure of threat, one of a particular kind of interaction and meaning, a contest mostly driven by domestic politics, or a mixture of all of these.) Realism might consider the specifics of obtaining the equipment to be secondary.

However, such a realist explanation has a hard time handling the very different initial French and German desires in the presence of roughly the same threat. In addition, the reasons why France and Germany came together in this key weapons program are out of the explanatory reach of realist views. This matters because, according to realist logic, Germany, in particular, should have gone about satisfying its security interests against this existential threat as quickly as possible, without risking any loss of time. With some 35,000–40,000 tanks at its borders and armed only with entirely inadequate and outdated (first-generation) anti-tank arming, security considerations had be paramount. Such a realist perspective would expect Germany either to buy the readily available American Apache helicopters or, as a second choice, to move ahead with Italy as quickly as possible. Indeed, there was a strong group within the *Bundeswehr* that wanted to buy American. But the political leadership rejected this option for a bilateral Franco-German program.

However, a strategic realist perspective gives more leeway to what France should have done in those years. On the one hand, French Cold War contingency plans predicted that—if NATO's forward defense collapsed—Warsaw Pact tanks would need some five hours to reach the Rhine and thus French territory. And the Rhine is not an ocean. On these grounds only, the realist expectation for France should resemble the one for Germany. On the other hand, until the mid-1990s France was reasonably equipped for such a scenario, with an anti-tank helicopter that the French considered adequate. There was no immediate pressure for France in the years under consideration here. For France, then, there is no clear prediction from this perspective for these years.

Perhaps we can derive expectations for France at that time from another variant of realism. A mercantilist-nationalist, political economy variant of realism might lead us to expect that economic nationalist motives of strengthening the domestic industrial base in this central strategic economic sector should have driven French (and German) combat helicopter interests and policies. According to this view, France should have embarked on a national program on its own. Indeed, the export motive loomed large in French interest formation: "France wants to develop and produce what also can fly in the South American pampas and in sand storms in the desert," as one German observer put it. The export motive helped to drive France's desire for two different and lighter helicopters. Furthermore, the French arms industry was largely state controlled or state run. Traditionally, together with agriculture and tourism, arms export is among the most important strongholds of French export revenues. It is likely that, in the absence of the Franco-German relationship effects, France would have chosen the "all national" option. But the dynamic of Franco-German relations channeled French interest formation in another direction.

It is not exactly clear what explanation a neoliberal institutionalist perspective would offer. Neoliberal institutionalist thought takes common interests as a necessary precondition for the possibility of cooperation. From such a perspective, there could perhaps have been some efficiency gains from helicopter cooperation between France and Italy. The interests of these two states indeed overlapped, and both states wanted helicopters that were probably similar enough to provide some overall gains from cooperation. However, this conceivable outcome did not become reality. France never seriously considered the option, and there is no empirical indication that Italy ever expected it to do so.

However, one can clearly derive an expectation of what should *not* have emerged as an outcome during these years according to a neoliberal institutionalist perspective: the initiation of a bilateral Franco-German program. Common interests in combat helicopter matters are precisely what were lacking for France and Germany during these years. If the institutionalized Franco-German relations had worked according to a neoliberal logic—that is, enhancing transparency and providing valid information for France and Germany that would have been unavailable otherwise—it should have become evident rather rapidly that sufficient common interests with respect to acquiring a fleet of new-generation helicopters, and the manifold specification and scheduling issues involved, were absent. Franco-German relations should have helped to clarify that a bilateral program could not satisfy the divergent French and German interests at once. These relations might further have helped to clarify that such a bilateral program bore significant risks of efficiency losses (as the program's future would show). Consequently, according to a neoliberal rationalist institutionalist view, France and Germany should have pursued their dissimilar desires in other ways.

However, by 1979, France and Germany entered the common definition phase despite the absence of common interests. The depiction of the political-historical developments in the six years covered above does not suggest an immediately intuitive answer to the question, as constituted by the answers "economic efficiency" or "congruent demands." Starting from the predefined wishes of the French and German armies, it is not clear what efficiency gains existed to be realized. From the beginning, interestingly enough, nobody expected such gains, nor did anybody think of the potential cooperation project in such terms. In fact, it seems that both France and Germany were willing to compromise efficiency and previously defined preferences in order to make Franco-German cooperation possible.

The causally effective factors during these years also lie outside explanations derived from a society-rooted liberal perspective on international politics. French and German interests and policies were not decisively shaped by the interests of domestic or transnational societal actors, however organized. For two main reasons, it is problematic to derive determinate expectations with respect to the outcome of case 1 from a domestic inside-out perspective: first, the Franco-German program was not initiated by the industries involved; and second, the French SNIAS (National Aircraft and Aerospace Company, as it was then called) was not an entirely independent societal-economic actor but state dependent and state controlled. Therefore, it is not clear what societal, industrial, or unionist interests the French and German governments could have adopted and translated into public policy.

Although both Aérospatiale and MBB signaled their interest in a joint development program, this was not the driving force behind the historical outcome in 1979. That the two companies' common history of defense-industrial cooperation was considered a good example for Franco-German industrial co-production, and so taken as socially desirable as well, is largely a function of the institutionalized social meaning and purpose between France and Germany. However, the evidence does not suggest that the intermediate outcome of 1979 could be traced to domestic French and German interests. Table 3.2 summarizes the expectations or predictions of alternative explanations derived from the major currents in international relations theory with respect to the possible outcomes of case 1 in the years 1974–1979.

Case 2: . . . and Being Unable to Cooperate (1979–1982)

The joint Franco-German combat helicopter definition phase began in April 1979. Yet, by October 1980 it had already become evident that, for various reasons, it was impossible to fulfill both French and German wishes, define a common helicopter, and remain within a financial frame that was halfway acceptable to the French and German governments. The second main question that needs explanation is: Why were France and Germany unable to get the program under way, once they had entered cooperation on the levels of technical experts and military representatives? The answer should also say something about the apparent perceived necessity to "save the program" after the definition phase had ended in failure.

Table 3.2 **Case 1: Alternative Explanations and Possible Outcomes**

	structural realism	*mercantilism or economic nationalism*	*neoliberal institutionalism*	*liberalism*
Germany	buy American (Apache) (co-develop and -produce w/Italy)	(all national program?)	NO bilateral Franco-German program	(self-develop?)
France		all national program	NO bilateral Franco-German program (co-develop and -produce w/Italy?)	not applicable

"[F]rom the beginning," Louet reports to the French National Assembly in mid-1986, "the political will to arrive at an accord was prevalent and has often obscured the difficulties and incoherence of this accord."[48] One set of difficulties, known already in 1979, was simply the radical differences in what the French and German defense planners wanted, and what the political leadership in the ministries had adopted as French and German needs. Pointing to the diverging concepts for the envisioned employment of the desired helicopter, defense analyst Dagmar Trefz correctly notes that during those early years of the helicopter project planning, there was anything but "clean military and industrial tuning."[49] Within the fixed frame of requirements, the interaction among the technical and military experts, assigned to tailor a joint helicopter at comparatively low hierarchical levels, could not mold the requirements that the French and German defense planners had fixed. The failure of the definition phase can only be properly explained through the direct and indirect effects of French and German historically shaped domestic constructions of their respective proper roles and conduct in the world.

The demands of the French and German militaries, adopted as initial interests by the French and German governments, correspond with these respective domestically constructed self-understandings. French specification interests, at the time, resulted from a mix of threat definition, a great power striving for cutting-edge military-technological prowess, all-around armament and defense technological self-sufficiency, and export goals. All of these motivations were fed, in important ways, by internal French constructions of France as France. One direct effect of such French domestic construction was its strong interest in self-developing and producing, as France saw fit, the technological core of a second-generation combat helicopter: its target and night vision system (TADS/PNVS). This interest stood in direct opposition to the German goal of having new helicopters available as soon as possible. In sharp contrast to French worries, to buy and include an American TADS/PNVS did not conflict with the German domestically rooted self-understandings.

Another direct effect of the French self-view's (symbolic) independence ingredient related to France's interests in two different and lighter helicopters. This element of domestic construction induced interests in future export potential, and thus in the industrial-developmental aspects of the respective specifications. It increased the state's interest in all-around armament and the highest possible degree of defense-technological self-sufficiency. Such effects were entirely absent from the German interest. The French domestic construction effects on the helicopter's basic physical configuration features stood in direct tension with German wishes following from its threat definition within NATO's defense doctrine.

An indirect effect of the French domestic self-view on its specification of the two helicopters was the need to fit its threat analysis within the concept of "two battles." Preparing the French army for such a scenario is in line with France's independent nuclear strategy and, closely tied to it, conventional defense doctrine. Both, in turn, have intimately related to French nonparticipation in NATO's integrated command, force structure, and defense planning ever since the state left the alliance in 1966—preceded by pulling first France's Mediterranean fleet, then its Atlantic fleet out of the unified NATO command, as well as its acquisition of a national nuclear force and adoption of a national nuclear deterrence doctrine. France's leaving of NATO, according to Raymond Aron, symbolizes the ultimate summary of Gaullist diplomacy as well as France's desire for (at least symbolic) "total independence." It expresses France's unwillingness to situate itself within one of the two blocs and its wish to elevate itself to the status of a great power of global rank.[50] Such deeper reasons, too, find their expression in the design and specification of conventional weapons such as new combat helicopters.[51]

German arms interests, on the other hand, were strongly informed by Germany's full NATO integration and its immersion in the alliance's doctrine of forward defense, both indirectly affected and fully compatible with domestically rooted constructions of proper German role and conduct at the time. As such, German military planners framed their interests according to what they considered the weak spots of this military doctrine, with the goal of strengthening NATO defense lines along the German-German border. In sum, even though "finding new technical and military mixes" was among the assignments of the experts participating in the definition phase, by the fall of 1980 it was clear that the differences were too drastic for the French and German positions to be redefined within the given time and financial frames, on this low level of political hierarchy.

Explanations in the realist vein could stress that German interests in helicopter specifications remained oriented according to objective power or threat imbalances in central Europe, or at least the German definition of that threat. The diagnosis is correct. But then again, according to this logic, Germany should have proceeded to buy available American machines or join with Italy, instead of wasting time with France in the difficult processes of attempted co-definition. The time-consuming "rescue attempts," including one by the German Defense Ministry, of a difficult and protracted development program sits uncomfortably with a realist logic, where security concerns should be the overriding motive informing the interests and policies of states.

A neoliberal rationalist-institutionalist explanation of this second case or observation will stress that the French and German inability to launch the program between April 1981 and September 1982 had to do with the absence of common interests—a precondition for international cooperation in neoliberal theory. That diagnosis, too, is not wrong. But similarly, according to a neoliberal logic, France and Germany should not have been in the situation at all, and this second case should never have emerged. The wide discrepancies in interests along all dimensions were already known before France and Germany entered the definition phase in September 1979. In a neoliberal rationalist-institutionalist world, there are no forces inducing states to formulate common interests, particularly in adverse situations like these. In addition, the sense that, one way or another, the program had to be saved after May 1981 does not fit with a neoliberal style of explanation. These "saving attempts" were not driven by the prospect of neoliberal efficiency gains.

Inside-out liberals, when looking at the outcomes of late 1982 (as well as 1974–1979), will stress the roles of the French Aérospatiale and the German MBB in the respective domestic policymaking processes. They further might focus on the somewhat shaky transnational links between the two, established through earlier programs of technological cooperation between them. Liberals will look for the impact of these domestic collective actors on French and German interest formation and policymaking.

That the two aircraft and helicopter companies had cooperated before and were interested in the development of a new helicopter did work in favor of the potential Franco—German armament project. It is important, however, to be clear about the actual causal impact of organized interests in the domestic spheres and about the direction of causal forces. Most important, at the time in question there existed in armament no independent "organized society" in France. Aérospatiale, like other key defense industries, consisted of publicly owned or publicly run industrial branches.[52] Thus, the usefulness of an inside-out liberal, or pluralist, view is severely undermined by the absence of an independent principal—here, the defense industry with its putative interests—and a government that is all but a mere agent. In this political-economic segment, there were no French collective societal actors who could act independently from the state.

In Germany, very much in accordance with historically rooted domestic construction, there was generally a low-key approach to the arms industry. The defense sector in Germany is not an object of industrial policy. Interests of the defense industry (also often not entirely autonomous elements of independent society) are generally not accorded great legitimacy in the public at large, or in administrative and governmental circles. Rather, the effects of the domestic-societal demands (at least to some extent in the German case) were more indirect. That their wish to cooperate bore legitimacy rested on the institutionalized reality that Franco-German cooperation a priori and by itself is something desirable and "good."

The empirical evidence strongly suggests that the helicopter project would have developed just as well in the absence of the well-established working relations between the two companies. The "domestic-societal" variable had, at most, a permissive effect, letting the effects of the public institutionalized meaning and interaction fully unfold. In other words, whereas there is not much evidence that domestic pressures (considering the circumstances in the two countries) had a major impact on the process and the outcomes so far, they also did not undermine or counteract the process that had taken shape by lobbying or actively opposing it (e.g., in rallying for a national solution). Such society-rooted lobbying had taken place not only in other arms procurement projects but also in other political domains, where such an "undermining from within" has occurred with empirically documented causal effect.

Whereas domestic interests and structures did not decisively condition French and German interests here, they also did not prevent or undermine the effects of the institutionalized relations between France and Germany or those of their respective domestic constructions. One might look at domestic interests and structures as a permissive cause. However, the swiftness and ease with which both French and German defense ministries rejected the joint Aérospatiale-MBB proposal in November 1981—as well as the alternative proposal in March 1982— very much conflict with liberal, pluralist, or liberal intergovernmentalist views of the making of foreign policies. This is even more the case where the material stakes are so high—all aside, for the moment, the huge French Aérospatiale is not an independent collective societal actor, as it would have to be in order to support an explanation in the society-rooted liberal vein.

Summary

The years 1974–1982 were about France and Germany coming together in combat helicopter matters, about embarking on the joint definition of a second-generation helicopter, and about discovering discrepancies after having entered the first common definition phase. Franco-German defense affairs are political processes charged with the political meaning and the institutionalized general desirability of Franco-German cooperation. Over the eight years of Franco-German dealings in armament issues covered by this chapter, both their relations and their respective domestic constructions underlay and decisively drove the processes of French and German interest formation and policy formulation. Combinations of interstate relations and dissimilar French and German domestic construction also account in important ways for the two main political outcomes of these years.

The first distinct political outcome to be explained for these years is why France and Germany initially came together—even though there were no obvious reasons in favor and some strong reasons against jointly embarking on combat helicopter cooperation. This case, covering the years from 1974 to 1979, shows how the Franco-German institutionalized relations and the two states' respective domestic constructions additively affected French and German interests and policies. During the five years of this first case, there were no tensions yet between these factors of interest and policy.

The second case, concerning the years 1979–1982, shows that in the subsequent Franco-German interaction on low governmental and administrative levels, diverging French and German interests, informed in important ways by their respective historically shaped domestically rooted views of self, led to stalled cooperation during the first joint definition phase. During that time, tensions materialized between the logic of the institutionalized relations and French and German interests and policies induced by their respective domestic constructions of French and German role and purpose in the world. The result was the failure of this first definition phase.

The outcomes of both cases are in accordance with the first two propositions that I have derived from the constructivist-institutionalist model of interest formation and policy formulation in chapter 2. In both cases, a sufficiently high degree of authority centralization and state autonomy are permissive underlying causes that allowed, to different degrees, institutionalized relations and domestic construction to take effect.

4

Bilateral Will and National Resilience
(1982–1984)

This chapter picks up where chapter 3 left off, reconstructing and analyzing the continuation of Franco-German combat helicopter dealings from October 1982 to May 1984. At the end of this critical period, Germany and France, via an intergovernmental agreement in the form of a Memorandum of Understanding (MoU), jointly embarked on the common development of a second-generation combat helicopter. The chapter first discusses the history of Franco-German defense affairs, beginning with the bilateral re-launch of the program at the fortieth Franco-German summit consultation in Bonn in October 1982 and continuing through the subsequent Franco-German interaction. It culminates in the initiation of the enormous joint armament project in May 1984, with the signing of the Franco-German MoU during the forty-third Franco-German summit in Rambouillet. It then investigates the contents of the MoU contract, as the definition or nondefinition of common interests, positions, and goals regarding all aspects pertaining to the helicopter program—including the machine's technical specifications, its delivery schedules, and its financing.

After focusing on the institutionalized meanings and purposes underlying the political processes of the period under review, the chapter presents as cases the three main outcomes that need explanation during this period: the revival of the program in the fall of 1982; the French and German interests and positions that were modified during the interaction processes between 1982 and 1984; and the interests and positions that have remained unaffected by the interaction in the same time period. It scrutinizes these outcomes and comparatively evaluates the hypotheses as derived from the constructivist-institutionalist model advanced above, as well as those derived from the major currents of international thought.

During the years covered in this chapter, the Cold War continued to dominate much of European politics. These were the years of the "missile gap," NATO's "double track" decision, the stationing of U.S. Pershing II missiles in Europe, mass protests, and much political ado. Below the surface of these upheavals, Franco-German institutionalization and construction held strong and continued to affect the definitions of French and German national interests and foreign policies. But these effects remained contingent and uneven, emerging in some instances and matters and lying dormant in others.

Bilateral Will for Renewal (1982–1984)

During the Franco-German summit consultations in October 1982, the French and German political leadership decided to revive the common helicopter program. In the months following the summit, France and Germany were able to sufficiently co-define common interests regarding major aspects of the program. At the forty-third Franco-German summit in Rambouillet in May 1984, the two states' defense ministers signed an intergovernmental agreement on the joint development of a second-generation combat helicopter; in the second half of that year, France and Germany jointly embarked on a phase of research and development.

"Bilateral Will" on the Top Political Levels

German Chancellor Helmut Schmidt and French President Valéry Giscard d'Estaing had been thinking about a tighter coupling of French and German policy formulation in security and defense affairs for some time, and expected to move ahead substantially after Giscard's reelection.[1] Although Schmidt's hopes for a second Giscard *septennat* (seven-year presidential term) were disappointed, François Mitterrand's assuming of the French presidency in May 1981 did not lead to the rupture of earlier plans. After the last Franco-German summit of Schmidt's chancellorship on February 24–25, 1982, in Paris, he and Mitterrand pronounced, in a joint declaration, a "yet closer" coordination of the French and German foreign policies and a deepened exchange between the two governments on security issues.[2] Schmidt and Giscard's, then Schmidt and Mitterrand's plans corresponded with a more widespread sense that Franco-German cooperation was underperforming in defense and security. That "something had to be done" in these policy domains, in particular with the Elysée Treaty's twentieth anniversary approaching, was a sense shared not only among the few top officeholders and their immediate foreign policy entourage. It did not depend on the "couple" Schmidt-Giscard or on Schmidt as a person. Helmut Kohl's succession as German chancellor in October 1982 did not interrupt the planned collaboration that was about to be set in motion.

In heading to Paris on October 2, 1982, to meet President Mitterrand, only three days after his election, Kohl followed the symbolic Franco-German "first visit" tradition that brings a new chancellor or president to the respective other country on the first trip abroad. By so ostentatiously stressing the significance

of close Franco-German relations, he instantly washed away skepticism that
Franco-German affairs had been overly contingent upon the personalities of
Giscard and Schmidt. Some twenty years after Adenauer's and de Gaulle's tri-
umphal voyages to the respective other sides of the Rhine, the dynamics of
Franco-German relations had taken on a life of their own. They had reached
stability and an (elevated) baseline of expectations that had, to a large degree,
emancipated them from specific personalities.[3]

The fortieth Franco-German summit meeting of October 21–22, 1982, in
Bonn was the first to take place under the joint leadership of Mitterrand and
Kohl. Many professional observers of the Franco-German scene were quick to
point out the significant differences between the two men in terms of looks,
habits, backgrounds, political socializations, personalities, and many other
more or less obvious and well-known criteria. There were few indications that
the massive, jovial, Rhineland-Palatinatian Christian Democrat and the grace-
ful, distinguished, Mediterranean Socialist were about to become one more
outstanding example of the already considerable collection of Franco-German
political and diplomatic couples.

Security, defense, and armament matters dominated the summit. The meeting
saw deepened exchanges between foreign and defense ministers—from which
developed the Franco-German Defense and Security Commission and, by the
end of the 1980s, the Franco-German Defense Council. Afterward, Mitterrand
and Kohl jointly announced their intention to revive Franco-German military
cooperation.[4] With the approach of the Elysée Treaty's twentieth birthday, a significant Franco-German anniversary, the two governments wanted to underline
the value of Franco-German rapprochement and cooperation with concrete
results. "Both sides naturally sought a tangible demonstration of the new relationship."[5] The hapless joint helicopter project was among the major concrete projects
discussed during the two-day consultations.

In this larger context of Franco-German political affairs, the previously
aborted project to commonly develop and produce a cutting-edge combat helicopter arrived at the top levels of the established Franco-German interaction and
communication net during the October 1982 consultations. The project was now
a matter among ministers, heads of governments, and heads of states, and it would
never again leave these highest levels of hierarchy of the bilateral Franco-German
institutionalization. During the consultations, the French and German political
leadership decided to refer helicopter matters to the working groups of the Franco-
German Security and Defense Commission, with the joint directive to enable the
realization of this highly visible and technologically as well as financially demanding Franco-German *Zukunftsprojekt*—a project pointing into the future. Deputy
Louet rigidly summarized this important step in his report to the French National
Assembly in headline style: "Bilateral will to reinvigorate the project" (*Volonté
bilaterale de relancer le projet*).[6]

Concretizing a Bilateral Will

In the months between the October 1982 summit and April 1983, the French and German political leaderships returned helicopter matters to the lower echelons of institutionalized Franco-German regularized intergovernmentalism, where the details to make the cooperation viable would be worked out. As overall plans for a tighter cooperation in defense and security were taking on sharper contours, the Franco-German Security and Defense Commission's working group on armament cooperation searched for ways to revitalize the moribund common combat helicopter activities. Defense analyst Rüdiger Moniac reported from the first experiences in the new Franco-German committees, including the armament working group, that "an atmosphere of trust" had begun to develop.[7] However, in such an atmosphere, he warned, "impatience and a call for quick results would be counterproductive."[8] While he pointed out that it remained "to date still entirely open whether an arrangement will be adopted," he also emphasized that especially after the futile attempts at a Franco-German combat tank, "in Paris and Bonn one knows to appreciate more the symbolic content of a major common armament project."[9]

Helicopter matters were again among the central subjects the French and German governments discussed during the forty-first Franco-German consultations in Paris on May 16–17, 1983, although defense and security did not dominate this summit as during the fortieth consultations a few months earlier. As a result of the summit talks and the preceding preparatory work in the Franco-German armament working group, Defense Ministers Charles Hernu and Manfred Wörner concluded a "basic agreement" on the communal construction of a helicopter to combat tanks. In a first estimate of the financial frame of such a demanding program, development costs were assessed at some FF 4 billion.[10]

After these consultations, several armament experts gave a telling overview of the state of Franco-German interaction. Analyzing Franco-German co-formulations of interests and differences in French and German positions, they documented the political and social reference frame of the activities in the late spring and early summer of 1983. Finally, they suggested that despite the previous and significant remaining differences regarding the entire range of dimensions that would define the helicopter, there was a strong sense that the program would take off and be jointly formulated very rapidly. I will look at three of these reports.

As defense journalist Rudolf Metzler concluded in a comprehensive analysis of the state of affairs of the fragile and at the same time seemingly tenacious Franco-German project, there still remained "many obstacles to be overcome" on the way to a common helicopter.[11] As is the case with most technologically high-performance machines, Metzler noted, the "devil is in the details"—in spite of renewed attempts by Defense Ministers Hernu and Wörner to bring the project along.[12] The (incomplete) list of "devilish details" that Metzler explicated in spring 1983 begins with which of the two states (or companies of the two countries) would function as "project leader." It continues with differences on arming and the inclusion of parts and components from third-country producers (most important, still, the targeting and night vision system as core component), as well as the seating arrangement with its several technical and operational consequences. Finally, there remained differences between MBB and SNIAS, which would undertake the lion's share of development and production regarding the materials for various parts of the would-be helicopter. In light of such differences, Metzler described the definition of a common helicopter type as an attempt to "square the circle."[13]

Le Monde reported, based on information from the entourages of the two defense ministers, that the two states were on "a good way that will lead to an accord on the common construction of a helicopter."[14] They "remain[ed] on the path" despite remaining difficulties after several months of attempts to harmonize differences, including intense consultations on the ministerial and subordinate levels of the Franco-German interaction net.[15] Reporting that Kohl and Mitterrand had jointly commissioned their defense ministers "to now prepare the common decisions for a Franco-German antitank helicopter," armament expert Walther Stützle reached the same judgment.[16]

During the spring of 1983, prior French and German positions on military performance could be approximated after MBB and Aérospatiale had worked out plans for the design of a common basic model, allowing some flexibility for customized finishing.[17] By May 1983, Bonn and Paris had agreed upon an approximate common schedule for the delivery of the helicopters to the two armies, both now desiring the helicopter by early in the 1990s. Simultaneously, due to the enormous rise in expected costs since the first calculations in the early 1970s, the financing of the helicopter was not yet secured. However, by the end of the year, it was clear that a draft for a governmental accord would be worked out.[18]

After intense working sessions during the forty-second Franco-German consultations on November 24–25, 1983, in Bonn, Defense Ministers Hernu and Wörner issued a joint declaration on the "preparation of a governmental agreement" on the development of a common Franco-German anti-tank helicopter. The ministers proclaimed "a large convergence of the positions on the technical and economic aspects and on the organization of the program" and signed a series of instructions destined for their military leaderships and armament divisions, which would participate in working out a governmental agreement "very shortly."[19] The ministers underlined their "intention to jointly develop and produce a Franco-German anti-tank helicopter" that was quite obviously to serve as a visible and symbolic kernel of the process of deepening and interlocking the security and defense policies of France and Germany.[20]

The declaration further stated that the delivery of the first helicopters to the German army would begin in 1992 and to the French army in 1991. Both armies would receive some 200 helicopters. For Germany, the helicopter would, due to its capability for night combat, contribute to the anti-tank ability of the army. France now wanted the machine to increase the efficacy of its new Rapid Reaction Force or *Force d'Action Rapide* (FAR), which it was in the process of assembling at the time.[21] The German company MBB and, as co-contractor, the French SNIAS were projected to lead the project as "general contractors."[22] France and Germany would share the development costs of the helicopter, estimated at some DM 900 million at the time. The acquisition costs for the helicopters for the German *Heer* were estimated at DM 3.2 billion.[23] This framework of November 22, 1983, was the basis for the governmental agreement that would be signed five months later in May 1984.[24]

Fixing—and Failing to Fix—Common Positions

Three obstacles remained before the program could take off. The first was the still unresolved issue of the targeting and night vision system—"the German wish to incorporate an American night vision system," as French sources described the problem. The second concerned the program's financing. The latest estimates went enormously "overboard" from the previously calculated costs.[25] The third, related to long-standing Franco-German disagreement on the export of jointly developed or jointly produced arms, only briefly surfaced. For the time being, France and Germany successfully suppressed the first problem by putting it off and jointly ignoring it. The second they could resolve by decreasing their respective financial contributions for the development phase to DM 475 million each, in harsh negotiations between the two governments on the one side and the industrial companies involved, most notably MBB and Aérospatiale, on the other.[26]

The third problem was, again for the moment, kept latent by mutually ignoring it and thus delaying it for the time being. It would surface later. However, during these months, French officials had made no secret of their objective to export the helicopter. In fact, as pointed out above, the export motivation had helped to shape French interests regarding a number of the helicopter's specifications, notably weight and functionality. On the other side of the Rhine, yet without confronting their French partners directly, a number of policymakers involved in arms procurement in Bonn stated—as the cooperation program became concrete—the German position as follows: "because of the much more restrictive guidelines for arms exports of the Federal Republic, the German government will keep an eye that future helicopter exports will only be possible with permission of the German partner."[27] These German ruminations regarding the long-standing Franco-German incongruity in its latest helicopter manifestation were conspicuously overheard in France.

Already, at a toast on the first day of the forty-second Franco-German summit consultations on November 24, 1983, in Bonn, Chancellor Kohl, recalling the celebrations of the twentieth anniversary of the German-French "Elysée Treaty" in January of the same year, underscored "the historical meaning that the treaty embodies for our two peoples."[28] And in an official press statement after the consultations, speaking for himself and Mitterrand as well as for the two delegations, Kohl declared: "We are deeply satisfied about the good progress of the cooperation in security between France and the Federal Republic of Germany. Already now it appears that the optimistic expectations which the French and German governments have in this context, will be by far surpassed." Detailing the results of the two days of recent consultations, the Chancellor continued: "As a first concrete result for the operational and technical need of the armed forces, an agreement on the common development of anti-tank helicopter for the German and French forces has been reached. We honor the overview on the possible future cooperative endeavors, which we have completed, and state that the investigation has generated a pleasantly large number of promising objects."[29]

After the cornerstone for the agreement had been laid in Bonn in October-November 1982, and after the clarification of some minor remaining issues after the forty-second consultations, by early 1984 France and Germany had worked out the bases of a program to jointly develop and produce a Franco-German combat helicopter of the second generation. On May 24, the German *Bundestag*'s Defense and Budgetary commissions approved the conclusion of a Franco-German accord on the program. After a final common working session, Defense Ministers Charles Hernu and Manfred Wörner signed the cooperation agreement on the development of a Franco-German anti-tank helicopter as the culmination of the forty-third Franco-German summit consultations on May 29, 1984, with a display of great satisfaction. The agreement was "celebrated with unparalleled media coverage."[30]

The Memorandum of Understanding of May 1984

Officially titled "Agreement between the Minister of Defense of the French Republic and the Federal Minister of the Federal Republic of Germany on the execution of a common development of a helicopter destined to fight against tanks," the MoU that Defense Ministers Hernu and Wörner signed at Castle Rambouillet in May 1984 is a comprehensive document.[31] It consists of three parts: the agreement itself and two annexes. Next to generally regulating the joint definition of a Franco-German combat helicopter of a new generation, the MoU's main part defines a variety of organizational additions to the net of bilateral Franco-German institutionalization, thus specifying the governmental-administrative and industrial execution of the helicopter program. Annex A is dedicated to regulating (or not actually regulating, as the future would show) the specifics of the national versions. Annex B addresses, yet leaves fundamentally unresolved, the difficult issue concerning the targeting and night vision system, the combat helicopter's central component. The May 1984 MoU summarizes the results of the bilateral combat helicopter activities of the preceding twenty months. Various prior French and German positions have evolved or been molded as a result of intense bilateral interaction over that period. Some have not.

Stipulations and Specifications as Interests and Goals

The May 1984 MoU formulates the technical, financial, and temporal frame of the research, development, and testing during the "development phase" leading to a common Franco-German combat helicopter. It regulates the public-administrative and industrial organization of the project and specifies the most important aspects of the physical configuration and performance characteristics of the helicopter-to-be. The cooperation included the development and testing of a total of seven prototypes within the eight and a half years following the signing of the accord. Upon a common basis-helicopter cell, three national versions, two for the French *armée de terre* and one for the *Bundeswehr*'s *Heer*, would be built.

Overall, the stipulations and specifications fixed in the MoU are closer to the original German wishes than to the French. However, in the course of the interaction to work out the program's ramifications between November 1982 and May 1984, both French and German positions regarding several technical and performance specifications of the helicopter itself, as well as scheduling and financing issues, were incorporated. Simultaneously, regarding a few yet important aspects, no modification or generation of prior French or German interests, positions, or goals took place at all during the interactions leading up to the May 1984 MoU.

The main part of the agreement comprises twenty-four articles, which delimit the general specifications of the helicopter, the schedule, and the broad lines of how the cooperation would be organized. Strictly speaking, this is the accord. This part establishes, Articles 1 explicates, the fundamental principles of cooperation in the course of the development phase, sets up the organizational structure and the further course of the development program, outlines the nature and roles of the organizational entities charged with the future flow of the development specifics, and launches the development phase. Together, the twenty-four articles define the joint research goals and the consecutive fabrication of the seven prototypes and their test flights, as well as the development and production of the helicopter's engines.

France and Germany, according to the MoU, would develop a common-basis helicopter of 5,400 kg weight, including its maximum load.[32] Pilot and gunner would sit in "tandem order" or "tandem position" (*i.e.*, one behind the other) whereby the gunner would be elevated, improving his vision. The helicopter would be motorized with two turbines (MTM 385 1R) of 830 kW each.

The accord also states that the German *Motoren Turbinen Union* (MTU) and the French *Turboméca* would co-develop the two engines for this "bi-motor" solution. The memorandum further defines other basic performance figures, including a flight autonomy of two and a half hours with some twenty minutes of reserve flight time. Article 2 states that the three national versions would be finished on the identical basic helicopter cell and stipulates that they must have the maximum number of elements in common. The three finished versions should differ as little as possible.

The German version of the helicopter, referred to as *Panzerabwehrhubschrauber 2* (PAH-2; Anti-tank Helicopter of the Second Generation), would at first be armed with eight HOT (second-generation) anti-tank missiles, as well as four air-to-air American Stinger missiles for self-protection purposes. Once ready, third-generation missiles would replace the HOT missiles. The PAH-2 would then also carry combinations of second-and third-generation missiles. Article 2 of the MoU previews that the first five PAH-2s would be delivered to the *Heer* in 1992; the German forces should be in possession of all 212 helicopters by the end of 1996.[33]

The French army would be equipped with seventy-five of the *Hélicoptère d'Appui-Protection* (HAP; Support and Protection Helicopter) finished versions, to be delivered between 1991 and 1995. The HAP version would be armed with a 30-mm cannon, four Matra air-to-air missiles of 4,000-meter range for self-defense, and twenty-two small 68-mm *"roquettes"* missiles. Further, the French forces would receive 140 anti-tank helicopters of the *Hélicoptère Antichars avec Missiles Antichars de 3e Génération* version (HAC 3G: Antitank Helicopter with missiles of the third generation). This last version would be armed exclusively with eight third-generation air-to-surface missiles (AC 3G) as soon as these missiles became available. The delivery of the HAC 3G version would stretch from 1995 to 2000. The PAH-2 and the HAC 3G versions' top speed would be about 260 km/h; the maximum speed of the HAP version would be increased to at least 280 km/h.

The contracting parties committed themselves to covering two kinds of expenses during the development phase: for the development of the common Franco-German basis helicopter, and for the finishing of the national versions. Adding these two cost items together, Germany committed to a total of DM 858 million (FF 2,574 million) for the development phase, and France to DM 1,058 million (FF 3,174 million). Article 9 of the MoU strictly stipulates that these figures (before taxes) are the maximum limits of the program's development costs.[34]

With respect to the potential export of the common helicopter to third states, Article 20 succinctly and formalistically refers to the Franco-German accord of February 17, 1972, on the export of commonly developed and produced armament material. This "Schmidt-Debré accord" legalistically states that the partner state has no veto over the other's export on jointly developed and produced arms.

The Unresolved Vision and Targeting Issue

Annex B is a joint declaration on the sensitive and difficult issue of the targeting and vision system.[35] In this annex, Germany states its preference, "in principle," for a European system. For the time being, however, *no choice* for either a European or an American vision and targeting system was made because of the risks of delay embodied by a commitment to a European system. Germany declared that it would choose a European (*read* French or Franco-German) system if it was superior to the American one, and if it could be available quickly enough. Annex B further previews a comparison between the two systems for the year 1989 or 1990 as a basis for choosing one of the alternatives, so that the first PAH-2 version helicopters could be equipped with the selected vision and targeting system without risk of delivery delays.

At the same time, the MoU makes clear that neither of the two French versions would be equipped either with an American targeting and visioning system, or with one produced under license, under any circumstances. Both French helicopters would be finished with a new "European" TADS/PNVS to be installed in the mast of the helicopter in the HAC 3G version; in the HAP version, cameras and a laser would be installed on the roof.[36]

Detailing the Execution of the Helicopter Program

The comprehensive Articles 6 and 7 of the MoU define the governmental-administrative and industrial organization of the helicopter program.[37] In order to specifically deal with the matters of the huge armament project, these two articles together outlined an organizational structure that was added to and plugged in below the permanent and regular Franco-German institutional structures in the security, defense, and arms procurement domains.[38] Article 7 assigns responsibility for the future direction of the program to a binational Franco-German steering committee comprising equal numbers of French and German officials from various governmental entities, ministries, and military staff.[39] Two co-presidents, one French and one German, would preside. The steering committee would take the basic decisions as necessary for the execution of the program, issue general directives to the executive agency (see below), detail for the executive agency the various elements of the development of the common helicopter, and control progress and management of the daily work as carried out by the executive agency. Further, it would approve the specified yearly budgets as proposed by the executive agency. It could also, if need be, set up a "harmonization committee" to align remaining or upcoming national differences within the directives issued, in order to assure the continuous execution of the program between steering committee meetings.[40] The steering committee would meet approximately every three to four months and would report to the MoU's contracting parties (*i.e.*, the French and German defense ministries).

The accord institutes, as the program's "executive agency," implementing the development phase and responsible for the day-to-day management of the project, the German *Bundesamt für Wehrtechnik und Beschaffung* (BWB; Federal Office for Defense Technology and Acquisition) in Koblenz.[41] Headed by a program director, the agency would negotiate and conclude the contracts with the industrial companies involved in the development of the helicopter's components, define helicopter and engine components, and oversee the work and advancement of the program.[42] A "connecting officer" represented the French general staff, and a "connecting engineer" representing the French government and military kept contact to the *Direction Technique des Constructions Aéronautique* (DTCA) of the general armament delegation.[43] These two newly established organizational bodies, the steering committee and the executive agency, were charged with getting the helicopter program under way.

Memorandum Article 7 designated the German MBB as "project leader" and the French SNIAS as "cooperator" for the ensemble of the program. From 1985 on, the general contractor of the program would be Eurocopter GmbH, Munich, founded on September 18, 1985, 100 percent owned by GIE Eurocopter, Paris, which in turn was co-founded by MBB and Aérospatiale in May 1984.[44] Further, Article 7 charges the German MTU and the French *Turboméca* with the development of the helicopter's engines.

The conclusion of the MoU in May 1984 was celebrated as a great bilateral achievement. As would become evident shortly after its signing, however, the memorandum could not resolve conclusively all the difficult issues of financing, scheduling, arming, and technical specifications to provide a smooth execution of the project. The unresolved disagreement over the helicopter's targeting and night vision system constituted just one thorny issue among others and was responsible for many of the difficulties to arise after the MoU had been signed.[45]

Such was the state of Franco-German combat helicopter affairs in May 1984.

Processes and Meaning

The fortieth Franco-German summit consultations of October 1982 marked a change in the combat helicopter's genesis out of the force field of Franco-German institutionalized interaction and constructed meaning. Combat helicopter matters had now arrived at the highest level of political hierarchy, to be discussed by chancellor, president, prime minister, and ministers. Consequently, the robustly institutionalized and highly regularized Franco-German intergovernmentalism with its rhythm of semiannual summit meetings now significantly affected Franco-German armament dealings. On the political level, potential future anti-tank helicopters became objects associated with the bilateral desire for "something tangible" to underscore Franco-German relations in defense and security.

More generally, and whether or not personally involved, neither those in favor of the program nor those (rather few) opposing it viewed the path to the MoU, its conclusion, or its stipulations as mere fixations of an asocial bargaining outcome, or as the mechanical execution of compatible or overlapping French and German armament interests. Rather, these processes were highly charged with meaning, chiefly resulting from Franco-German interstate institutionalization and construction as well as the (partially incompatible) French domestic construction.

The comments and remarks from policymakers personally involved in Franco-German helicopter dealings, or from professional observers of Franco-German affairs, both express and mirror the socially constructed value frame and baseline of expectations at the time. These testimonials outline a frame of social meaning that takes common Franco-German (armament or other) programs as serving an undefined value and Franco-German cooperation as a "good" in itself. If cooperation fails, it is a fiasco from which to learn; if cooperation takes off, it is a reason for celebration, irrespective or decoupled from the realization of clearly definable technical, economic, or military gains. These statements also give us a sense of how this bilateral meaning and social purpose helped to steer political processes toward arming in a certain way and not in others.

Many of those personally involved in the political process refer to this value frame with respect to the evolving cooperation—for example, when Chancellor Kohl expresses his "deep satisfaction" with the progress in Franco-German defense cooperation, which now finds a "concrete result for the operational and technical demand for both armed forces . . . with the development of an anti-tank helicopter."[46] In reverse, "the temptation to give preference to national solutions is large," especially when army leaders are allowed too much say in the formulation of the goals and specifications, warns a long-standing observer of Franco-German security affairs reporting on the ongoing definition process; however, he declares, the chances of success are high, since "all signs indicate that politics will keep the upper hand with respect to the anti-tank helicopter."[47]

On the background of a failed Franco-German combat tank project in early 1982, a defense journalist reports in November 1983 that "both sides have learned from the fiasco in which the tank cooperation got stuck," growing to appreciate the value of a major common armament project for the security relations between the two states.[48] In the same vein, a political commentator approvingly notes that the two states found a solution whenever the problems threatened to get out of control, even if it meant that one of the two would "have to jump over its national shadow."[49] Political scientist Stephen Kocs points out that, not least because of continual German complaints regarding France's nuclear strategy, the French government wanted to underscore its respect for the demands of the Franco-German relationship and thus "found itself anxiously searching for some impressive, tangible demonstration of progress in Franco-German defense relations."[50]

There were few exceptions to the near consensus on the desirability of the program. One interesting dissenting voice from France's communist Left, however, passionately criticized the colossal cooperation project and its Franco-German accord. Jean-Pierre Ravery condemns the collaboration with not uncommon nationalism from the French far Left: Instead of improving French international competitiveness in this strategically important and commercially potentially lucrative business through a purely national route, he criticizes, the cooperation project compromises this branch of French defense industry's future and "at the same time weakens our country's capacity for independence. . . . The Germans," he finds particularly unacceptable, "still have not given up the option of installing the American target and night vision system, even though French companies are in the process of developing such a system on the same level of technical performance and . . . in every respect comparable."[51] Ravery clearly understands that Franco-German institutionalization and construction affect the French definition of interests. He states his case from a purely domestic construction-informed view of what should drive France's interests and policies. His is the domestic construction critique against the logic of the institutionalized external relations.[52]

In the end, the May 1984 MoU document itself is a product of political processes driven by the meaning-charged processes of Franco-German institutionalization and construction on the one hand and French and German national domestic construction on the other. It bears traces of both sources of interest and policy as well as the tension between the two. For example, the institutionalized meaning and social purpose of the Franco-German relationship finds a most conspicuous manifestation in the highly value-charged Article 2 of the MoU. Framing the "objective of the program," it is a striking example of how institutionalized interstate interaction and meaning translate into state interest and goal definition. "The three national versions" of the helicopter "must have the maximum number of elements possible in common." As politically desired and conceptually conceived, "they must be finished on the common and identical basis helicopter" and differ as little as possible.[53]

Many of the stipulations of Annex B express French domestic construction effects. The political management of the diverging effects, it turned out, succeeded in enabling France and Germany to begin joint development after the MoU signing. Yet it failed, as the program's further history would show, to specify them well enough for a smooth development history after May 1984. For example, the failure to develop a common position on the pivotal targeting and visioning system issue could not be treated in as much isolation from other issues as the signatories of the agreement had hoped.

A particularly pernicious consequence was that keeping the option to install the Martin Marietta TADS/PNVS in the PAH-2 version would cause technical difficulties and incompatibilities that would severely increase costs and strain the schedule as laid out. Consequently, the differences among the three versions built upon the common base helicopter could not be minimized, as the MoU had dictated as the guiding principle of the entire venture. Too many tensions remained among incompatible effects of institutionalized interstate logic and domestic constructions—not in spite of the MoU, but on its very pages. This led to an entire list of unsound consequences that would soon move the joint development into an impasse and near cancellation.

Outcomes and Explanations

Three (sets of) outcomes need explanation in the period between October 1982 and May 1984: the revival of the program in the fall of 1982; the French and German interests and positions that were modified during the interaction processes between 1982 and 1984; and the interests and positions that have remained unaffected by those interaction processes. Why did France and Germany reanimate the supposedly dead program in the fall of 1982? Why did some prior French and German interests evolve and shift, while other positions proved unmalleable?

Case 3: Bilateral Will for Renewal (October 1982)

During the fortieth Franco-German summit in Bonn on October 21–22, 1982, and in the few weeks that preceded and followed it, France and Germany re-launched the Franco-German helicopter project. The potential project had reached the top political levels in each government, discussed among the French president and German chancellor, the French and German foreign ministers, and the French and German defense ministers, as well as among all six of them during the consultation sessions of the summits. Especially after the faltering of a Franco-German combat tank project, there was an increased sense that the Franco-German relationship was underperforming in defense and security and that "something tangible" should come out of this relationship in these policy areas. The deepening and intensification of Franco-German security relations had been in the offing for some time and was already the subject of the February summit in 1982.

In the joint press conference of the German chancellor and the French president that concluded the fortieth Franco-German summit consultations, Chancellor Kohl first emphasized that, on the basis of the continuity and calculability of German foreign policy, neither a new German top officeholder nor a new German government would affect the continuity of the close Franco-German relations.[54] The new German chancellor re-emphasized the importance of the Franco-German Treaty by recalling its twentieth anniversary in January 1983. Kohl further pointed out that he and the French president had deliberated together on how to "adequately celebrate this anniversary, and to properly honor it in both Paris and Bonn."[55] Kohl went on to transmit an invitation, formally issued by the president of the German parliament, for Mitterrand to address the German *Bundestag* on the day of the twentieth anniversary of the Elysée Treaty—"the opportunity to speak to the German people via their representatives," as Mitterrand would phrase it in his statement following Kohl's.[56]

Subsequently, both Mitterrand and Kohl emphasized the common Franco-German determination to deepen French and German exchanges on security, defense, and arms matters. Mitterrand then expressed his appreciation of "the manner of his and the French delegation's welcoming and reception."[57] He thanked the chancellor for the gesture of visiting him immediately after his election, and concluded the press conference by summarizing: "We have progressed on the trajectory of Franco-German friendship and alliance, which history had already delineated (*vorgezeichnet*), and which is more real and stronger than ever."[58] The common decision—after all—to jointly develop and produce a second-generation combat helicopter, thus viewed, was almost a side product of the 1982 fall summit.

In the otherwise detailed and meticulous account of the Franco-German helicopter project that he presented to the French national assembly's defense commission in 1986, RPR Deputy Louet writes a striking phrase regarding the October 1982 events: "Bilateral will to re-launch the project."[59] What is a "bilateral will"? Inadvertently, presumably, Louet conceptualizes social interaction, which is helpful in summarizing the argument up to this point. The concrete result of the institutionalized Franco-German relations is not simply bargaining outcomes of certain pre-existing "win-sets," nor a collection of minimal consensuses. Instead, in the case here, institutionalization and construction help to generate what the actors involved adopt as their interests. Their *will* emerges out of a political process based on structures of institutionalized interaction, meaning, and social purpose, without which these interests could not have taken shape. That Louet, at other times sharply critical of the tormented defense project, does not comment or pass judgment on such a "bilateral will" suggests that he is familiar with this view of Franco-German reality—as numerous other passages of his report of some seventy pages imply as well. What Louet refers to is what John Searle and, following him, John Ruggie, describe as "collective intentionality." These are socially consequential phenomena that cannot be reduced to the sum of separate wills or overlapping interests of atomized actors.[60]

"Bilateral will" as a form of collective intentionality is more than and different from the combining of formerly separate wills. It is also more than and different from a minimal overlapping consensus, the result of tit for tat, or the bargaining outcomes resulting from power differentials or asymmetric opportunity costs of a non-outcome. Neither can the interest to *together develop and produce* be reduced to threats as given or defined. Collective intentionality in this instance means that neither France nor Germany would have wanted to revive the joint development of a combat helicopter without the institutionalized relationship. Louet's "bilateral will" comprises aspects of French and German national interests that would not have formed at all, or not in this way, without the institutionalized interaction, meaning, and social purpose with the respective other.[61] This study's institutionalist-constructivist model of interest formation attempts to grasp such phenomena and to incorporate their effects in explanation and theory.

In the face of the still increasing tank asymmetries in Europe in the early 1980s, according to realist views, Germany's overwhelming preference in particular should have been to have available powerful anti-tank helicopters *as soon as possible*. That would have meant either buying American Apaches and finishing them for German needs or turning to Italy. Turning to France and reanimating the joint development implied a delay of up to a decade, or, given various uncertainties, even longer. It is the opposite of what we should expect from realist premises.

Neoliberal institutionalism cannot capture the social phenomenon that does the explanatory work here. The deeper political forces driving the "getting back together" are outside neoliberalism's view and conceptualization of international institutionalization. Cooperation-inducing efficiency gains of the neoliberal kind did not drive the program's re-launch; to the contrary, the resumption of the bilateral program would most likely imply higher costs than developing alone. It also risked tremendous delays and certainly meant that they would acquire the helicopters significantly later than if they had bought them in the international marketplace. Sufficient "common interests" did not pre-exist but were generated and molded as part of Franco-German institutionalization and construction. According to neoliberal institutionalist precepts, France and Germany should not have re-launched the program.

In an inside-out society-centered liberal view, the revitalization of Franco-German cooperation should have resulted from domestic (or transnational) societal interests, however organized. Even leaving aside for the moment that Aérospatiale and much of the rest of the French armament industry were not independent societal actors but state owned or state controlled, there is no evidence that Aérospatiale preferred to develop with the German MBB rather than going it alone. It is also not clear why Aérospatiale should prefer a bilateral development over an all national one. On the German side, furthermore, the evidence does not suggest that MBB's development or other economic interests, or those of any of the other German companies that would be involved in a development program, had been the causal force behind the late 1982 outcome. The decisions to re-launch the combat helicopter program were taken on high political levels, largely autonomously from the impact of organized society, or from state-owned or state-controlled companies on the French side.

In sum, no explanation of the October 1982 Franco-German armament revival is effective without the impact of the logic of the Franco-German relationship itself, institutionalization and construction at the interstate level, as an explanatory factor. Franco-German relations have full causal efficacy because both of the other two sources of the constructivist-institutionalist model functioned as permissive causes:

There were no tensions with domestic construction of either of the two countries yet. None of the more difficult specifics affected by domestic construction were of concern to the upper hierarchical levels where the political action took place. While not driven by domestic interests, neither dispersion of political authority nor lack of autonomy encumbered the effects of institutionalized Franco-German relations.

Case 4: Endogenous Interest Formation (October 1982–May 1984)

Taking the respective French and German interests in the summer of 1982 as a baseline for comparison, between November 1982 and May 1984 a miscellaneous set of French and German interests had been molded. This section explains which interests evolved and why they did so.

By May 1984, the German side had reframed its positions in numerous ways to make viable a major project with France. Most dramatically, Germany redefined the delivery schedule of the new-generation helicopters. The German *Heer* would now receive the first machines no sooner than 1992, at least six years after the latest original target date. In other words, to make the cooperation with France feasible, Germany had agreed to delay delivery of the most efficient anti-tank weapon in the face of a most dire threat to its territory. With acquisitions from a third supplier, even in 1984, Germany could still have received the machines much more quickly.

Further, Germany was now willing to allocate substantially increased financial resources for a joint development program than it initially expected or was willing to commit during the first, failed definition phase. It was very likely that the new joint development would not only *not* save costs but most likely run critically higher than separate developments or outside acquisitions. However, the German Ministry of Defense underscored the larger "alliance-political dimension" of the cooperation and put "particular stress on the political gain of the cooperation" for Franco-German relations.[62]

Finally, the German side agreed to postpone its final decision about which TADS/PNVS to incorporate, in turn affecting both timing and costs. Still, with respect to the TADS/PNVS as the new helicopter's core component, the MoU's Annex B constitutes only a slight modification to Germany's prior position. Fully committing to the French-European night vision and targeting system would have meant tying the delivery of the helicopters entirely to this decisive component—with all of the many risks, financial and temporal, involved for a highly complex technological part that had yet to be developed. Expecting that security concerns would override the priority of Franco-German cooperation, a group of German industrial companies around Siemens had bought the license from Martin-Marietta in order to adjust and build the TADS/PNVS for German purposes.[63] Siemens subsequently lobbied to build an American system under license for the helicopters. However, without the 1982–1984 processes, Germany would not have stated in Annex B that "in principle it preferred a European" vision and targeting system. Not insisting on the quickly available, fully functional, and financially calculable American TADS/PNVS is a minor process-endogenous preference modification. Without the institutionalized bilateral interstate relationship, this would not have happened either. It did so in spite of the overwhelming prior German interest to have second-generation helicopters available as fast as possible.[64]

The modifications of prior French goals, as expressed by MoU stipulations, were yet more far-reaching. They included issues of motorization, seating arrangement, weight, speed, unit costs, and higher overall development costs.[65] Together they constituted four major revisions of prior positions: weight; unit costs; overall development costs; and, by lowering the speed, reduced military performance of the "support helicopter version" that France now desired. That the helicopter was now designed to be propelled by two motors, instead of the one-turbine solution that was strongly favored by the French general staff, had consequences for both weight and unit costs. The tandem seating (as opposed to side-by-side seating of pilot and gunner) increased the helicopter's height and weight and changed the machine's center of gravity. The initially desired smaller, faster, and cheaper attack helicopter would have been much more competitive in world markets and could have been exported in larger numbers than the helicopter as now defined, with its higher weight, lower speed, and higher unit costs.[66] Like Germany, finally, France greatly increased the allocation of resources to the bilateral development program. By 1984, the French helicopters had traveled far from what the French military planners initially sketched as most suitable for much less money, in terms of both development costs and ultimate unit price.

Taken together, French and German interests evolved in numerous substantive ways during the bilateral interactions between the fall of 1982 and spring of 1984. The dynamic inherent to the relations between two countries at the time, institutionalizing bilateral interaction and constructing a certain bilateral meaning and purpose, explains these modifications. This explanatory factor could take effect because there were no direct clashes with interest-inducing effects from French or German domestic construction of self-understanding or international role in any of these single issues. Furthermore, sufficient degrees of authority centralization and state autonomy permitted, as an underlying cause, the institutionalized relations between France and Germany to be effective.

With respect to the permissive effects of state strength (degrees of political authority centralization and state autonomy) as the third variable of the constructivist-institutionalist model, it is important to consider what did *not* happen in the spring of 1984 but very well could have. When on May 24 the *Bundestag*'s Budgetary Commission endorsed the financing of what the French and German governments had worked out as a bilateral development program, it allowed the interest and policy inducements of the institutionalized relationship to take effect. Had political authority been dispersed, and had the Budgetary Commission not confirmed these results, then a domestic political feature would have demolished the causal effects of systemic social structure. This has at times happened in the Franco-German context (usually on the German side). For example, in 1982 the German Budgetary Commission shattered a major joint tank development project that Chancellor Schmidt had worked out with President Giscard because Schmidt could not secure a majority for the project within his then shaky SPD-FDP coalition.

However, under the new Chancellor Kohl, chairman of the ruling CDU and in tight control of both his party and parliamentary faction, the political authority to fix interests and policies was much more centralized than, for example, under his predecessor Helmut Schmidt—especially toward the end of Schmidt's chancellorship. In May 1984, the *Bundestag* commissions were very unlikely to refuse Chancellor and party leader Kohl, and the Budgetary Commission authorized the substantial funds involved at the stage. State strength, the combination of political authority centralization and state autonomy in a political system at a given time period, as part of this book's constructivist-institutionalist model of interest formation and policy formulation, subsumes such constellations among executive and legislative branches of government.

It is important to comprehend these French and German adjustments as modifications of their preferences, not as mere variations of behavior. Under the impact of their institutionalized relationship, both France and Germany reframed *what they wanted*. The changes in their positions were not externally coerced, and they did not simply choose to use fixed preferences under different constraints. Nor were their governments merely executing shifting domestic interests. The conceivable opportunity costs of a break-up in the program could not explain their sticking together and jointly redefining to get the development program under way. In fact, if one wants to put it in such terms, the opportunity costs of break-up would have been positive: Alternatives more closely matching prior preferences could have been realized more quickly and very likely more cheaply. Those were often difficult negotiations. But they took place on the institutional stage of the shared understanding that the wishes of both states had to be re-formed in order to make viable the joint development program.

Realist perspectives can stress that Germany, in the face of the overwhelming tank threat at its borders, did not definitely agree to incorporate the French TADS/PNVS in its helicopters and was unwilling to take any greater risks of delays. However, that Germany was willing to accept any delays at all, especially such major ones, sits uncomfortably with realist logic, as does both countries' willingness to commit more resources in order to facilitate cooperation. That France, in a state-run or state-controlled sector of the French national economy, compromised its export prospects in order to make viable the cooperative development of a new weapon runs counter to a mercantilist hypothesis derived from the political economy variant of realist thought. According to realist views of international affairs, France and Germany should not have modified their interests, thereby compromising aspects of national security and accepting unnecessary and inefficient allocations of national resources.

The Franco-German interaction between November 1982 and May 1984 was about the common reformulations of "want." It was not about *prior* common interests, independently from the institutionalized interaction and meaning, but about bringing about common interests. According to neoliberal expectations, the absence of common or overlapping interests in the very "wants" should a priori have been a strong incentive *not* to cooperate. The key problem for a neoliberal institutionalist perspective, it seems, is that that the institutionalization and construction of Franco-German relations does not seem to be international institutionalization of a neoliberal kind. According to a neoliberal view of international affairs, France or Germany should not have modified its interests in order to permit the embarkation of the program. Due to the absence of sufficient common interests prior to their redefinition during the period in question, France and Germany should not have cooperated at all on combat helicopter matters.

Finally, a liberal perspective could argue that domestic interests would either trump the external threat and French statist-mercantilist propensities or frame them in such a way as to make them compatible with the interests of the domestic societal actors. However, domestic or transnational societal actors should have driven both processes and outcomes of case 4. Yet the evidence suggests that the processes were driven by sufficiently autonomous state governments (in Germany's case) or by the state executive in a state-run armament sector (in France's). A liberal position still could stress that German industries' interest in producing the TADS/PNVS under license at least partially found expression in Germany's hesitation to take France's position on the matter. That indeed might apply. Yet, Siemens only bought the right to produce the American system under license knowing that the German government would give decisive priority to having the TADS/PNVS available as soon as possible. Given that the German government's preferences were not crucially shaped by domestic societal or economic actors, from a society-based liberal perspective it is not clear what German interests should have emerged regarding the matters of case 4. And since the French industrial companies most prominently involved in helicopter construction and arming were not autonomous societal actors altogether, the liberal perspective might not really apply for explaining French national interest formation in the time period and policy areas in question.

Case 5: Positions Not Affected (October 1982–May 1984)

Three important and ultimately incompatible French and German interests in helicopter matters remained more or less unaffected by the bilateral definition processes between late 1982 and spring 1984. With respect to these, little French or German national interest modification can be identified: German interest in a "polyvalent" multifunctional combat helicopter, German export skepticism, and the French categorical insistence on a "European," *read* French or, at best, Franco-German targeting and night vision system.[67] The first—the German desire for of a "polyvalent" machine—could, at least for the time being, be accommodated within the larger reformulation of the development program and increased development costs. The second—German export skepticism—was successfully postponed, only to surface forcefully more than a decade later during the Tiger's serial production. "Annex B" dealt with the TADS/PNVS. The Franco-German MoU recognizes the last two major differences and treats them in the same manner: It puts them off to be dealt with later. To allow the development phase to begin, France and Germany agreed to jointly ignore these issues for the moment.

German insistence on an all-purpose helicopter was tied to West Germany's defense along the German-German border—entirely formulated within NATO and NATO's defense doctrine for Western Europe. It remains tied most closely to the Federal Republic's threat definition within NATO—the threat of Warsaw Pact tanks behind its eastern borders. Germany's NATO integration was compatible with the domestic construction of its proper role and conduct in the world. Germany's "polyvalent helicopter" interest remained largely unaffected by the dynamic of its relations with France. However, neither German domestic construction nor insufficient degrees of political authority centralization and state autonomy in conjunction with domestic interests satisfactorily explains why. The institutionalist-constructivist model formulated in chapter 2 at best partially captures the non-modification of German national interest with respect to a "multifunctional" kind of combat helicopter.

The other two issues—German export skepticism and French insistence on its own targeting and night vision system—are interests that directly derive from core elements of the two states' domestically constructed views of self and roles in the world. As a result, they are barely malleable through the dynamics of the institutionalized relations between France and Germany. Regarding German export skepticism, the MoU's Article 20 refers mechanically and legalistically to the 1972 "Schmidt-Debré Accord," which states that one state cannot veto the export of armament material commonly developed or produced with the other state. However, it was clear for both partners that basic differences in such important issues were of a deeply political nature, hardly solved legalistically by one-sentence references as in Article 20. German arms export attitudes closely intertwined with dominant domestic interpretations of the meaning of its national past. Particularly connected to the "responsibility" and "stability" elements of its domestic construction at the time, Germany's arms export policies were highly limiting.[68] German policy circles voiced the view that "because of the much more restrictive guidelines for arms exports of the Federal Republic, the German government will keep an eye that helicopter exports will only be possible with permission of the German partner."[69] With the French overhearing the familiar German position,

France and Germany, for the time being, agreed to disagree on this long-standing and well-known Franco-German incongruity in its latest manifestation. Because potential future export differences did not concern the immediate future, France and Germany successfully put off a problem that could not be expected to go away, yet by delaying it allowed joint development to begin.

The strong French interest in a "European" targeting and night vision system (and its strong objection to choosing an American one) are overwhelmingly driven by French domestic construction. "The helicopter to be developed in this project," as Louet, for example, explicates, "is entirely new. It must integrate the most modern technologies, equally including new composite materials as well as in aeronautics, electronics, and the targeting and vision systems. This is a new generation, not the modernization of machines which are in service."[70] The targeting and night vision is the pivotal technological part of this new generation helicopter. The French view of self, a core element of French domestic construction at the time, made it a matter of course that France should not only possess such helicopters but be able to develop and self-produce the decisive component of this prestigious and powerful weapons system.

A new-generation helicopter with a targeting and night vision system is a demonstration of technological prowess fit for a power like France, in its view of itself and its proper role in the world: an active-independent major power in possession of the most advanced weapons and with the capability to independently develop and produce such technology.[71] Relating to several elements and terms of French domestic construction, all French governmental and administrative entities involved assumed from the very beginning that France would participate in developing and producing all major elements of the new weapons system. Similarly, the French domestic construction *proscribed* the inclusion of an American core element. The fundamentally different German domestic construction induces neither effect and does not translate into interests similar to France's regarding the meaning of incorporating high-tech components from foreign producers in the development and planned assembly of a high-tech weapons system. The divergence of the French and German domestic constructions explains the extremely different respective attitudes toward the new helicopters' central component.

Annex B of the MoU, entirely devoted to the matter, leaves the TADS/PNVS issue fundamentally unresolved. It reads as the expression of the hope that this troublesome topic might somehow go away as the incipient development work gained momentum. It does not represent any modification of the prior French interest regarding the matter, and only a slight modification of the German one. France's fundamental interest in developing its own system in this cutting-edge, high-end element of defense technology directly clashed with the German interest in having the helicopter as soon as possible. The additional helicopter history should forcefully underscore that the desire for its own night vision technology and system would remain an unmodifiable French national interest. With respect

to German export skepticism and French insistence on the domestic development and production of the new helicopter's pivotal component, it seems that
functioning relationships also manage to jointly put off or mutually ignore—for a
while—important problems. Yet some differences, especially if rooted in divergent understandings and views of self, do not go away easily.

From different realist currents, one can develop two different explanations for
the absence of process-endogenous interest formation that I have discussed here.
Realists on the security studies end of international affairs would find Germany's
non-modifiable insistence on a "polyvalent" helicopter easily explained with external power or threat imbalance. And, indeed, the German political leadership considered such a helicopter to be the most suitable weapon to match the danger that
Warsaw Pact tank cohorts posed to its territorial integrity and political survival.

From a mercantilist realist position in international political economy, in turn,
derives the hypothesis that France would insist on developing the technological
capability to produce the TADS/PNVS in order to reap future export benefits.
Such a consideration might have played a role *as well*. Yet, the strongest motivation for France's non-modifiable interest in this respect related to the prestige of
this technology in conjunction with a French self-view. Germany's hesitation to
export runs strongly against such a statist-mercantilist expectation. Why two
states with such momentous differences, then, should enter a major cooperation
program remains enigmatic for the various realisms as much as for a rationalist
institutionalist perspective. Still, on balance, realist perspectives capture a great
deal of case 5's outcomes.

A rationalist institutionalist perspective here could point out that, in its conception, international institutions do not reconstitute interests, as they have
not in this case. However, with major remaining differences, the actors should
not enter into an enormously expensive cooperative armament development
program either. Germany's inclination *against* exporting its own products,
counterintuitive from an economic point of view, and France's categorical
opposition to a much cheaper and readily available targeting and visioning system could be considered to run against neoliberalism as a larger perspective
with economic motivation at its core.

A society-rooted liberal view expects irreconcilable national interests, such as
the French and German interests of case 5, to originate in diverging domestic
societal interests. The positions of governments, in this general perspective, will
mirror such differences. The resilience of divergent national interests should thus
be rooted in divergent societal demands and pressures. Case 5's evidence does not
support the theoretical expectation. German export skepticism runs against the
general export interests that one would, from such a perspective, tend to deductively attribute to the defense industry. The French insistence on their own
TADS/PNVS should have been decisively driven by domestic economic interests, but it was not. The key French military technological companies involved

were state run or state controlled as "national champions." In this specific case, pertaining to development that includes high-tech laser electronics and second-generation infrared technology, this is particularly true for Thomson CSF—the company that would take on most of the TADS/PNVS research and development. The interests discussed in this section were not decisively shaped by the influence of diverging interests of French and German domestic collective actors.

Summary

The years 1982–1984 saw the re-inauguration of Franco-German combat helicopter cooperation. By the fall of 1982, helicopter matters had arrived at the highest political levels. The subsequent bilateral definition of common Franco-German interests and positions ushered in the May 1984 MoU. With this formal governmental agreement, France and Germany entered the joint development program of a Franco-German combat helicopter of the second generation.

Three main outcomes need explanation in these years: why France and Germany re-launched common work toward joint helicopter development; why some French and German interests and positions were modified through the Franco-German political processes leading to the MoU of May 1984; and why other French and German interests and positions were affected little or not at all by these processes.

The institutionalized relations between France and Germany, along with the two states' domestic constructions, were the key forces driving the processes and outcomes in helicopter dealings in the years covered here. Without the institutionalized bilateral relations with their interaction, meaning, and social purpose, France and Germany would not have re-engaged in cooperation on this expensive and advanced key weapon against tanks. And the different constellations between the effects of the institutionalized Franco-German relations and French and German domestic constructions explain many, albeit not all, of the variable outcomes in interest formation and definition between late 1982 and May 1984.

The evidence of this chapter's three cases supports the first three hypotheses regarding the constellation between institutionalized relations and domestic construction that I have derived from the constructivist-institutionalist model in chapter 2. If the effects of domestic constructions and the interstate relationship were not in tension, French and German preferences were modified. If interstate relationship logic and domestic construction clashed, the effects of the domestically anchored role view kept the upper hand. This chapter's empirical investigations, furthermore, furnish at least suggestive evidence for the propositions regarding the constellation between institutionalized relations and political authority centralization and state strength. The institutionalist-constructivist model grasps many, although not all, aspects of French and German interest formation and policy formulation in the year and a half of Franco-German armament researched here.

5

Cost Explosions, Delays, Obstacles, Restoration (1984–1987)

Chapter 5 covers the turbulent years from 1984 to 1987. The chapter examines why and how the Franco-German combat helicopter program—due to mushrooming costs, massive delays, and multiple other obstacles—slid into a financial and technical impasse between late 1984 and mid-1986. The chapter also scrutinizes why and how the program, barely escaping cancellation, survived deadlock and paralysis, and finally escaped the impasse in a yet further modified and revised form ultimately codified by the French and German governments in November 1987.

The twenty-four months following its conclusion and celebration show that the May 1984 Memorandum of Understanding (MoU) was not a thought-through, well-balanced, or realistic formula according to which France and Germany could develop and construct a combat helicopter. Shortly after its signing, numerous difficulties had already surfaced that, in combination, moved the development into an impasse with no obvious way out. By the early summer of 1986, it had become clear that the technical demands and specifications, the financial frame, or both required fundamental redefinition or significant adjustment. Nor, it soon turned out, was the MoU's schedule realistic or tenable. Too many factors spoke against the program as designed at the time, amounting to "the impossibility of respecting the accord of May 29."[1]

By 1986, many sharply criticized the program. Some considered it obsolete. Once again the program was practically dead, again France and Germany revived it, and the Franco-German answer to all of the calamities that plagued the program was, again, a Franco-German solution. On the way out of the impasse, France and Germany moved, as one commentator put it, from a Franco-German French and a Franco-German German to a Franco-German Franco-German helicopter. In November 1987, the two countries signed an agreement that substantially modified the regulations of the May 1984 MoU. The combat helicopter would ultimately be developed based on this November 1987 covenant. The result was a product yet further removed from the initial conceptions of the

1970s, and yet further molded by the political forces of French, German, and Franco-German institutionalization and construction.

This chapter's four case studies tackle the four key outcomes that need explanation during the three and a half years that the chapter covers: why the program so quickly drifted into paralysis and near-cancellation; why it was *not* canceled in spite of numerous reasons to do so; why France and Germany settled the onerous issue regarding the night vision and targeting system the way they did, defining their interests to accept the enormous costs that this settlement implied; and, finally, why France and Germany defined their interests and positions regarding the much revised joint development program in its entirety. The stipulations of the agreement they signed in November 1987 expresses how French and German interests and goals had evolved since May 1986.

Drifting into Deadlock (June 1984–May 1986)

By early 1985, it had already become clear that, given the military and technical demands, the budgetary frame set for the armament project in the May 1984 MoU could not hold. The project's cost explosions were so massive that, according to some estimates, the acquisition of American Apache helicopters might have saved Germany DM 2 billion without sacrificing any decisive military or technological performance.[2] In addition, numerous other obstacles surfaced in the year and a half after the MoU's signing. Together, they made its smooth execution impossible.

Into the Impasse

After the program's steering committee had convened for the first time in June 1984 to set the helicopter program on its way, MBB and Aérospatiale co-founded and owned in equal shares the *Groupement d'Intérêt Économique* (GIE) Eurocopter, a loose organizational connection according to French law, to facilitate a more flexible response in realizing the program.[3] However, by the steering committee's second meeting in September 1984, the first difficulties in translating the MoU into a working program had already begun to surface. Some tensions originated in the lack of clarity of some of the MoU's stipulations—for example, regarding the exact role of GIE Eurocopter and those of the harmonization committee and the German military acquisition authority (BWB). Specifically, the French steering committee members wanted the harmonization committee to play a larger role in the daily management of the project than the German BWB was willing to grant.

More profound frictions, however, concerned the divergent views on the choice of equipment, components, subcomponents, and material to be bought and assembled in the course of the program. The French participants in the steering committee hoped to limit the competition to French and German producers.

Taking a more market-oriented approach, the Germans favored opening it equally to outside suppliers. According to French National Assembly *rapporteur* Louet, hardly hiding his deprecation, the Germans hoped for a "total international competition that would favor quite evidently the United States."[4] The MoU's Article 5 had stipulated that the most important equipment and components for the helicopter should ideally be produced cooperatively by French and German companies. Yet, it also stated that economic aspects, notably competition, would be considered. Although France and Germany had signed the same formulations, French and Germans interpreted the words quite differently in the daily practice of implementing the memorandum.

Such frictions aside, however, the program advanced quickly in other areas. Commonalities in many major and minor details developed and were incorporated. For example, France and Germany quickly agreed to welcome the eventual participation of other states in the program, provided this would neither involve major modifications of the specifications reached nor cause cost increases or delays in the realization of the program.

At the third gathering of the steering committee in February 1985, however, technical experts indicated that the projected power of the two engines of some 900 kW each would probably not suffice at the moment of take-off, for a machine now expected to have a mass of 5.5 tons. "It is amazing," as Louet commented on the problem with dashing acidity, "that one takes notice of that only six months after the signing of the accord."[5] By the steering committee's fourth meeting in May 1985, the engines' capacity could have been increased. However, the issue of the targeting and vision system, unresolved in the MoU, and the ongoing "competition between the two vision systems," as some newspapers had it, continued to strain the evolution of the project.

The steering committee's fifth meeting in October 1985 marks two important events. First, French and German governmental and industrial representatives agreed on the creation of Eurocopter GmbH, Munich, as a joint Franco-German subsidiary of Eurocopter GIE. This entity, founded specifically for the purposes of the Franco-German combat helicopter project, would become the main contractor for further development and construction work.[6] Second, the industrial companies chiefly involved in the technical realization of the program submitted, for the first time, an integral estimate of the expected expenses for the entire development program as specified in the May 1984 accord. This latest cost estimate, which the steering committee judged competent and realistic, made it clear that that the development program's financial framework as laid out in the May 1984 MoU had become obsolete.[7] As a first reaction to this sobering reality, the committee set up two reflection groups assigned to reduce costs and technical demands—one composed of the Franco-German military leaderships and another of representatives of the industrial companies involved. These double consultations, however, did not immediately yield significant results.

At the steering committee's sixth meeting in January 1986, the industrialists for the first time presented a precise estimate of the "cost overrun" (*surcoût*). In these figures, the helicopter development costs alone had risen to FF 4,317 million for France—constituting an increase of 36 percent over the costs estimated for the May 1984 MoU—and FF 3,963 million (DM 1.32 billion) for Germany—a cost increase of 54 percent over the figures on which the MoU had been concluded only eighteen months earlier. Further, it became manifest that the MoU's timetable would almost certainly not be tenable. In January 1986, the project was an estimated two and a half years behind the schedule set out less than two years before.[8]

In the Impasse

In February 1986 the helicopter's program difficulties, which had accumulated and aggravated on the operational levels since June 1984, again reached the ministerial level. Without yet indicating any possible solutions, Defense Ministers Manfred Wörner and Paul Quilès both expressed their personal worries about the projected cost increases. Simultaneously, MBB let it be known that, in its present state, the project had become unrealistic; according to some information, it was no longer interested in continuing the program.[9]

"War with the bursar," defense journalist Wolfgang Hoffmann entitled an article, in which he sharply criticized the program's planning and management and posed even the militarily most basic question—namely, whether the French and German forces needed an anti-tank helicopter at all. Given the massive delays and reports about the development of electronic missiles on the other side of the Iron Curtain, Hoffman warned that the helicopter might already have become obsolete by the time of delivery, now expected by the German army in 1995 at the earliest. Irrespective of military considerations, he judged the helicopter a "cost scandal." In light of the "cost explosions and considerable delays," Franco-German armament observer Alexander Szandar deemed the situation much more dramatic than the responsible ministers did, judging the project to be "drifting towards a fiasco." Prematurely, as shall be seen, Szandar declared that the "Franco-German communal production will not take off."[10]

In March 1986, neither the new French defense minister André Giraud (who had taken office after the French parliamentary elections in the same month yielded a majority for a new government under Prime Minister Jacques Chirac) nor the German *Bundestag*'s Defense Committee (*Verteidigungsausschuß*) was willing to continue the project with massive cost increases in the billions of marks range. According to one report, when Giraud took office in the defense ministry, he found four different helicopter dossiers on his desk.[11] Some commentators called for "pulling the emergency brake."[12] Unlike Giraud and the *Verteidigungsausschuß*, however, Chancellor Kohl and President Mitterrand remained favorable toward the program, albeit without commenting on its details.[13] Nonetheless, the mood of almost all those closely or peripherally involved in the program had reached its nadir. "The helicopter," as one observer put it, not only "has trouble taking off, [but] has lead in its blades."[14]

At the seventh meeting of the helicopter project's steering committee, the industrial contractors presented the program's definitive "overcost" calculations. The total costs of the French share for developing, constructing the prototypes, and testing was now fixed at FF 4,443 million (an increase of 40 percent) and the German share at FF 4,066 million (an increase of 58 percent over the approximate calculations of early summer 1984). Only two years after the two countries' defense ministers had signed the memorandum setting the project on its way, the total costs for the development alone had reached FF 8.5 billion.

By late spring of 1986, it was an open secret that the German army leadership—diverging sharply from the official position of its government—now much preferred to buy the more readily available American Apache helicopters for the *Bundeswehr*.[15] Although he did not fully line up with the position that some of his defense planners now (more or less openly) promoted, the German defense minister reminded the public that the German army had initially wanted a helicopter capable of fighting at night by 1986. The delivery date of the first Franco-German helicopters, Wörner recalled, had first been postponed to the end of the 1980s, then scheduled for 1992. Now, 1995 was the earliest the helicopters could be available.[16]

Only two years after the inauguration of the program had been celebrated with so much satisfaction and sense of achievement, the Franco-German helicopter project reached an impasse with no obvious escape. Disastrous cost explosions and massive delays plagued the program, and even its military purpose had become contested. Such was the context and mood on May 12, 1986, when André Giraud met his German counterpart Manfred Wörner in Bonn for a first "introductory visit" to be held, as an official source in Paris informed the press, "in a spirit of openness."[17]

Out of the Impasse (May 1986–November 1987)

After the ministerial meeting between Giraud and Wörner on May 12, various French and German governmental units at different hierarchical levels executed wide-ranging program revisions. Between March and July 1987, the two defense ministers, with the backing of their heads of governments and state, pinned down the main results of this reopened redefinition. At the fiftieth Franco-German summit consultations in Karlsruhe in November 1987, France and Germany formalized these results, moving the project, in much revised form, out of the deadlock. The reinvigorated joint undertaking was less French, less German, and yet more Franco-German.

Moribundity and Revival

The meeting of Defense Ministers Giraud and Wörner on May 12, 1986 yielded the scheduling of two extra sessions between the French and the German armament directors, in order to "deblock the situation":[18] one in Paris on May 30, and a second in Bonn ten days later. These activities brought a Franco-German governmental agreement to give the main industrial companies two months to prepare definite propositions on how to deal with the central complications of the project. Further, the two governments agreed to reexamine the entire program with respect to its technical specifications and costs by July 1, 1986.[19] At the same time, the French government let the public know that "at no price" would it accept integrating into the combat helicopter a vision and targeting system from an American supplier.[20]

By mid-June, the course of the French and German armament directors' discussions, "in a cooperative fashion," gave "reason for cautious optimism for a solution." According to some information, the program was again "on a good way."[21] At the same time, Chancellor Kohl and President Mitterrand announced that they would again discuss the helicopter program during one of the frequent working meetings in Rambouillet on June 17.[22] There, in a joint press conference following their discussion, Mitterrand announced that "the common will of the Chancellor and myself, the political will, must allow us to overcome the difficulties toward an anti-tank helicopter." Both Mitterrand and Kohl further stressed their more general will "to overcome the difficulties that have appeared for some time in the bilateral relations." *Le Figaro* condensed the outcome of the Kohl-Mitterrand session with the headline, "Political accord for a Franco-German helicopter."[23]

In July 1986, after the talks on the armament directors' level and the common Mitterrand-Kohl declaration in favor of the program, helicopter affairs returned to the ministerial level. On July 25, Defense Ministers Wörner and Giraud worked hard in a four-hour session, consulting various military and technical experts on the state of the program and on potential modifications to enable its perpetuation in a re-tailored form. The participants, according to French sources, "expressed their will to arrive at a compromise."[24] As an immediately palpable result, the Giraud-Wörner session yielded the joint commission of two studies, charging the two states' armament directors and their administrations with the express mission of reaching conclusions rapidly.

The first of these studies aimed at resolving "the irritating problem of the visioning system."[25] Again, the two main issues were, first, where to get it—that is, buying American or developing their own; and second, where to install it in the helicopter—that is, in its nose or in the mast. Postponing a decision on these questions, as the 1984 MoU had done, implied tremendous costs and delays. If the program was to have a common Franco-German future, these troubles required decisive resolution soon. The second study would deal with the issues of seating (pilot and gunner "in tandem" or side by side) and motorization (one or two engines). Although the 1984 MoU had established the development task regarding these two technical configuration issues, Giraud and Wörner agreed to reopen and potentially rework the positions on these matters.[26]

With these results, the helicopter project seemed to escape deadlock and cancellation. The Giraud-Wörner meeting of July 1986 once again opened doors for the resolution of the manifold problems and difficulties. The subsequent months would be filled with intensive bilateral collaboration at the "working levels" in order to complete the two studies that the ministers had commissioned.

Revamp

By early spring 1987, the work on the two studies had progressed satisfactorily enough to present their results to the defense ministers. In a number of working sessions during the preceding weeks, the French and German armament directors and the two ground forces' generals had carefully prepared for the ministerial meeting.[27] At the German Defense Ministry at the *Hardthöhe* on March 20, 1987, Giraud and Wörner accepted and adopted their joint propositions and took the "fundamental decisions" to (re-)inaugurate the helicopter program, agreeing that definite decisions would be made on the technical, industrial, and financial specifications by July.[28] Although the earliest delivery date was now set for 1996, the agreement was readily viewed as a "breakthrough."[29]

Most important, the preliminary results of these studies specified that "all vision and targeting system electronic components will be European"—that is, as the daily *Libération* rightly comments, "truthfully speaking altogether French."[30] The French electronics companies Thomson CSF and Eltro would undertake the development of this central part of the helicopter. The helicopter would be propelled by two turbines, and gunner and pilot would sit "in tandem." Aérospatiale and MBB would continue to take the lead for the development of the helicopter's cell, and MTU and Turboméca for the engines. Regarding arming and finishing, France and Germany would now develop a single anti-tank version (PAH-2 *and* HAC) to be armed with eight anti-tank air-to-surface missiles and four air-to-air missiles.[31] The arming of the combat support and protection version (HAP) would remain the same. The costs for the development phase were set at DM 3.5 billion (before taxes), and the further studies indicated France's and Germany's continued intention to acquire 215 and 212 helicopters, respectively.

After the session in Bonn, Defense Ministers Giraud and Wörner "praised the Franco-German spirit of cooperation" and congratulated each other.[32] A meeting "behind closed doors" between Chancellor Kohl and President Mitterrand, scheduled for March 28, and a conference between Kohl and Prime Minister Chirac a few days thereafter would underline the significance that both governments accorded to

Franco-German defense and armament cooperation and endorse the ministerial re-adoption of the mammoth joint development program at the highest political level.[33] "Finally one knows what one talks about," summarizes political commentator Pierre Darcourt, considering the results a "decisive step." Before, he finds, the helicopters really "did have nothing in common but the name. There was a Franco-German German helicopter and a Franco-German French helicopter."[34] Now, the story found a happy ending with a truly Franco-German helicopter. The formal adoption of the new program had become only a question of time.

Simultaneously, however, cost and financing issues kept fermenting. In April, new estimates reached the public that the helicopter's unit price—that is, the ultimate acquisition cost per helicopter (excluding the preceding costs for research, development, testing, and serial production preparation)—would be over FF 100 million. "The very elevated costs of that program," remarked the president of the national assembly's defense commission, "will very certainly lead to a modification of the doctrine of [the helicopter's] employment, notably for the imperative necessity to protect at all costs a piece of equipment that is so expensive."[35]

In early June, the program's planners on the working levels of military experts and industrialists estimated the ultimate unit price per helicopter at FF 120 million. In a telling example of French statism, Defense Minister Giraud first sent a "warning" to the planners in the industrial companies involved, stating that the helicopter program "will only be launched next summer if its price is acceptable. Therefore, a convergent plot" (*complot convergent*) among the general staffs and industrialists was needed in order to lower the price of the weapon.[36] Sharply attacking the military leaders and industrialists, especially the Aérospatiale planners, for defining "too often technical characteristics without caring about the costs," Giraud admonished: "if the numbers that are in the process of being worked out leave me fearing that industrial propositions do not take into account the budgetary provisions, . . . we will not make this helicopter. . . . There is no absolute necessity for a weapon of this sort."[37]

With the main purpose of completing the general framework agreement, German Defense Minister Wörner traveled to France on July 15–17, 1987. Wörner's visit began with "intensive talks" with Prime Minister Chirac and the chairman of the National Assembly's Foreign Affairs Commission, former President Giscard d'Estaing.[38] Wörner's most important talks, however, in several sessions over the three-day period, were again with his ministerial counterpart Giraud. The single most significant and difficult issue was how to concretize and fix what had been worked out over the winter, and what had been generally adopted in March, regarding rejuvenating the helicopter program. On July 16, 1987, Giraud and Wörner announced in Cannet-des-Maures (Var) that they had concluded a "definitive agreement" on the development and construction of a combat helicopter.[39] Although its financing had yet to be secured in the German defense budgets and in the Federal Republic's budgets at large, Wörner's three-day trip brought about the re-inauguration of the Franco-German helicopter program in a new form. France and Germany saved the formal adoption of the revived and revamped development program—"the most important Franco-German cooperation in the domain of arms fabrication since the beginning of the 1970s"[40]—for the fiftieth Franco-German summit consultations, scheduled for November in Karlsruhe.

The new machine would be equipped with an all-European vision and targeting system to be installed in the helicopter's mast; it would be propelled by two turbines, and gunner and pilot would sit one behind the other ("tandem seating"). The helicopter would have a mass of about 5.4 tons, with slight variations depending on the finishing and arming. France and Germany would share the program leadership, and a permanent Franco-German "program office" would manage the program.[41] In order to inhibit renewed cost explosions, the two governments included special clauses on "fixed price contracts" with the industrial companies, stipulating that at least half of any cost increase that surpassed the sums fixed in the contracts would have to be shouldered by the companies themselves.[42]

The numbers that circulated in Bonn in the summer of 1987 calculated the German share of the development costs at DM 2.1; the ultimate acquisition costs for the *Heer*'s 212 helicopters were estimated at some DM 6.1 billion. Furthermore, there were plans to either update the first-generation anti-tank helicopters (PAH-1) in use or to buy fifty to sixty Apache AH-64's in order to bridge the temporal gap until the new Franco-German PAH-2 was available—either of which would consume significant extra resources.[43] The expenses for the third-generation missiles were not included in these calculations. Considering these missiles as an integral part of the weapons system, the total price of the new helicopter-missile combination, the *Frankfurter Allgemeine Zeitung* computed in 1987, lay well above DM 10 billion for Germany alone.[44]

During October, a few members of the *Bundestag*'s Defense Committee (*Verteidigungsausschuß*) asked whether the supremely expensive helicopter program should be continued in times of financial shortage and a general necessity to curtail spending in the military sector. Chancellor Kohl rebuked such doubtfulness with the stoicism of the political leader in control of his party (CDU) and aware of the stability of his ruling party coalition (CDU/CSU-FDP). On November 11, the *Bundestag*'s Budget Committee (*Haushaltsausschuß*) approved the program on the basis of the defense ministers' agreement of July 16.

The fiftieth Franco-German summit meetings in Karlsruhe took place in an atmosphere of expectation of the twenty-fifth anniversary of the signing of the Elysée Treaty in January 1963. Chancellor Kohl alluded to the helicopter program in his speech at opening dinner on November 12 at Castle Bruchsal: "we are aware that we must not remain standing where we are. We have no reason to rest on what has been achieved. The Franco-German cooperation is asked anew every day to again unfold its dynamic. . . . We are ready to accord a new dimension to the Franco-German relationship. To the latter belongs in particular a deepening of the Franco-German cooperation in defense and security. . . . Germans and Frenchmen have to make efforts again and again to bring their policies into accord."[45] On November 13, 1987, Defense Ministers Giraud and Wörner signed a governmental agreement on the joint development of a Franco-German combat helicopter of a new generation.

Understanding Processes: The Meaning of Blame, Failure, and Success

The political processes between the summer of 1984 and November 1987 were strongly guided by bilateral interstate institutionalization and construction. Some aspects of socially constructed meanings and value judgments stood out during these years: the meaning of "failure," "blame," and "success" regarding the course of the tormented armament program. All of these value-charged notions need some intersubjective preconception in order to be comprehensible to the actors involved. Few things inherently or by nature are failures or successes or deserve blame. Charging these terms with meanings, and politically anchoring them, is part of the Franco-German historical institutionalization and social construction of the period. As social constructions, such notions help to shape expectations and function as reference points of judgment. Those personally involved in decision making, or close observers commenting upon Franco-German armament affairs during these years, virtually took for granted the value frame within which these processes took place—ultimately paving the way toward the physical emergence of one of the most sophisticated weapons systems in European military history.

When by late spring 1986 the discontinuation of the project had become a realistic possibility, policymakers and political commentators immediately raised the question of who would have to shoulder the political responsibility for a possible failure in the Franco-German relationship.[46] "Narrow national egotism" and "overly nationally charging" armament interests "that lead to major difficulties in Franco-German armament collaboration," as one defense analyst put it, are surely one reason for blame.[47] But the question of whom to blame applied not only to the two nation-states, but also to entities within the political systems, governments and administrations of the two states, or even single persons.

Note how incoming conservative Defense Minister André Giraud conceives of the cleavage of those working toward the realization of a Franco-German combat helicopter and those causing problems, sharply warning the industrialists and military leaderships of both states involved. Together with his German colleague Wörner, he forced "fixed-price" clauses in the contracts with the industrial contractors—common practice in the civil air industry but unusual in arms procurement contracts—in order to make the survival of the future Franco-German prestige weapon viable. Within the same value frame, when all of the problems associated with the helicopter program aggravated and accumulated during mid-1986, Giraud did not focus specifically upon the ills and difficulties of the helicopter program itself. For him, the trouble was not with the specific project. Rather, he was quick to express his worries about the broader state of Franco-German armament cooperation and of Franco-German relations in general.[48]

On July 2, 1986, the French National Assembly's Committee for National Defense and the Armed Forces discussed RPR Deputy Henri Louet's detailed report on the Franco-German helicopter project.[49] Louet meticulously presented the problems that had plagued the bilateral project since first consideration in the 1970s, putting forth a number of devastating criticisms regarding the planning, management, and execution of the program. Overall, the report is indeed perhaps a "shatter gun critique" of the project.[50] However, all of Louet's criticisms related to *how* the project was conducted. Louet never targeted the Franco-German aspect of the program, which he appreciated and supported. As solutions to the manifold troubles that he identified, he advised a joint Franco-German review and a bilateral reformulation of the program.

In reverse, making cooperation viable is considered a "success." Accordingly, the results of German Defense Minister Wörner's trip to France in July 1987, which confirmed the revised re-inauguration of the cooperation project, was celebrated as a "breakthrough,"[51] welcomed with "this time it's official," and praised as a "spectacular relaunching."[52] Notwithstanding all of his scathing criticisms of the program management, *rapporteur* Louet had already declared the conclusion of the 1984 MoU an "undeniable success for the co-signing Defense Ministers Charles Hernu and Manfred Wörner."[53] Accordingly, on its front page *Le Monde* celebrated the importance of the March 1987 Giraud-Wörner agreement for a tight Franco-German coupling within an integrating Europe: "Today the product is defined, the objective fixed, and the conditions of the realization determined."[54] After all major stipulations had been pinned down in July 1987, the paper applauded that entering the revised project meant "defeating the skepticism and the incredulity of those who think that the Franco-German cooperation, so abundantly venerated, results too often in words only, but not enough in concrete realizations."[55]

In the same spirit, German Defense Minister Wörner boasts, "we have succeeded, in spite of the obstacles, in contradicting all those who do not believe in the Franco-German military cooperation,"[56] adding with relief that now there is "no way back anymore" (*kein Zurück mehr*).[57] Wörner's French counterpart Giraud recalled with satisfaction the successful conclusion of his agreement with his German colleague, especially given that "historical differences between France and Germany can lead to difficulties."[58] Observers of various backgrounds shared the value frame of the policymakers and leading papers: Moving ahead with the cooperation was a "positive decision for the relations of the two countries."[59] "The development [of the helicopter] is for both countries prestigious, and is publicly considered a symbol that Franco-German cooperation indeed progresses."[60]

Such were the ways in which those involved in and those observing Franco-German arms procurement between 1984 and 1987 referred to the large program on a combat helicopter of a new generation. These references included highly charged expressions of value and meaning regarding what is good, preferable, or undesirable in the relations between Germany and France. "Failure" and "success" are social constructions that institutionalize value and purpose. As part of a larger institutional setup, they help steer the course of actions, choices, and events in particular directions and not in possible others.

Explaining Outcomes

Four main outcomes need explanation in the 1984–1987 time slice:

1. Why did the program so quickly slide into complete paralysis and near cancellation?
2. Why, between 1986 and November 1987, did the project "move out of the impasse" and *escape* cancellation—although there were enough good reasons to quit? This case requires an explanation of what did *not* happen.
3. Why did France and Germany settle the onerous issue regarding the night vision and targeting system the way they did, defining their interests in ways that accepted the enormous costs that this settlement implied?
4. Why did France and Germany define their interests and positions regarding the much revised joint development program in its entirety as expressed in the agreement of November 1987?

Case 6: Drifting into Deadlock (June 1984–May 1986)

Perhaps there is a threshold of inefficiency that fundamentally undermines the continuation of international cooperation projects, no matter what the international or domestic causal force that drives them. By late spring 1986, the stipulations of the May 1984 MoU had become illusionary and the MoU as a whole obsolete. Neither the explanatory hypotheses derived from chapter 2's constructivist-institutionalist model nor alternative explanations derived from neoliberal or liberal perspectives on international relations theory deal well with the program's drift into complete deadlock and near cancellation between June 1984 and May 1986. A realist view, on the other hand, helps to shed light on the outcome of case 6.

As this book's constructivist-institutionalist perspective can account for many of the results of the 1984 MoU—including its tensions—it might be expected to explain the planting of the seeds that led to the difficulties driving the program "into and in the impasse." Furthermore, the respective French and German domestic constructions at least partially capture the two countries' divergent approaches to the same stipulations. For example, according to a French historically rooted self-understanding, the state leads the economy, with economic activity much more tightly connected to the purpose of the nation-state. West Germany, on the other hand, is in this field more market oriented. The difference finds expression in the Franco-German frictions about how and where to acquire numerous component parts for the helicopter. However, when the main contractors estimated the development costs for each country at around FF 4 billion in early 1986—along with a project schedule that had become unpredictable—the program was no longer viable. As case 8 below suggests, which costs are acceptable and which are unacceptable can in important ways be social constructions. However, on balance the constructivist model does not accommodate well to the period of mid-1984 to early 1986.

Case 6's empirical evidence also fails to support a neoliberal view. "Into and in the impasse" was about excessive inefficiencies, *not* the lack of efficiency gains. That both France and Germany judged the cost explosions after May 1984 unacceptable, and, by May 1986, prohibitive does not suit neoliberal institutionalist efficiency arguments. Unlike the tenets of neoliberal institutionalism, this finding suggests that cooperation can take place largely unaffected by neoliberal views of efficiency. Yet, once a certain threshold of inefficiency is crossed, international cooperation becomes strained and may tumble into deadlock or rupture.

Nor do the particularistic interests of domestic groups turning against the program explain the development program's drift into deadlock—as a liberal position would surmise. Rather, the issues of "costs and delays" and to a lesser degree, contested purpose—independent of the particularistic interests of societal groups and industrial interests—made the program in its two-year-old MoU formulations impossible to realize. Also, the impact of subsidiary governmental entities, such as pressures from the German army or any other German or French domestic collective public actor, does not empirically explain the program's drift toward deadlock. The German military's turning away from the program at the time was a reaction against its incalculable delays, not their cause.

A realist view, on the other hand, helps us to capture important combat helicopter developments between June 1984 and May 1986 and, indeed, to expect the huge program ultimately to tumble into deadlock and toward cancellation. Realism might stress that until June 1984, the possibility of Franco-German cooperation in helicopter matters had been in words and on paper: The real business of reshaping distinct and disparate national interests only began after the May 1984 MoU was translated into reality. A realism-informed view of case 6 will thus find it little surprising that reshaping national armament interests—especially when security and national economic stakes are so high—would turn out to be extremely difficult. That distinct national interest would not be easily malleable is exactly what realism would expect, and in fact is a key reason why realists generally remain cautious and skeptical about achieving cooperation among politically independent units. According to realist precepts, France and Germany should never have been in the situation in which they found themselves between June 1984 and May 1986 but, rather, should have parted ways in new-generation helicopter matters a long time before. Still, if considered an independent case or observation, realist expectations help us to capture important aspects of why the Franco-German development program drifted into deadlock and tumbled toward cancellation during the twenty-four months covered by case 6.

Case 7: What Did Not Happen, but Could Have (January 1986–July 1987)

Why was the program *not* discontinued between January 1986, when it reached full deadlock, and July 1987, when the French and German defense ministers pinned down its re-inauguration in a much revised form? Why was it *not* canceled, as many expected and some had already pronounced? Then, the two countries were more likely to abolish the problem-ridden project than to steer it out of its impasse. Thus, this case scrutinizes a very probable outcome that did *not* occur. The causal effects of bilateral Franco-German institutionalization and construction again helped to shape French and German interests in important ways. However, the logic of the bilateral dynamic in steering the program away from elimination between early 1986 and summer 1987 rested on high degrees of French and German "state strength" in the relevant policy fields. As defined in chapter 2's institutionalist-constructivist model, as a combination of political authority centralization and state autonomy, state strength is indispensable to an explanation of what did not happen during the period in question but very well could have.

Reasons to discontinue the project were plenty. And there were many ways that the Tiger could have been brought to an end long before the first Franco-German helicopters had become physical reality. First, there were the tremendous cost explosions, including the stiff rise in the estimated development expenses and estimates of the helicopter's eventual unit price. All French and German estimates agreed that the ultimate price for each single helicopter would be dramatically higher than calculated in 1984. Second, there were the troublesome delays. Less than two years after the MoU, it was evident that the schedule laid out there would not be even remotely tenable. By early 1986, it was clear that the helicopter could not be available before 1995.[61] Third, given these delays, some defense experts questioned the paramount military purpose of the helicopter. Both France and Germany had intelligence reports that the Warsaw Pact was attempting to develop electronic missiles that might undermine the helicopters' military functionality—particularly if they were not available before the second half of the 1990s.

Aware of these reasons, yet also sensitive to the institutionalized social meaning and symbolic value of the program, defense analyst Alexander Szandar suggested giving up the project in the interest of the taxpayers and military leaderships, before "reasons of prestige will proscribe that option." Instead, Szandar advised Germany to turn to the readily available Italian or American products. By so doing, "the Franco-German cooperation would probably not suffer lasting damage," he surmised, if "Kohl and Mitterrand could agree on the next Franco-German summit in the end of February to bury the helicopter in all friendship." The program, he concluded, would not take off.[62]

In addition to various reasons why Franco-German dealings in combat helicopter armament could have been disrupted, there also were numerous ways in which that could have taken place. Various governmental entities or private actors could have put an end to the project through various constitutional or political mechanisms in either of the two states. Given the overall structure of the German political system, the decisive blow was more likely to come from within Germany. On the German side, the preferences of subsidiary governmental entities— including the parliament, in particular the Budgetary Committee—could have finished off the future Tiger; the program could have become an issue between the coalition parties in government or among ministries; or private domestic interests could have triggered disruption.

To begin, by early 1986, a majority of the German army leadership preferred the immediate acquisition of American Apache helicopters. Initially, the Bundeswehr had demanded the second-generation helicopters by the mid-1980s. It saw its military projections of the 1970s confirmed: The Warsaw Pact tank threat had not abated and continued to pose the risk it had about a decade earlier. Most German military strategists did not want to wait any longer—particularly with so many uncertainties as to when the Franco-German machine would finally be available, and even as to how powerful the new creation would ultimately be. They wanted helicopters now. If the German military had had more authority to influence the definition of German national interests, the program would have been canceled in the course of 1986.

Next, if the German government had had a weaker backing in the *Bundestag*, the program could have ended there just as easily. When the Bundestag's Budgetary Committee approved the financing of the revised program on November 11, 1987—although not without unease—the last hurdle toward the realization of the combat helicopter was overcome. Had the Committee refused to back up what French and German experts worked out under the supervision of the armament directors and with the endorsement of the defense ministers, president, prime minister, and chancellor, the proposal and the cooperation program would have died there.

Further, conceivable tensions within the coalition parties (CDU, CSU, and FDP) and among individual ministries (e.g., between the finance and defense ministries, or between the foreign affairs and defense ministries) could have undermined the renewed pursuit of the program. "Because of the *Ressortprinzip*," notes political scientist Leimbacher—referring to the fair degree of ministerial independence from the influence of other ministries and to some degree even the chancellor, as anchored in the German constitutional Basic Law—"it was more difficult for the chancellor than for the French president to make sure that a politically desirable joint project would receive the necessary financial means."[63]

Finally, the effects of organized domestic interests with access to political authority centers could have caused a complete erosion of the program. Most notably, a group of powerful industrialists around the Siemens electronics company had bought the rights from Martin-Marietta to produce a targeting and night vision system under license.[64] While they pushed for a faster and, most likely, cheaper German (-American) solution for the helicopter's technical core, the French insistence on self-developing such a system remained unyielding. If France and Germany had not been able to agree upon a system, a Franco-German helicopter divorce would have been inevitable.

And yet, none of these potential disruptions found its way to kill the revival (and revamp) of the gigantic armament program. Both authority centralization and state autonomy were high enough to prevent any of these various forces from finding necessary access to those parts of the political machinery that ultimately set national interests and armament policies. The German military's impact on the overall definition of interests was too cumbersome at the time to get the majority of the army leadership on its side. Chancellor and CDU Chairman Kohl was in a strong position, in his roles as both party leader and government chief executive. He was in charge of his parliamentary faction and kept tight relations with the members of the *Bundestag's* key foreign policy committees. Kohl's Napoleonic style of leading the CDU has been widely commented upon. And the coalition government among CDU, CSU, and FDP was too stable to allow a significant rift between the chancellor's office and FDP parliamentarians on such a major foreign political issue.

The nonchalance with which Kohl rebutted even the strongest skeptics of the price tag attached to the combat helicopter correlated with the strength of his position. Continually and imperturbably, he underlined the high priority he accorded to corroborating the good relationship with France with concrete projects, including the anti-tank helicopter.[65] And finally, the German electronic sector around Siemens could not decisively permeate the German government with its interest in producing the American night vision and targeting system under license. High degrees of authority centralization and state autonomy in the policy area during the time period under review explain why Germany did *not* cancel the program through any of these possible pathways.

Due to the strong French state with its generally high centralization of political authority, it is overall less likely that a subsidiary governmental unit or organized society could execute a decisive blow to France's external cooperative relations. Both aspects, authority centralization and autonomy, were high for France in this policy domain and time period. The French state largely controlled the armament sector; it was not only highly autonomous but also actively involved as a driving force behind its industry's defense economic activities. When, on May 8, 1988, Jacques Chirac became prime minister of a conservative government with social-ist President Mitterrand, Franco-German armament cooperation could have become a contentious issue in the divided *cohabitation* ruling France. Yet, neither the new prime minister nor incoming Defense Minister Giraud decisively under-mined the institutionalized Franco-German relationship from within.

In a comprehensive review of the Franco-German helicopter negotiations of the preceding month, *Le Monde* presents a view on Franco-German relations in which frictions and difficulties do not predominantly originate between the French and the German states but from the particularistic interests of the two states' military leaderships and industrial companies. The main cleavage it identi-fies is between the French and German governments on one side and particular-istic domestic interests in both countries on the other. One important aspect of managing Franco-German relations, thus, is that the two governments together push back particularistic domestic interests in order to arrive at the true French, German, and Franco-German interests. "The Europeans finally understand," the paper concludes, "that their collective security is founded in the first place on an armament community, and that implicates a very strong political will to put to an end the particularisms of the general staffs and the industrialists."[66]

In sum, the degrees of French and German political authority centralization and state autonomy in the policy area and time period covered here were both high. Along with the logic of bilateral institutionalization and construction, these political system features explain what *did not* happen, between January 1986 and July 1987—when discontinuation of the project was a very probable outcome.

According to a realist-informed explanation, the political outcome of the period should have been program disruption and cancellation. But this is not what hap-pened. For France, perhaps, with the immediate security threats not quite as dire given its fleet of somewhat adequate anti-tank helicopters, it is not clear how its government should have acted according to realist precepts. Germany, however, once and for all should have cancelled the hapless Franco-German project and acquired either American Apaches or new Italian combat helicopters as quickly as possible. Militarily matching the tank threat along its Warsaw Pact borders, accord-ing to realist thinking, should have been paramount and trumped possible other considerations. Cancelling France-Germany and buying American or Italian was a position advocated by many among the German military. But this was not the position that the German government adopted.

For the question at the core of this case study, neoliberal institutionalism is not really applicable. Neoliberalism is not equipped to explain the non-occurrence of the probable outcome of program abortion. The enormous armament program had never decisively been driven by efficiency considerations or expectations of absolute gains to begin with. Accordingly, in the time period that case 7 reviews, none of the observers and nobody directly involved believed that the cooperation program would allow the reaping of otherwise unattainable gains, either as the project had been previously formulated or in its revised form.

A liberal perspective will seek to explain a potential disruption of the program via the influence of domestic constituencies, perhaps in combination with governmental fragmentation. However, case 7's empirical record does not suit liberal expectations. The German defense company MBB's apparent loss of interest in the potential program under the ever-aggravating conditions did not bring about disruption. The French defense companies chiefly involved were under governmental ownership or control. And neither German nor French taxpayers' associations either lobbied for program discontinuation or engendered cancellation for the French and German taxpayers' sake.

Case 8: Acceptable and Unacceptable Costs (November 1987)

"*A aucun prix*"—at no price—would France include a night vision and targeting system from an American supplier.[67] The French government categorically preempted any attempts to reduce costs by dropping the plan to self-develop the technological core of the second-generation military helicopter in the upcoming general reexamination of the program in 1986. Producing the readily available American system under license, and including it in the Franco-German helicopter, could have saved money and time. Even when the cost explosion brought the entire program near cancellation in April-May 1986, doing so lay outside the conceivable in Paris. France categorically ruled out the option to save on the helicopter's single most expensive component.

The French historically rooted domestic construction of self-understanding and proper place in the world induced a strong interest in the capability to produce this central technological part. France had long associated its strong leanings toward national political and military independence as well as its aspirations for world political presence with the ability to independently develop and possess the most advanced weapons systems. It has striven to produce and independently operate armaments that only the leading powers possess, such as aircraft carriers, nuclear submarines, and advanced combat aircraft.[68] A highly advanced night vision and targeting system as the centerpiece of military helicopters of a new generation only followed suit. France was determined to possess this technology and the ability to self-produce such highly advanced vision and targeting systems. This strong domestic construction-induced interest also overruled the logic of the Franco-German relationship: Even though interrupting the program would save costs and accelerate the undertaking, to facilitate cooperation with Germany, France chose to drop the entire project rather than incorporate the American-made alternative. French domestic construction prescribed self-development and proscribed the inclusion of an American vision system. Accordingly, one French observer stresses that Louet in his National Assembly report "invites Mr. André Giraud to demonstrate to Bonn France's capacity to realize such a flying vision and targeting system."[69]

The institutionalized relationship transmitted the willingness to accept these enormous extra costs—along with further delays—to Germany. At the ministerial meeting on March 20, 1987, Germany ultimately and definitely gave up its option to incorporate the American TADS/PNVS into the helicopter. Because of the importance of the matter, a separate document would be signed on the development of the vision system. The decision was formalized in November 1987, with far-reaching consequences for Germany. It now tied the availability of the new helicopters to the technical insecurities related to the development of such a complex technological part. In framing its interests, Germany found that the logic of the institutionalized Franco-German relationship clashed with its interests to have the helicopters available as quickly as possible, and to save expenses. The logic of the relationship won. For both France and Germany, "unacceptable costs" had become malleable: For France, acceptability was decisively framed by its domestic construction of French self-view; for Germany, "acceptability" was defined in the context of the Franco-German relationship.

Perhaps there are limits beyond which costs—as numbers or "facts" by themselves—become unacceptable, as case 6 suggests. However, the question of which costs are acceptable and which are not is also a function of institutionalized social meaning. The politicking around the financial matters of the readjusted helicopter program demonstrates the degree to which attitudes toward costs are a question of political priorities. Interests that derive from core elements of an internally firmly established view of self-help to *define* which costs are acceptable and which are not. The French domestic construction-induced interest to self-develop and produce this key part did not so much overrule financial considerations; it decisively framed them. At a time when both France and Germany considered the program's costs "unacceptable"—expenses that had taken the entire enterprise hostage—France considered paying dearly for the single most expensive item to be a matter of course. In the course of the manifold and multilevel interaction via the Franco-German transmission belt, Germany ultimately adopted the same position. Choices about which costs are acceptable and which are not are partially rooted in institutionalized relations with others and in social constructions of their meaning.

The effects of the French domestic construction first trumped the logic of the institutionalized Franco-German relations. Its prescriptive and proscriptive effects were then diffused via the Franco-German net of interaction and meaning to affect German interest formation and positions on the matter as well. The effects of the German domestic construction were permissive. State strength, the third factor of my constructivist-institutionalist model, was sufficiently high, and functioned as a permissive underlying cause. Together, these factors explain the TADS/PNVS outcome of 1987, including the definition of acceptable costs.

Alternative explanations from the other major perspectives on international politics can be readily derived regarding the positions France and Germany adopted on the TADS/PNVS issue. From a strategic-realist point of view, the continued immediacy of the Warsaw Pact threat at Germany's borders should have overruled all other considerations, including those of a tightly institutionalized and meaning-charged interstate relationship. A realist-informed view would predict that Germany would acquire helicopters at this point *as fast as possible*, which would have meant buying Apaches and finishing them for German purposes. A mercantilist-realist position, however, might hold that France insisted on the technological capability for a TADS/PNVS for national industrial developmental reasons. Such a perspective conflicts with the empirical observation that for Germany, at the same time, this aspect was a complete non-issue. Still, a mercantilist-realist view can claim to capture some aspects of France's position on the night vision and targeting system, the central component of the combat helicopters-to-be.

According to all expectations that can be derived from a neoliberal perspective, France and Germany should have parted ways at this point, at the very latest. If one applies a neoliberal logic of cooperation, there was nothing to gain and a lot to lose for both France and Germany—on all accounts. Following a neoliberal rationalist-institutionalist perspective, parting ways and program disruption should have been the outcome of case 8.

According to a liberal view, Germany should have produced the Martin-Marietta vision system under license. The electronic giant Siemens had already bought the license rights to do so and was, together with a group of other German industrial companies, ready to move ahead. Between 1984 and 1987, this powerful industrial group strongly lobbied the German government to move ahead on the matter,[70] but the logic of the Franco-German relationship overruled their efforts. Further, the bossy tone with which incoming Defense Minister Giraud pushed around, and even outright threatened, the large French state-controlled industrial conglomerates involved in the helicopter program does not sit well with a liberal perspective.

Case 9: Interests Defined (November 1987)

This case investigates the ensemble of French and German interests and goals as *defined* by July and formalized in November 1987. They include the revised scheduling, financial allocations, and various other specifications. The document fixed the expenses for the development phase at DM 3,464 million (taxes excluded), of which Germany committed to about DM 1,500 million (taxes excluded). The program costs were not only significantly higher than estimated anytime before but also higher than the alternatives on the international marketplace. The document now set the delivery of the PAH-2 machines to the German forces for 1998. France would receive the first helicopters of the HAP version by the end of 1997 and those in the HAC version in 1999. In order to overcome the difficulties that had surfaced after May 1984, the agreement of November 13, 1987, defined, in multiple ways, "new mixes" for the helicopter to be developed. Most conspicuously, the German PAH and French HAC were now defined as the same, common Franco-German anti-tank helicopter. All helicopters would be propelled with two engines, increasing their weight and unit price. Both, France was fully aware, would infringe on the helicopters' export prospects.

The Franco-German helicopter had gone a long way since the initial sketches of the early 1970s. It evolved and permutated, in many respects, away from interests prior to institutionalized interaction. At the decisive junctures, both France and Germany defined their interests to formulate a Franco-German answer to the complete deadlock and near-cancellation of the program in the first half of 1986. The result was a further "Francogermanization" of the project instead of a "re-nationalization" or buying abroad.

The constellation among the factors of chapter 2's constructivist-institutionalist model of interest formation and policy formulation explains these outcomes. The effects of the institutionalized relationship could have impact because they were not, except in the TADS/PNVS issue discussed above, in direct conflict with the interest-and policy-inducing effects of French or German domestic constructions. Concurrently, sufficiently high levels of political authority centralization and state autonomy permitted the bilateral interstate institutionalization and construction to become effective: Domestic institutional structures or domestic society did not weaken the interstate relations' effects from within.

The results that Giraud and Wörner formalized at the fiftieth Franco-German consultations in Karlsruhe underline the impact of bilateral Franco-German institutionalization and construction. What the two countries ultimately fixed as their interests and goals cannot be explained with overlapping exogenously predefined preferences, or mirroring the two states' relative bargaining power. These outcomes cannot be understood without the difficult political processes that had preceded the ministers' signatures. Many of them only emerged endogenously to the processes between the two states—"because of the continuing process of bilateral rapprochement," as one official source put it.

Le Figaro, in a review of Franco-German military cooperation since Defense Minister Pierre Mendès-France, concluded that the July 1987 agreements had "most of all political significance and range, going largely beyond their economic and military aspects."[71] Sharing the diagnosis, the Swiss Neue Züricher Zeitung viewed them as "mainly *politically motivated*" and serving to "underline the tight Franco-German defense cooperation."[72]

Henri Louet's report on the helicopter program to the French National Assembly, notwithstanding its frequently scathing criticisms, in many ways shows what is taken for granted in dealing with frictions in Franco-German affairs. It also shows what was intuitively plausible as a measure to "exit the impasse" into which the program had drifted—as well as what was *not* conceived of as immediately intuitive or plausible. Louet did *not* suggest getting out of the hapless project with as little damage as possible, cutting losses, and discontinuing the program. To the contrary, his policy prescriptions aimed at a closer coordination between France and Germany and at jointly dispelling the differences that constituted obstacles to the program's feasibility. The members of the National Assembly's Defense and Armament Committee shared the logic of Louet's problem-solving suggestions, as the transcript of its discussion demonstrates.[73] Both are paradigmatic for the institutional stage on which Franco-German cooperation unfolded, and the outcomes that this stage helped to materialize.

In order to improve the overall coherence of the project, Louet first demanded greater adjustment of French and German positions. "France and Germany both want an anti-tank helicopter," he wrote with respect to the scheduling, for example, "but Germany wishes to receive it much more quickly than France." Regarding this and other differences plaguing a successful realization of the program, he thus concluded, "it is *necessary* to arrive at constructing the *same* anti-tank helicopter."[74] This is exactly what happened. Very much in the same spirit, and despite his criticisms, Louet summarized in the introduction to his shattering report to the *assemblée nationale*, "the program is nonetheless essential for the good health of Franco-German cooperation."[75]

When André Giraud took office, he stressed his basic valuation of Franco-German cooperation in general and in this case in particular. Yet, he pointed out that for successful cooperation in the combat helicopter case, two conditions had to be fulfilled: a common view on the goals for the weapons system and reduction of the costs of the project. In its present form, Giraud elaborated in late May 1986, the helicopter program did not meet these conditions.[76]

In order to reach "common views," France and Germany first tried a common medicine for dealing with their bilateral problems: switching hierarchical levels of interaction. During their first meeting, Giraud and Wörner decided to delegate the helicopter troubles to French and German Armament Directors Chevalier and Schnell for a comprehensive review. The results of the subsequent dealings are recorded in the November 1987 agreement.

Realist expectations with respects to the set of outcomes summed up in this observation are congruent with those above regarding the TADS/PNVS case; they do not need to be recounted here. To make the cooperation viable, Germany again postponed the dates when the helicopters could finally be delivered, even though the existential tank threat to its territory had not abated.

Propositions derived from a neoliberal approach again have difficulty relating to the empirical observations. The evidence so far has overwhelmingly shown that the various neoliberal, efficiency-enhancing explanations for international institutions and cooperation have not driven the collaboration. However, by the beginning of 1985, it had become unmistakably manifest that keeping up the joint project not only would *not* save costs but would make the endeavor very expensive. "A resource-sparing common production was no longer conceivable," summarizes political scientist Urs Leimbacher.[77] According to official calculations, supplying the German forces with American Apache helicopters would have saved Germany some DM 2 billion, without necessarily trading in military performance. The French government, too, was aware that the costs of a common project were higher and that the development would take longer than a national program, as Defense Minister Giraud testified before the National Assembly's Defense Commission on April 23, 1986.[78] The Louet report, published in July 1986, strongly underscores that neoliberal explanations were not driving the combat helicopter cooperation. In fact, two of Louet's main criticisms addressed the ever-mushrooming expenses and the subordinate role that the initial wishes of the armed forces had taken from roughly the second half of the 1970s onward.

The results of July-November 1987 emerged independent of, or in opposition to, organized domestic interests. In France, Defense Minister Giraud harshly pushed around and even threatened the French industrialists. In tone and style, his management sometimes seemed to resemble issuing orders—unusual even for the dealings of the French state with its state-owned Aérospatiale in a state-led economy. Thomson CSF, the company that would take over, together with Eltro, most of the electronic development work (including the vision system), was a French "national champion" under public tutelage. On the German side, there is no evidence that MBB's interests helped to shape the November 1987 stipulations in major ways. France and Germany's conclusion of "fixed price contracts," shifting much of the financial risk to the industrial companies involved, further mirrors the weakness of the industrialists (to the extent that they were not state-dependent in the first place). Very much in contrast to the rough tone with which Giraud chided the industrial companies (and to a lesser degree the general staffs), spokespersons from the German Chancellor's Office and from the Elysée Palace continually underlined the value and relevance of Franco-German cooperation as Wörner traveled through France. And German Chancellor Kohl repeatedly expressed his will "to reinforce the Franco-German relationship with concrete projects."[79]

Summary

Due to enormous cost explosions, massive delays, and numerous other problems between June 1984 and May 1986, the Franco-German combat helicopter program drifted into an impasse with no obvious way out, barely escaping cancellation.

Subsequently, between May 1986 and November 1987, France and Germany jointly re-formulated the program and formalized the revamped and yet further "Francogermanized" project at the fiftieth Franco-German summit consultations in Karlsruhe on November 13, 1987. By then, France and Germany had moved from Franco-German French and Franco-German German to Franco-German Franco-German helicopters, as one journalist put it.[80] Compared with the initial French and German positions in the first half of the 1970s, Franco-German dealings between 1984 and 1987 yet further molded the future helicopter, the objectives and the stipulations of the program. "Development and production of this anti-tank helicopter," the Federal Republic's Press and Information office reported, "are an expression of strengthened Franco-German relations."[81]

The four cases that this chapter has presented concern the main outcomes needing explanation during the forty months that it covers. This chapter's first case suggests that neither the propositions derived from chapter 2's institutionalist-constructivist model nor neoliberal institutionalism nor society-focused liberalism can effectively explain why the program drifted into deadlock between the summer of 1984 and the spring of 1986. A view of this case informed by realist thought, on the other hand, helps shed light on the empirical outcome that the case reconstructs.

This chapter's second case study demonstrates that high degrees of political authority centralization and state autonomy explain why the program was *not* canceled between January 1986 and July 1987—a time during which several observers had already declared the project dead. The evidence supports the fourth and fifth hypotheses put forth in chapter 2 concerning the constellation between institutionalized relations on the one hand and state strength on the other.

The third case, in turn, supports the first two hypotheses as formulated in chapter 2. This case shows how institutionalized relations and domestic construction together explain the outcome regarding the night vision and targeting system, underscoring how these two factors in important ways define acceptable costs for actors. The prescriptive and proscriptive effects of the French domestic construction were diffused via the institutionalized Franco-German relationship to ultimately affect German interest definition regarding the matter as well. State strength, the third factor of this study's constructivist-institutionalist model, was sufficiently high and functioned as a permissive underlying cause.

Finally, this chapter's fourth case, again in accordance with this book's first two hypotheses, shows that the French and German interests and positions, as defined in the intergovernmental agreement between the two states in November 1987, have been decisively shaped by the interplay between the effects of their institutionalized relations and historically shaped domestic constructions. The sufficiently high degree of state strength, in this case, has again worked as an underlying permissive cause.

6

Becoming Reality (1988–2009)

This chapter covers Franco-German political developments around the Tiger combat helicopter from 1988 to 2009. At the beginning of this period, France and Germany implemented their intergovernmental agreement from November 1987, jointly completing the helicopter development work while the various Tiger prototypes collected flying time and steered the program toward serial production. Yet various kinds of political tensions, both between and within France and Germany, again accompanied the project during the 1990s. At the beginning of the decade, troubling financial issues were back on the scene. They culminated during 1996, when severely aggravating budgetary pressures once again led to a fundamental questioning of the entire program. After France and Germany confirmed the project's continuation late in 1996, the way toward the physical emergence of the Tiger had ultimately been paved. In 1999, France and Germany each placed a definite order for a first batch of eighty Tiger combat helicopters.

The 1990s also saw questions emerge regarding the potential export of the highly advanced Franco-German combat helicopter. The export question became particularly politicized during the mid-1990s, with the bids for Dutch and British helicopter orders, and particularly after Turkey expressed interest. In the end, the Franco-German helicopter failed to win the Dutch and British contracts. German hesitation to sell the machines to Turkey contributed to turning away the Turkish government as a potential customer. Early in the new century, however, France and Germany won the bids of both Australia and Spain to acquire combat helicopters on the international marketplace. The Tiger's international career had begun. Over the course of the 1990s, in the wake of the Tiger program, the French and German helicopter industries integrated and became fully fused as the Franco-German "Eurocopter." By the early twenty-first century, Eurocopter had become the world's largest helicopter manufacturer. In the same vein, as France and Germany integrated the management of their bilateral armament dealings, the nucleus of a European armament agency (OCCAR, or *Organisme Conjoint de Coopération en Matière d'Armement*—Common Organization for Armament Cooperation) took shape. France and Germany instituted fully integrated Tiger pilot and mechanic training schools, jointly training staff to operate the new combat helicopters. Finally, the first series-produced Tiger-helicopters were officially delivered to the French and German armed forces in 2005. Three French Tigers flew their initial combat missions in 2009.

Focusing on these years' historical processes illustrates—notably through the evolving Franco-German pride regarding the high-end armament product and their joint salesmanship of the Tiger—that institutionalized relations may bring about events that in turn reflect back on the meaning of an institutionalized relationship itself. These years also demonstrate—particularly through the fusion of the French and German helicopter industries into "Eurocopter," the foundation of the Franco-German Helicopter Office and then the armament agency OCCAR, and the institution of joint Franco-German helicopter pilot and mechanics training schools—how institutionalized relations can generate further institutional elements and affect social organization more broadly. Three particular sets of outcomes need explanation during these years leading up to the Tiger's becoming a physical reality: the French and German export interests in the Dutch, British, Australian, and Spanish export episodes (which I discuss together as one case); the quite different French and German interest formation in the Turkish export episode; and the outcomes of the difficult year 1996, when the program's existence was questioned once again.

Implementation and Export Skirmishes (1988–1995)

During the years covered in this section, France and Germany honored the Elysée Treaty with splendid celebrations of the twenty-fifth anniversary of its signing; the Berlin Wall crumbled; the two Germanys unified; the Warsaw Pact dissolved; the Soviet Union imploded; and Germany won the World Cup in soccer. In Franco-German combat helicopter terms, on the other hand, the years from 1988 to 1995 were a rather quiet time, as France and Germany installed the necessary institutional infrastructure to implement the working program with technical specifications as defined in the November 1987 memorandum.

On September 28, 1988 in Koblenz, the German armament acquisition office BWB and Eurocopter GmbH, the program's main contractor, concluded a contract that covered the first eighteen months of the development work. At a volume of DM 270 million (FF 920 million), it scheduled the first prototype flight for 1991 and the beginning of serial production for 1997.[1] After delays due to quarrels between the German Finance and Defense Ministries,[2] France and Germany installed the Franco-German Helicopter Office (DFHB) in May 1989 to take over the role of program executive agency in the same year.[3] Lacking legal status (*personalité juridique/Rechtspersönlichkeit*), however, the BWB continued to formally conclude the contracts with the industrial companies involved.[4]

On November 30, 1989, the BWB and Eurocopter signed the "contract on the global development" (*Hauptentwicklungsvertrag*) of the Franco-German helicopter, financially securing the second and main segment of the helicopter's development phase toward serial production. France and Germany together committed to a total payment of DM 1.885 billion (FF 6.41 billion) for the development phase. Simultaneously, the participating companies and ministries agreed on the ultimate installation of two assembly lines for the final serial production of the helicopter in the Aérospatiale and MBB plants in Marignane (Bouches-du-Rhône) and Donauwörth. The development work began to gain momentum. With French and German co-pilots, the first Tiger prototype made its initial flight of some thirty minutes in Marignane on April 27, 1991.[5] This machine and the four other prototypes subsequently collected flying time during the first half of the 1990s.

During the late 1980s and the first half of the 1990s, a number of issues began to set the stage for the continuation of this history in the following years:

1. Over the cooperation work on the Tiger program, Aérospatiale and MBB began to integrate their helicopter divisions. This integration consolidated and deepened in several stages during the early 1990s, amounting to the full fusion of the French and German helicopter industries later in the decade.
2. With the first reports on the development work, the late 1980s and early 1990s brought to the surface a certain Franco-German pride regarding the common high-tech program.
3. Concomitantly, increasing budgetary pressures again began to plague the project, escalating during 1996.
4. The German government decided upon a number of technical adjustments for the finishing of the German Tiger helicopter version, which had little impact on the program as a whole.
5. France and Germany founded a bilateral armament agency that would become the cradle of the emerging European arms agency OCCAR.
6. The politics around the export of the new weapons system moved to center stage, with France and Germany trying to win major helicopter orders from the Netherlands and Great Britain.

These issues are discussed in the paragraphs that follow.

Industries Integrating and the Franco-German Roots of a European Armament Agency

In the fall of 1988, in the wake of the Tiger program, Aérospatiale President Henri Martre began to advocate a joint company that would bind together Aérospatiale and MBB's helicopter divisions and specialize in the fabrication of civil and military helicopters.[6] After "having received warm approval of the governments of the two states,"[7] Aérospatiale and MBB set up a reflection group to deliberate on the integration of their helicopter units. By February 1990, the two companies had announced the creation of a Franco-German helicopter company, Eurocopter S.A., with Aérospatiale S.A. holding 60 percent and MBB 40 percent.[8] Taking the French legal form of a GIE (*Groupement d'Intérêt Économique*), explained MBB's helicopter division director Heinz Plückthun, the new creation would constitute a "structural unification without fusion," with management headquarters located in La Courneuve near Paris.[9] On April 6, 1990, Aérospatiale and MBB signed a protocol detailing the "harmonization" of their helicopter divisions and envisioning the creation of a common holding.[10] Approving the agreement, the European Commission's competition control legally cleared the way for the industrial regrouping on February 26, 1991.[11] In May 1991, Aérospatiale and MBB jointly founded Eurocopter International GIE—to be supervised by the common Eurocopter S.A.—an independent agency to oversee the marketing and sales of the joint Franco-German helicopter production.[12] In the course of 1992, Daimler-Benz/DASA/MBB and Aérospatiale fully merged and streamlined their helicopter activities into a Franco-German conglomerate, dubbed "Eurocopter." From that point on, Eurocopter would be the world's largest helicopter exporter (of civil and military machines taken together), and the world's second-largest helicopter manufacturer after the American Boeing Sikorsky, which strongly focused on the protected American military market.[13] With the production of seven helicopter models, available in twelve different versions, the new Franco-German Eurocopter corporation met 85 percent of the global demand.[14]

Around the same time, based on the first reports about the development program's progress and likely results, a certain pride began to evolve as France and Germany together prepared to develop the most advanced combat helicopter yet. On all measures of performance, including the new night vision and targeting system's "visibility range and focus," the Tiger was about to set new standards superior to its U.S. competitor Apache. At the fortieth air and space exhibition in Le Bourget in 1993, the Tiger made a "sensational impression" as both French and German aerospace and defense journalists applauded the "trumps of the Tiger"— its high survivability, difficulty of detection by radar thanks to its thin silhouette, its high self-protection potential, and its military capacity. Its new vision system, according to the state of development, was expected to detect and designate four targets simultaneously and fire four missiles within eight seconds.[15]

Between 1988 and mid-1991, discussions on the enormous overall costs of the project had quieted, both in public debate and within the governments of the two countries. In late 1991, however, with initially anonymous informants from high German governmental and military circles reporting that the German government might have difficulty financing the continuation of the Tiger program, financing troubles were powerfully back on the scene. In its entirety now priced at above DM 10 billion for Germany alone (including the expenses for definition, development, and serial production preparation, and ultimate production costs, yet excluding the machine's expensive arming), such information from "well informed circles" confirmed that increasing budgetary pressures might constitute a serious peril for the perpetuation and completion of the helicopter program. Jörg Schöhnbohm, German Defense Ministry *Staatssekretär*, was one of the first to comment openly on the matter, noting that he might have to abandon the Tiger if he did not receive more money for the armed forces.[16]

During 1992, again, bits and pieces of information leaking from the relevant official circles implied that financial difficulties might continue to strain or endanger the costly helicopter program. With military budgets continually being cut for a range of reasons—including the budgetary rigor necessary to meet the "Maastricht criteria," in addition to Germany's enormous costs for "inner unification"—the Tiger's future did seem less secure than it had since November 1987. When German Defense Minister Volker Rühe traveled to Paris in September 1992, meeting his French counterpart Pierre Joxe to discuss how European security cooperation could be pushed ahead and to review Franco-German security matters, some observers deemed the Tiger's future uncertain.[17] However, nine months later, in reaction against renewed rumors that Germany might consider cutting the Tiger program for budgetary reasons, the new French Defense Minister François Léotard affirmed on June 30, 1993, before the National Assembly that "France assigns the greatest importance" to keeping up the combat helicopter program.[18] Budgeting issues would continue to simmer on a low flame until the end of 1995; by 1996, they would once again bring the program's existence into question.

Toward the mid-1990s, furthermore, following a planning conference chaired by Defense Minister Volker Rühe in December 1992, the German political leadership decided to modify the finishing of the predominantly anti-tank-focused German PAH-2 Tiger version toward a more versatile "multi-role capable" or multi-purpose UH-Tiger (*Unterstützungshubschrauber Tiger*— "Support Helicopter Tiger").[19] At the signing of the global development contract in 1989, the German PAH-2 Tiger had still been conceived as a second-generation combat helicopter centering on the destruction of tanks and other major objects on the ground. The future UH-Tiger would still be the most advanced weapon against tanks, but it could also cover a wider range of military tasks including combat support for ground troops and armed reconnaissance, as well as escort and protection of other helicopters. Accordingly, the UH-Tiger's arming may flexibly include various mixes of weapons, including (unguided) 70mm rockets; HOT 2 and HOT 3 anti-tank missiles; third-generation long-range "fire and forget" missiles (PARS 3LR); air-to-air Stinger missiles; and a 12.7mm cannon.[20] The adjustments leading from PAH-2 to UH-Tiger only applied to the German version; they neither affected significant specifications of the identical Franco-German "basis helicopter," nor interfered with the French HAC and HAP versions. By June 1993, all necessary modifications had been coordinated with the plans for the respective French helicopter finishing plans, and the fifth adjustment of the global development contract in 1998 confirmed these decisions.[21]

Furthermore, during these years France and Germany installed a Franco-German arms agency, thereby paving the way for an emergent European arms agency. Defense Ministers Léotard and Rühe had already discussed how to simplify the management of Franco-German armament projects as early as December 1993 and at the summit consultations of May 30–31, 1994, in Mulhouse/Alsace. In September 1994, the French General Armament Delegation (DGA) announced that France and Germany intended to create a common armament agency, to integrate the management of existing projects and the planning of future programs while running Franco-German armament programs "with the same rigor as national programs," before the end of 1995.[22]

Finally, during the sixty-sixth Franco-German consultations on December 7, 1995, in the Black Forest resort of Baden-Baden—post-war headquarters of the French forces in Germany—Chirac and Kohl established "a new cooperation structure to rationalize the existing bilateral programs and to take charge of the future bilateral programs."[23] Whereas the ("Maastricht") Treaty on European Union had previewed the creation of such a European agency, Chirac and Kohl considered their Baden-Baden creation the "kernel" (*noyau*) of a future European armament agency, and from the beginning intended to keep this (initially) bilateral "structure" open to other interested European states. After Britain and Italy joined the agency's "precursor team" in the summer of 1996, OCCAR, a European arms agency, was born of the Franco-German Baden-Baden initiative.[24]

The (Failed) Dutch and British Export Episodes

After France and Germany had successfully evaded the traditionally difficult matter all through the 1980s, in 1991 the "export issue" conspicuously entered the scene in combat helicopter matters: what would it mean for the potential export of the Tiger that the Franco-German helicopter company Eurocopter S.A. had *legally* become a French company? In formal legal terms, this *might* mean that the restrictive German arms export laws no longer applied, although the Tiger was a partially German-made weapons system. The significance, however, was not of a legal nature at all but deeply political, and it touched the core of historically rooted German constructions of self-understanding and proper role in the world.

Particularly worried about potential Tiger sales to non-EU member states, German IG Metall union functionaries publicly raised the matter in 1991, wondering whether the new legal constellation (with Eurocopter S.A.'s base location in France) might be an elegant organizational setup allowing the German arms industry to circumvent the restrictive German export laws. "All ruminations," MBB's chief public relations executive Willi Vogler rebutted sharply and promptly, "that German arms export controls are to be circumvented via France lack any basis, and are utter nonsense" (*Quatsch*), and stressed Eurocopter's desire to succeed especially on the highly competitive world market for civil helicopters.[25] The course of events during the mid-1990s would initially dampen the potentially controversial nature of the issue, as the first two prospective Tiger customers were equally desirable for France, Germany, and the Franco-German Eurocopter: the Netherlands and Great Britain.

In late 1994, the Netherlands announced it would acquire thirty-two combat helicopters for its armed forces, specifying the Franco-German Tiger and American Apache helicopters as contending alternatives. Eurocopter immediately accorded great importance to the Dutch government's statement. Such an order would be worth more than FF 3 billion; but it could also be expected to influence the acquisition decision of the British government, which had stipulated the need for ninety-one combat helicopters valued at some FF 9.5 billion.[26] British and French officials had talked about a potential British association with the Tiger program as early as the winter of 1988. After discontinuing somewhat secretive talks, Britain then began to consider developing a light anti-tank and attack helicopter (LAH) along with the Netherlands, Italy, and Spain. These plans, in turn, had become definitely buried by 1990.[27] By the mid-1990s, it was clear that Britain would purchase helicopters abroad.

Since too much doubt remains for potential customers until an armament is produced or formally ordered by the producing country's government, Eurocopter president Jean-François Bigay began 1995 by calling for the start of the Tiger production in series as soon as possible. The uncertainty about the exact date of the Tiger's serial production and thus its definite availability compromised its export chances and constituted a major disadvantage against its main competitor, the American-made Apache AH-64.[28] Other than the Netherlands and Great Britain, various other possible customers had not yet explicitly stated their interest. Eurocopter and the French military administration then calculated the potential worldwide export market for the Franco-German Tiger helicopter at around 500 machines.[29] Although the fourth Tiger prototype had already been constructed by 1995, the machines had accumulated only 650 flying hours. Expecting the Dutch decision by the end of January 1995, Eurocopter co-president Siegfried Sobotta characterized the Tiger vs. Apache choice as "a decision for or against Europe."[30]

During late 1994 and early 1995, The Hague was the scene of active lobbying by the "two camps"—high-ranking French and German politicians and public servants on the one hand and Americans on the other. Top-level lobbyists included American President William Jefferson Clinton, French Prime Minister Alain Juppé, and German Chancellor Kohl. "You want to approach the Franco-German couple? Let your words be followed by deeds," one French reporter characterized an overarching Franco-German lobbying theme.[31] Some observers described the vigor with which French, Germans, and Americans courted the Dutch government as an "air battle above Holland."[32]

With his cabinet divided on the matter, Dutch Minister President Wim Kok decided on January 30, 1995 to postpone the decision until March 31. On April 7, 1995, Kok announced that the Netherlands would buy thirty American Apache helicopters for some FF 4 billion. "This is neither a choice against Europe, nor a choice for America," Kok insisted, explaining that Apache helicopters would be available more rapidly than Tigers, and, despite their age, had proven their quality.[33] Eurocopter and the French and German governments were disappointed. Apart from losing the Dutch order, French and German officials and industrialists feared that the Dutch decision would affect Great Britain's choice later in the same year, with the potential contract estimated at a total value of FF 15 billion.

In mid-June 1995, Sobotta announced during the air fair in Le Bourget that the contract on the final production of the Tiger combat helicopter was ready to be signed.[34] On July 1, 1995, committing DM 770 million (FF 2.7 billion), German Defense Ministry State Secretary Schönbohm and French General Armament Delegate Henri Conzé signed a letter of intention stating that France and Germany would provide the financial means to enter the "serial production preparation phase," expected to last from 1996 to 2000. The next remaining step to expedite the beginning of the Tiger's industrial production would be the signing of the series production contract with the manufacturers. Competing against the Cobra-Venom of the British-American GEC-Bell-Textron and the Rooilvalk of the South African manufacturer Atlas Denel, in addition to the Apache, "the Franco-German axis thus signals clearly to London," French commentators emphasized, "its will to remedy the delivery schedule problems that were fatal for the Tiger with respect to the Netherlands." The British decision was expected shortly.[35]

Simultaneously, lobbying of the British government by high-ranking Franco-German representatives including French Defense Minister Charles Millon continued, again involving the "Europe vs. America" theme. British Defense Secretary Malcolm Rifkind strongly refuted the idea that the choice constituted a test of Britain's commitment to Europe, instead stressing that the British choice would be based "on the operational effectiveness, cost and industrial implications of the decision."[36]

The "helicopter battle"[37] ended with British Defense Minister Michael Portillio's announcement on July 13, 1995—one day before France's national holiday—that the British government had decided to acquire only sixty-seven combat helicopters instead of the original ninety-one; and that it would satisfy its demand with American Apache machines. The total value of the acquisition would be about £2.5 billion (DM 5.6 billion, or $4 billion). After much disagreement within the Major administration, the British defense ministry, which had favored the Apache, prevailed over a coalition of other ministries and a group of "European-ists" around Michael Heseltine, who would have preferred the newer and techni-cally more advanced Franco-German product. Other factors in favor of the Apaches included the weak dollar (which worked as an "export subsidy" for the American helicopter, as some in France and Germany put it); that British indus-try would participate to a significant degree in the Apache construction and the production of components; and the promise that the Apaches could be delivered as early as 1998. Some observers pointed to John Major's political weakness as a factor allowing the British military to prevail.[38]

The reactions in France and Germany oscillated between disappointment and outright anger; the tone was sharper on the Rhine's left bank than on its right. Jacques Chirac, who had personally intervened with John Major on behalf of the Tiger, "bitterly disapproved" of the decision.[39] Charles Millon clarified that "the Franco-German armament axis clearly appears more solid than the Franco-British one."[40] Pointing out that "this is not the first time the British turn away from Europe in favor of the United States," some French observers saw "the British . . . boy-cotting Europe."[41] The British decision to buy American concluded these first two Tiger export episodes with Eurocopter failing to win a second major order from a European NATO state. A quite different export episode would follow in 1997.

Policymaking Under Extreme Budgetary Pressure (1996)

The year 1996 was again a turbulent one for the Franco-German combat helicop-ter. In some ways, it is an abstract of the leading themes of the entire preceding quarter century of Franco-German helicopter affairs. During the course of the year, the continuation of the project was questioned yet again and several observ-ers considered the program untenable. The institutionalized relations between France and Germany were an important factor with impact on the domestic allocation of budgetary resources within the two states. By the end of the year, ultimately, the way to the physical appearance of the helicopter would be paved. Nine years after the ultimate 1996 breakthrough, the first series-produced Tiger helicopters would be delivered to the French and German forces.

Collecting Flight Time and Ever-Mounting Budgetary Pressures

By 1996, all five prototypes had been assembled and, to different degrees, tested. One of the prototypes, favorably displayed in a product placement of its own kind, starred in the 1995 James Bond movie *Golden Eye*. By February 1996, the machines had together accumulated a total of 1,100 hours of flying time.[42] In order to improve the Tiger's competitiveness especially against the American Apache, after losing the bid for the valuable Dutch and British combat helicopter orders, Eurocopter president Bigay in January asked the French and German governments to sign the treaty on the Tiger's industrialization (serial production preparation) as soon as possible. Because of increasing financial strains during the preceding year, France and Germany had repeatedly postponed this last step toward the ultimate manufacturing in series.

Simultaneously, rationalizing Franco-German armament affairs, Eurocopter—supported by the French and German governments—worked on plans to fully integrate the various Eurocopter units. "In order to symbolize their will to cooperate, Germany and France envisage concentrating Eurocopter in one single company, if European law permits." Still, during February 1996, the French government began to consider reducing the number of helicopters it had planned to acquire for its army, or postponing some acquisitions, if the Tiger's unit price could not be curtailed.[43]

At the same time, German Finance Minister Theo Waigel repeatedly announced the need for deeper cuts in the 1996 budget. According to some figures, the 1996 German defense budget alone, fixed at DM 48.4 billion during the preceding year, might face cuts of some DM 2 billion. Waigel, *Le Figaro* remarked, "considers cutting primarily the budget for Franco-German armament cooperation."[44] By May, the sense of a serious malaise in Franco-German armament had once again become widespread. That the treaty on the Tiger's preparation for production had remained unsigned for months only symbolized the crisis faced by Franco-German armament cooperation.[45]

In the first place, the crisis was financial. By 1996, French and German budgetary pressures had become imposing. The strict (while self-defined) Maastricht criteria for European monetary union, and, in the German case, the mushrooming costs of "inner unification" dramatically aggravated the financial difficulties of the mid-1990s. The French and German Defense Ministries simply had no money and had to economize in areas that began to touch the core of the two states' defenses. The dramatic budgetary pressures strained Franco-German armament cooperation in this inherently expensive policy field.

The difficulties of the Franco-German Eurocopter conglomerate added to the overall atmosphere of dissatisfaction and malaise. Eurocopter suffered severely under the worldwide shrinking defense budgets and the weak dollar, which favored its American competitors, as Eurocopter and governmental officials repeatedly emphasized. Eurocopter finished these years with painful and damaging financial losses.

Moreover, the new French president Jacques Chirac began restructuring the French military in February 1996. The reform included a reworking of defense and security planning, organization, and strategy, in turn resulting in the phasing out of conscription, downsizing of the army, and concomitant tighter procurement constraints—thus straining the Franco-German relationship in defense. German military planners felt irritated and insufficiently informed and consulted by Chirac's "top-down" reform style. German Defense Minister Rühe publicly lamented being confronted with "a certain number of French decisions, unilateral decisions" about recent French propensities in political domains that he considered partially Franco-German business.[46] Paris took the German complaints about inadequate consultation very seriously. "The primacy of France's cooperation with Germany in defense, as in all other fields, remains unshaken," President Chirac assured Chancellor Kohl during a visit to Bonn in May, attesting that his reforms and the planned cuts in armament would neither endanger Franco-German military cooperation nor damage France's involvement in the Tiger (or the NH-90) helicopter programs.[47]

At the same time, in a transnational lobbying effort, Manfred Bischoff, Daimler-Benz Aerospace (DASA) chief executive, warned the French government against "endangering cooperations," demanding that the important programs in air and space navigation be maintained. The "postponements and stretches" in the acquisition of military material, including helicopters, would hit "the Franco-German cooperation in its core," added Werner Heinzmann, DASA board member responsible for civil and military air technology. He reckoned that "the German politicians and representatives of the industry must now argue their case in Paris on all levels, so that the common Franco-German programs shall not be endangered."[48]

In late May, some very unlikely bedfellows united behind the Tiger, as the several French unions representing the Eurocopter workers of Marignane and La Courneuve joined the Daimler-Benz managers in lobbying in defense of Franco-German armament and high-tech programs. Led by the union alliance FO-CFE/CGC and supported by CGT, CFDT, and CFTC, French unionists calculated that the new military program law as discussed by the French national assembly deputies on May 5–6, the likely French and German cuts in military spending, and the intention to push back the beginning of the combat helicopter production from 1999 to 2003 could cost more than 1,000 high-tech jobs in France alone. Such plans, according to the unions, would further aggravate the situation of the already struggling young Eurocopter group, possibly even threatening the future of the factory in La Courneuve. Following the calls of their union leaders, 5,000 Eurocopter employees demonstrated in Marignane, demanding that the new military program law maintain allocations for the Tiger program.[49] Still, in late May and early June, the figures circulating regarding the Tigers that France would eventually acquire ranged from 180 to 168 to 120, of the initially envisioned 215.

This was the situation at the end of May 1996: Chirac and the French executive worked on military reform plans with likely considerable impact on Franco-German security relations in general, and upon the Tiger program in particular.

After blunt criticisms, however, Chirac and his Elysée entourage were careful not to adopt final positions without first consulting with their German partners. The French *assemblée nationale* worked on a financially restrictive new military program law (*loi de programmation militaire*), setting out budgets and procurement plans for 1997–2002 that sought to "place a tighter overall cap on equipment spending" and previewed a reduction of the defense budget of about FF 20 billion (DM 6.5 billion) per year until 2002.[50] Eurocopter, suffering under the worldwide contraction of defense budgets, was cutting jobs and planned to cut more. German industrialists, in unanimity with French unions representing Eurocopter personnel, outspokenly lobbied for maintaining Franco-German armament cooperation. In order to prevent France and Germany from drifting apart too widely, the manifold communication channels of Franco-German interstate institutionalization below the top political and diplomatic levels were highly frequented, while the fiercest fights within the German government about limiting public spending during the current and following years were just about to start. However, given the importance of the matters involved, conclusive decisions had to be worked out on the highest levels of state and government. There was more than enough work waiting for the upcoming Franco-German summit meeting scheduled for early June in Dijon, in the heart of Burgundy.

From Dijon to Nuremberg

In preparation for the Dijon summit, Defense Ministers Rühe and Millon met secretively in Strasbourg on May 28, a week before the sixty-seventh Franco-German consultations, to engage in "frank discussions" on armament matters—a diplomatic formulation signifying a rather "rude conversation."[51] Rühe again criticized France for insufficiently consulting Germany when working on plans that affected Franco-German matters, and for its irritating volition with respect to joint projects. Of the twenty-seven armament programs under way, the ministers ordered their armament directors to list the difficulties of the most troublesome projects, especially the Tiger helicopter, in order to be better able to "reinvigorate" (*relance*) armament cooperation in Dijon.

During the Dijon consultations on June 5, France and Germany decided jointly to "reexamine the ensemble of their common armament programs," setting up Franco-German working groups to identify new rules, to be fixed by the next summit, which would improve the functioning of bilateral armament programs.[52] Regarding the Tiger helicopter project specifically, France and Germany underscored the importance of continuing the program, yet agreed "to consider decreasing the number of Tiger combat helicopters" and to stretch the timetable of orders, production, and delivery.[53] They further decided to increase the pressures on the industry to produce the helicopters at prices fixed at the time of the order. Although it is uncommon in armament procurement to fix prices when the product is still under construction, they thus forced much of the financial risk upon Eurocopter and other industrialists. Together, these results decisively helped to structure the ongoing French, German, and Franco-German policy- and decision-making processes toward the Franco-German winter summit in Nuremberg.

In the weeks and months following the Dijon summit, French plans circulated to reduce France's ultimate order to about 120 Tigers (50 instead of 140 of the HAC version, and 70 rather than 75 of the HAP version).[54] At the same time, however, referring to the value of joint armament programs for Franco-German relations in general, prominent personalities within France sharply argued against too severe cuts in spite of the extraordinary financial pressures. Xavier de Villepin, president of the Senate's Commission for Foreign Affairs and Defense, for example, warned that harsh cuts would not only limit the French forces' air mobility and endanger up to 1,000 jobs at Eurocopter but would strain the Franco-German relationship: "The fact that these programs are the object of cooperation with Germany, our principal political and military partner on the way toward a European defense industry, could also have awkward consequences in the future."[55]

Meanwhile, in a politically highly charged atmosphere, the several Eurocopter unions continued their campaign, pushing especially for the realization of the Tiger (as well as the NH-90 transport helicopter). Struggling to preserve the armament programs, the interunion alliance of FO, CFDT, CFTC, and CFE/ CGC published a leaflet in mid-June quoting the famous phrase from de Gaulle's June 1940 call: France had "lost a battle but not the war." The pamphlet bore the title "L'Appel du 18 Juin."[56] Simultaneously, joint bodies from the lower echelons of Franco-German interstate institutionalization voiced their positions. After a bilateral consultation conference among fifty high-ranking French and German officers in Berlin, military leaders of both forces spoke strongly in favor of tighter cooperation in military and defense. Demanding that units of the two forces exercise together more frequently and coordinate their missions abroad more tightly, conference chairs Generals Hans Speidel and Philippe de la Mettrie also pushed for keeping up the current twenty-seven joint armament projects.[57]

The intra-German struggles on defining priorities more rigidly and economizing in times of shortage culminated during the summer of 1996. They were fought along numerous cleavages: among federal ministries; between federal and *Länder* levels; between West (read: richer) and East *Länder* (poorer); between Southern (richer) and Northern (read: poorer) *Länder*; and several others. For the "consensus democracy" standards of former West Germany, the contenders' positions were particularly rigid, the tone of the debate sharp and ruthless. Wary of "Weimar conditions" (*Weimarer Zustände*), some observers worried about Germany's democracy and "political culture" in general. In fiscal terms, then perhaps the tightest in the almost fifty years of post-war German democracy, and tailored under the top priority of meeting the convergence criteria for monetary union as set out in the Maastricht Treaty (TEU), the federal budget was to be reduced by some 2.5 percent from 1996 to 1997 (to about DM 440 billion)—as one French commentator put it, "cut with Maastricht's big scissors."[58] Having incessantly repeated the monetary stability mantra all over Europe for years, Germany itself now had severe difficulties in meeting Maastricht's budgetary criteria. The mushrooming and radically underestimated costs of Germany's "inner unification" dramatically aggravated the situation, as public transfer payments from former West to former East Germany reached above DM 100 billion annually.

The fiercest German fight took place between Finance Minister Waigel and Defense Minister Rühe. The two ministers were plainly unable to find common ground to discuss the size of the defense budget. Waigel sought to decrease the budget to DM 46 billion, a sum that Rühe considered utterly unacceptable. Given the German military's fixed costs plus the "fixed variable costs" (including wages and minimal expenses to keep the forces operational), "after yet further cuts"[59] of its budget, the Defense Ministry had no money for "major ventures" (*Großvorhaben*) in 1996 and subsequent years. The *Frankfurter Allgemeine Zeitung* hypothesized, apparently based on discretionary official information, that keeping up the costly Franco-German Tiger helicopter project would be impossible under such circumstances, surmising that the helicopter orders would be postponed for an indefinite period and thus, de facto, be canceled.[60] In his struggle for funding, Rühe personally wrote a letter to Kohl. Pointing out that the envisioned budgetary reductions for 1997 threatened several Franco-German armament projects, including the Eurocopter-Tiger project, he asked for the Chancellor's support in circumventing such postponements or cancellations.[61] "Paris cuts, Bonn economizes," a European security observer summarized in the summer of 1996.[62] The fierce 1996 budgetary struggles had once again put into question continuing the Tiger combat helicopter program.

During the second half of July, finally, under Chancellor Kohl's engaged arbitration, Rühe and Waigel set the 1996 German defense budget at DM 47.1 billion and reduced the 1997 budget by 1.3 percent, to DM 46.5 billion. While managing to escape yet more severe cuts with Kohl's support, in real terms, Rühe stressed that with the cuts of 1997, the defense budget had been reduced by 24 percent within the last five years.[63] In one work titled "A tough German budget for France," a budget analyst highlighted the potential menace of the German 1997 "austerity plan" for several Franco-German programs including the Tiger, predicting that Franco-German cooperation would have to "overcome a phase of unpleasant financial settlements."[64]

Simultaneous to and intertwined with French and German domestic priority-setting politics, French and German experts jointly "re-examined" the financing of several programs for a report at the next summit consultations in Nuremberg in December. These working groups—set up after the Dijon summit—along with French and German civil servants of the defense ministries sought to allocate resources such that the Franco-German component of arms procurement would be given adequate attention. The Tiger program thereby played an important role, and they prepared a separate Tiger dossier for the approaching December summit.

With various numbers of helicopters to be ultimately ordered and dates of how to stretch these orders circulating in Bonn and Paris, by October it had become clear that the Tiger program would be kept. Simultaneously, French officials pushed Eurocopter to reduce the ultimate unit price, as well as the costs of the ongoing development, as much as possible. French armament acquisition director (DGA) Jean-Yves Helmer, for example, plainly stated that with a mix of different measures, including for example establishing only one final assembly line in either France or Germany instead of one in each country (an idea dropped later), it was feasible for Eurocopter to reduce the Tiger's unit price by up to 10 percent.[65]

At the sixty-eighth Franco-German summit consultations on December 9, 1996, in Nuremberg, the governments concluded a turbulent year in French, German, and Franco-German politics. There, they formalized the results of both domestic and bilateral work following the Dijon summit in June. Specifically for the Tiger combat helicopter, Chirac and Kohl together adopted the following positions: First, they decided to sign the contracts on the serial production preparation and the production itself shortly, thus promising to assure the financial means necessary for the perpetuation and completion of the program. Second, Chirac and Kohl adopted an agreement to order a "first batch" of eighty helicopters each for the French and German armed forces. The first of these were to be delivered to the *Bundeswehr* in 2001 and to the French army two years later.

Third, the two statesmen confirmed that France and Germany would ultimately acquire a total of 215 and 212 helicopters, respectively—in spite of severe budgetary pressures. This joint decision surprised most observers of the scene, who had expected the ultimate number of helicopters to be reduced or left undefined given the financial and strategic circumstances. Finally, as a Franco-German answer to the numerous difficulties regarding arms cooperation that had surfaced particularly strikingly during 1996, France and Germany agreed to expand their attempts toward a common arms and equipment acquisition calendar to help harmonize equipment demands in the future.[66]

"Helicopter Tiger takes off," one German daily newspaper summarized.[67] Indeed, by the end of crisis and breakthrough year 1996, it was only a matter of time before France and Germany would sign the treaties on the serial production preparation and the manufacturing itself. After a year of frequently tumultuous politics in which the continuation of the program was questioned anew, the Nuremberg summit ratified that the Tiger would indeed become a physical reality.

Becoming Reality, Export Politics, and the Initial Combat Missions (1997–2009)

Between the decision of the December 1996 Franco-German summit and the end of the century, France and Germany successively prepared the Tiger's serial production. In the process, they fully integrated Eurocopter's four branches and moved ahead with the new long-range, third-generation missiles to arm the Tigers-to-be. In June 1999, France and Germany ordered the first batch of Tiger combat helicopters. Between 1997 and 1999, in parallel, another and quite different export episode drew great political attention, as Turkey announced its interest in acquiring Tigers for its forces. The years 2000–2009 conclude the Tiger's history for the purposes and inquiries of this book. These years brought two more export episodes—Australia and Spain—launching the Tiger's career as an export item on the international marketplace. They also saw the opening of a Franco-German pilot helicopter school as well as a Franco-German mechanics school instituted to train specialized technicians for Tiger operations and logistics. By the early twenty-first century, four different versions of the Tiger combat helicopter were being developed and assembled. The first Tigers were officially delivered to the French and German armed forces in March and April 2005, respectively. Over thirty years after the first "tactical demands" for a new-generation combat helicopter and initial Franco-German discussions about developing and constructing such a machine, the combat helicopter Tiger had become physical reality. In 2009, three French Tigers flew their first combat missions in Afghanistan, far from the battlefields in continental Europe that had been their original destination.

Toward Production

In January 1997, Eurocopter announced that it would fully integrate its four branches—Eurocopter S.A., Eurocopter Deutschland GmbH, Eurocopter France S.A., and Eurocopter International—into one single company with a unified management structure. The new Franco-German Eurocopter S.A. would establish its seat in Marignane (Bouches-du-Rhône), near Marseille.[68] It would be, as Eurocopter S.A. Chairman Bigay pointed out, "the first integrated aeronautic group in Europe."[69]

In the same month, after the development and testing of the new Trigat (AC3G-LP) third-generation long-range anti-tank missiles had been completed, Defense Ministers Rühe and Millon delegated to their armament directors a first order of 1,800 missiles for each of the two forces. Germany had fixed its total demand at 2,544 and France at 3,600 of these arms, designed to be the Tiger's central arming component and to succeed the second-generation HOT missiles.[70]

A few days after a meeting between Defense Ministers Rühe and Millon in Lyon in April 1997, the two defense ministries announced that the contract on the industrialization of the Tiger helicopter would be signed in June. At the Eurocopter factories, the manufacturing and finishing of the necessary tools and machines had begun. The ultimate unit price per Tiger (acquisition costs excluding development expenses) was now calculated at around FF 115 million (about DM 33 million), varying somewhat with the specifics and equipment with which each helicopter would be finished.[71]

On June 20, 1997, during the forty-second *Aérosalon* in Le Bourget, in the presence of Defense Ministers Alain Richard and Rühe, BWB President Peter Koerner signed the "serial production preparation contract" with Eurocopter for the Franco-German Tiger combat helicopter. The contract had been ready for signature since December 1995, yet this penultimate step toward the physical birth of the helicopter had been postponed several times due to the turbulences of 1996. The serial production preparation contract, valued at DM 733.6 million (FF 2.5 billion, $430 million), covered all expenses (such as the design and acquisition of tools, machines, infrastructure, materials, etc.) to prepare for the ultimate manufacture of the highly advanced combat helicopter.[72] It also confirmed that a contract for an initial batch of 160 helicopters would be signed the following year and reaffirmed the prior schedule, according to which the German *Bundeswehr* would receive the first helicopters by 2001 and the French army two years later.[73] By June 1997, the Tiger's five prototypes had together accumulated a total of 1,700 flight hours and had fulfilled or surpassed all of the technical performance specifications.[74]

On May 20, 1998, during the International Aeronautic Fair (ILA) in Berlin, DGA Jean-Yves Helmer and Defense Ministry *Staatssekretär* Gunnar Simon signed a new document, officially titled "Agreement on the common entrance into the acquisition in series of the helicopter Tiger." France and Germany "pluriannually"—read: over several years—ordered a first batch of eighty helicopters each. France ordered ten Tigers in the pure anti-tank (HAC) version and seventy in the combat support and protection version (HAP). All of Germany's eighty combat helicopters would be finished in a "polyvalent" multifunctional anti-tank and support UH-T version.[75] The agreement again confirmed 2001 as the delivery date of the first helicopters to the German forces, and 2003 to the French forces. The last of this first batch of 160 Tigers were to be delivered by 2011.

However, with the creation of the European defense agency OCCAR, in its embryonic state after Italy and Great Britain joined the initial bilateral Franco-German arms agency, the formal Tiger ordering procedure had become complicated and confusing. After the Franco-German 1998 ILA agreement in Berlin, the official order would be passed from OCCAR to the German BWB and from there to Eurocopter.[76] Yet, due to remaining difficulties with the night vision system and other technical problems, the BWB had not yet signed the contract on the series production of the Tiger with Eurocopter by the fall of 1998. The delivery dates scheduled in May 1998 were already obsolete by the fall of the same year.

Furthermore, the German federal election of September 27, 1998, brought about a new German government, with Chancellor Gerhard Schröder leading a coalition between the German Socialdemocratic Party (SPD) and the Greens. By December, the SPD-Green government's new Defense Minister Rudolf Scharping and his French colleague Alain Richard announced that France and Germany would review their armaments programs. While Scharping underscored that the "Tiger programme was guaranteed," this review might delay confirming the order of the 160 Tiger helicopters for some six months. Later in December, Richard pronounced that the Tiger production treaty would be signed in 1999.[77]

Finally, on June 18, 1999, at the aeronautics fair in Le Bourget, the armament directors of both countries, Weise and Helmer, signed the Tiger production contract and confirmed the first order of 160 Tigers, eighty each for France and Germany. Passed on to Eurocopter later in 1999, the series production contract alone was worth some €3.3 billion.[78] Some twenty-five years after the two states' army leaderships had first voiced a desire for third-generation anti-tank helicopters, the act marked the official entering of the production in series of the Franco-German combat helicopter.

Tigers for Turkey?

A few days after the Nuremberg summit of December 1996 had secured the physical advent of the Tiger combat helicopter, the export issue again moved to center stage. This time, however, it took a different guise. A Franco-German company would soon produce a highly advanced combat helicopter that would be competitive in the international marketplace but, as the French economics newspaper *La Tribune Desfossés* carefully stated, "the two countries do not have the same policy in terms of armament export." Indeed, whereas German arms export regulations are highly restrictive, France's selling of arms of any kind is commonplace. It would only be a question of time before a potential buyer would enter the scene, triggering incompatible French and German responses toward selling arms abroad.[79] The issue had not yet become acute. It soon would.

In 1997, the Turkish government announced its intention to acquire 145 new combat helicopters, calling internationally for offers. The entire package had a value of some DM 5 billion. During the last few months of 1997, a noticeable silence dominated from all sides: Eurocopter, France, and Germany. On February 3, 1998, the French press reported that Eurocopter, with the approval of the French government, had made an offer to Turkey. On the same day, the Turkish defense minister visited the Eurocopter factory in Marignane. The issue became highly politicized, as Eurocopter acknowledged the "juicy Turkish helicopter market" as a potential "target" for Tiger sales.[80]

Observers of the scene immediately evoked the 1972 Debré-Schmidt accord, which required "consultation," but which also stipulated that one partner of a Franco-German arms cooperation program cannot veto the export of the equipment by the other. Yet, it was clear that the issue was of a political, not of a purely legal, nature. Though the notion of "veto" existed nowhere in the legal framing of the Franco-German interstate institutionalization, France considered a German "veto" of the potential Tiger sale to Turkey to be politically legitimate and conceivable.

As the contours of the deal became more concrete and Turkey confirmed its intention to utilize the helicopters in its "combat against the guerrilla" (read: in the Kurdish areas in Turkey's southeast), the fundamentally different French and German attitudes toward arms export lay fully bare. Seen in purely legal terms, the deal could be managed via France alone. However, such a formalistic evasion of the issue would not satisfy German concerns, nor would France entertain this option. On the contrary, the French Defense Ministry "underscored that France and Germany would seek agreement even before the issue of export could become imminent."[81]

As a North Atlantic Treaty Organization (NATO) member state and long-term European Union (EU) candidate, Turkey is in fact not the type of weapons export destination that Germany categorically rules out. Turkey is not a systematically repressive human rights violator, nor is it generally considered a "tension area," in German legal diction. Yet, arms exports to Turkey have long been a highly contested issue in German domestic political debate. Now, although the German government did not hide its inclination to preclude the deal, it did not immediately formulate a categorical position. Throughout 1998, Germany criticized Turkey for human rights violations and demanded remediation, just as it did on the Kurdish minority problem. Further, in May 1998 the French national assembly adopted a proposition that publicly recognized the 1915 slaughtering of Armenians as genocide, further straining Turkish relations with France.[82] Simultaneously, the Turkish government hinted repeatedly that it would prefer the Tiger to several other competitors.

In December 1998, the German government forbade Eurocopter for an unlimited period from giving a flight demonstration of a Tiger prototype to Turkish officials, who naturally were eager to see the likely product of their choice in the air.[83] Although not strictly a "veto," the measure significantly reduced Eurocopter's chances of winning the valuable order. Berlin's "reticence" to export the Tiger to Turkey, reported the center-right French daily Le Figaro, was only reinforced with the 1998 change in government.[84]

The situation could have provided an interesting observation of how Franco-German institutionalized relations, together with the fundamentally divergent positions on arms export stemming from the different historically rooted domestic constructions of self-view and proper role and conduct in the world, would somehow produce a position that had to be—one way or another—a Franco-German one. However, this process was interrupted by Turkey early in 1999. In a demonstration of its rejection of French, German, and Franco-German concerns and criticisms, Turkey decided to buy American Apache helicopters. The continued German censure of Turkey's human rights record led the Turkish government to turn away from its initially preferred supplier and toward the American helicopter company, where no questions were asked and no criticisms were voiced regarding what the Turkish government considered to be domestic matters.

Tigers for Australia and Spain

On December 18, 2000, the Australian government announced its intention to acquire some twenty to twenty-five combat helicopters in order to build up two squadrons. It sought a contract for the most modern and competitive helicopters available, to be signed before the end of 2001, and was willing to spend up to 1.2 billion Australian dollars. Building up a helicopter fleet was just part of a major military reform through which Australia intended to develop the capability for a larger regional and international role in security affairs. Australia desired to be more militarily operational outside its borders.[85] To that end, it wanted a versatile, "multi-role," multipurpose helicopter for "armed reconnaissance."[86] It was clear that, next to the Tiger, the competition would include Boeing's Apache, Bell's Cobra, and the Italian company Agusta's Mangusta.[87]

The competition and lobbying that followed was as intense as in the Dutch and British instances just a half-decade before. Unlike in those episodes, however, and in spite of intense pressure from Washington, the Australian government decided in favor of the Tiger. On August 10, 2001, Australian Defense Minister Peter Reith publicized that his government would acquire twenty-two Tigers and expected to sign a formal contract by December.[88] The Australian general staff, Eurocopter Director Bigay reported, particularly valued the Tiger's maneuverability, speed, and versatility, with the capability for a wide range of missions ranging from peacekeeping to heavy combat.[89] On December 21, Australia signed an acquisition contract for twenty-two Tiger combat helicopters at 1.1 billion Australian dollars (some €730 million) and an additional Through-Life-Support Contract (covering a three-year pre-implementation phase and a fifteen-year in-service period) of another 410.9 million Australian dollars (€340 million).[90]

The Australian Tiger version, Tiger ARH (Armed Reconnaissance Helicopter), is based on the Franco-German Tiger base cell. The ARH specifically meets Australian safety requirements, communications, avionics, and weapons configurations. It carries two primary weapons systems, the Hellfire missile system and a 70mm rocket system, as well as a 30mm cannon for self-defense. The first four ARH Tigers are to be entirely completed in the Eurocopter factory in Mariagne.

The remaining 18 will be manufactured in France and then assembled in Brisbane.[91] The Tiger's career as an international export item had begun.

In its call for offers for some twenty combat helicopters, the Spanish government underscored its particular interest in a combat helicopter that was as versatile as possible. It wanted machines that could perform multiple roles in the "entire spectrum of missions."[92] In their subsequent talks, by the summer of 2001, the Spanish, French, and German governments had baptized the possible Spanish version HAD—*Hélicoptère d'Appui et Destruction* in French, and *Helicoptero d'Apoyo y Destrucción* in Spanish.[93] While sharing much with the French HAP and Australian ARH versions, this "multifunctional," "multi-role" "combat support and destruction" version would be "yet more polyvalent" (read: versatile and capable of various missions and purposes) than all of the Tiger's prior versions. From early on, the three negotiating governments entertained the possibility that Spain would participate in the Tiger program more comprehensively than just assembling its Tigers at home (as Australia would partially do).[94]

The Spanish government posed three conditions for Tiger acquisitions: (1) that the Spanish Tigers comprise a more powerful engine that could propel a somewhat heavier machine; (2) that they include the new Trigat LP (long-range) missile; and (3), that at least one of the two Tiger producers (France or Germany) themselves acquire machines of the version that Spain would receive. The French army and government agreed to the third condition, which Spain termed a "political signal."[95] By June 2002, Spanish and French Defense Ministers Federico Trillo and Michèle Alliot-Marie had officially confirmed their will to co-develop a version of the Tiger that would also comprise part of France's Tiger fleet. The costs of developing such a version were estimated at between €150 million and €250 million; the total costs of the some twenty-four Spanish machines at €650–760 million. The issue now seemed to be whether Spain would exclusively buy Tigers or split its total order between Tigers and American Apache helicopters.[96]

On September 5, faster than expected, Spain announced that it had decided exclusively in favor of the Tiger: it would acquire twenty-four Tigers of a new and yet to be developed "HAD" version.[97] The deal involved the inclusion of Spain in the Tiger program, both in administrative terms through the arms agency OCCAR and by partially integrating its own aeronautics industry into Eurocopter, now part of EADS. Furthermore, part of the Tiger's cell would be produced in Spain, where the Spanish Tigers would be assembled. In September 2003, the total contract value was estimated at over €1.35 billion.[98]

After Spain's September 2003 decisions in favor of the HAD Tigers, France adjusted its prior intentions to receive Tigers in the pure anti-tank (HAC) version. France would now receive 37 HAP Tigers, along with 43 Tigers to be finished in the Spanish HAD version.[99] The HAD shares much with the French HAP and Australian ARH Tiger. Among other differences, however, the HAD incorporates a more powerful engine, new ballistic protection, and Air-to-Ground

Missile (AGM) capability.[100] It can be armed with up to four air-to-air Mistral missiles; a 30mm cannon; small guided and non-guided missiles; and second-and third-generation missiles for the destruction of objects on the surface, including but not limited to tanks.[101] Following the signing of a trilateral administrative arrangement in March 2004, Spain joined the program. On November 30, 2005, Eurocopter and OCCAR signed a formal contract on the development and production investments for a new Tiger HAD version for France and Spain.[102]

Expanding Franco-German Defense Infrastructure, World Markets, Delivery, and Baptism by Fire

As early as the 1991 Franco-German summit in Lille, President Mitterrand and Chancellor Kohl had discussed the creation of a Franco-German helicopter school to train future Tiger pilots. After the Nuremberg summit in December 1996 had cleared the way for the Tiger's physical emergence, the two defense ministries moved ahead with their plans. On April 11, 1997, ministers Millon and Rühe announced after a meeting in Lyon that the armies of their two states would establish such a school in Le Luc (Var) in Provence. The new helicopter pilot school, a "great premier" of complete common formation of pilots of different armies, would be commanded alternately by French and German officers.[103] The Franco-German summit in Vittel in November 2000 saw the signing of the official administrative act to create a Franco-German helicopter pilot school. The school's foundation stone was set in December 2001, and it was officially inaugurated on July 1, 2003. The administrative agreement signed by the French and German defense ministers makes express reference to the Elysée Treaty on Franco-German cooperation and friendship, in the spirit of which the new school would serve.[104]

The helicopter training school was devised to host some twenty-eight Tiger helicopters of various versions (each country contributing fourteen), along with twenty helicopter training simulators. More than 300 persons work at the school at one time, about half of them Tiger pilots in training. The school's "daily functioning is fully bilateralized." Its training purposes focus on close joint instruction, perhaps laying the groundwork for future side-by-side missions abroad.[105] Jointly trained Tiger helicopter pilots and squadrons may eventually constitute the basic building blocks of more tightly integrated, "European" armed forces in the decades ahead.[106]

Paralleling the helicopter pilot school in Le Luc, France and Germany instituted a joint technical training school in Fassberg in Lower Saxony to train all French and German specialized mechanics and technicians. Its graduates are trained to provide technical and logistical support for the Tiger helicopters in their respective French and German military units. Inaugurated on September 27, 2003, the mechanics' school would be "embedded in the comprehensive cooperation between France and Germany within the frame of the Tiger project."[107]

Then the Tigers themselves appeared. On March 22, 2002, some 500 guests, mostly from French and German politics, armed forces, industry, and media, attended the "rollout" of the first series-produced UH-Tiger from the Eurocopter factory in Donauwörth.[108] During 2003, a UH-Tiger was delivered to the Fassberg school.[109] Eurocopter officially delivered the first Tiger (one of the HAP version) to the light aviation of the French army (ALAT) on March 18, 2005, and the first serial UH-Tiger was officially handed over to the German armed forces on April 6.[110] However, a series of technical difficulties has kept the Tiger's German UH version from reaching operational capability in the ensuing years. Three French HAP Tigers, on the other hand, flew their first combat operations in August and September 2009 in the fight against the Taliban in Afghanistan. The Tigers' "baptism by fire in the field" included, as one French military officer summarized, "find, attack, suppress, seize, raid, and support."[111]

By the beginning of the twenty-first century, orders for a total of 206 Tiger combat helicopters had been confirmed. These were developed and assembled in four different versions: eighty "support" Tigers (UH-T) for Germany; thirty-seven "support and protection" Tigers (HAP) for France; twenty-two "armed reconnaissance" Tigers (ARH) for Australia; and sixty-seven "support and destruction" Tigers (HAD) for France and Spain. All of the various Tiger versions are built upon the same basic helicopter cell and share most of their features.[112]

Tigers will take on a wide range of helicopter missions including armed reconnaissance and monitoring; anti-tank combat; ground troop support; and escort and protection for transport and other helicopter operations. Capable of multiple fighting tasks, they will operate day and night, in all weather conditions, and perhaps even in nuclear, biological, or chemically contaminated areas.[113] They will be armed in a range of mixes, comprising cannons, small unguided missiles, and air-to-air and air-to-surface missiles of various types, including self-guiding long-range "fire and forget" missiles of the third generation.

It is now highly unlikely that Germany will ultimately acquire 212 Tiger helicopters as it initially intended and restated even in 1996. Officially, it "keeps open the option" of adding to the 80 machines that it ordered in 1999.[114] In November 2005, the French defense ministry announced the reduction of its ultimate order from 215 to 120. These machines of the HAP and HAD versions would be delivered over a decade or decade and a half. Thus, by around 2015 or 2020, 120 Tigers might equip the French armed forces.[115] However, in light of the enormous budgetary pressures and significant debt in the wake of the economic and financial crisis, it remains uncertain whether France and Germany will ultimately acquire 120 and 80 Tigers respectively, per the contracts at the time of this writing, or whether for financial reasons they might end up reducing these numbers.

In 2002, Eurocopter President Bigay estimated the size of the world market for combat helicopters like the Tiger at between 200 and 400 machines in the next few decades. With the Tiger, Eurocopter hopes to win about half of the worldwide combat helicopter orders in that period, including such potential customers as Norway, Sweden, and Finland; Malaysia and Singapore; the United Arab Emirates; as well as some other states in South America and Asia.[116] Turkey may also reappear as a potential customer.[117] The U.S. military market, the world's largest for combat helicopters, is likely to remain closed for Tigers. China will be the second largest helicopter market. In 2003, Eurocopter opened a permanent office in Beijing to represent all of Eurocopter's products, most of which, at least for some time to come, will remain civil helicopters.[118] By the year 2020, some 250 Tiger helicopters might populate the globe; toward the middle of the twenty-first century, perhaps some 300 to 500.

Processes and Implications

Focusing on the processes of the years covered in this chapter brings to light two observations in particular. First, institutionalized relations may bring about events that reflect back on the meaning of the relationship itself. The "evolving pride" in the cutting-edge high-tech weapon over the course of the 1990s, the joint Franco-German salesmanship, and the opening of a joint Franco-German pilot helicopter school in the early new century illustrate such process-endogenous implications. Just as failures or disappointments produced by the relations can undermine or change the meaning that relations embody, joint success or endeavor in turn may shape an interstate relationship's texture. Second, institutionalized relations can generate further institutional elements or affect social organization more broadly. The fusion of the French and German helicopter industries into "Eurocopter," the foundation of the Franco-German Helicopter Office and then the armament agency OCCAR, and the institution of a the two joint Franco-German training schools are examples of such processual effects. Such new institutionalization or social organization can in turn be meaning charged. However, this newly institutionalized meaning is not necessarily entirely identical with the institutionalized meaning that helped to bring it about.

Regarding the first observation above, the evolving pride over the common product in the early 1990s is an example of how such meaning can be generated within institutionalized relations themselves. Those involved, as well as many outside observers, characterized the helicopter development as an achievement. In doing so, they underscored the Franco-German element of the accomplishment. Before the 1991 air fair exhibition in Le Bourget, for example, Aérospatiale President Martre called the Tiger "the youngest child of the exemplary

Franco-German armament cooperation based on the Elysée Treaty." A Tiger prototype, celebrated as "one of the stars of the fair," was portrayed as the "fruit of the Franco-German collaboration."[119]

Later, with regular production of the Tigers about to commence, French armament director Gleizes interpreted the rollout of the first series-produced Tiger from the Eurocopter factory in Donauwörth as "an important symbol for Franco-German cooperation." A long-term observer of French, German, and European armament politics viewed the "helicopter Tiger at the heart of Franco-German cooperation."[120] In all of these instances, the Tiger helicopter was not simply depicted as a cutting-edge weapon that France and Germany developed for more or less sound reasons. Rather, the helicopter was about common Franco-German achievement and success in a much broader sense that mirrored and reproduced the social purpose of Franco-German relations.

The joint Franco-German salesmanship, especially during the mid-1990s but also in the early new century, exemplifies how dealing with third parties may reflect back on and perpetuate signification of a certain type of institutionalized relations. France and Germany structured their joint lobbying of the Netherlands and Great Britain very much around the theme of "approaching the Franco-German couple" or "tandem." After both countries decided against the Tiger, French and German public officials depicted them as "choices against Europe" (with a Franco-German kernel) or, in the British case, as "dumping Europe and privileging the United States." As the commentaries by French and German officials seem to underscore, even if jointly dealing with third parties ends in failure or rejection, the process can reinvigorate meaning structures of institutionalized relationships and seems to confirm who was really tightly connected with whom.

Finally, the symbolic meaning associated with the bilaterally conceived training schools illustrates how institutionalized relations may generate meaning that reflects back on the relationship itself and at the same time becomes part of it. German Defense Minister Struck, for example, in a speech delivered at the Tiger mechanics' school opening, underlines that the "institution of the binational training facility" in Fassberg "represents a great opportunity that in its importance extends far beyond its military Dimension."[121] In the same vein, at the helicopter school in Le Luc, French President Chirac calls Fassberg and Le Luc a "strong symbol" of both French and German common security and of a "concrete manifestation of the will that animates us to build a Europe in all of its dimensions."[122] Indeed, as an observer for the German economics daily *Handelsblatt* put it, the French and German capitals "celebrate the joint Tiger-pilot training as pathbreaking."[123]

Furthermore, the years covered in this chapter also show how institutionalized relations can bring about further institutional elements. Such "institutionalization out of institutionalization" is the product of the interaction, meaning, and purpose that interstate relations can embody. In turn, it is also a manifestation, prolongation, or residue of such meaning and social purpose. However, the meaning of such newly generated institutionalization is not necessarily entirely congruent or identical with the institutionalized meaning of the relationship that helped to bring it about. Such process-induced institutionalization, as exemplified by the successive integration of the French and German helicopter industries or the foundation of the Franco-German arms agency OCCAR as a nucleus of a future European arms agency, can affect social organization more broadly. On the other hand, as the newly instituted pilot training and mechanics schools illustrate, it may add to the bilateral institutionalization from which it chiefly emerged. All of these developments exemplify aspects of process-endogenous institutional structuration: structures of institutionalization and construction generate processes that in turn reproduce, yet also develop, such structures themselves.

The successive integration and then full fusion of the French and German helicopter industries was decisively lubricated by the Franco-German combat helicopter program. This industrial fusion can be neither explained nor understood without the logic of Franco-German interstate institutionalization and construction. The making of a major European transnational actor has its roots in the May 1984 Memorandum of Understanding (MoU) in the wake of which Aérospatiale and MBB strengthened their cooperative ties. Whereas corporate representatives of Aérospatiale and DASA/MBB worked out this and successive integration steps, the process could not have unfolded without the support and agreement of the French and German governments. This support and even promotion was of decisive relevance, especially on the French side. Aérospatiale was a publicly owned French "national champion," its activities under special surveillance of the respective ministerial bureaucracy.

After the successive stages of increasing integration outlined above, the French and German helicopter industries became fully fused during the second half of the 1990s. The process is closely tied to Franco-German purpose, and the political dimension of cross-border industrial integration is conspicuous. Already during the late 1980s, Eurocopter chief Martre stressed that while with respect to joint Franco-German helicopter ventures he likes to speak of "a privileged axis within the European cooperation," there is "no cooperation in sight with the United States."[124] During the 1990s, Eurocopter Chairman Bigay stressed that this fusion is so far singular in the European aircraft industry.[125] In the 2000s, Eurocopter became the helicopter division of EADS, the new European conglomerate in aeronautics, defense, and space technology. In addition to acquiring Tiger helicopters, Spain joined both the helicopter program and Eurocopter in the early twenty-first century. However, as one European armament analyst insisted in an extensive report on the state of European defense, Eurocopter's success story begins with the Tiger.[126] The history of the Tiger's emergence thus also contributed in important ways to the establishment and consolidation of a transborder European defense industry that, although still in its infancy, may ultimately help to bring about more comprehensive and truly European defense structures.

OCCAR provides another example of (bilaterally) institutionalized interstate relations affecting social organization more broadly. OCCAR's nucleus emerged in a series of Franco-German summit meetings and tight consultations during the first half of the 1990s. In the wake of the Tiger program, Kohl and Mitterrand's December 1995 "Baden-Baden" declaration marks its official beginning. An off-spring of Franco-German intergovernmentalism, OCCAR took over the management of the Tiger program in February 1996. In the same year, Italy and the United Kingdom joined OCCAR's previously all Franco-German "precursor team" to institute the foundations of a European arms agency-to-be. From the beginning, France and Germany had invited other Europeans to join the agency, instituting a catalogue with a number of principles that potential participants had to accept. Chief among them was the two governments' determination to renounce the principle of "just return" of armament projects on a program-to-program basis, instead seeking a rough "global pluriannual equilibrium." OCCAR became a legal entity (*personalité juridique/Rechtspersönlichkeit*) in 2001, and Spain joined in 2005 after choosing to acquire Tiger helicopters and participate in the Tiger program.[127]

The Tiger program was key in consolidating the embryonic European defense agency. Until the integration of the Airbus A400M military transport aircraft program into OCCAR, the Tiger project was by far its largest, most comprehensive, and most expensive program. The Tiger program has been a major lubricant not only for the fusion of the French and German helicopter industries but also toward engendering the nucleus of a future European armament and defense agency.[128]

Finally, the institution of a fully integrated Franco-German helicopter flying school in the wake of the Tiger program is yet another example of "institutionalization out of institutionalization." It expresses and perpetuates institutionalized value and purpose. A side product of the Tiger program's history, the pilot school is very much a product of the rhythms of Franco-German regularized intergovernmentalism with the semiannual summit meeting at its core, along with the institutionalized Franco-German meaning. It is "just one of numerous common creations following the Franco-German Treaty of January 22, 1963 that concretize the privileged relationship between the two countries."[129] "We will not only have a common technology" but also "a common training and common deployment," commented German Defense Minister Rühe on the school's wider scope and ramifications during its planning stage. French Defense Minister Richard praised the foundation of the school as "the continuation of a long tradition in confidence building cooperation" between France and Germany.[130] In instituting the joint pilot school, "France and Germany have decided to open a new stage in their long-term military cooperation." The school "is a premier" in that it "closes the complete cycle of cooperation between two armies . . . that began with the joint fabrication of the helicopter."[131]

Outcomes and Outcome

Three main outcomes need explanation in the period 1988–2009: the French and German interests and according policies to sell Tigers to the Netherlands, Britain, Australia, and Spain (since all of these export episodes are similarly structured, I discuss them together as one case); the French and German hesitation to sell their combat helicopters to Turkey; and the overall outcome with respect to the Tiger program at the end of 1996, after a tumultuous political year that once again could have terminated the Tiger's history.

Case 10: For Sale! The Dutch, British, Australian, and Spanish Export Episodes (1994–2005)

For the overall history of Franco-German defense cooperation generally and the Tiger's history specifically, the export episodes involving the Netherlands and Great Britain (both 1994–1995), Australia (2000–2001), and Spain (2001–2005) constitute important political milestones, not least because they launched the Tiger's career as an export item. As distinct political outcomes, the French and German interests in selling the Tiger to these four countries are causally overdetermined. Although for different reasons, all of the propositions derived from the major currents of international relations theory, as well as from chapter 2's constructivist-institutionalist model, predict French and German interests in selling to these states. Indeed, France and Germany were intensely interested in selling Tigers in all four of the episodes. That they won the order in only two of the four potential sales stemmed from reasons unrelated to their motivation. Case 10 is an important reminder that at some junctures, the dissimilar political and economic factors emphasized by commonly competing macro-perspectives on world politics may in fact pull toward the same political outcome. Although rooted in diverging general views of how the world works, the hypotheses generated by the main theoretical currents in international relations may offer the same expectation or prediction. History is not always and not necessarily the result of various forces in one intellectual tradition getting the upper hand over those in other currents but sometimes may be driven in the same direction by all of these forces at once.

From a mercantilist-realist perspective, the interest to sell stems from national developmental reasons. Such a realist position would especially point at France, where the weapons industry is under tight control of the state. State-controlled or state-owned industries immediately benefit from weapons sales. Both France and Germany were strongly interested in selling their combat helicopter during all four export episodes.

A neoliberal institutionalist position could observe that the institutionalized relations between France and Germany serve both states if they help to boost and coordinate French and German (public) lobbying for Franco-German products abroad. Such a perspective could assume the underlying interests to sell these products as exogenously given.

A liberal society-based inside-out perspective will also predict French and German interests in such sales because they are in the interest of the industrial companies that produce the weaponry. A liberal perspective would especially focus on Germany. MBB and Daimler-Benz are private companies. Indeed, in unison with the German as well as the French governments, the companies chiefly involved in the Tiger's production wanted to sell in all four export instances.

The constructivist-institutionalist model advanced in chapter 2 also predicts France's and Germany's interest in selling their high-tech development to all four potential customers. The key elements of German domestic construction do not imply any proscriptive effects on German interests regarding arms sales to these four states. The Netherlands, Great Britain, Australia, and Spain are stable democracies with impeccable human rights records. The three European states, in addition, are EU and NATO members. All four are welcome customers for Germany. Selling to them does not conflict with historically rooted elements of German domestic construction of proper German role and conduct. The French domestic construction induces prescriptive effects toward the sale, allowing the machinery of Franco-German political lobbying to sell the Franco-German product to take full effect.[132] France, Germany, and the Franco-German Eurocopter were keen to sell to these unproblematic arms export destinations. That the Netherlands and Great Britain decided to buy American and turn down the Eurocopter offer had nothing to do with German public policies of restrictive export guidelines or a German Tiger "veto."

Absent any tensions between respective French and German domestic constructions and institutionalized relations, and without the undermining effects from French or German political systems or domestic societies, the model hypothesizes that both France and Germany would be strongly interested in acquiring these orders. The model, however, insists that the interests relate to a public-governmental consent in both countries. Interests in these sales are neither apolitical nor merely industry driven. The case becomes interesting if compared with the other export episode, the politics around the potential export of Franco-German combat helicopters to Turkey. The model argues that the varying effects of the German domestic construction affected the different interest formations and policies in the Turkey case in important ways.

Case 11: For Sale? The Turkish Export Episode (1997–1999)

In 1999, this third export episode ended in the same way as the two before: Eurocopter did not sell the Franco-German Tiger helicopter. However, the factors that produced the same surface outcome were very different. French and German interest formation and actions contributed, in important ways, to Turkey's choice to buy from the United States. From 1991 on, the problematic Franco-German arms export issue in its Tiger incarnation had been on the table. At that point the matter was not yet concrete enough to become fully virulent because there was not yet a customer interested in buying the Tiger, colliding with German self-understanding and internally anchored construction of proper conduct. That changed during 1997–1998 when Turkey expressed interest in buying Franco-German combat helicopters.

"Border case Turkey" is a hard case on which to test the causal implications of German domestic construction elements on export interests and policies. In fact, it appears to be a clear potential destination for German (or partly German) arms. The Turkish state is neither regularly repressive nor a systematic human rights violator, and it is not really situated in a "tension area" (*Spannungsgebiet*). Since Atatürk, the Turkish state has been secularized, and the Turkish military establishment has remained Western in its values and orientation ever since. Turkey is a NATO member, with NATO also being a community of values—at least according to German consensus. As a rule, Germany exports arms without hesitation to NATO and EU states, as well as to a number of other stable democracies including Australia, New Zealand, and Switzerland.

However, Germany had long criticized the overall Turkish human rights record. Yet more relevant for a potential Tiger export was the unresolved Kurdish minority problem in the southeastern part of Turkey, in the areas toward its borders with Syria, Iraq, and Iran. The combination of the two issues immediately politicized the potential export issue. From a military point of view, it was clear that the Franco-German combat helicopter would be a perfect weapon to combat the PKK and other Kurdish organizations, as well as to bomb territory populated by Kurds. In May 1998, the Turkish government confirmed, in an official statement, what German officials knew and feared: Turkey intended to utilize especially the first batch of forty-five helicopters in "combat against the guerrilla."[133]

The different interests and policies induced by the German domestic construction set the Turkish case apart from those of the Netherlands and Great Britain before, and from those of Australia and Spain thereafter. All other factors in these export episodes are the same. The divergent effects of German domestic construction with their implications for arms export explain the different interests and policies. Turkey's strong interest in the Tiger relative to the Netherlands and Great Britain underscores the efficacy of the factor. "To whom and for what purpose?" were important questions for Germany in trading arms, tightly connected with the foreign policy notion of "politics of responsibility," a major element of domestic construction at the time.[134]

Rooted in the differing historically shaped and domestically anchored elements of self-view and proper role in the world, the German attitude diverged widely from the French one with respect to a potential Tiger export. What was immediately a weighty political issue for Germany was a non-issue for France—which largely considered Turkish problems internal matters of another sovereign state and none of France's business.

Yet, France and Germany were "in it together." It is only due to the robustness of the institutionalized Franco-German relationship that France, with an entirely different position on the matter, respected and accepted the German domestic construction-induced interest. Absent the institutionalized relationship, France could simply have sold unilaterally. The effects of the German domestic construction were diffused via the institutionalized net of Franco-German relations, and so ultimately helped to shape not only the German position but the French one too. (In this sense, this case mirrors the strong effects of French domestic construction regarding the TADS/PNVS system of case 8 above. In that case, elements of French domestic construction ultimately affected both French and German policy definitions regarding the matter.)

However, the effects of the German domestic construction did not categorically rule out a potential deal; nor did they directly clash with the Franco-German relationship, although they were in strong tension with it. One would have to locate this case between hypotheses 2 and 3 as formulated in chapter 2. However, the German domestic construction of proper conduct does the explanatory work, with the troubles and frictions about the potential deal that it induced. Germany's forbidding Eurocopter to perform demonstration flights of the helicopter for Turkish officials was nothing less than a "semi-veto" of the valuable deal, although reserving the last word on the matter.

From an analytic point of view, it is perhaps regrettable that the Turkish government turned away from its initial preference for the Franco-German combat helicopter. Indeed, Ankara's decision meant that "the SPD-Green government could evade a definite answer to the question of whether or not to sell arms to NATO-partner Turkey."[135] For theoretical reasons and in order to more sharply evaluate the different theoretical hypotheses, it would have been preferable if history had taken a slightly different course: Turkey's lasting insistence on Franco-German Tigers rather than turning to American Apache helicopters in 1999 would have been yet more illuminating. A further escalation of the political matter would have allowed us to observe the forces within and between France and Germany more thoroughly. This would have been particularly interesting with respect to the French government, the Eurocopter management, and the unions representing the interests of Eurocopter workers. As history turned out, while strongly suggestive, the evidence is not fully conclusive. However, even using the evidence that is available, the Turkish export affair is an important case.

Nonetheless, although for different reasons, explanations derived from realist, neoliberal, and liberal approaches to international affairs have difficulty grappling with the historical evidence of the Turkish export episode. A mercantilist version of realism is poorly equipped to explain why a government would undermine the performance of its economy by encumbering its export chances in such a lucrative industry. This is true whether the state is directly involved in the economic sector, as in France, or whether the industry is largely under private control, as in Germany. Yet, the German government strongly undermined the Tiger's export chances to Turkey, and France made no attempts to sell unilaterally.

From a neoliberal point of view it is striking that, at least for France, the institutionalized relationship with Germany in this case in fact decreases economic efficiency. Both states had long been aware of this chronic disagreement on export. Nonetheless, both repeatedly strongly promoted the cooperation program. According to neoliberal expectations, given the prospect of dealing once again with the troublesome difference—now in such an extremely expensive weapon—both France and Germany should have abandoned the joint project long ago. They should never have ended up in this situation. However, such efficiency sacrifices due to cooperation with Germany are well known and understood in France. They do not hinder Franco-German cooperation even in this instance. The cooperation on the helicopter project has begun and developed not only in the absence of common interests but even in the presence of contrary interests with respect to ultimately exporting the product.

Finally, the case also cuts against domestic or transnational society-rooted liberal expectations. When the government of one state acts in a way that precludes its own industry from entering a valuable international market, and the government of another state at least passively goes along despite the same results for its own industry, it turns liberal inside-out reasoning on its head. The German government's actions made an extremely valuable potential deal for the German (and indirectly the French) industry a great deal less likely. The German government's quasi-veto directly contradicts liberal inside-out modes of explanation.

Case 12: "1996"—Showdown and Ultimate Breakthrough

The year 1996 was another tumultuous helicopter year. Almost as if an abstract, it brings to light many of the leading themes that shaped the processes and outcomes of the preceding twenty-five years history. The year began with new "turbulences around the Tiger" and ended with "reinforced armament cooperation" between France and Germany.[136] By the end of the year, finally, everything was set for the new combat helicopter to move toward production. In a time of most severe budgetary pressures, exacerbated by the stipulations of the ("Maastricht") Treaty on

European Union, the Tiger created interests in maintaining its original funding, even though the expenses forced states to make painful cuts in other areas. The French, German, and Franco-German political processes during 1996, leading up to the decisions jointly made at the December summit in Nuremberg, cannot be understood without the logic of interstate institutionalization and construction, in combination with domestic-internal political structures and processes. The patterns of interaction and constructed purpose inherent to Franco-German affairs did not only give meaning to an otherwise bare physical world. They also seem to have added palpable physical matter to it—in the form of a highly advanced combat helicopter.

The year 1996 was then perhaps the toughest budgetary year for the German post-war democracy, and surely one of the most tenuous for the Fifth Republic as well. Both states struggled toward the self-defined goal of meeting the strict "Maastricht convergence criteria" in order to join the Economic and Monetary Union (EMU). In the German case, the overwhelming costs of "inner unifica-tion" gravely aggravated these extraordinary financial constraints. The choices that the two governments had to make regarding the allocation of very scarce financial resources during 1996 were exceptionally difficult ones. Under such cir-cumstances, one would not expect an armament project of the Tiger program's magnitude to remain untouched. However, even during the financial difficulties of the budgetary politics in both states, the armament year 1996 strikingly shows that the Franco-German relationship was one important factor in the two govern-ments' priority setting, interest definition, and the public policymaking of domes-tic resource allocation. The bilateral relationship logic was an important factor in shaping French and German positions even in very dire political circumstances and in the solutions arrived at by the end of that year. In December, at least for the time being, France and Germany maintained the original scheme to ultimately acquire a total of 427 helicopters.

With respect to the role and impact of Franco-German institutionalized rela-tions on French and German interest formation and policy formulation, three aspects become particularly salient during the political struggles of 1996: how much the institutionalized meaning and value incorporated by the Franco-German relationship had become a reference point for various political actors involved in the political process; how much the Franco-German summit consul-tations had become an element of the French and German policy processes; and how much these processes prestructured avenues that appear quite natural and intuitive to both France and Germany.

First, the empirical record strikingly shows how various actors—for example, German Defense Minister Rühe, struggling with the Finance Ministry and the Daimler-Benz/DASA/MBB management on their lobbying the French govern-ment for the continuation of the program—referred to the value of Franco-German cooperation for their respective goals. Rühe succeeded, and with the support of the chancellor and the chancellor's office received extra funding to keep armament cooperation with France viable. The public admonitions of the DASA management put France in the position of having to take responsibility for the downturn of such cooperation. This apparent value in itself was not called into question within Germany or France, or between them. The confidence with which such diverse actors—Rühe and armament managers—refer to such ends signifies how much the institutionalized value was internalized and taken for granted.

Already in 1991, as financing troubles returned to accompany the Tiger project, French armament analysts Thierry d'Athis and Jean-Paul Croizé referred to this institutionalization of meaning and value, hypothesizing that "our neighbors know very well that this program will have to be continued, cost it what it may. . . . The helicopter Tiger represents the backbone of Franco-German cooperation," they explained, and "abandonment of the Franco-German anti-tank helicopter would put into question the military cooperation between France and Germany." Because "this abandonment would practically mark the end of Franco-German military cooperation," as they somewhat dramatically put it, as a matter of course the shared Franco-German understanding of the necessity to prevent such an outcome made it improbable that the program would be cut or abandoned.[137]

When during the summer of 1996 the financial strains culminated and the future of the entire Tiger program was again questioned, the generally market-liberal British *Financial Times* characterized the state of affairs along the same lines: "It is no coincidence that the cuts in German defence spending follow hard on the heels of similar reductions in France. Both countries are trying hard to squeeze their bloated budgets into the tight corset of conditions set for joining a single currency programme. . . . Defence spending is a natural target for finance ministries, not least because such spending is partly discretionary when threats are hard to spot." Yet, the paper astutely added, "[n]either country wants to be blamed for outright cancellation of a programme."[138]

Second, the 1996 case demonstrates how much the regularized intergovernmentalism around the Franco-German summit meetings have become a part of French and German policymaking. They help to frame interest formation processes, not only for the dealings between France and Germany but also for their domestic policy-and decision-making. They are structural elements that generate collective intentionality. Already before the Dijon summit, when the difficulties culminated as outlined above, Defense Ministers Rühe and Millon had met in order to level the field for the upcoming summit meeting. During the summit France and Germany discussed armament matters, including the Tiger program, on the highest political levels including president, chancellor, prime minister, defense ministers, and foreign ministers. These consultations resulted in the shared will to find common positions allowing continued joint armament policy formulation. The governments set up working groups to review Franco-German armament projects in detail. These groups, under the tight supervision of the defense ministries, guided the ongoing bilateral interest formation process and so affected the policymaking process of both states. They aimed at producing outcomes that could be settled by the French and German heads of state and governments by the next summit in December.

The eventual results of the Nuremberg summit—the categorical endorsement of the Tiger program along with other outcomes in the security domain—are an expression of these institutionalized processes of regularized intergovernmentalist interaction and institutionalized meaning. That Chancellor Kohl during the summit promised his defense minister additional money for Franco-German armament projects underlines the degree to which their institutionalized relations had become a part of French and German priority setting and resource allocation.[139]

Third, this case shows how strongly the institutionalized relations between France and Germany, even with concomitant tensions and frictions between the two states, induce solutions that appear self-evident and intuitive to both of them. One solution that France and Germany worked out to address the difficulties in their armament cooperation was a further decoupling and insulating of their cooperation from the potentially distracting influences of the two countries' domestic political arenas. As a consultant to the French defense minister put it, "[t]he cooperation needs to be more constraining; each partner should not be exposed to the fluctuations of the other as is the case today."[140] France and Germany thus set up regulations to make future armament cooperation more resistant especially to temporary, volatile, and unpredictable domestic political influences—including the vicissitudes of domestic budgeting. There is no indication that French and German officials on any hierarchical level found that to be an inadequate solution to the problem.

The parallel development toward a Franco-German arms agency, beginning after the consultations in Baden-Baden in December 1995 and fully outlined by November 1996, underscores this conclusion. After all the difficulties and the extraordinary financial strains through which armament cooperation had passed in 1996, France and Germany did not consider a split, downsizing, or tighter national controls to be appropriate responses. Instead, they desired deeper and stronger institutionalization, increased efforts toward integration of planning, and more insulation from the respective domestic spheres of their two countries, including from budgetary pressures. "Armament cooperation keeps moving ahead," arms expert Puhl correctly noted, ". . . *in spite of* the general financial shortages in the defense budgets."[141] Such "natural solutions" demonstrate the bilateral determination to make Franco-German defense and armament cooperation succeed, irrespective of persistent or circumstantial intricacies. They are widely taken-for-granted solutions—as an entire range of other conceivable trajectories is not.[142]

In sum, during 1996, the institutionalized Franco-German relations were an important factor influencing internal French and German processes of interest formation and policymaking. As a result, the Tiger program was neither discontinued nor cut, even under the exceptional budgetary constraints in the wake of Maastricht and German inner unification. Due to sufficiently high degrees of both political authority centralization and state autonomy, the institutionalized relations could be effective even while their logic frequently interfered with domestic politics related to cutting expenses and allocating resources. There was no tension between either the French or the German domestic construction and the institutionalized logic and meaning of the bilateral Franco-German relationship. The "1996" case thus speaks to the institutionalist-constructivist model's hypothesis 1 and falls between the model's hypotheses 4 and 5.

What sits uncomfortably with a realist perspective, in the 1996 case, is that the changed strategic environment and threat perception, while not irrelevant, did not move to center stage as the key causal factor with respect to the Tiger helicopter program. After the dissolution of the Warsaw Pact, German unification, and the implosion of the Soviet Union, an entirely new security environment had materialized. Yet, the new security context remained a subsidiary issue regarding Franco-German combat helicopter dealings. Particularly for the German side, realist approaches will point out, the original interest in new "anti-tank" combat helicopters was sparked by the Warsaw Pact tank threat along its Cold War borders. However, as 1996 shows, both French and German interests in the helicopter remained, whereas power imbalance and threat perception, central realist variables, had fundamentally altered in the meantime. By the end of 1996, France and Germany even confirmed the total numbers of helicopters they would ultimately acquire.

On the other hand, with respect to the changed strategic environment, a realist perspective can properly point to the consecutive technical adjustments of the German helicopter version during the 1990s. These modifications moved the German Tiger version away from the predominantly anti-tank (PAH-2) combat helicopter toward a more versatile multipurpose machine (UH-T). A realist position will correctly point out that the changed military-strategic context drove these changes. Furthermore, although in 1996 both France and Germany stated their intentions to acquire the initially envisioned numbers of Tigers beyond the first batch of eighty helicopters each, in the succeeding years it became increasingly unlikely that the two countries would ultimately obtain a total of 427—particularly given the enormous costs of each helicopter. Yet, realists will underscore that if the intense security pressures of several tens of thousands of Warsaw Pact tanks had persisted, France and Germany would very possibly have committed to carry the enormous burden.

Three observations on the events of 1996 are incompatible with a neoliberal perspective. Together, they suggest that neoliberalism is not applicable to this case. First, French and German interests with respect to the Tiger helicopter program were not fixed during 1996. Rather, they formed as part of the political processes that this chapter has documented. However, exogenously given interests are a precondition of neoliberal theorizing. Second, it is not clear what absolute gains France and Germany would realize with the continuation of the program by 1996. Third, the lesson that France and Germany drew from the year's frictions and difficulties, namely, to further insulate their armament cooperation from the French and German political shifts and potential vicissitudes, also does not fit nicely with a neoliberal point of view. According to a neoliberal institutionalist view, we should expect states to keep their options open, to defend their ability to transparently assess international institutions' efficiency, and to react flexibly based on their assessments.

Focusing on the lobbying of both the German armament industry and the entire collection of French unions, explanatory propositions derived from a society-centered liberal inside-out perspective would predict the continuation of the program. The outcomes of 1996 are in accordance with a domestic and transnational society-based liberal point of view. However, the empirical record suggests that such an explanation only accommodates part of the politics leading to the outcomes at the end of 1996. Additionally, the pressure that especially the French state exerted on Eurocopter to reduce the Tiger's ultimate unit price runs in the reverse causal direction from the one preferred by such a liberal perspective. Nonetheless, DASA's interests find their expression in the results fixed by the French and German governments in Nuremberg in December 1996.

Summary

This chapter has reconstructed the French, German, and Franco-German politics related to the Tiger combat helicopter politics between 1988 and 2009. These years were marked first by the new-generation combat helicopter's development and production preparation in full swing, implementing the stipulations as set forth in the memorandum of November 1987. Further developments of the 1990s and the early twenty-first century included the successive integration of the French and German helicopter industries, the first steps toward a European armament agency, various adjustments of the exact versions in which the Tiger helicopters would be finished, and the institution of fully integrated Franco-German Tiger pilot and mechanic training schools.

With financial pressures and budgetary constraints mounting, however, by 1996 the survival of the program had once again reached deadlock and faced significant cutbacks or cancellation. After confirming the continuation of the program at the Franco-German summit meeting late in 1996, the way toward the physical emergence of the combat helicopter had ultimately been secured. In 1999,

France and Germany definitely ordered a first batch of eighty Tiger helicopters each. In 2005, some thirty years after the first considerations of jointly developing a new-generation combat helicopter, the first series produced Tiger helicopters were delivered to the two countries' armed forces. In 2009, three French Tigers flew their first combat missions in Afghanistan.

The years covered in this chapter also saw questions about the potential export of the Franco-German high-tech weapon enter the scene. During the mid-1990s, France and Germany failed to win helicopter orders from the Netherlands and the United Kingdom. The potential export of the joint Franco-German combat helicopter became strongly politicized, particularly after Turkey expressed interest. German hesitation contributed to turning away the Turkish government as a potential customer. Early in the new century, however, France and Germany won the bids by both Australia and Spain to acquire combat helicopters on the international marketplace, and the Tiger's international career had begun.

The political processes around the Tiger program during these years particularly illustrate how institutionalized relations may bring about events that reflect back on the meaning of an institutionalized relationship itself; and that institutionalized relations can help generate or affect political and economic organization more broadly. The fusion of the French and German helicopter industries into "Eurocopter" and the emerging European armament agency OCCAR exemplify such implications beyond a bilaterally institutionalized interstate relationship.

The three case studies in this chapter analyze the main outcomes that need explanation during these years leading up to the physical appearance of the combat helicopter: varying French and German export attitudes toward the Netherlands, Great Britain, Australia, and Spain on the one hand, and Turkey on the other and the outcomes of 1996, a year when extraordinary budget pressures strained the program once again and even put it in question altogether.

During the Netherlands, Great Britain, Australia, and Spain export episodes, there were no tensions between either the French or the German domestic construction with effects on interests and policies originating in the institutionalized bilateral relationship. Both France and Germany had strong interests in selling the common product. These outcomes are in accordance with the first three propositions that I have derived from the constructivist-institutionalist model as formulated in chapter 2. However, the French and German interests in these four export episodes are overdetermined: All predictions derived from the major perspectives in international relations would expect French and German interests to sell.

The Turkish export case shows how the effects induced by German domestic construction brought about hesitant attitudes toward the sale of the helicopter. Interest- and policy-inducing effects of German domestic construction, in this episode, transmitted to the French point of view via the institutionalized relationship. It affected the German and indirectly the French sales attitude, undermining the potential sale. In that case, the tension between the effects of the German domestic construction and the logic of the institutionalized relations allowed the effects of the former to predominate. The politics around the potential Turkish deal, furthermore, were characterized by high levels of political authority centralization and state autonomy from societal interference. The Turkish export episode speaks to hypotheses 2 and 3 as well as 4 of chapter 2's institutionalist-constructivist model of interest formation and policy formulation.

The "1996" case, finally, shows that the institutionalized relations as institutionalization of interaction, meaning, and social purpose at the interstate level affected French and German domestic priority setting regarding budgetary resource allocation, even during what was for both states one of the financially most constrained years in their post-war histories. With no tensions between domestic construction and institutionalized interstate logic, fairly high levels of political authority centralization at the time and policy areas in question enabled the bilaterally institutionalized purpose to take effect at times of severe domestic political struggles in both states.

7

Findings, Conclusions, Implications

Frequently highly charged with meaning and value, the historical and political processes of Franco-German security relations investigated in the preceding chapters helped to bring about an extremely expensive piece of material reality in policy areas in which we should expect it the least. However, these processes were also prominently driven by rather dissimilar, historically shaped French and German domestic constructions and their respective impacts on the two states' interests and policies. This book's institutionalist-constructivist model sheds much light on the processes and outcomes of French and German national interest formation and policy formulation in the historical investigations of chapters 3–6. However, the model does not explain equally well the outcomes in all of the twelve case studies that these chapters present, and it fails altogether to explain the outcome in one of these cases.

Realist, neoliberal institutionalist, and liberal thought in international relations direct our attention to different facets of Franco-German security and armament dealings between the mid-1970s and the early twenty-first century. These theoretical approaches help to shed light on some aspects of the political processes documented in chapters 3–6, and they are useful for explaining and comprehending several of the outcomes on which these chapters have focused. However, expectations and explanations derived from these macro-perspectives also frequently have difficulty in capturing what decisively shaped French and German interests and policy, and thus in accounting for the key outcomes as they emerged over these decades. While differing in their relative usefulness in the processes and outcomes in question, overall the explanatory propositions derived from these macro-perspectives on international affairs fare less well than those derived from chapter 2's institutionalist-constructivist model.

This book's inquiries and findings entail a number of general implications for our knowledge of international relations, notably regarding institutionalization and construction in the international sphere as well as the interplay of various political factors at different levels of analysis. Furthermore, this book identifies hitherto little recognized factors and mechanisms of state arming and arms procurement generally. Its conceptualizations and theoretical approach point to a comprehensive and conceptually robustly grounded perspective on the grand sources or reservoirs of the forces that shape international history and world politics. This perspective offers new and creative ways of connecting causal factors of different types and from different levels of analysis, and it promises to pose novel questions regarding the workings of international affairs. All of these findings and implications speak to a fairly general view of international history and world politics.

At the same time, this book's investigations show a different sort of European integration which, for the most part, lies outside the multilateral EU framework, and which underlies and perhaps functions as a catalyst for the multilateral European Community (EC) or European Union (EU) frame of European integration. This book's empirical reconstructions also show important yet neglected aspects of European international relations from the mid-1970s into the new millennium, which are not reducible to the logic of the Cold War or its demise. This study has focused on the Tiger helicopter as the physical result or outcome of many years of French, German, Franco-German, and European politics. However, the history of the vast program and highly advanced weapons system also itself affected Franco-German and European political and industrial evolutions in a variety of ways, and it is likely to leave its own imprint on European and international affairs for many decades to come.

Processes and Outcomes

The processes of French and German bilateral and domestic planning, politicking, negotiation, developing, and finally producing and delivering the Tiger helicopter were charged with meaning, significance, and social purpose. The particular institutionalization and construction of Franco-German relations—in important ways constituted by their regularized intergovernmentalism with the rhythms of their semiannual summit and ministerial meetings and beyond, the meaning and social purpose of Franco-German symbolic acts and practices, and a web of parapublic underpinnings—incorporated and generated such meaning and purpose. It affected the history and politics of Franco-German combat helicopter dealings, particularly during the decisive Tiger years between the mid-1970s and the early twenty-first century. Such historical meaning and social purpose is irreducible to domestic French and German politics, whether resulting from constructions of collective selves or features of the political system, state-society relations, or domestic interests.

Already during the early years, when the potential common project initially entered the magnetic field of the Franco-German institutionalized relationship, the non-realization or discontinuation of the program would not have been seen as "more or less sound" but, rather, a "fiasco," a "catastrophe," at least a "failure"—attributed to the mistakes or lack of commitment of those crafting the project. In the same vein, the successful conclusion of the cooperation project or the ulti-mate definite French and German orders of a first batch of series-produced Tigers at the end of the century would not be considered "more or less sound" but a value-charged undertaking serving an institutionalized social purpose. In 1984, it was called "a spectacular re-launching of Franco-German military coopera-tion"[1] or an "undeniable success for the co-signing Defense Ministers Charles Hernu and Manfred Wörner"[2]—an achievement in any case. Such value judg-ments make no sense in a historical vacuum bare of social meaning and political significance. The (Franco-German) institutionalization and construction supply the reference point for all of these "catastrophes" and "fiascoes," as well as the "spectacular (re)launches" and "bilateral achievements."

Almost all observers, commentators, and policymakers find that the program was driven by a shared sense of the need to come up with "something visible" (*etwas Vorzeigbares*) that would underline the continuing, and after 1983, increas-ing proximity between France and Germany in defense, military, and security matters. They all stress the "political will," the "primacy of the political"; they judge that, for example, the May 1984 agreement had been dictated by political will, even seeing the "political will on a high level" as leading to the "quasi-coerced ini-tiation of the joint project."[3] That the Franco-German partnership should find its expression in a new major joint arms procurement project was accentuated because no such project had taken shape since the early 1970s Alpha-Jet—considered too long a time lag. Although France and Germany had undertaken numerous smaller scale projects and were in the process of doing so, no major armament program had been initiated in recent years. France and Germany shared the sense that such a project was missing, as well as the view that such a "success" had to be initiated.

The institutionalization and construction of Franco-German relations in the period under review implied elements of collective identity at the international level and aspects of collective intentionality—however tenuous or incomplete at any moment in time. Collective intentionality may mean that "my doing is only part of our doing."[4] It may also mean that actors form interests only in being inter-twined with other actors. Their individual wills are only possible as part of "our will." Collective intentionality implies that "'we intend,' and 'I intend only as part of our intending.'"[5] This book's historical inquiries and empirical investigations have documented Franco-German collective intentionality at several important junctures of the almost four decades covered in chapters 3–6. To be sure, French and German interest formation is not fundamentally integrated; and France and Germany do not formulate their foreign policies together. There remains an "us" and a "them." There is no common amalgamated "we," either between French and German societies or between French and German elites. However, there are rudi-ments of collective intentionality. Failing to grasp such phenomena and their causal implications means missing important forces that drive political processes and engender political outcomes.

Franco-German historical institutionalization and social construction had an immediate impact on the history of what would become the Tiger helicopter as soon as the would-be program entered its force field. That force field profoundly shaped the political processes and outcomes of the Tiger's development and affected the formulation of French and German objectives and desires in the policy areas and questions involved. Along all key dimensions—political and military, technical, financial, and temporal—the institutionalization and construction between France and Germany in important ways affected the evolution of this major arms program and the history of the Tiger's ultimate emergence.

Under the influence of its institutionalized relations with France, for example, Germany repeatedly framed interests and formulated policies that delayed the delivery of the powerful combat helicopters to the German forces, making feasible the huge program with France—even in light of the existential tank threat along its eastern borders. France, in reverse, traded in much of the machine's export potential in the decades to come, by defining and developing a heavier and much more expensive helicopter than it would have by itself. Both Germany and France occasionally framed and reframed their military requirements with respect to this key weapon in light of their institutionalized relationship. Both Germany and France repeatedly modified their budgetary allocation to allow the program to take place or to continue. As a result of their institutionalized relations, they both allocated tremendously more resources than each would have if not motivated by a desire to work together on the common project. In the end, over thirty-five years after the first considerations about a new-generation combat helicopter, the first Tigers flew their initial combat missions in Afghanistan. They did so in a global political and strategic context thoroughly transformed from the Cold War environment that crystallized along the Iron Curtain in continental Europe in the 1970s, when France and Germany embarked on developing a radically new and immensely powerful weapons system to defend their territories.

Without the two countries' relationship and the effects of its particular institutionalization and construction on their national interest definition and policy formulation, those interests and policies would have taken quite different shapes overall, as well as in most of the twelve cases. Without these effects, in many instances the outcomes of these cases would have been very different. First, the combat helicopter project would never have been initiated as a Franco-German program. Germany would either have bought the American Apache AH-64, or co-produced with or bought a combat helicopter from the Italian company Agusta in the course of the 1970s. During the same period, France would have, in a purely national program, begun to develop and produce two different helicopters, both of which would have differed significantly from what ultimately became the Tiger.

Second, France and Germany would not have persevered in spite of the many adverse circumstances and reasons. Instead, they would have discontinued or at least chosen not to relaunch or re-invigorate the common project on several occasions.

There would never have been a Franco-German combat helicopter of the second generation. Their institutionalized relations independently helped to shape French and German interests, goals, positions, and policies in a way that not only brought them together in this key arms procurement program but also kept them together, and kept them going together.

Third, this cutting-edge weapon also would not have become *what* it became, with its ultimate specifications and configuration. Along all of the machine's dimensions including its physical configuration, technical specifications, financing, and delivery schedule, the relationship also shaped the helicopter itself, affecting the definition of French and German positions on a diverse set of issues that surfaced in the course of the decades of politics around combat helicopter matters. In the end, the highly advanced weapons system that ultimately came into being is neither French nor German, nor additively French *and* German, nor the result of a minimal overlapping consensus—but Franco-German, read *Francogerman*. It is a product generated and shaped by the institutionalized relations between France and Germany with their specific mixture of interaction, meaning, and social purpose.

At the decisive junctures, the Franco-German institutionalization and construction affected French and German interests and policies. These effects came out particularly clearly in the cases on the original initiation of the program (case 1); the bilateral renewal of the program (case 3); the subsequent joint Franco-German definition and specification period (case 4); partially in the acceptance of the enormous, yet avoidable, costs of the development of a new targeting and night vision system (case 8); and the Franco-German politics during 1996 (case 12). Only by including the impact of this relational interstate factor of national interest and security policy can we make comprehensible the political processes of and around the enormous Tiger armament program, explaining many of the specific outcomes in the integral episodes.

Yet, Franco-German institutionalization and construction at the interstate level alone did not drive the processes of Franco-German combat helicopter affairs and charge them with meaning. They intertwined with domestic construction. The historically anchored meanings and understandings of the French and German domestic constructions, too, left their imprint on the processes of the two countries' interest formation and policy formulation. French and German attitudes toward the role of armament in their respective overall political frames differed greatly. France's insistence on self-developing and producing a complete high-tech cutting-edge weapons system, which it considered desirable for a major power, is but one example. This interest inducement sharply crystallized in the politicking around the core technological part of the second-generation helicopter, its target designation and night vision system.[6]

The contrast with Germany is striking. Whereas within France the striving for military technological prowess and independent capacity was deeply shared, there are few such leanings in Germany. "The all-around armament of the single partner countries is in the first place a sign of distrust that has to be overcome most urgently," expresses a German view. Instead of "all-around armament," Germany aimed at stabilizing the alliance through the cohesive effects of complementary task fulfillment, including the development and production of arms.[7] As much as the French squabbled and jostled in their own formulation of positions in military strategy, tactics, and armament policy, such criticisms were unheard of on the left bank of the Rhine, and in fact they were hard to imagine. Domestic divergence in historically rooted construction both explains and makes comprehensible many differences and dire difficulties between French and German inclinations and attitudes, including on issues of arms export.[8] The interstate logic of bilateral institutionalization and construction, together with historically shaped respective French and German domestic meanings and understandings, make intelligible the political processes of Franco-German defense and armament affairs reconstructed and analyzed in this book.

Hypotheses, Explanations, Comparisons

The twelve cases studies presented in chapters 3–6 provide strong empirical support for chapter 2's constructivist-institutionalist hypotheses regarding the effects of the constellations between interstate institutionalization and domestic construction. These cases also support the hypotheses on the constellations between interstate institutionalization and features of the domestic political systems of those states involved in such interstate relations. While suggestive, however, the empirical support for these three hypotheses is overall not as strong as for the first three. On the whole, the model outlined in chapter 2 fares well in shedding light on *why* and *how* institutionalized relations generated, modified, or adjusted some French and German interests and policies, as well as why others have remained fixed and unaffected by these institutionalized relations. This model captures many of the important aspects of these almost four decades of history in security and armament affairs.

Although analytically very useful overall, however, the model does not explain all of the processes and outcomes equally well. The factors and constellations on which chapter 2's model focuses explain processes and outcomes in chapter 3–6's case studies to varying degrees. In one instance (case 6 on the Tiger project's drifting into deadlock beginning in June 1984), the constructivist-institutionalist model does not effectively explain the outcome, nor does it shed light on the processes that brought it about. Other factors and forces outside the model's reach drove process and outcome in this case. Chapter 2's institutionalist-constructivist model also has a difficult time capturing Germany's strong insistence on a "polyvalent" all-purpose helicopter between October 1982 and May 1984, which is one part of the outcomes that case 5 presents. This interest was not modified during the Franco-German interaction processes during the period. Yet, this insistence cannot be directly explained by the effects of the German domestic construction, by the impact of domestic political authority fragmentation, or by insufficient state autonomy from economic or societal lobbying or other undermining interference from within either France or Germany. That Germany continuously framed its interest within the North Atlantic Treaty Organization (NATO) defense strategy was in accordance with key aspects of German domestic construction at the time and the interests they induced. However, the causal chain to Germany's insistence on an all-purpose helicopter in May 1984 is too long and too indirect.

However, throughout its empirical investigations, this study pays careful attention to "non-events" or "negative cases," that is, to processes and to outcomes that did not emerge but could have. Historical institutionalist and constructivist approaches to politics and history have been criticized for their relative weakness in dealing with potential realities that have *not* become real, that have *not* been institutionalized or constructed, but could have. The criticism holds that these approaches, as broad perspectives on world affairs, are not very good at studying such "non-events" and "negative cases"—for example, social entities and their interests that did not emerge, or cases when meanings did not produce certain outcomes even though they could have or possibly should have.[9] Chapters 3–6 frequently consider what did *not* happen, what France and Germany ended up *not* wanting, and policies that France and Germany did *not* formulate.

Case 7 is entirely devoted to explaining a very likely outcome that did *not* occur during the period it covers: the cancellation of the Tiger program. Other case studies, too, pay due attention to outcomes that did not emerge. The inquiry on the initial coming together (case 1), for example, also investigates why Germany did *not* co-develop with Italy and why France did *not* pursue a purely national program. In cases 8 and 9, I also explain why Germany did *not* produce its own night vision and targeting system even though the German electronic company Siemens had already acquired the rights to such a system. Moreover, the 1996 case (case 12) very thoroughly investigates why France and Germany did *not* cut back the program and did *not* cancel it. This book's historical investigations did not underestimate the likelihood of the non-real. Frequently, studying what did *not* happen turned out to be quite accessible to empirical inquiry.

Table 7.1 summarizes the various propositions regarding the outcomes of the twelve cases in chapters 3 to 6. Each cell very briefly (and sometimes in somewhat simplified form) indicates the proposition derived from each of these theoretical points of view regarding the case at hand. If applicable, I distinguish between separate French (F) and German (G) interests. A question mark (?) indicates that it is not clear what explanatory position the respective theoretical perspective puts forth with respect to the empirical material of the case and its outcome. A

Table 7.1 **Summary of Propositions and Outcomes**

	constructivist-institutionalist model: evidence for	realism	neo-liberalism	liberalism
coming together (case 1)	hypothesis 1 (hypotheses 4 and 5)	not cooperate; G: buy; F: self-develop (?)	not cooperate	G: self-develop (?) F: —/? (state-led)
frictions, stalling, disruption (case 2)	hypothesis 3	G: buy or self produce F: ?	not cooperate	?
relaunch project (case 3)	hypothesis 1 hypothesis 4	not relaunch	not relaunch	G: ? F: — (state-led)
stipulations of 1984 MoU (modified interests) (case 4)	hypothesis 2 (hypotheses 4 and 5)	not modify interests	not cooperate; not modify interests	G: ? F: — (state-led)
stipulations of 1984 MoU (interests not modified) (case 5)	partially hypothesis 3	varied	not modify interests; not cooperate	not modify interests for other reasons
drifting into deadlock (case 6)	?	drifting into deadlock and toward cancellation	?	? or non-deadlock due to domestic pressure

non-cancellation (case 7)	(hypothesis 2) hypothesis 4	G: cancel; buy abroad F: ?	—	G: cancel; license-produce TADS/PNVS F: ?/—
TADS/PNVS and enormous avoidable costs acceptable (case 8)	hypothesis 3 hypothesis 4	G: cancel; buy abroad F: costs acceptable (?)	disrupt; G and F part ways	G: disrupt; self produce TADS/PNVS (Siemens) F: accept (?)
stipulations of November 1987 agreement (case 9)	(hypothesis 1) hypothesis 2 hypothesis 4	G: cancel; buy abroad F: costs acceptable (?)	disrupt; G and F part ways	G: —(state-led) F: —(state-led)
interest to sell (case 10)	hypothesis 1	interest to sell	interest to sell	interest to sell
hesitation to sell (case 11)	hypothesis 2 (3) hypothesis 4	interest to sell	interest to sell	interest to sell
confirmation and continuation of program (case 12)	hypothesis 1 hypothesis 4 (hypothesis 5)	adjust to new strategic environment	—	confirmation and continuation of program

dash (—) suggests that the perspective, for whatever reason (and as explicated in chapters 3–6), is not applicable to the specific case.

Hypotheses 1–3

The cases over the entire period of almost four decades show that Franco-German interstate institutionalization and construction substantially affected French and German interests and policies, as long as the tensions between the relations' effects and those of the two states' domestic constructions did not become too strong. In cases of strong tensions or direct clashes, the impact of the domestic construction tended to predominate.

The first hypothesis that I derived from chapter 2's constructivist-institutionalist model holds that the potential effects of institutionalized relations on national interest and foreign policy are strongest if there is no conflict between the effects of the institutionalized relations and the respective domestic constructions of those involved. In this constellation the two factors, interstate institutionalization and domestic construction, will additively affect interest and policy. The independent impact of the interstate logic will be strong. This first hypothesis is supported by the outcomes of the cases on the initial coming together (case 1); on the bilateral relaunch of the project (case 3); and parts of the outcomes of case 9 on the stipulations of the November 1987 agreement. The outcomes of case 10 on French and German interests to sell the common product to the Netherlands and Great Britain, and of case 12 on the confirmation and continuation of the program in 1996, are also in accordance with hypothesis 1. In all of these cases, the logic of interstate institutionalization and construction could become effective without the interference of causal effects stemming from either French or German domestic construction. Neither French nor German domestic constructions encumbered the effects of Franco-German relations on the two countries' interests and policies in any of these cases.

The second proposition derived from the constructivist-institutionalist model states that with increasing tensions between the effects of institutionalized relations and aspects of either one or both domestic constructions, the effects of interstate institutionalization and construction will weaken. In this constellation, institutionalized relations will still affect interests and policy, but their impact will be dampened or associated with frictions. The evidence of case 4 on the modified interests after joint definition as mirrored in the Memorandum of Understanding (MoU) of 1984; of case 9 on the stipulations of the November 1987 agreement; and partially of case 12 on the confirmation and continuation of the program during and at the end of 1996 support this second hypothesis. In these cases, there were, to somewhat differing degrees, tensions between the effects of institutionalized relations and those of either one or both domestic constructions. The institutionalized relations remained effective as a causal force. However, their impact was weaker, and frictions with domestic construction effects diminished their efficacy.

The third hypothesis derived from chapter 2's model suggests that if the effects on interest and policy from institutionalized relations and from elements of domestic construction directly clash, the impact of institutionalized relations will decline. In such a constellation, domestic construction effects will generally be preponderant. This third hypothesis is supported by case 2 on the stalling and disruption of the emerging common project between 1979 and 1982; by two of the three nonmodified interests as cast in the stipulations of the 1984 MoU (case 5) regarding French insistence on a native TADS/PNVS and remaining German export skepticism; and in particular by case 8.

In case 8, the effects of the French domestic construction overrode any effects from the institutionalized relations between France and Germany. It was clear that France would rather discontinue the common undertaking than give up the incorporation of a native night vision and targeting system, the core technological component of the weapons system. France's intense interest in the ability to self-produce a core kit of great-power arms systems, as induced by its historically shaped and domestically anchored self-view, could not be affected or transformed by the Franco-German relationship's institutionalization or construction—even if buying from allied states would be much more efficient without undermining France's technological capability. Aspects of French domestic construction decisively undermined the causal significance of the institutionalization and construction of Franco-German relations.[10]

The Turkish export episode (case 11) falls between the second and third hypotheses. German domestic construction, inducing reluctance to export arms to regimes with questionable human rights records, affected German attitudes toward arms export. However, although very strong, the effects of German domestic construction in this case did not directly *clash* with those stemming from the institutionalized relationship. Moreover, in accordance with this third (and second) proposition, the domestic construction effects seemed to prevail. The case offers indicative evidence for both the second and third hypotheses. For analytic purposes, it is regrettable that Turkey ultimately pulled out of the bid and decided to buy American combat helicopters. The empirical evidence that the Turkish export case offers is strong; however, it is only suggestive, not conclusive.

Hypotheses 4–6

Propositions four, five, and six that I have derived from the constructivist-institutionalist model focus on the interplay between institutionalized relations and domestic political system features in given time periods and policy areas. The fourth hypothesis proposes that high degrees of both authority centralization and state autonomy from organized domestic or transnational societal interests are conducive to institutionalized relations taking effect upon national interests and foreign policies. Hypothesis five maintains that "medium" degrees of authority centralization and state autonomy are likely to negatively affect the impact of institutionalized relations among states on their national interests and foreign policies. Finally, the sixth hypothesis holds that decentralization and dissipation of political authority in the system, and low state autonomy, undermine the potential for the independent causal impact of institutionalized relations among states to affect interests and policies.

The outcome of case 7, where only high degrees of both authority centralization and state autonomy explain the "noncancellation" of the project between January 1986 and July 1987 despite numerous reasons for termination, underscores the general plausibility of these hypotheses. Lower degrees of authority centralization or state autonomy from societal and economic pressures, in this case, would most likely have led to program cancellation. A number of counterfactual considerations across several of the other cases further support hypotheses 4–6, most notably in case 3 (project relaunch); case 8 (self-development of TADS/PNVS and enormous avoidable costs); case 11 (German hesitation to sell in Turkey export episode); and case 12 (confirmation and continuation of program in the "1996" cases).

However, the evidence that chapters 3–6 provide for these three hypotheses is only suggestive, not conclusive. In general, it is not as strong as the empirical support for hypotheses 1–3. This study's twelve cases do not provide sufficient variation, or different constellations between interstate institutionalization effects and "state strength" as defined, to consider these propositions confirmed in the same way as the first three discussed above. In all cases there were sufficient degrees of state strength so that neither lack of political authority centralization nor absence of state autonomy could fully undermine the potential impact of Franco-German relations' institutionalization and construction. State strength was high for France in all of these cases. It was also rather high for Germany. Cross-case comparisons and the historical reconstructions of chapters 3–6 alone do not make the case for hypotheses 4–6 as strongly as for hypotheses 1–3.

However, there is plenty of additional circumstantial evidence, both from French and German contexts and beyond, that supports propositions 4–6 as derived from the constructivist-institutionalist model. For example, that the Franco-German Council for Economics and Finance, instituted in the late 1980s, was officially declared only a Franco-German "consultation-" rather than a "decision-organ" (in contrast to the Council for Defense and Security) was exclusively related to the low degree of political authority centralization in the German system in this policy area, specifically the completely independent status of the German central Bundesbank. The fragmentation of authority within the German system in this policy area has subsequently affected the work of the Council since its inception. Bilateral Franco-German institutionalization and construction thus could only produce weak and encumbered results in these policy areas.

Another example is a major common Franco-German tank project that was discontinued and transformed into separate national programs during the early 1980s. The fragmented political authority within the German government under Helmut Schmidt's last years as German chancellor (when he was barely in charge of his party members in parliament and parliamentary committees), in combination with the weakness of the SPD-FDP coalition, strongly undermined the effects of the institutionalized relations between France and Germany. The project had been conceived and initiated at the top political levels, and the two governments signed an agreement regarding the project at the Franco-German summit in February 1980 in Paris. However, the project had faltered by September 1982, before Helmut Schmidt's departure from power. The German positions in interacting with their French counterparts were undermined, and freedom of action was limited by the Bundestag and its Defense Committee (*Verteidigungsausschuß*), as well as by deviating views among the major parties and within the SPD, Chancellor Schmidt's own party. The *Bundestag's Verteidigungsausschuß* ultimately gave the program the decisive blow. Fragmentation and dissipation of political authority in the policy issue during the decisive period undermined the realization of the tank program from within Germany.[11]

In reverse and in contrast, the high degree of centralization and autonomy during the Kohl-Mitterrand years was a decisive precondition that allowed the "bilateral will building" regarding several aspects of the *Tiger/Tigre* helicopter project during the 1990s (e.g., the program's difficult financing, with costs exceeding the double-digit billion DM range). In this sense, it was an underlying permissive cause.

Further, the observation that weak states in general seem less likely to form strong and lasting collective identities at the international level appears to provide circumstantial evidence for these hypotheses beyond the Franco-German context. The political systems of the United States and Switzerland are possible examples that generally illustrate the effect (with their respective domestic constructions presumably further contributing to the outcome). The perhaps classic example of Woodrow Wilson's failure after World War I to secure Congress's ratification for the United States to join the League of Nations—a system of order that Wilson himself decisively engineered and promoted—is a case in point. A domestic political system less strongly characterized by checks and balances and by the fragmentation of political authority, here through a strong and independent legislative branch, might have allowed the anchoring of the United States in the League of Nations system.

All of these examples, as circumstantial evidence, support hypotheses 4–6. However, a more conclusive judgment regarding the accuracy of propositions four, five, and six would require the systematic analysis of more cases that would together provide more variation in constellations between institutionalized interstate relations' impact and the "state strength" factor, resulting from variable degrees of political authority centralization or state autonomy or both.

Realism

Realist perspectives—either of the strategic version focusing on external security threats or of the nationalist-mercantilist political economy version—help us to comprehend some aspects of the political processes reconstructed in chapters 3–6, and to fully or partially explain some of the outcomes of these chapters' twelve cases. A realist view sheds light on Germany's insistence on an all-purpose helicopter as stipulated in the May 1984 MoU (case 5), a position that was not modified during the preceding joint Franco-German helicopter definition. Realist precepts also help us to explain the program drifting into deadlock and tumbling toward cancellation between June 1984 and May 1986 (case 6).

A mercantilist-realist view, in addition, may also at least make partially comprehensible why, for France, the enormous yet avoidable costs were acceptable in cases 8 and 9. Perhaps independently possessing the new night vision and targeting technology would pay off some time in the future; and France was under much less time pressure to possess the all-new anti-tank helicopters than Germany was. The common Franco-German interest in selling the Tiger to the Netherlands, Great Britain, Australia, and Spain (case 10) suits a mercantilist-national developmental realist perspective and does not run counter to a strategic realist logic focusing on immediate external security threats. Furthermore, a realist view focusing on the Cold War security context may help us to understand the initial impetus for the two states to acquire new-generation combat helicopters, as well as the adjustments to the various Tiger versions in the 1990s and early twenty-first century in light of changed and changing security environments.

However, realism is ill-equipped to account for the tremendous differences in the kinds of machines France and Germany initially wanted. Nor can realist perspectives account for the dynamic of the unfolding process with its impact on French and German interests and policies, driven by domestic factors along with the systemic relationship. In particular, the outcomes of the cases on the initial Franco-German coming together (case 1), the relaunch of the common program in late 1982 (case 3), the French and German interest modifications between 1982 and 1984 as fixed in the 1984 MoU (case 4), and the noncancellation of the program between mid-1986 and July 1987 (case 7) run against realist expectations. The hesitation to sell to Turkey (case 11) also remains outside of mercantilist-nationalist realism's explanatory range. Further, realism has a hard time dealing with the politics and outcomes of the 1996 case (case 12), in which realist thinking should expect more flexible armament adjustment to a radically changed security environment. Regarding the enormous avoidable extra costs that both France and Germany ultimately defined as acceptable (case 8) and the reformulation of the program as mirrored in the 1987 agreement between France and Germany (case 9), at least the respective German positions sit uncomfortably with realist expectations. Given the immediacy of the pressure on German territorial security through Warsaw Pact tanks, according to realist priorities, in cases 8 and 9 Germany should have canceled the bilateral Franco-German helicopter program and bought anti-tank helicopters abroad as quickly as possible. None of these outcomes can be satisfactorily explained with factors or logics that realism generally prefers.

Neoliberal Institutionalism

The outcomes of the disruption of the program after the failed definition phase by 1982 (case 2); those French and German interests that did *not* modify during the months before the signing of the May 1984 MoU (case 5); and the French and German interest in selling the helicopter to the Netherlands, Great Britain, Australia, and Spain (case 10) may be brought in line with neoliberal institutionalist expectations or at least do not contradict a general neoliberal outlook on international relations. However, overall, propositions derived from neoliberal institutionalism have not fared well in explaining the outcomes of chapter 3–6, or in making comprehensible the processes that generated these outcomes. Most of these cases are difficult to explain with a view of utility-maximizing states with exogenously given preferences interacting instrumentally in a neoliberal sense. That cooperating through Franco-German institutionalization would save resources or increase efficiency in other ways was hardly a widely shared expectation or motive. The empirical record does not suggest that considerations of economic or other efficiency were among the driving forces of the potential realization of the collaboration. From the very beginning in the 1970s, nobody seemed to expect resources to be saved through cooperation. In fact, it was likely from early on that the project would be more complicated and time-consuming, as well as more expensive, than other possible routes for both France and Germany to acquire new cutting-edge combat helicopters. In the course of the project, the enormous costs involved were only used as arguments *against* the program.

In fact, had the institutionalized relations between France and Germany properly functioned in their information-providing and efficiency-maximizing capacity as they should have according to neoliberal precepts, they would have made it evident to both countries as early as the 1970s that they did not share enough common interests in this matter to make cooperation feasible. However, particularly the outcomes of case 1 (initial coming together); case 3 (project relaunch in October 1982); case 8 (rendering acceptable for both France and Germany the enormous and avoidable costs of self-developing an all new night vision and targeting system); and case 9 (the stipulation of the November 1987 agreement bringing the Tiger project on its way) directly contradict neoliberal expectations on the efficiency-increasing logic of interstate institutionalization. Furthermore, in case 7 (program noncancellation between mid-1986 and July 1987) and case 12 (domestic and interstate politics related to the program and its ultimate confirmation and continuation during 1996), the distinct focus of the neoliberal perspective does not seem applicable. In case 6 (program drifting into deadlock and toward cancellation), it is not clear which expectation or proposition would be derived from neoliberal institutionalist thinking with respect to the politics and outcome of the case.

Neoliberalism's difficulty with these cases stems to a large degree from its conception of international institutions. Franco-German institutionalization and construction, while undoubtedly forms of international institutionalization, are not, or not in the first place, international institutionalization in the neoliberal conception. During the period covered in chapters 3–6, Franco-German interstate relations institutionalized and perpetuated fairly stable and comprehensive patterns of interaction, meaning, and social purpose. These patterns were highly charged with political and historical significance. However, this bilateral institutionalization does not seem to stem from efficiency considerations of the neoliberal kind.

Liberalism

The outcomes of case 10, on French and German interests to sell the Tiger to the Netherlands, Great Britain, Australia, and Spain, and case 12, on the confirmation and continuation of the program after German DASA and French union lobbying in 1996, are in line with a domestic and transnational inside-out liberal explanatory propositions. However, the outcomes of especially the German positions in cases 7 (noncancellation) and 8 (enormous avoidable costs for self-developing a new vision and targeting system rendered acceptable) run directly counter to liberal expectations. Siemens had already bought the rights to produce the American TADS/PNVS under license from Martin-Marietta. Together with a group of other German electronic companies, it lobbied strongly for a domestic (cheaper and quicker) production of a night vision and targeting system for the combat helicopter. Yet, the German government decided to go along with the new French development of such a system in order to make the joint program viable. The export hesitation in the Turkey export episode (case 11), decisively driven by effects of the German domestic construction, also does not suit expectations derived from a liberal inside-out perspective.

What further sits uncomfortably with a liberal perspective is that especially in the 1970s and 1980s, through different political and legal forms, the French armament sector was heavily state led. Aérospatiale was under tight control of the French Defense Ministry with its General Armament Delegation, as well as the presidential administration in the Elysée. Aérospatiale and other segments of the French defense industry hardly constituted independent, autonomous private actors positioned to approach governments in order to translate economic interests into national interests and state policy, as a basic precept of liberal thinking assumes. French domestic political-economic organization in the time period and industrial area was not like that. This renders, for the French side, a liberal inside-out perspective not really applicable for case 1 (initial coming together); case 3 (project relaunch); case 4 (stipulations of 1984 MoU); case 7 (noncancellation); and case 9 (stipulations of the November 1987 agreement).

A distinctly society-rooted liberal perspective has difficulty in capturing the frequently autonomous effects of interstate institutionalization and construction, which come out strongly in the data. These effects neither originate in nor can be reduced to French and German domestic interests or transnational societal links among businesses, unions, or other economic or societal groups. However, domestic and transnational society-rooted liberal propositions are likely to gain explanatory leverage in contexts where state strength is low. Especially with state autonomy decreasing, liberal explanations are likely to complement the explanatory model advanced here and vice versa.

World Politics and International Relations Theory

This book's investigations reveal important findings and implications regarding the general workings of world politics and various aspects of international relations theory broadly. These pertain to the causal connections and interrelations between factors from the interstate and the domestic levels; the apparently loose coupling of construction and institutionalization at different levels, with lastingly discordant and inconsistent causal implications; and the crystallization of a hitherto little recognized factor of state arming and arms procurement generally. This book's conceptualizations and theoretical approach further point to a broad and comprehensive perspective on the grand sources or reservoirs of the forces that shape history and politics. All of these theoretical findings and implications speak to a fairly general view of international history and world affairs.

Interstate Institutionalization and Domestic Politics

This book reveals important reasons why even strong and durable international institutionalization and construction may affect only weakly, or not at all, what states define as their interests and how they conduct policy. It uncovers how domestically rooted factors, either domestic constructions or aspects of domestic institutional structures, may impede or undermine the institutional logics at the interstate level. In turn, this finding—well beyond the French and German experiences—helps us to comprehend why collective identity building at the international level is difficult to achieve and to stabilize.[12]

For example, the impact of decentralized political authority and frequently limited state autonomy—especially from domestic society—explains some impediments to the United States' immersion in deep and lasting collective identities, and its integration into larger international political contexts. Structural obstacles are represented by America's comparatively weak state with its fragmented political system, pervasive federalism, checks and balances on the federal level with an often parochial congress as a forum of representatives' local interests, and generally low levels of autonomy from a great variety of societal actors and influences. Such domestic political features help to explain the efficacy or nonefficacy of international processes, without even considering key components of historically rooted domestic construction regarding America's proper role and purpose as a state in the international sphere.[13] One famous example of the causal implications of a decentralized political system with checks and balances on the possibility of entering international institutional arrangements is surely the United States' remaining aloof from the League of Nations after World War I, after President Wilson failed to gain the necessary majority in Congress for accession into the League system that he had so prominently helped to design and shape.

In terms of the effects of domestic political features in this regard, the American superpower perhaps resembles Switzerland. The Alpine republic's politically decentralized state has similar effects that undermine a deep integration into international collective identities. Clearly, such domestic and historically rooted constructions as "neutrality" and "staying aloof" make it yet more impervious to collective identity building at the international level. Switzerland has joined neither the European Union nor NATO. It became a member of the United Nations only in 2002, after a referendum in the country's twenty-three cantons yielded just a slender majority in favor. The perspective presented here clarifies outcomes for countries like the United States and Switzerland—surely not commonly named together for their similarities in international involvement. Provided that key elements of domestic construction do not strongly collide with the logics of interstate institutionalization and construction, states with more centralized domestic political authority and a higher degree of state autonomy from societal interests are more likely to build strong and lasting collective identities with other states on the international level.[14]

Loose Coupling and Durable Coexistence with Incompatible Causal Effects

A striking related finding of this book's empirical investigations is that institutionalization and construction at the interstate level on the one hand, and construction at the domestic level on the other, can in fact be quite loosely coupled. Simultaneously effective factors of national interest and foreign policy at different levels of analysis may be discordant and inconsistent with one another. In various ways, for example, the effects of the institutionalized relations between the two states were frequently in tension with those of either French or German historically rooted domestic construction, or both. France and Germany have gone to great lengths and often succeeded in accommodating the often diverging effects of these different sources of interest and policy. Indeed, the two countries have learned to live with these inconsistencies and the tensions they generate. We can assume that, without their institutionalized relationship, France and Germany would frequently have drifted much further apart over the past four decades and arrived at interests and policies even more at odds with each other. In the absence of these institutionalized relations with their regularized intergovernmentalism, symbolic acts, and parapublic underpinnings, French and German interests and policies would have been more incompatible in many instances.

In addition, there remains the simple empirical observation that different types of institutionalization and construction, while frequently pulling state interests and policies in different directions, have by and large successfully coexisted over quite extended periods. While not central to this book's objectives and inquiries, the interesting question of whether or not this is the case for yet longer slices of time does emerge out of these findings and considerations. For periods of three or four decades, however, the empirical record clearly shows that even if not nicely compatible, factors with quite dissimilar causal implications for national interest and policy may coexist in a fairly dissociated manner without many mutual effects upon each other's substance:

1. Neither French nor German domestic construction has excluded or fundamentally undermined the institutionalized relationship between France and Germany.
2. The institutionalization and construction of the Franco-German relationship have not fundamentally altered the basic aspects of French and German domestic constructions, their respective views of themselves as social collectivities, or their individual roles in the international arena.
3. Nor have the two different domestic historical constructions fundamentally transformed or eliminated one another.[15]

This, too, is a finding of this book: social relationships among quite unlike actors can be fairly stable and endure over extended periods of time. Such relationships can persist and affect the interests and behavior of their component actors. At the same time, the actors involved remain in many ways very dissimilar characters.

Factors and Mechanisms of State Arming

With respect to security studies and state arming more narrowly, in focusing empirically on almost four decades of Franco-German defense politics, this book's analyses and findings identify hitherto little recognized factors and mechanisms of state arming and arms procurement generally. These historical investigations document how the institutional logic inherent to the particular institutionalization and construction of an interstate relationship—along with factors from domestic politics—lead states toward certain arming interests and policies and away from others.

Thus, in addition to the factors that the literature on state arming has established—prominently including external security pressures or factors entirely rooted in domestic political affairs, such as industrial and union pressures or local industrial politics, among others—this study offers new pathways and causes that help us to comprehend why states arm and why they sometimes do it together.[16] Its findings underscore the frequently highly charged political nature of international armament cooperation between states. Rather than rather mechanical responses to external threats or power asymmetries, or more or less smooth state responsiveness to domestic industrial or other pressures, the historical processes reconstructed here show how much political significance and conflicting social purpose state arming—as well as its difficulties or failures—may carry. This is not to argue that types of interstate institutionalization and construction, whether by themselves or in combination with factors from domestic politics, will always function as causal forces for arms procurement, or that such forces are even necessarily among the most common factors or mechanisms of state arming. However, this book's empirical findings document them as having important causal effects over extended periods of time, and in historical situations and security contexts that we might expect to be especially impervious to such influences.

Grand Sources of National Interest and Policy, and Types of Historical Forces

From a rather broad perspective, this book's conceptualization and theoretical approach direct our attention to what may be the grand sources of national interest and policy—the major reservoirs of the historical forces that shape world politics, international history, and the foreign policies of single states. In pursuing its research questions and inquiries, from each main source this book defines one specific and distinct explanatory factor of national interest and policy, which, accordingly, it treats conceptually separately: Out of the international sphere—the level of the international system broadly, comprising material structures as much as a range of different types of institutionalization and construction—it shapes a particular kind of interstate institutionalization and construction; out of the realm of domestic construction—inclusively comprising the domestic-cultural context and potentially including various types of such construction—it defines a particular kind of historically rooted construction of self and proper role and purpose in the world; and out of the domestic system broadly—political, economic, and societal structures that include features of the political systems, organized society, and state-society relations—it focuses on political authority centralization and state autonomy, which together shape "state strength" (see Figure 7.1).

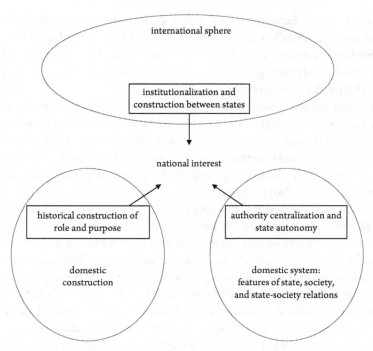

Figure 7.1 Grand Sources of Historical Forces and Specific Factors

If one thinks of the state as a (collective) actor (as is common in both international relations practice and scholarship), and imputes to this conceptual unit interests and identity (as is equally common), then in a variety of ways one might think of the international sphere as states' external social and physical relations and (among others) as the realm of the "society of states" (or altogether the realm of the external aspects of identity and interests). Various possible kinds of domestic construction in this metaphor would be the actor's psyche or its spirit or soul; and features of state, society, and state-society relations represent the actor's flesh and bones—its "corporate identity."[17]

On the one hand, such a broad view promises new and creative ways to connect factors and forces from the various grand sources, and to think about how specific factors or variables from these three grand sources hang together—whether they, for example, by themselves shape interests and policies or mediate or condition the effects of others. Rather than exclusively focusing on one or the other or playing them against one another, this may fruitfully involve connecting internal and external factors of political outcomes, as well as integrating variables from different levels of analysis.[18] On the other hand, such a perspective may also sharpen our grasp of the general interplay among different factors from the same grand source or reservoir. Either way, such a perspective offers a more comprehensive and perhaps conceptually more robustly grounded view of the forces that shape world politics and international history. This general view also promises to help us to pose new and interesting questions, test potentially important causal connections, and formulate new hypotheses.

This book's inquiries have demonstrated the analytic value of conceptualizing certain patterns of interaction and meaning in the international sphere as institutionalization and construction between states. Thereby, this book's conceptual apparatus and empirical examinations contribute to a better understanding of the materials potentially making up and thus constituting particular relations between some states. Rather than understanding such relations as series of single, dissociated actions and events, this conception allows us to grasp their particular nature as well as their (contingent) causal implications.

Tied to its original research questions and hypotheses, this study explores empirically the causal implications of the *overall* logic of a bilateral relationship over extended periods and in diverse political and historical settings. Indeed, various aspects of the overall logic of the relationship come out clearly in the specific empirical investigations of chapters 3–6 in ways that have proved analytically valuable and revealing. In this book, I did not test for the causal impact of the single components that together make up interstate institutionalization and construction. Doing so would be a separate undertaking, and a potential continuation, extension, and specification of this book's explorations. Depending on the particular research questions at hand, it might yield interesting results.[19]

This book's conceptualizations thus bring to light important and causally consequential aspects of institutionalization and construction at the level of the international system. These differ from other such factors or aspects, as well as from the material systemic forces on which scholars have focused.[20] In particular, the book's conceptualization of relations between states seeks to advance our knowledge of an interesting phenomenon of systemic institutionalization and organization that differs from a great variety of research that focused on historically grown, socially constructed, or politically designed institutional components of the international sphere and the world polity.

Sociological institutionalists, for example, have explored the content and effects of a set of system-wide institutions enmeshed in an expanding and deepening Western world culture. Such global social structures constitute actors, shape actors' properties, and define legitimate goals for them to pursue. For example, they define the meaning of modern statehood, with both organizational and behavioral implications for international relations.[21] Adherents to the English school of international relations, in turn, have investigated formal and informal rules, procedures, and principles constituting and regulating modern international relations. Originating in early modern Europe, these historical creations have become defining institutions of the global society of states.[22] And in his brand of systemic constructivism, Alexander Wendt broadly distinguishes among three systemic macro-cultures (Hobbesian, Lockean, and Kantian). Distinct logics of anarchy, they are defined by variations in basic relationship patterns among states as enemies, rivals, or friends, respectively.[23]

However, much international institutionalization and construction is considerably more variable—regionally and or even bilaterally or otherwise—than allowed for by sociological institutionalism's focus on the world polity's dominant cultural constructions. The same applies to the scope of the set of European and then global institutions and organizing principles that the English school has explored. And many patterns of interaction and meaning in the international system are historically and spatially more differentiated than Wendt's tripartite vision or other constructivist system-wide perspectives are able, or even aspire, to grasp. Furthermore, the institutionalization and construction between the states scrutinized also differs from formal international organizations or informal regulatory institutions, whether conceived in a Weberian, constructivist, or rationalist mold, as well as from world order analyses in a broadly liberal vein.[24] Finally, the relations between states are in many cases more diverse and multidimensional than the research on enduring rivalries in world politics postulates.[25]

In a similar vein, in pursuing its research questions, this book has concentrated on a specific kind of domestic construction: dominant interpretations of the meaning and implications of historical experiences for one's proper role and purpose in international arena—historical constructions of role and purpose. This approach differs from other types of domestic construction on which, for a variety of explanatory purposes, scholars have focused, including daily practices and routines; strategic thought and strategic culture; organizational cultures of state and military; ideas about policymakers' proper role in particular policy areas such as monetary policy, or with respect to certain policy projects such as regional integration; varying types of nationalism; particular kinds of domestic cultural norms; or various types of dominant domestic discourses not necessarily tied to one's history or to historical experiences and interpretations of their implications.[26]

One set of research questions that this view of grand sources generates with respect to domestic construction is whether there might be particular kinds of complementarity, affinity, or aversion between domestic constructions of role and purpose across different states. Thus, similar or different constructions might either facilitate or undermine cooperation or breed or condone conflict between states—with or without the additional impact of a certain interstate institutionalization and construction or other system-level institutionalization. The evidence of chapters 3–6 shows that implications of key elements of the French and German domestic historical constructions of role and purpose frequently implied conflicting or incompatible interests and policies. However, such divergent domestic constructions of role and purpose regarding some political issues might prove complementary; similar constructions, in contrast, may also imply conflicts regarding specific questions.[27] Relatedly, thinking in terms of grand sources or reservoirs of historical factors and forces leads us to ask how different types or sorts of domestic construction that scholars have identified increasingly systematically over the past decade and a half within the same country may hang together or interrelate with one another, either at a given moment in time or over more extended historical periods: Do different sorts of domestic construction in the same country require certain (minimal?) levels of compatibility or similarity? Will they, over time, affect each other or interact with one another, perhaps as some sort of melting pot of domestic construction? Or, can pockets of divergent domestic construction at different locations in the same country (say at different branches or bureaucracies of the state, ideas at the elite level vs. in the broader publics, or different forms of nationalism at different national or regional segments of domestic communities) coexist fairly isolated from one another and perhaps not necessarily with consistent causal implications? (Whether there ever will be a general theory of domestic construction, to be sure, remains a separate issue.)

Finally, the general perspective of grand sources or reservoirs of historical forces enables us to think coherently about possible interrelations between factors and features from domestic construction(s) on the one hand and characteristics of the domestic system—that is, state, organized society, and state-society relations broadly—on the other. For example, are only some combinations of domestic construction and key aspects of domestic systems successful or viable? In the longer run, do key elements of domestic construction interact with constitutional features of domestic structures? Are there particular "fits or misfits" between certain types of domestic construction and features of the domestic system? In the period covered here, for example, France's ambitious and activist construction of role and purpose seems to fit well with important features of state organization, notably the strong executive and the concentration of political authority with the president especially in foreign affairs, security, and defense. Similarly, key elements of German domestic construction apparently suit a federal system in which the strong tendency toward government by party coalitions often leads to a slow and incrementalist style of policymaking.

However, the historical roots of the political systems of the Fifth Republic and the Federal Republic only partially explain such seeming affinities. In neither case are key features of state and society organization just the result of the dominant domestic construction of self and purpose—or the other way around. Generally, factors from the two grand reservoirs of factors seem anything but causally tightly connected. As a comparison between the United States and Switzerland suggests, there seems to be enormous (unrestricted?) leeway between domestic systems characteristics and domestic construction. These two countries' political systems clearly share certain important features: pervasive federalism; both horizontal and vertical checks and balances in the system; and a perhaps generally fragmented political system. At the same time, they differ widely in the respective domestic constructions of their roles and purposes in the world. These brief thoughts and examples only begin to illustrate the conceptual and explanatory research potential that systematic thinking about interconnections and combinations among factors from the two grand domestic sources of historical factors and forces might hold.[28]

While empirically focusing on France and Germany, this book puts forth general concepts to properly capture and expose institutionalization and construction that links states in certain ways and not in others, thus characterizing certain periods and places. Neither regularized intergovernmentalism or symbolic acts or practices nor types of international parapublic underpinnings are Franco-German idiosyncrasies. Rather, for each of these categories, just as for interstate institutionalization and construction as a whole, France-Germany represents only one particular instance of a set of diverse manifestations of the same or similar phenomena. Properly grasping Franco-German institutionalization and construction, and comprehending their effects and limitations, helps us to identify and properly capture other such examples. The particular realities of institutionalization and construction constitute an important yet overlooked and underappreciated aspect of connecting states and structuring interstate conduct at the heart of Europe as well as beyond, and appear to be a prominent aspect of how the world is organized.

Obviously, the ability to research the seemingly variable impact of interstate institutionalization and construction on national interest and policy requires a minimum of such interstate institutionalization and construction. On the one hand, France-Germany, as it appeared and evolved during the twentieth century's second half and stretched into the twenty-first century, may exemplify a particularly developed and robust instance of an institutionalized relationship between states. On the other hand, given the fundamental security stakes involved as well as and the financial and industrial ones, the policy areas that this study considers are domains in which we should expect the autonomous effect of such institutionalization and construction to materialize the least. The combination—fairly solid institutionalization and construction and least likely policy areas—makes France-Germany in security, defense, and armament an ideal terrain to explore the ways and contingencies through which interstate relations may affect the formation of national interests and the formulation of policy, thus shaping political outcomes. If we can identify causal effects in such unlikely historical and political contexts, we might assume similar effects in less unlikely policy areas between France-Germany and between others as well.

Other instances of institutionalization and construction between states will likely display diverse manifestations and mixes of regularized intergovernmentalism (whether formal or informal), symbolic acts and practices (of whatever kind, intensity, or with whatever reference points), and (potentially) international parapublic underpinnings. However, to name but a few examples, comparable bilateral examples of such connections may include the ("special") relationship between the United States and Britain, with particularly tight while often informal connections in military, defense, and intelligence matters; the regularized cooperation between Australia and New Zealand; or the close ties between the United States and Israel, especially but not limited to the areas of security, defense, and intelligence, partially formalized with the Joint Political Military Group that the two states established in 1983. Modeled after its practices and experiences with Germany, France has instituted regularized intergovernmental relations with its southern neighbor Spain, holding (annual) Franco-Spanish summit meetings that involve the heads of state and government, and the two states' foreign, defense, interior, and justice ministers; they celebrated the twentieth Franco-Spanish summit in January 2008. The relations between Germany and Israel, to name but one more example, has long involved particular meanings not least perpetuated by a host of symbolic acts and practices as well as a variety of bilateral parapublic activities. In 2008, to mark the sixtieth anniversary of the foundation of Israel, Germany and Israel agreed to institute regularized annual governmental consultations at the political top levels, to include the heads of government and key ministers.[29]

In the multilateral realm, the EU's intergovernmental parts display elements of all three components that this book has conceptualized and identified: regularized intergovernmentalism, symbolic acts and practices, and (multilateral) types of parapublic underpinnings. (So do the EU's supranational parts, but, arguably, these might conceptually be treated differently.) Testing for the causal impact, contingencies, and limitations in the EU's intergovernmental policy areas (perhaps especially in foreign policy, security, and defense) in ways that this book has done for France-Germany appears analytically promising and might capture a good part of the workings of the interconnections between nation states and Union in Europe. Furthermore, formations such as the northern European countries around the Nordic Council (*Norden*); the British Commonwealth of Nations; the *Hispanidad*, the connections between Spain, Latin America, and the Caribbean; or the *Francophonie*, perhaps especially the ties between France and the francophone states in West Africa, might represent comparable instances of institutionalization and construction.[30]

A View of History

Finally, and quite generally, this book's inquiries and findings speak to a certain view of history—one that sees political actors, their goals, and their relations with one another as historically contingent products. Commonly propounded by social constructivists and historical institutionalists, this perspective tends to be enmeshed in a larger project: the denaturalization and de-essentialization of the social world. In the fields of international relations and foreign policy, this prominently applies to the "denaturalization" and historical contextualization of what states want and what they do: their national interests and foreign policies. Survival perhaps aside (possibly along with some minimal levels of stability and wealth), there is nothing natural about what states want and do. To considerable degrees, state interests and policies are historical creations resulting from both international and domestic institutionalization and construction. Insisting, however, that national interests are political products of historical processes has a long tradition that predates the emergence of the theoretically explicitly formulated positions of social constructivism and historical institutionalism. In the spirit of these intellectual positions, Raymond Aron reflects with respect to states as political entities: Their ends are not immanent.[31]

There is also nothing natural about the specific quality or substance of the relations between states. Such relations, too, are products of history, institutionalized practice, and constructed meanings. Friendship, enmity, and indifference between states are all types of historically contingent institutionalizations. Which of these applies depends largely on the inherent logics of the interstate relations themselves, and on domestic affairs. There is nothing natural, for example, about an institutionalized Franco-German proximity that during a particular period of history generates terms such as "couple," "tandem," or "axis," as during the second half of the twentieth century, and that produces a physical reality in terms of cutting-edge weaponry. It is the result of a particular type of regularized intergovernmentalism, symbolic acts and practices, and a weave of parapublic underpinnings—perhaps complemented by a certain private-societal interaction. The Franco-German proximity of that time is the work of two generations of French and Germans who, after the catastrophes of the first half of the twentieth century, believed that the future must not be a repetition of social patterns that led to battlefields. Perhaps, at the beginning of a new century, French and Germans should recognize more clearly the historical contingency of a reality that is human-made and must be reproduced in order to endure.

But there is also nothing natural about enmity between politically independent units, or between France and Germany. Today, it appears preposterous or ludicrous to many young Europeans that it was common in both countries, only some half century ago, to refer to the relationship between France and Germany as "hereditary enmity"—*enmitié héréditaire* and *Erbfeindschaft*. Enmity is not at all hereditary—nor is indifference, another type of institutionalized meaning. Friendships, as much of this book's empirical findings suggest, are not, or not necessarily, cost-effective. We do things with our friends not only to maximize our separate utilities, the pre-existing preferences exogenous to our external relations. Rather, the relations often help to define our interests and thus what we find worthwhile. But neither is enmity cost-effective. In fact, enmity is often more expensive than friendship. Perhaps a-sociality or "a-historicity," the complete absence of any meaningful institutionalization of interaction and construction of meaning or purpose, would be the most efficient state of affairs among actors.

Perhaps in such an a-social world, efficiency would be easier to define or to recognize, and easier to cast into policy. However, the history and politics at the time and place that this book has covered was not like that.

Such a broader view of history, to be sure, is not opposed to analyzing the emergence or reemergence of historical patterns or structures. Moreover, it certainly does not rule out the recognition of some possibly enduring logics in world politics and international history. However, it will remain doubtful regarding all too handy unhistorical and perhaps antiseptic assumptions of necessary sameness across too many places or huge slices of time. And it will remain deeply skeptical about suggestions of mechanical historical determinism, no matter of what kind.

European Politics and History, European Integration, Franco-German Affairs

With respect to European politics and Franco-German affairs, this book's investigations show a different sort of European integration that underlies and perhaps functions as a catalyst for the multilateral EC- or EU-centered European integration on which much post-war research on European affairs has centered. They also show an important aspect of European international political history that spans post-war and post-Cold War periods, and that, while irreducible to either, is part of both. Finally, this book's findings suggest that Franco-German affairs seem at once better and worse than is commonly believed.

European Politics and History, European Integration

In substantive terms, this book's empirical reconstructions represent a particular kind of European history and politics, stretching from the mid-1970s into the first decade of the new millennium. This is French, German, and Franco-German history. It is also part of the history of international relations in Europe. Yet, it is European international politics outside and different from the multilateral EU-centered integration experience. This book's empirical chapters reconstruct a slice of European history that is part of the post-World War II international affairs of binding together the European states in new and different ways, yet has received too little attention in international relations and European integration scholarship.

The complex and adventurous history of the Tiger, as the evidence of chapters' 3–6 documents shows, is not a function of the wider (multilateral) process of European integration, which largely remained in the background. None of its various aspects, for example the prospect of future pan-European armament politics or potential French, German, or French-German master plans to play an avant-garde role therein, decisively explains the history of this armament politics—at least not until the mid-1990s. For most of this book's twelve cases, the historical record shows, the broader frame of European integration was entirely or almost entirely absent as an explanatory factor or driving force of the Tiger helicopter project.

In fact, almost in reverse, as some of chapter 6's empirical findings illustrate, broader European integration in defense (the founding of Eurocopter, EADS, and other aspects) emerged out of the Tiger's complex history. It is perhaps surprising how bilaterally this politics unfolded, and how dissociated and largely independent from the multilateral EU Brussels-centered European integration history and politics of the period. There clearly seems a different, perhaps concealed aspect of European integration here, which has remained almost entirely unexplored in the scholarly literatures on international relations and European affairs. This particular and underexplored European integration reality seems to underlie and importantly fuel the wider frame of European integration, and in many ways it might be its kernel and catalyst.[32]

Perhaps the strong focus on multilateral EU-centered integration or the foreign policies of single states have led international relations scholars to neglect other important aspects of the European international history and politics during these decades, not least in the areas of foreign policy relations, security, and defense. (That armament politics and weapons procurement might seem a somewhat recondite and perhaps secretive area of national and international affairs might be another reason.) Still, this finding is striking, especially since it was exactly these policy domains in which EC/EU-centered integration remained weakest and least developed throughout the second half of the twentieth century, while European affairs in these policy areas, as chapters 3–6 document, also have not remained strictly national. This book shows important aspects of international relations in Europe, which, while in important ways part of Europe's regional polity, lie outside the multilateral EU framework, but which are also not identical to the sum of the separate foreign policies of single European states on which comparative foreign policy analysts concentrate.[33]

At the same time, this part of European politics is not reducible to the logic of the Cold War or its demise, or to some larger logic of post-Cold War politics. The history that this book's empirical chapters present is not just about translating external Cold War pressures into national policy. Neither the Soviet and Warsaw Pact threats, nor U.S dominance within the Western alliance, nor German security dependence on the United States conclusively drives this history or satisfactorily explains its various outcomes.[34] Rather, while in its politically decisive years set within the Cold War and early post-Cold War periods, this is political history strongly driven by a particular kind of bilateral institutionalization in conjunction with domestic forces. This history reaches back deep into the Cold War of the 1970s yet stretches across the Cold War's collapse into another era with entirely different security and defense challenges and political contexts. Its product, a stunningly powerful weapons system of a new generation, will be part of the physical security environment in Europe and the world for many decades to come—irrespective of the endurance or decline of the particular historical forces that brought it about.

Franco-German Relations: Better and Worse

Given the apparent stability of Franco-German institutionalization and construction on the one hand and the lasting and at least partially incompatible implications of the French and German domestic constructions of proper self and role over time on the other, this book's findings may also suggest that during the period covered the relations between France and Germany were at once better and worse than is commonly believed. Franco-German relations are "better" than posited in much general international relations literature, because they are a fairly robust and enduring social structure of institutionalized interaction, meaning, and social purpose. They are quite independent from short-term political shifts, squabbles, or swings in the management of circumstantial political difficulties. They are also rather unaffected by changes in governments, parties or party combinations in power, or single key officeholders. In fact, not even such momentous historical transformations as the end of the Cold War and Germany's second unification seem to have fundamentally altered their basic setup and quality.

This pivotal European interstate relationship has grown into a tenacious structural constituent of European international political affairs. It is not merely the succession of single, dissociated incidents between France and Germany. The Elysée Treaty at the core of this relationship was not, as Charles de Gaulle put it in his disappointment after the German *Bundestag*'s addition of the preamble to the Franco-German treaty before its ratification, "like roses and young girls, who only blossom one morning." Rather it turned out, as Konrad Adenauer responded, like the rose plant itself—an utterly sturdy variety that survives the hardest winters and continues to produce new blossoms thereafter. The institutionalized Franco-German relations have indeed survived some cold winters over the last half century. They have also continued to produce new blossoms. In brief, Franco-German relations are a fairly stable and durable institutional reality. They are a social-structural component of contemporary Europe. And they make a difference in that they have the potential for autonomous causal effects on French and German national interests.

At the same time, however, Franco-German relations were also "worse" than held by other customary views. They were more difficult and problem-laden than acknowledged by perspectives that fail to recognize the effects of the diverging French and German domestic constructions during the period under review. Differences in French and German national interests and foreign policies, and the resulting tensions, are not just minor misunderstandings among political leaders, diplomats, or French and German governmental units. Difficulty or impossibility in arriving at sufficiently similar positions in important or secondary international matters frequently does not simply spring from politicians' shortsightedness, bureaucrats' managerial shortcomings, or petty national narrow-mindedness. Rather, at their source, the frequently dissimilar French and German interests and diverging foreign policies are mainly driven by the profound forces of deeply rooted domestic constructions of self. What so often sets France and Germany apart frequently stems from fundamentally disparate internally anchored views regarding the proper role and purpose of one's collectivity in the international sphere. These are historically grown and domestically dominant interpretations of who one is, wants to be, and should be—and they have significant implications for the definition of one's interests and policies.

Tiger as Outcome and Cause

This study has focused on analyzing the Tiger program and the physical emergence of the Tiger combat helicopter as a product or outcome of the institutional logic of the bilateral Franco-German relations, in conjunction with the modulating impact of various domestic factors between the mid-1970s and the first decade of the twentieth century. The almost four decades of history and politics that brought about this extraordinarily expensive high-tech weapon is as remarkable on its own terms as it is revealing for broader and more general thinking about international relations and history. At the same time and in turn, however, the vast Tiger program has itself had manifold political, organizational, and industrial implications. Thus viewed, the program is also a cause or factor affecting Franco-German and European political affairs, political-economic structuring, and French and German military structures in important ways. The enormous program will have lasting impact beyond its own confines.

For one, the Tiger helicopter program and the physical emergence of this immensely powerful machine was an important lubricant for the successive integration and then full fusion of the French and German helicopter industries, and subsequently for the ongoing integration of the European defense and aerospace industries. Over the cooperation on the Tiger program, Aérospatiale-Matra and Daimler-Benz/DASA/MBB began to combine and then fully amalgamate their helicopter divisions in the course of the 1990s. Their merger in 1992 marks Eurocopter's birth. In 2000, Eurocopter became part of EADS, the European Aeronautic, Defense, and Space Company, a conglomerate initially formed by tying French, German, and Spanish industries in these areas into a major defense and aerospace group. Eurocopter counts among EADS's most deeply integrated branches. By the early twenty-first century, Eurocopter had become the world's largest helicopter manufacturer, with the military share of its sales steadily rising. The increasing number of permanent Eurocopter representations around the world is a visible sign of the company's ascent. At home, the Tiger's main construction sites belong to the kernel of Europe's aeronautic and defense industrial base. The history of the Tiger's formation has critically affected the establishment of Eurocopter, then EADS, thus contributing in important ways to the establishment and consolidation of the nucleus of a European defense industry.

In organizational and managerial terms, furthermore, the Tiger functioned as a catalyst for the development of the European arms agency OCCAR. In the wake of the Tiger program, France and Germany, soon to be joined by other European states, took decisive steps toward the foundation of an integrated European armament agency. The Franco-German Helicopter Office, bilaterally installed in 1989 as the Tiger program's executive agency, was only OCCAR's embryonic stage. An offspring of Franco-German regularized intergovernmentalism around the semi-annual summit meeting, OCCAR emerged in a series of consultations during the first half of the 1990s and was formally introduced in Chancellor Kohl and President Mitterrand's December 1995 "Baden-Baden declaration." It took over the management of the Tiger program in February 1996 and assumed legal status in 2001. OCCAR grew rapidly, and the United Kingdom, Italy, Belgium, and Spain joined it for various arms programs. The Tiger program was central in establishing and consolidating OCCAR, and, through the magnitude of the combat helicopter program, in giving it weight. The Tiger thus also importantly helped to engender the nucleus of a European armament and defense agency.

The institution of the fully integrated Franco-German helicopter flying school in Le Luc, France, and the mechanics' training school in Fassberg, Germany, exemplify further outcomes of the Tiger's history that are likely to have lasting implications. In the wake of developing and constructing Tiger combat helicopters, the plans to institute a joint Tiger pilot school date back to the beginning of the 1990s, taking concrete shape in the decade's second half. When the schools officially opened in July and September 2003, respectively, French and Germans celebrated them as bilateral achievements. Shaped by the rhythms of Franco-German regularized intergovernmentalism, the schools themselves became part of the Franco-German web of institutionalization. Not least symbolizing Franco-German association in security and defense, they will continue to keep the training of French and German armed forces intertwined. Products and part of the Tiger's history, they also may in turn represent the nuclei of common training facilities for more deeply integrated European forces in the future.

Finally, there is the physical reality of the Tiger combat helicopter itself, a supremely powerful high-tech, high-end weapons system. Tiger helicopters will be central components of the equipment of French and German armed forces for a long time to come. By 2020 or so, Germany might possess 80, and France 120 (although the enormous budget pressures and debt crisis in the wake of financial and economic crisis might lead either one to reduce those numbers). These arms, along with the Australian and Spanish Tiger fleets as well as those of other future customers, will also shape military capabilities and help to define military options for some decades. In the further course of the century, Tigers that European states possess or acquire may form central pieces of more deeply integrated European forces. How many Tiger combat helicopters will populate the globe later in the century, we do not yet know. But however many there may be, they will contribute to characterizing state arming in the twenty-first century.

Having emerged as part of the Tiger combat helicopter program's history, these and other ensuing historical outcomes—industrial, organizational, institutional, and military—will last and will have enduring impact. Political choices and embarkation on certain courses of action—as opposed to possible others—have implications. Further down the road, they make some subsequent decisions and developments more likely to emerge, and they constrain others. Some may call this "path dependence." Others, simply "history."

Appendix

COSTS, PHASES, NAMES

Costs

The Tiger combat helicopter program's total costs and volume are and will remain difficult to calculate; frequently, they involve some secrecy. One reason for the difficulty of calculating a reliable total cost estimate is that official figures typically offer separate estimates for each "phase" (or sub-phase) in the long process leading from "starting from scratch" to series production of such a complex weapon. (For an overview of the main phases of such a major weapons development program, see below.) The ultimate acquisition costs at delivery, its "unit price," in turn, are calculated independently of the prior costs of defining, developing, and preparing the helicopter for serial production.

In addition, the various parts or components of such a weapons system—most important, the helicopter itself, its propulsion turbines, and its very expensive arming—frequently come as separate items. Figures may include or exclude the propulsion turbines (again broken down into various phases of definition, development, and ultimate production) when calculating costs and volume. However, figures commonly exclude the immense development and production costs of the Tiger's variable arming, most notably of the very costly third-generation "fire and forget" missiles. Furthermore, they commonly leave out various taxes that have to be added to the program's overall volume. The Tiger's incipient career as an international export article further complicates calculations of the program's overall volume.

Indeed, the expenses directly or indirectly involved in this program are immense and will figure in the multibillion euro range. Overall costs have also steadily risen since the earliest projections and program sketches in the 1970s. The following figures, drawn from reliable sources of the Franco-German combat helicopter's four-decade-long history, indicate actual costs, or politically relevant cost estimates or projections of various aspects of the Tiger combat helicopter weapons system.

During the first half of the 1970s the German Ministry of Defense, perhaps already unrealistically, estimated the development costs of a second-generation helicopter at about DM 250 million (for Germany only) and the ultimate acquisition costs at below DM 10 million per helicopter.[1] In 1983, during the definition phase, the joint Franco-German development costs were calculated at about DM 900 million for each country.[2] The Memorandum of Understanding (MoU) of May 1984 set the costs of the development phase, to begin subsequently, at DM 1,916 million as an upper limit—to be split by France and Germany (with taxes to be added to all of these figures). Germany then calculated the (separate) ultimate acquisition costs for the 212 machines to lie around DM 3.4 billion.[3] By January 1986, the expenses for the development phase were estimated at FF 4,317 million for France and FF 3,963 million for Germany.

After several major efforts to control the program's exploding financial demands, the Franco-German agreement of November 1987, which ultimately initiated the development of the helicopter, set the costs of the development phase at DM 3,464 million (taxes excluded). As for prices and numbers, at the time of signing the memorandum in Karlsruhe in November 1987, the unit price per helicopter was estimated at between DM 36 million and DM 42 million, and some FF 140 million—depending on the finishing in terms of technology and arming.[4]

When the development phase approached completion in 1995, the additional costs for the serial production preparation phase were, bilaterally, calculated at about DM 1 billion. By 1999, when both France and Germany definitively ordered a first batch of eighty combat helicopters each, costs had risen further and continued to do so into the twenty-first century. A 2004 French National Assembly Report estimates the total program costs (still apparently excluding the development and production of the helicopters' turbines as well as the development and production of the arming) at €7.5 billion.[5] Whereas these figures resemble the estimates of the European armament agency OCCAR's 2006 business plan, some commonly well-informed sources calculate the Tiger's development and production costs at some €3.9 billion for Germany alone (again apparently excluding the development and production costs of the aircrafts' turbines and arming).[6]

The program ultimate costs, evidently, will also depend on the number of Tigers France and Germany eventually acquire. That the French and German forces will receive 215 and 212 machines, as initially envisaged and still confirmed in 1999, is now highly unlikely. As of 2008, France projects ultimately obtaining 120 Tigers (yet may reduce these figures to 80) and Germany at least 80.[7] Depending on the version and exact finishing, in the early twenty-first century the Tiger's unit costs are expected to figure between around €24 and €30 million or more, although these figures are likely to rise. The Tiger HAD version will be the most expensive, followed by the UH-T version, and the Tiger HAP and Tiger ARH types.[8] Including definition, development, and production of the helicopter as well as its turbines and arming, together with various taxes, the Tigers' overall costs for France and Germany are likely to extend into the double-digit-billion

Euro range. The Tiger's incipient career as an international export article will further add to make Tiger matters a multibillion Euro affair.

Phases

Chapters 3–6 present the history of and around the Franco-German combat heli-copter and armament politics, both chronologically and by topic according to political and historical relevance. This breakdown and presentation, however, is not entirely identical to the program's (partially overlapping) various official-administrative phases with their respective technical denominations:

Table Appendix 1 **Phases of Development and Production**

Phase	Original French/German	Dates
preparation	*phase préparatoire, Vorbereitungsphase*	November 1976
conception	*phase de conception, Konzeptionsphase*	April–June 1978
(failed) definition	*phase de définition, Definitionsphase*	October 1979–April 1981
definition	*phase de définition, Definitionsphase*	November 1982–May 1984
(first) development	*phase de développement, Entwicklungsphase*	May 1984–1987 (then adjustment and redefinition)
(second) development	*phase de développement, Entwicklungsphase*	after November 1987–ca. 2001/03
serial production preparation	*préparation de production en serie* or *phase de industrialisation, Serienvorbereitung*	1998–2005/08
serial production and delivery	*phase de production en série, Serienfertigung*	beginning 2005

Note: (1) Series production preparation (or "industrialization phase") and series production itself ("series production phase") overlap; the first helicopters may thus already be delivered while the "prep-aration phase" for the serial production is not formally fully concluded. (2) Series production prepara-tion as well as series production itself vary somewhat for the four Tiger versions assembled in the early twenty-first century. The first series-produced Tigers are of the French HAP and the German UH-T versions. Series production preparation and series production for the (Australian) ARH Tigers and the French and Spanish HAD Tigers lag behind somewhat.

Names

The Franco-German combat helicopter and its various versions have had several names during the period over which it evolved. Until the mid-1980s, the program commonly carried the machine's technical denominations and was generally referred to as the Franco-German combat helicopter. In 1987, the helicopter was baptized *Tiger* (in German) and *Tigre* (in French). That has remained the generic name of the helicopter and helicopter program since, in spite of various different versions and arming of the helicopter with additional, more specific technical names. When referring to the Franco-German helicopter, or the helicopter program as a whole or in a general way, I use the names *Tiger* or *Tigre*. I employ the more technical names or denominations of particular versions only when making specific reference to these versions at the time (irrespective of whether they were ultimately produced or plans were aborted).

From early on, the Germans referred to their potential machine as PAH-2 (*Panzerabwehrhubschrauber 2*—Anti-tank Helicopter of the Second Generation). The French in turn denominated the version destined exclusively for combat against tanks, as HAC or HAC 3G (*Hélicoptère Anti-Char 3G*—Anti-tank Helicopter capable of carrying third-generation missiles). The addendum "3G" was dropped or became lost in the course of the years. The more versatile French version as defined in the 1984 Franco-German Memorandum of Understanding— which in addition to attacking tanks was to be finished particularly for a variety of combat support tasks—became known as HAP (*Hélicoptère d'Appui et de Protection*—Support and Protection Helicopter).

With the 1987 adjustments and the "Francogermanization" and streamlining of the helicopters' physical features, although they kept their separate names, the former German PAH-2 and French HAC versions had now become almost identical. This similarity led to some confusion in terms of references to the helicopter versions among military, journalistic, and academic observers. Some spoke from late 1987 of only two versions, an anti-tank version (with HAC *and* PAH-2 as only different names for the same thing) and a combat support and protection version (HAP).[9] Others continued to speak of three versions—PAH-2, HAC, and HAP.[10] Furthermore, after 1987 the French HAP version frequently became called the *Tiger-Gerfaut* (or simply *Gerfaut*), although the name was later dropped.

With the mid-1990s changes in the German Tiger version, the Germans moved from PAH-2 to calling their "multi-role capable" or "multipurpose" version the UH-Tiger (*Unterstützungshubschrauber Tiger*—"Support Helicopter Tiger"), or initially sometimes also the UHU- or Uhu-Tiger, UHU-T, Uhu-T or UH-T. Subsequently, it again became standard to speak of three Tiger versions: Tiger-HAP, Tiger-HAC, and Uhu-Tiger or Uhu-T.[11]

The names of the four different Tiger versions assembled and delivered in the early twenty-first century denote each version's specific finishing, particularized for its specific or general missions and purposes: (the French) Tiger HAP; (the German) UH-Tiger or UH-T; (the Australian) ARH Tiger or Tiger ARH (Armed Reconnaissance Helicopter); (and the French and Spanish) Tiger HAD (*Hélicoptère d'Appui et Destruction* in French, *Helicoptero d'Apoyo y Destrucción* in Spanish—Support and Destruction Helicopter). If referred to in general terms, the "Eurocopter Tiger" now often carries its company designation: "EC665" or "EC665 Tiger."

NOTES

Chapter 1

1. For influential constructivist groundwork, see Jepperson 1991; Johnston 2008; Katzenstein 1996a; Kratochwil 1989; Reus-Smit 1999; Ruggie 1998a; Wendt 1999. For social constructivism's theoretical roots and philosophical underpinnings, see Ruggie 1998b; Searle 1995. Intersubjective structures may have different components: norms, understandings, meanings, knowledge, culture, identities. These may be located at the system-level or sub-systemic level. Wherever located, these components help to shape actors and specify the interests that motivate action.

2. Katznelson and Weingast 2005; March and Olsen 1989, 1998; Pierson 2004; Pierson and Skocpol 2002; Steinmo 2008.

3. Friend 1991, xix.

4. Delattre 1997.

5. Bock 1989, 160.

6. Compare, for example, Abdelal and Kirshner 1999/2000; Burchill 2005; Finnemore 1996a; George and Keohane 1980; Krasner 1978, 12–13, 2009; Moravcsik 1997.

7. Checkel 2008; George and Bennett 2005, chapter 10; Gerring 2007, chapter 7; Hall 2003, 391–395.

8. George and Bennett 2005, chapters 3, 4, 8, and 10; Gerring 2007, chapters 3 and 7.

9. See Sverdrup 1994.

10. For a more extended conceptual and empirical discussion and a historical overview of how Franco-German "regularized intergovernmentalism" has evolved since the early 1960s, see Krotz 2010.

11. For a conceptual discussion of "predominantly symbolic international acts and practices" and a thorough historical examination of such practices in the Franco-German case—including acts that initially installed a new Franco-German meaning in the post-World War II era and a review of practices that reproduced and perpetuated it—see Krotz 2002a.

12. For a comprehensive conceptual discussion of international relations' "parapublic underpinnings" and much Franco-German parapublic empirical detail, see Krotz 2007.

13. In the following overview, I rely on figures from Aerospaceweb.org 2008; *Archiv der Gegenwart* 1983, 272209; *Archiv der Gegenwart* 1984, 27726; Carrez 2004 (October 13), 108; *Les Echos*, March 25, 2002, 13; Louet 1986; OCCAR-EA 2006, 16; Schmalz 1997; *Wehrpolitik* 2002.

14. I did not "select" France-Germany. Because of their historical and political relevance, studying Franco-German relations was part of the initial research project, not of the case selection.

15. This breakdown is not entirely identical to the (partially overlapping) official administrative-technical denomination of the program's various phases. On these, see Appendix.

16. Such or similar slicing or "casing" is common practice in this kind of historically minded social science. See, for example, Lindley 2007; Moravcsik 1998; Zakaria 1998. For methodological reflections on this practice, see also King et al. 1994, 217–228; Ragin 1992.

17. For presentational reasons, some of these cases treat several outcomes collectively, where the outcomes are similar and the constellations among the factors of chapter 2's institutionalist model are the same. Case 10, for example, collectively considers the combat helicopter export episodes to the Netherlands, Britain, Australia, and Spain. In all instances, Germany and France desired to export their combat aircraft. Thus, the total number of outcomes analyzed in chapters 3–6 is in fact larger than twelve. The historical slices most important for this study's analytic goals lie between the mid-1970s and mid-1990s, stretching from the initial Franco-German discussions of the possibility of a joint new-generation helicopter development program to their final decision to produce the machine in series.

18. The considerations here draw from a number of important works on case studies, their nature, their various methodological aspects, their purposes and uses. These notably include Bennett and Elman 2006; George and Bennett 2005; Gerring 2007; Mahoney and Rueschemeyer 2003; McKeown 2004; Ragin and Becker 1992. More specifically, on "casing," note Ragin 1992; Ragin and Becker 1992; on case studies design and case selection, see Collier and Mahoney 1996; Gerring 2007, chapter 5; George and Bennett 2005, chapters 3, 4 and Appendix; on "process tracing" or "systematic process analysis," which chapters 3–6 employ for these chapters' intra-case analyses, see Checkel 2008; George and Bennett 2005, chapters 8 and 10; Gerring 2007, chapter 7; Hall 2003, 391–395.

19. This, in their own way, makes these cases "structured" and "focused" in the sense of George and Bennett's influential formulation of the "method of structured, focused comparison." See George and Bennett 2005, chapter 3.

20. For both historical and theoretical purposes, I am very careful to report empirically the findings that support or challenge each of the various theoretical propositions drawn from the main currents in international relations theory, and to clarify the strengths and limits of each, including the hypotheses of chapter 2's "institutionalist-constructivist" model. In most of the cases, the major theoretical perspectives in international relations offer diverging hypotheses on what should happen (or should have happened). However, at some historical junctures or with respect to some outcomes, they may produce the same expectation (or "prediction"). In case 10, for example, all hypotheses derived from the various theoretical macro-perspectives would predict France and Germany's interests in exporting their *Tiger* combat helicopter. In this sense the political outcome is causally overdetermined. However, not only for the historical record, but also to elucidate that at some historical junctures diverse political forces commonly emphasized by often competing perspectives on world politics may in fact pull toward the same political outcome, I consider it mandatory to report so. In the same vein, chapters 3–6 aspire to make the best analytic use of the evidence available, even if for purely theoretical reasons it would have been preferable if history had at times taken a slightly different course than it did. In case 11, for example, in order to more sharply evaluate the different theoretical hypotheses, Turkey's lasting insistence on Franco-German *Tigers* rather than turning to American *Apache* helicopters would have been yet more illuminating. As history turned out, while strongly suggestive, the evidence is not fully conclusive. Again, for this adventurous history's overall reconstruction, and to bring the historical record to bear analytically as strongly as possible, it is vital and a matter of intellectual honesty precisely to document what happened.

21. On counterfactuals and counterfactual analysis, see Capoccia and Kelemen 2007; Fearon 1991; George and Bennett 2005, 167–170, 230–232; Tetlock and Belkin 1996; on

within-case and cross-case analysis, see George and Bennett 2005, chapters 3, 4, and 8; Gerring 2007, chapters 3 and 7.

22. On qualitative and historical data in international relations, see Lustick 1996; Thies 2002; on the qualitative-historical approach to international relations, and on the craft of fruitfully integrating international relations theory and international history—especially with empirical work using primary sources of various kinds—note Trachtenberg 2006.

23. Next to a variety of other press products, I have mainly drawn from the following sources: *Der Spiegel, Die Welt, Die Zeit, Financial Times, Frankfurter Allgemeine Zeitung, Frankfurter Rundschau, Handelsblatt, Le Nouvel Observateur, La Tribune, Le Figaro, Le Monde, Le Monde Diplomatique, Le Point, Les Echos, L'Humanité, Libération, Neue Züricher Zeitung, New York Times, Stuttgarter Zeitung, Süddeutsche Zeitung, The Economist, Wall Street Journal.*

24. In the following overview, I draw from Casamayou 1993; Louet 1986; Martini 1997; Metzler 1983; Officers of the Führungsstab des Heeres im Bundesministerium der Verteidigung 1986; *Frankfurter Allgemeine Zeitung;* and *Le Figaro.*

25. *Tiger* (in German) or *Tigre* (in French) became the generic name for the program and the machine in 1987. X.X.X. (Anonymous) 1990, 44. I use these names when referring to the Franco-German helicopter or program as a whole and in a general way. I employ the numerous technical names that machine and program have carried or the denominations of the various Tiger-types of sub-versions only in direct reference to these particular machines.

26. On levels of analysis, classically, see Singer 1961; Waltz 1959; more recently, note Fearon 1998; Gourevitch 2002.

27. Compare Bull 1977; Bull and Watson 1984; Meyer et al. 1997; Ruggie 1998a; Wendt 1999.

28. On arming and arms production, see for example, Buzan and Herring 1998; Eyre and Suchman 1996; Jones 2007, chapter 5; Krause 1995; Kurth 1973, 1995; Sagan 1996/97.

29. For example, de Weck 1997; Delors 1998; Kohl 1988. The manifold writings on all aspects of Franco-German affairs importantly include Calleo and Staal 1998; Gordon 1995; Haglund 1991; Leblond 1997; Pajon 2006; Simonian 1985; Soutou 1996; Ziebura 1997.

Chapter 2

1. "The conduct of states or of militarily independent political units, even if one assumes them rational, does not refer to a single objective. To say that states act on the basis of their national interest is to say nothing, as long as one has not defined the content of that interest." Aron 1983, 454–455.

2. "However, the more sharply the significance of a cultural phenomenon is to be brought to cognizance, the more imperative the desire becomes to operate with unambiguous concepts that are not only particularistically, but generally defined." Weber 1988 (1922), 194. For this translation, I have partially relied on Edward Shils and Henry Finch's translation of Weber's essay. Weber 1949, 93.

3. For a more comprehensive discussion of the concept, its usefulness and implications, see Krotz 2010.

4. For a historical overview of Franco-German regularized intergovernmentalism across policy areas, see Krotz 2010. See also there for additional Franco-German regularized intergovernmentalism beyond and below the Elysée Treaty as a main framework. For additional views, particularly focusing on regularized Franco-German intergovernmentalism in security and defense, see Gareis 2008; Pajon 2006.

5. *Cohabitation* denotes a governmental configuration in which the president on the one hand and prime minister and ministers on the other are from different political camps.

The Fifth Republic's political system permits this constellation, and, since the mid-1980s, electoral results intermittently have produced it.

6. For a more extended discussion of the historical significance of the Franco-German regularized intergovernmentalism and its political implications, see Krotz 2010, especially 168–177.

7. de Murville, 1983, 1, 12.

8. For a more extensive discussion of "predominantly symbolic acts and practices" in world politics, see Krotz 2002a.

9. For a history and analysis of Franco-German symbolic acts and practices, see Krotz 2002a.

10. On parapublic underpinnings of international relations generally, see Krotz 2007.

11. On the history and make-up of the parapublic underpinnings of Franco-German relations in greater detail, see Krotz 2007.

12. The latter is a different undertaking, and perhaps a continuation or extension of this book's inquiries. For some hypotheses and initial findings with respect to regularized intergovernmentalism, see Krotz 2010, 151–155 and 168–177; with respect to parapublic underpinnings, see Krotz 2007, 389–390 and 400–404.

13. On process tracing, causal mechanisms, within-case analysis, and cross-case analysis, see Checkel 2008; George and Bennett 2005, chapters 3, 4, 8, 10; Gerring 2007, chapters 3 and 7; Hall 2003. On the view that concepts "embed" causal hypotheses or imply causal mechanisms, see Goertz 2006.

14. This formulation of "historically rooted domestic construction" resembles the concept of "national role conceptions." Notably, see Harnisch and Maull 2001; Holsti 1970; Krotz 2002b; Maull 1990; Walker 1987. However, here the focus is entirely on the domestic level and the internal aspects of national role views as rooted in national historical experience. Similar and compatible conceptualizations of domestic construction for political analysis include Abdelal 2001; Hopf 2002; Johnston 1995; Katzenstein 1996b; Kier 1997; Krotz forthcoming; Ruggie 1997; Walker 2004.

15. Domestically anchored historical constructions must be extracted from *general* statements of proper role and purpose in the world from as broad a range of empirical materials as possible (e.g., speeches of policymakers across parties and offices, various government documents from offices involved in foreign and security affairs, or statements of political parties). Thus they are concentrations of role and purpose broadly shared across persons and offices during particular periods of time. On various conceptual and methodological aspects underlying this notion of domestic historical construction as well as its usage within international relations theory and comparative foreign policy generally, see Krotz forthcoming, chapters 1 and 2.

16. For comparative studies on the impact of such historically rooted domestic constructions on national interests and foreign policy over extended periods of time, see Krotz forthcoming, chapters 5–8; Krotz and Sperling 2011.

17. In addition to prescription and proscription, historically rooted domestic constructions may affect preferences of a certain procedural style of interest formation and policy formulation. See Krotz forthcoming, chapters 1, 5, and 6. However, the potential impact on process and style is of subsidiary relevance for the institutionalist-constructivist model formulated here.

18. In the following paragraphs, I draw from Krotz 2002b; and Krotz forthcoming, chapter 4. For more extended discussions of French and German domestic constructions and their implications, see there. During the time period covered here, the key components of France's and Germany's domestic constructions of their proper international role were fairly robust. If contested, it was along their fringes, not at their cores. Infrequent deeper contestation came only from isolated political outsiders and proved neither viable nor successful. The depiction here focuses on the most basic elements of domestic

construction over the decades in question; it does not aim at an exhaustive historical characterization and therefore does not include a range of other, less basic or less enduring elements of national role and purpose construction that might have emerged alongside, complementary to, or in specification of those portrayed here.

19. See, for example, Genscher 1981, 1995; Maull 1992b; Schmidt 1994; Schweigler 1985, 1996.

20. Kinkel 1998; von Weizsäcker 1992, 111. Further, for example, see Hacke 1996, 4; Haftendorn 1993; Schweigler 1996.

21. See, for example, Maull 1992b; Maull 1992a; Schweigler 1985.

22. As in the diction of Hans-Dietrich Genscher, German foreign minister from 1974 to 1992. Genscher 1995; similarly, Genscher 1981.

23. See, for example, Baring 1997; Hacke 1996; Hellmann 1996, 1997; Kinkel 1998; Vernet 1998a. From the mid-1990s on, the German foreign policy discourse and its vocabulary began to evolve and modify, while in many respects still carrying the flavor of the preceding decades. On evolution, modification, and continuity, see Hellmann et al. 2008; Krotz forthcoming chapter 8.

24. Quotes, in this order, are from Walker 1987, 270 (appendices); Becker 1983; Walker 1987, 270; Gordon 1993, xv; Nonnenmacher 1986.

25. Rouget 1989, 68. See also Hermann 1987, 136; Holsti 1970, 262; Sampson and Walker 1987, 117.

26. de Gaulle 1970, 177.

27. Védrine 1996, 7.

28. Walker 1987, 270 (appendices).

29. Quotes, in this order, are from Gordon 1993, 1; Vernet 1997; DePorte 1991, 253.

30. Compare, for example, de Montbrial 1989, 288–290; Savignac 1995, 210–216.

31. Scholl-Latour 1988, 88–99.

32. von Weizsäcker 1998. On "France's right and duty to act on a world scale," see also de Gaulle 1970, 177–180.

33. Compare, for example, Cerny 1986; Vaïsse 1998; Vernet 1998b.

34. Quotes, in this order, are from Frank 1991, 68–69; DePorte 1991, 254; Kramer 1991, 962.

35. de Gaulle 1954, 5. For further terms that became standard reference vocabulary, see ibid. 5–7. On the same theme, note Malraux 1971, especially 21–23; and, three presidents later, Kramer 1991, 962. For continuity and evolution of basic aspects of French domestic construction and its impact on national interest and policy from the mid-1990s on, see Krotz forthcoming chapter 7; for translating some major elements of such domestic construction into national foreign policy, security, and defense strategies in the emerging twenty-first century, note the two White Books: *Défense et Sécurité Nationale: Le Livre Blanc* 2008; Juppé and Schweitzer 2008.

36. For a grand outline of the historical raw materials from which France and Germany selected, see Krotz, forthcoming, chapter 3.

37. For similar views on the period relevant here, see Banchoff 1996; Berger 1998; Duffield 1999; Katzenstein 1997; Krotz forthcoming, chapters 3–6; Schweigler 1996.

38. DePorte 1991, 251–252, emphasis in the original.

39. Cerny 1994, 99. On the chief constituents of this "national consensus" Frank 1991, 92 and its endurance, see further, for example, Aron 1983, chapter 16; Gordon 1993; Nonnenmacher 1999; Rouget 1989, 67.

40. Baums 1992, 259. Further, for example, Rémond 1982; Sauder 1995, chapters 7 and 8.

41. Why should we expect domestic construction to "trump" interstate institutionalization and construction? This proposition is deductively plausible because, overall, we expect the strength and the density of constructions of meaning in domestic settings to be greater than institutionalization and construction at the interstate or international level. General systems theory and cybernetics, as adapted by Karl Deutsch and his followers

and applied to the analysis of nationalism, internationalism, and collective identity formation, provides a theoretical footing for this expectation. See Deutsch 1953, 1963, 1969; Deutsch et al. 1957. Stephen Krasner echoes the point, in line with his own observations regarding the matter in Krasner 1999, chapters 1 and 2.

42. "Domestic structures" in particular have been the turf of historical institutionalist scholars of comparative politics and comparative foreign policy. Standard works in these veins of inquiry include Evangelista 1999; Evans et al. 1985; Hall 1986; Huntington 1968; Katzenstein 1978, 1985; March and Olsen 1984, 1989; Steinmo et al. 1992. For reviews of the literature, note Evangelista 1997; Gourevitch 2002; Hall and Taylor 1996; Pierson and Skocpol 2002; Thelen and Steinmo 1992.

43. On "veto points" and "veto players," see Immergut 1990, 1992; Tsebelis 2002.

44. Duverger 1974.

45. Mény 1996.

46. Among the standard texts on the French political system are Culpepper et al. 2006; Duhamel 2009; Flynn 1995; Hoffmann 1963; Mény 2008; Savignac 1995. Texts on France of particular relevance for the issues of authority centralization and state autonomy include Dunn 1995; Duverger 1974; Lüger 1996; Mény 1996; 1998, chapters 5 and 6; Rémond 1982; Wilsford 1988.

47. Schmidt 1996.

48. Katzenstein 1987, 58–80.

49. Among the standard texts on the German political system are Ellwein and Hesse 1987; Rudzio 1991; Schmidt 1992. Works on Germany of particular relevance for the issues of authority centralization and state autonomy include Haftendorn et al. 1978; Katzenstein 1987; Lehmbruch 1987; Niclauss 1988; Schmidt 1996. For comparisons of France and Germany regarding the issues discussed here, see especially Gladstone 1986; Kriesi 1994, chapters 11 and 12; Sauder 1995, chapters 8 and 9; Trefz 1989, 97–115.

50. The most influential realist texts of the past three decades include Mearsheimer 2001; Posen 1984; Van Evera 1999; Walt 1987; Waltz 1979. Good overviews and reviews of realist thought include Doyle 1997, Part One; Guzzini 2004; Jervis 1998; Smith 1986; Wohlforth 2008.

51. For varieties of contemporary realist thought in international relations, including, among others, defensive realism, offensive realism, balance-of-power realism, balance-of-threat realism, neoclassical realism, state-centered realism, see Kapstein and Mastanduno 1999; Lobell et al. 2009; Mearsheimer 2001, chapters 1 and 2; Rose 1998; Zakaria 1998.

52. On political-economic views of realism, see Abdelal 2001; Abdelal and Kirshner 1999/2000; Brooks 2005; Drezner 2007; Gilpin 1987, 2001; Kirshner 1999; Mastanduno 2008.

53. Mearsheimer 1994/1995; Mearsheimer 1995.

54. Snyder 1997; Walt 1987.

55. Key neoliberal institutionalist formulations, frequently with applications to Cold War- and post-Cold War European politics, include Haftendorn et al. 1999; Keohane 1984; Keohane 1989a; Koremenos et al. 2004; Martin and Simmons 2001; Wallander 1999. Other significant works on international institutionalization and organization importantly informed by liberal international thought, notably include Deudney and Ikenberry 1999; Ikenberry 2001, 2009.

56. Keohane 1989c, 3–4; Keohane 1989b, 164.

57. For basic outlines, see Keohane 1984, 14; Keohane 1989c, 2.

58. Keohane 1989b, 166.

59. Keohane 1983.

60. In my remarks here and in the following chapters, I focus on this recent social science systematization, "liberal intergovernmentalism" or "new liberalism," as propounded in the work of Andrew Moravcsik. For basic outlines, see Moravcsik 1993; 1997; 1998,

chapters 1 and 2; 2003; 2008. For general overviews of liberal thought in international affairs, note Doyle 1997, Part Two; Hoffmann 1987; Zacher and Matthew 1995. For an interesting blend between liberalism and constructivism in analyzing foreign-and security policymaking in Western democracies in the post-World War II era, see Risse-Kappen 1995.

61. Moravcsik 1993, 483; see also Moravcsik 1997, 516–517; 2008.
62. Moravcsik 1993, 474; 1997, 518–520.
63. Moravcsik 1998, 24.
64. Moravcsik 1993, quotes from 487, 496–497.

Chapter 3

1. In the following discussion, I especially draw on Bundesrechnungshof der Bundesrepublik Deutschland 1998; Leimbacher 1992; Louet 1986; Officers of the Führungsstab des Heeres im Bundesministerium der Verteidigung 1986; *Sicherheitpolitik* 1986.
2. In 1983, for example, the West estimated the Warsaw Pact forces to be in possession of some 42,000 tanks, whereas NATO *and* France taken together only possessed some 14,100. See Stützle 1983. On the delivery schedule priority, see Officers of the Führungsstab des Heeres im Bundesministerium der Verteidigung 1986, 210. See also Lecacheleux 2003, 136.
3. For more details and specifics, see Louet 1986, 8–9.
4. See Leimbacher 1992, 92.
5. See Officers of the Führungsstab des Heeres im Bundesministerium der Verteidigung 1986.
6. For more details on desired arming, see ibid., 212.
7. Kocs 1995, 168; SALSS 1985, 62.
8. Officers of the Führungsstab des Heeres im Bundesministerium der Verteidigung 1986, 212. There also more details on technical and other performance issues. See also Louet 1986, 8–9.
9. Bundesrechnungshof der Bundesrepublik Deutschland 1998, 5, 10–11, 18.
10. Bundesrechnungshof der Bundesrepublik Deutschland 1998, 11.
11. Louet 1986, 10.
12. Grosser 1988.
13. Trefz 1989, 98.
14. Louet 1986, 12.
15. Ibid.
16. For these and other details, see ibid., 11–12.
17. Ibid., 14.
18. Regarding French-German divergences with respect to the future helicopters' roles in military and defense, the types of machines desired, and scheduling issues, see also Seiffert 2004, 91–92.
19. SALSS 1985, 61.
20. Ibid.
21. Louet 1986, 16. In the following depiction of the early years of the helicopter project, I draw extensively on the detailed description of the political developments in Louet's substantive report on the project to the French National Assembly.
22. See Guisnel 1986a; Leimbacher 1992, 92; and especially Louet 1986, 20. When titles (such as president or defense minister) accompany a name, they always refer to the office-holder at the time.
23. Mathieu 1996, chapter 8.
24. I rely heavily in this section on several parts of Louet 1986.
25. Kocs 1995, 168.

26. *Handelsblatt,* April 28–29, 1978, 15.
27. Ibid.
28. *Frankfurter Allgemeine Zeitung,* April 20, 1979, 1; *Le Monde,* April 21, 1979, 16.
29. For example, *Frankfurter Allgemeine Zeitung,* April 20, 1979, 1; *Le Monde,* April 21, 1979, 16.
30. *Süddeutsche Zeitung,* June 12, 1979, 24.
31. Then between Bölkow Entwicklungen KG and Sud-Aviation. By 1979, Bölkow had become part of MBB, which in turn belonged to DASA, the aerospace division of the Daimler-Benz group. After fusing with Nord-Aviation, Sud-Aviation had become part of SNIAS. Among the products resulting from the established cooperation between the French and German companies were components for earlier German and French helicopters (although produced separately) and cooperation in missile systems, including the integration of the Franco-German HOT missile into French and German helicopters.
32. Bittner 1986, 120–121. See also Kocs 1995, 169.
33. Louet 1986, 21.
34. Kocs 1995, 170.
35. Louet 1986, 22.
36. Ibid.
37. Ibid.
38. SALSS 1985, 61–62.
39. Louet 1986, 22.
40. *Süddeutsche Zeitung,* October 1, 1982, 8, emphasis added.
41. Louet 1986, 21.
42. A tripartite cooperation at the time, possible for Germany, was then apparently encumbered by French domestic construction effects. That there is no indication of a French interest in such a trilateral cooperation, or in French-Italian cooperation for that matter, is worth noting. In terms of ideal flying weight, French preferences were about the same as the Italian and in fact corresponded to the weight of the helicopter that was developed and produced by the Italian company Agusta in the course of the 1970s.
43. See Louet 1986, 17–18 and 40–41.
44. Louet 1986, 17.
45. SALSS 1985, 61.
46. Hoffmann 1987. Another reason for the Italian-German "mismatch" was divergent wishes regarding the physical configuration of the helicopter. For example, Italy wanted a significantly lighter helicopter than did the German defense planners. However, the Italian wishes differed from the German ones no more than the wishes of the German military differed from those of their French colleagues.
47. Louet 1986, 23.
48. Louet 1986, 19.
49. Trefz 1989, 127–128.
50. Aron 1983, 439–448.
51. Leimbacher 1992, 60–68 and 92–93. French military and defense planning remained strongly influenced by the "two battles" concept, at the very least until the second half of the 1970s. This planning was relativized during the 1980s with the staffing and arming of the *Force d'Action Rapide* (FAR) and the 1981 decision to replace the short range *Pluton* nuclear missiles (120 km range) with new *Hadès* missiles (first to 350, then to 480 km range). However, these doctrinal modifications neither abruptly nor decisively altered the technical demands of the French army, or those of France at large, regarding new combat helicopters.
52. State-owned or -controlled French companies come in different legal types and have various legal forms such as *arsenaux d'Etat, Groupements Industriels des Armements Terrestres,* and *sociétés nationales.* For details, see Trefz 1989, 99. The armament industry

has been state owned or controlled in France for some 200 years, often dating back to before Napoleon.

Chapter 4

1. Schmidt 1990, especially 241–294.
2. Deutsch-Französisches Institut and Deutsche Frankreich-Bibliothek 1995 (and after), 70.
3. On the continued widening and deepening institutionalization of the "regularized inter-governmentalism" of Franco-German bilateral relations during the 1980s, including on the top political levels, see Filser 1996; Guérin-Sendelbach 1993; Krotz 2010; Sverdrup 1994.
4. Deutsch-Französisches Institut and Deutsche Frankreich-Bibliothek 1995 (and after), 72–73.
5. Kocs 1995, 170.
6. Louet 1986, 22.
7. Moniac 1983a.
8. Ibid.
9. Ibid.
10. Deutsch-Französisches Institut and Deutsche Frankreich-Bibliothek 1995 (and after), 75
11. Metzler 1983.
12. "Der Teufel steckt im Detail" (German proverb). Ibid.
13. Ibid.
14. *Le Monde*, May 19, 1983, 3.
15. Ibid.
16. Stützle 1983.
17. Bundesrechnungshof der Bundesrepublik Deutschland 1998.
18. *Stuttgarter Zeitung*, November 24, 1983, 2.
19. *Libération*, November 26–27, 1983, 17.
20. *Süddeutsche Zeitung*, November 26–27, 1983, 6.
21. *Archiv der Gegenwart* 1983. Whether the FAR would have been assigned the task it now was—to potentially support the defense of German territory in case of a Warsaw Pact attack "earlier and further ahead"—without institutionalized Franco-German interaction is highly questionable. Whereas France had partially adjusted the helicopter's designated military tasks, the social reasons for desirability of the Franco-German program have remained a constant.
22. Deutsch-Französisches Institut and Deutsche Frankreich-Bibliothek 1995 (and after), 77–78.
23. See *Archiv der Gegenwart* 1983, 27209; Moniac 1983b.
24. Bittner 1986, 119.
25. See Kageneck 1984.
26. Ibid.
27. *Stuttgarter Zeitung*, November 24, 1983, 2.
28. Kohl 1984 (1983)-b, D 43.
29. Kohl 1984 (1983)-a, D 49.
30. Hoffmann 1986.
31. It is reprinted in Louet 1986, 43–64.
32. Louet 1986, 26.
33. For a summary, see Louet 1986, 24–29. For details see Articles 2 and 3, and the annexes of the governmental agreement. Reprint in ibid.
34. These "development phase" expenses do not include the costs of the preparation, conception, and definition phases; the serial production preparation phase and the serial production itself; the design, development, and production of the third-generation

missiles; and the ultimate actual acquisition of helicopters by the two states. In May 1984, for example, the acquisition costs alone for the 212 German PAH-2 were estimated at some DM 3.4 billion. *Archiv der Gegenwart* 1984, 27726.

35. For a discussion, see Isnard 1984, 3.
36. See Article 3 of the MoU and Louet 1986, 26–28.
37. For overviews and discussions, see Kessler 1988, 274; Leimbacher 1992, 101.
38. Krotz 2010.
39. For details, see Louet 1986, 31–32.
40. See article VII, 1.4.
41. The BWB would function as executive agency of the helicopter program until mid-1989, when the authority for daily management was transferred to a newly founded Franco-German Helicopter Office (DFHB). Leimbacher 1992, 101, footnote 68.
42. Article 6, section 2.
43. See, for example, Kessler 1988. For details see MoU Article 6, sections 2.3 and 3.
44. Kessler 1988, 274; Leimbacher 1992, 101, footnote 68.
45. Kocs 1995, 171.
46. See Kohl 1984 (1983)-a, D 49; 1984 (1983)-b.
47. Stützle 1983.
48. Moniac 1983b.
49. Metzler 1984
50. Kocs 1995, 189–191, quote is from 191.
51. Ravery 1984.
52. Interestingly enough, Defense Minister Hernu considered Ravery's critique sufficiently important to respond that "the cooperation in armament contributes to the independence of our defense policy and preserves our industrial and technological capacities." The quote is from *Le Monde*, June 12, 1984.
53. See Louet 1986, 45–46.
54. Kohl and Mitterrand 1982, D 627.
55. Ibid., D 628. For the symbolic pertinence of celebration and commemoration of "Franco-German anniversaries" and specifically for the celebration of the twentieth Elysée Treaty anniversary that indeed was turned into a "Franco-German memorial day," see Krotz 2002a.
56. Kohl and Mitterrand 1982, D 630.
57. Ibid., D 630.
58. Ibid.
59. Louet 1986, 22.
60. On collective intentionality, see Searle 1995, 23–26 as well as Ruggie 1998b, 869–870 and Ruggie 1998c, 20–21.
61. In the same context, very tellingly, see, for example, Kohl's remarks, documented above, at the forty-second Franco-German summit a year later in November 1983. Kohl 1984 (1983)-b.
62. Bundesrechnungshof der Bundesrepublik Deutschland 1998, 13–14.
63. *Sicherheitpolitik* 1986, 13.
64. Bundesrechnungshof der Bundesrepublik Deutschland 1998, 13.
65. See Louet 1986.
66. Louet 1986, 26.
67. As above, I treat these outcomes collectively as a case. They also could be presented as three separate observations.
68. Krotz forthcoming, chapters 4–6.
69. *Stuttgarter Zeitung*, November 24, 1983, 2.
70. Louet 1986, 33.
71. Krotz forthcoming, chapters 4–6.

Chapter 5

1. Louet 1986, 35.
2. Leimbacher 1992, 100.
3. *Frankfurter Rundschau*, July 19, 1984, 2; Kessler 1988, 274.
4. Louet 1986, 35.
5. Ibid.
6. Kessler 1988; *Soldat und Technik* 1991, 100–101.
7. Louet 1986.
8. Ibid., 37.
9. *Le Monde*, February 19, 1986.
10. Hoffmann 1986; Szandar 1986.
11. Darcourt 1987b.
12. Leimbacher 1992, 101.
13. Ibid., 100.
14. Guisnel 1986b.
15. Ibid.
16. *Frankfurter Allgemeine Zeitung*, May 14, 1986, 2.
17. Guisnel 1986b.
18. *Libération*, June 4, 1986, 8.
19. Isnard 1986.
20. *Libération*, June 4, 1986, 8.
21. *Die Welt*, June 16, 1986, 4; *Süddeutsche Zeitung* June 16–17, 1986, 25.
22. Deutsch-Französisches Institut and Deutsche Frankreich-Bibliothek 1995 (and after).
23. *Le Figaro*, June 18, 1986, 4.
24. *Le Monde*, July 27–28, 1986, 8.
25. Louet 1986, 39.
26. *Le Monde*, July 27–28, 1986, 8; *Neue Züricher Zeitung*, July 29, 1986, 2–3.
27. *Le Monde*, March 19, 1987.
28. See Kocs 1995, 204; *Le Monde*, March 22–23, 1987, 1.
29. *Neue Züricher Zeitung*, March 24, 1987, 4.
30. *Libération*, March 23, 1987, 15.
31. *Die Welt*, March 23, 1987, 5.
32. *Le Monde*, March 22–23, 1987.
33. Ibid.
34. Darcourt 1987a, 3.
35. Quoted in Guisnel 1987b. On the same worry, see Louet 1986, 69.
36. As quoted in Isnard 1987b, 16.
37. Quoted in Guisnel 1987c; see further Guisnel 1987d.
38. *Frankfurter Allgemeine Zeitung*, July 18, 1987, 2.
39. Guisnel 1987a.
40. *Le Monde*, November 13, 1987, 4.
41. Brühmann 1995; Guisnel 1987a; Heckmann 1993; Moniac 1987a; *Soldat und Technik* 1991.
42. Casdorff 1987; Darcourt 1987b; Guisnel 1987a; Leimbacher 1992.
43. Moniac 1987b. Numbers from there and from other sources.
44. *Frankfurter Allgemeine Zeitung*, July 17, 1987, 1–2.
45. For the complete speech, see Presse-und Informationsamt der Bundesregierung (Bulletin) 1987, 1070.
46. Leimbacher 1992, 101.
47. Ruge 1986.
48. *Frankfurter Allgemeine Zeitung*, June 14, 1986.
49. Louet 1986.

50. Guisnel 1986a.
51. Casdorff 1987.
52. Darcourt 1987b.
53. Louet 1986, 5.
54. *Le Monde*, March 22–23, 1987, 1.
55. *Le Monde*, July 18, 1987, 1.
56. Quoted in Isnard 1987a.
57. Puhl 1987, and *Frankfurter Allgemeine Zeitung*, July 18, 1987, 2.
58. Quoted in *Frankfurter Allgemeine Zeitung*, July 18, 1987, 2.
59. Picaper 1987.
60. Moniac 1987b.
61. Szandar 1986.
62. Ibid.
63. Leimbacher 1992, 102.
64. *Sicherheitpolitik* 1986, 13.
65. *Süddeutsche Zeitung*, October 21, 1987, 8.
66. *Le Monde*, March 22–23, 1987, 1.
67. *Libération*, June 4, 1986, 8.
68. Krotz forthcoming, chapters 4–8.
69. Guisnel 1986a.
70. *Sicherheitpolitik* 1986, 13.
71. *Le Figaro*, July 19, 1987, 6.
72. *Neue Züricher Zeitung*, July 19–20, 1987, 5, emphasis in the original.
73. Louet 1986, 35–39 and 65–70.
74. Ibid., 38.
75. Ibid., 5.
76. *Neue Züricher Zeitung*, May 31, 1986, 4; *Süddeutsche Zeitung*, May 18, 1986, 8.
77. Leimbacher 1992, 99.
78. Ravery 1987.
79. *Süddeutsche Zeitung*, July 16, 1987, 6.
80. Darcourt 1987a, 3.
81. Presse-und Informationsamt der Bundesregierung (Bulletin) 1987, 1071.

Chapter 6

1. *Neue Züricher Zeitung*, October 2–3, 1988, 2; *Le Monde*, October 2–3, 1988, 8.
2. *Süddeutsche Zeitung*, January 28, 1988, 2.
3. Leimbacher 1992, 101, footnote 67; *Soldat und Technik* 1995, 332–333.
4. For more details on the working of the helicopter office, see the article written by its two co-directors Weiand and d'Antin 1995.
5. Heckmann 1993; *Le Figaro*, May 14, 1998, 1; *Le Monde*, April 30, 1991, 36; *Wehrpolitik* 2002.
6. *Le Monde*, September 6, 1988, 3.
7. *Le Figaro*, October 25, 1988, 6. MBB belonged to DASA, the aeronautic branch of the (then) Daimler-Benz group.
8. *Le Monde*, February 22, 1990.
9. Quoted in Isnard 1990a.
10. Isnard 1990b. In the early 1990s, the new company would employ some 12,700 workers, 5,000 in Germany and the rest in France. Initially, it would have a yearly turnover of some DM 3.3 billion (FF 11 billion).
11. *Le Monde*, February 28, 1991, 12.
12. *Die Welt*, May 7, 1991, 15; *Le Monde*, May 8, 1991, 19; *Stuttgarter Zeitung*, May 8, 1991, 15.

13. *Financial Times*, June 12, 1995, 11.
14. *Handelsblatt*, June 17, 1992, 28; Prämaßing 1996, 298.
15. Ruge 1990; Casamayou 1993.
16. d'Athis and Croizé 1991.
17. *Stuttgarter Zeitung*, September 23, 1992, 2.
18. Quoted in *Le Monde*, July 2, 1993, 10.
19. Brühmann 1995, 21; Prämaßing 1996, 300.
20. On the many different arming options of the versions, see Brühmann 1995; Gouvernement de France 2003; Heckmann 1993; Lecacheleux 2003, 130; Prämaßing 1996; *Wehrtechnik* 2003; Wennekers 2001.
21. Brühmann 1995; Heckmann 1993; Prämaßing 1996.
22. *Le Monde*, September 13, 1994, 13, quoting the official *Info-DGA*.
23. Aubert 1996a.
24. *Le Monde*, November 10–11, 1996, and *Stuttgarter Zeitung*, November 14, 1996; Isnard 1996a. On OCCAR as a European armament agency and its Franco-German roots, see in particular Le Drian 2002 (October 10); Sauvaget 2007.
25. Kanalmüller 1991.
26. *La Tribune Desfossés*, December 19, 1994, 14.
27. Guisnel 1989; *Le Monde*, November 25–26, 1990, 13.
28. *Le Figaro*, January 25, 1995, 6.
29. *Handelsblatt*, June 14, 1995, 13.
30. Quoted in *Le Monde*, January 26, 1995, 18.
31. Quotes from Franco 1995.
32. Weidemann 1995.
33. Quoted in *Le Monde*, April 9–10, 1995, 13.
34. *Handelsblatt*, June 14, 1995, 13.
35. Quoted in *La Tribune Desfossés*, July 3, 1995, 10; see also *Handelsblatt*, July 4, 1995, 12; *Le Monde*, July 4, 1995, 19; *Süddeutsche Zeitung*, July 1–2, 1995, 1.
36. *Financial Times*, June 28, 1995, 10.
37. *Le Figaro*, July 11, 1995, 2.
38. Moniac 1995.
39. *L'Humanité*, July 17, 1995, 5; similarly, *Financial Times*, July 15–16, 1995, 2; *La Tribune Desfossés*, July 17, 1995, 2.
40. Roland 1995.
41. Berlioz 1995.
42. Prämaßing 1996, 300.
43. Isnard 1996a.
44. *Le Figaro*, April 9, 1996, 6. In the mid-1990s, Franco-German armament cooperation encompassed some thirty projects; seven of them were commonly viewed as "major ventures" (*Großvorhaben*). Feldmeyer 1996.
45. Isnard 1996d.
46. Quoted in Isnard 1996d.
47. *Financial Times*, May 11–12, 1996, 2; *Financial Times*, May 9, 1996, 16.
48. *Handelsblatt*, May 13, 1996, 18; *Handelsblatt*, May 15, 1996, 20; *Süddeutsche Zeitung*, May 15, 1996, 31; *Frankfurter Rundschau*, May 15–16, 1996, 17.
49. *La Tribune Desfossés*, May 29, 1996, 15; *L'Humanité*, May 30, 1996, 9.
50. *Financial Times*, May 9, 1996, 16.
51. Isnard 1996e
52. *Le Figaro*, July 9, 1996; Aubert 1996b.
53. *La Tribune Desfossés*, June 7, 1996, 13.
54. Isnard 1996c.
55. *Libération*, June 17, 1996, 19; see also *La Tribune Desfossés*, June 17, 1996, 15.

56. Published in *Le Monde*, June 19, 1996, 20.
57. *Die Welt*, June 19, 1996, 2.
58. Millot 1996.
59. *Frankfurter Allgemeine Zeitung*, June 27, 1996, 1.
60. Ibid.
61. *L'Humanité*, July 1, 1996, 24.
62. Feldmeyer 1996.
63. *Frankfurter Allgemeine Zeitung*, October 10, 1996, 2.
64. Millot 1996.
65. *Le Figaro*, December 3, 1996, 8.
66. Isnard 1996b.
67. *Die Welt*, December 13, 1995, 15.
68. *Die Welt*, January 23, 1997, 16; *Frankfurter Allgemeine Zeitung*, January 23, 1997, 20.
69. Quoted in *Le Monde*, January 24, 1997, 18.
70. *Le Monde*, January 14, 1997, 17.
71. *La Tribune Desfossés*, April 18, 1997, 10; *Die Welt*, April 23, 1997, 15; *Süddeutsche Zeitung*, May 9, 1997, 23.
72. Isnard 1997; Provost 1997; Taverna 1997.
73. *Süddeutsche Zeitung*, July 7, 1997, 2; Taverna 1997.
74. Schmalz 1997.
75. *Le Monde*, May 22, 1998, 4. For the intended finishing of the different versions, and the arming options and combinations, see Brühmann 1995; Heckmann 1993.
76. Marx 1998.
77. *La Tribune*, December 22, 1998, 13; Owen 1998a, 1998b.
78. Aubert 1999; *Frankfurter Allgemeine Zeitung*, June 23, 1999, 4; Gouvernement de France 2003; OCCAR-EA 2006, 16; Owen 1999; *Wehrpolitik* 2002.
79. *La Tribune Desfossés*, April 18, 1997, 10.
80. Schwartzbrod 1998.
81. Puhl 1998.
82. Isnard 1999; *La Tribune Desfossés*, February 8, 1999, 15.
83. *La Tribune Desfossés*, December 22, 1998, 13.
84. *Le Figaro*, April 4, 2000, 7.
85. Australian National Audit Office 2006, 31, 35, 41; Pivet 2001; Sabatier 2001a.
86. Wennekers 2001.
87. Sabatier 2001a.
88. Isnard 2003a; *Le Figaro*, August 11, 2001, 1; Neu 2001; Sabatier 2001b.
89. Neu 2001.
90. Australian National Audit Office 2006, 13, 32, 35; EADS 2006 (August 10); EADS 2006 (January 18); Migault 2002.
91. Australian National Audit Office 2006, 11, 34, 47, 76.
92. Isnard 2001.
93. EADS 2006 (August 10); EADS 2006 (January 18); Eurocopter 2005 (March 18); OCCAR-EA 2006, 16.
94. Isnard 2001, 2003a.
95. Cabirol 2001.
96. Cabirol 2002, 2003b; *Les Echos*, January 8, 2003, 10.
97. Cabirol 2003a; EADS 2006 (August 10); EADS 2006 (January 18); Eurocopter 2005 (March 18); OCCAR-EA 2006.
98. *Frankfurter Allgemeine Zeitung*, September 16, 2003, 21; Migault 2003.
99. Carrez 2004 (October 13), 108; see also Lecacheleux 2003, 129.
100. EADS 2005 (December 5); OCCAR-EA 2006, 16; Neu 2001.
101. See the French government's financial planning, Projet de Loi de Finances pour 2006 (PLF 2006): Défense; DBGNORMALMSNDA.doc (accessed September 30, 2005).

102. EADS 2005 (December 5); EADS 2006 (January 18).
103. *Le Figaro*, April 12–13, 1997, 7; *Le Monde*, March 1, 1996, 8; *Le Monde*, April 13–14, 1997, 4.
104. Gouvernement de France 2003; Peiron 2003; Salendre 2007.
105. Beaulieu 2005 (October 12), 22; Gouvernement de France 2003; Peiron 2003; Salendre 2007.
106. Isnard 2003b.
107. Bundesministerium der Verteidigung 2003a; Bundeswehr 2003 (September 27); Gouvernement de France 2003.
108. *Les Echos*, March 25, 2002, 13; *Wehrpolitik* 2002.
109. EADS 2006 (August 10).
110. Australian National Audit Office 2006, 12; EADS 2006 (August 10); Eurocopter 2005 (March 18); Projet de Loi de Finances pour 2006 (PLF 2006): Défense; DBGNOR-MALMSNDA.doc, 244 (accessed September 30, 2005).
111. Guhl 2009; MacKenzie 2009; Ministère de Défense (France) 2010; Schubert 2010; Tran 2010; quote is from MacKenzie 2009.
112. Neu 2001.
113. OCCAR-EA 2006, 16; *Süddeutsche Zeitung*, March 8, 2001, 2; *Wehrtechnik* 2003.
114. *Wehrtechnik* 2003
115. Cabirol 2005b; Gouvernement de France 2003; Projet de Loi de Finances pour 2006 (PLF 2006): Défense; DBGNORMALMSNDA.doc, 243–244 (accessed September 30, 2005).
116. Cabirol 2003b, 2005a; *Les Echos*, March 25, 2002, 13; Migault 2002, 2003.
117. Cabirol 2003a, 2005a.
118. De Grandi 2003.
119. *Süddeutsche Zeitung*, June 11, 1991, 24; Croizé and d'Athis 1991.
120. *Les Echos*, March 25, 2002, 13; Isnard 2003a.
121. Bundesministerium der Verteidigung 2003b.
122. Chirac 2005.
123. Nesshöver and Rinke 2003. As Philippe Delmas underscores, parallel to this new production of bilateral meaning endogenous to Tiger dealings during the 1990s, avoiding a return of the past—with its sorry record of warfare among Western Europeans and notably between France and Germany—continued to hold significant underlying social meaning justifying and propelling tight bilateral cooperation in defense and security, including in armament production. In spite of his book's lugubrious title, his is really a plea for continued reconciliation and cooperation in order to keep the specter of intra-European war a distant one. Compare Delmas 1999. Such historically rooted meaning and social purpose between France and Germany during the 1980s and 1990s continued to be expressed and perpetuated in a series of symbolic acts and practices. On such symbolic acts and practices as part of the fabric of French-German inter-state institutionalization and construction, see Krotz 2002a.
124. Quoted in *Le Figaro*, October 25, 1988, 6.
125. Bigay 1992.
126. Alich 2007.
127. Aubert 1996a; Le Drian 2002 (October 10); *Les Echos*, January 8, 2003, 10; Kerdraon 1999 (December 7); Migault 2003.
128. Lignières-Cassou 2000 (December 12), 108–110; Nesshöver and Rinke 2003; OCCAR-EA 2006.
129. Gouvernement de France 2003.
130. Quotes from *Die Welt*, June 21, 1997, 14; see also *Neue Züricher Zeitung*, July 26–27, 1997, 1–2.
131. Isnard 2003a, 2003b.
132. Krotz forthcoming, chapters 4 and 6. For further background and details of German arms export and arms export policies through the end of the Cold War, and the importance of arms exports for the German defense industrial base, see Huebner 1989.

133. As quoted in Puhl 1998.
134. Krotz forthcoming, chapters 4 and 6; for additional background and detail on German arms exports through the end of the Cold War, see Huebner 1989.
135. Seibert 2000. It is quite possible, of course, that the future will again produce a similar Tiger export episode, perhaps with Turkey or with other potential customers.
136. Aubert 1996a, 1996b.
137. d'Athis and Croizé 1991.
138. *Financial Times*, July 10, 1996, 11.
139. Puhl 1997.
140. Quoted in Aubert 1996b.
141. Puhl 1996, emphasis added.
142. Presse-und Informationsamt der Bundesregierung (Bulletin) 1997; *Stuttgarter Zeitung*, December 6, 1996, 2; *La Tribune Desfossés*, December 10, 1996, 4.

Chapter 7

1. Isnard 1984.
2. Louet 1986, 5.
3. Leimbacher 1992, 93. See also Kocs 1995, 171.
4. Compare Searle 1995, 23. On social relations and their potential effects, see also Weber's concept of the "social relation" or "social relationship." Weber 1972 (1921), chapter 1.
5. Ruggie 1998b, 870. Compare also Searle 1995, 26.
6. Krotz forthcoming, chapters 4 and 6.
7. See SALSS 1985, 50.
8. Krotz forthcoming, chapters 4 and 6.
9. Checkel 1998, 339; March and Olsen 1989, 40.
10. Krotz forthcoming.
11. On the aborted tank project and related issues, see Baums 1992, 376; Bée et al. 2004; Kocs 1995, 162–163.
12. On different sorts of collective identity at the international level, however tenuous or fragile, see Deutsch 1954; Deutsch et al. 1957; Krotz 2007, 2010; Ruggie 1998a; Wendt 1994. The same causal connection might help us to comprehend important domestic inhibitors or permittors of the international socialization of states. On "state socialization," note Checkel 2007; Johnston 2008; Wendt 1999, chapters 6 and 7.
13. For compatible findings on the causal connection in the area of U.S. human rights policy, note Moravcsik 2001, 2005; for aspects of U.S. domestic construction during the twentieth century's second half, see Krotz and Sperling 2011.
14. On the Swiss political system and Swiss domestic construction, including some implications for Switzerland in international affairs, note Kriesi and Trechsel 2008; Lane 2001.
15. On remarkably enduring aspects of domestic construction and the implications of such historical domestic construction on foreign and security policy, see Krotz forthcoming.
16. On various perspectives and different explanations for state arming and arms production, see Buzan and Herring 1998; Eyre and Suchman 1996; Jones 2007, chapter 5; Krause 1995; Kurth 1973, 1995; Moravcsik 1991; Sagan 1996/97.
17. On such "anthropomorphization" of the state for analytic or conceptual reasons, and the "society of states," note especially Bull 1977; Bull and Watson 1984; Krasner 1978, 2009; and Wendt 1999; on "corporate identity," treating states as purposive actors, and "states are people, too," see especially Wendt 1999, chapter 5.
18. On levels of analysis matters and the role of domestic politics in international affairs, see Evangelista 1997; Fearon 1998; Gourevitch 2002; Singer 1961; Waltz 1959.
19. For some steps in this direction, and some hypotheses and initial findings, see Krotz 2002a, 5–8; Krotz 2007, 389–390 and 400–404; Krotz 2010, 151–155 and 168–177.

20. For such work in the realist vein, whether predominantly or entirely conceived in material terms or whether including variables such as intentions or perceptions of intentions, on the distribution of capabilities in the system, geography, or offense-defense balance, most importantly compare Mearsheimer 2001; Van Evera 1999; Walt 1987; Waltz 1979.

21. See, for example, Meyer et al. 1997; Scott and Meyer 1994; Thomas et al. 1987; for an overview, see Finnemore 1996b.

22. Notably see Bull 1977; Bull and Watson 1984; Dunne 1998; Reus-Smit 1999.

23. Wendt 1999, chapter 6. In a related perspective of "systemic constructivism," John Ruggie examines the institutionalization of "embedded liberalism" in the post-war international economy and the nature and effects of multilateralism as social form. Ruggie 1983, 1993.

24. On the former, note Barnett and Finnemore 2004; Finnemore 1996a; Keohane 1984, 1989a; on the latter, see Deudney and Ikenberry 1999; Ikenberry 2001, 2009.

25. Goertz and Diehl 1993; Thompson 2001. Whereas all of these research strands focus on some kind of institutionalization or construction in the international sphere and its causal implications, it is striking that most of them devote little attention to interrelating such system-level endeavors with factors from the other grand sources, or making connections across levels of analysis. A notable recent exception is "neoclassical realism," which begins from the formally anarchic international system materially conceived, then adds a great variety of factors from domestic politics broadly. See Lobell et al. 2009; Rose 1998.

26. Commonly, "domestic constructivists" employ one or more domestically constructed phenomena as independent variable(s) to explain a wide range of international or foreign policy outcomes. For various types of domestic construction and implications in a great variety of states and times note, for example, Abdelal 2001; Berger 1998; Hopf 2002; Johnston 1995; Katzenstein 1996b; Kier 1997; McNamara 1999; Parsons 2006. For the analytic value of domestic construction for comparative foreign policy analysis, see Krotz forthcoming.

27. Certain similarities between the French and the American domestic construction of international roles and ambitions, for example, seems an underlying cause for recurrent tensions in the relations between the two states. Compare Krotz and Sperling 2011.

28. Scrutinizing the nature and impact of the domestic features of state, society, and state-society relations has been the turf of scholars of comparative politics and comparative foreign policy. For a brief discussion of aspects of these literatures and their import for this book's inquiries, see chapter 2.

29. On United States-Britain, see, for example, Baylis 1981; Danchev 1998; Dumbrell 2006; Hollowell 2001; Louis and Bull 1986; Svendsen 2010; on Australia-New Zealand, see Ayson 2007; Ball 1986; on United States-Israel, see Ben-Zvi 1993; Schoenbaum 1993; Stephens 2006; U.S. Department of State 2007; on Spain-France, see Spain-France Forum 2008; on Germany-Israel, see BBC 2008; Feldman 1984; Pallade 2005; Wolffsohn 1993. In addition, Germany has over time established regularized intergovernmental relations with several states of particular importance for the country, such as Italy, Spain, Poland, Russia, and, most recently, China. Compare Krotz 2010. Especially Germany's relations with Poland have persistently included various symbolic acts and practices as well as an expanding web of parapublic underpinnings. On the tight and intensified coordination of EU and other policies among the Benelux countries as a trilateral example of regularized intergovernmentalism, see Stein 1990; Wouters and Vidal 2008, 3–26.

30. Compare Barrat and Moisei 2004; Brysk et al. 2002; Majza 2005; McIntyre 1978, 2009; Roy and Galinsoga 1997; Srinivasan 2008; Weaver 1998.

31. Aron 1983, 454–455.

32. For (pan-)European integration in foreign policy, security, and defense, which only began to gain real momentum during the second half of the 1990s, see Howorth and Keeler 2003; Jones 2007; Krotz 2009; Krotz and Maher 2011a; Smith 2004; Wallace 2005.

33. For a comprehensive discussion of the factors and forces working for and against Europe's emergence as a coherent actor in the areas of foreign policy, security, and defense, see Krotz 2009; for Europe in the world and Europe's foreign relations in the emergent post-post-Cold War world broadly, see Krotz and Maher 2011b.

34. For French, German, and European international relations and foreign affairs within the wider contexts of either Cold War or post-Cold War politics, see, for example, DePorte 1987; Haglund 1991; Katzenstein 2005; Risse-Kappen 1995; Trachtenberg 1999.

Appendix

1. Bundesrechnungshof der Bundesrepublik Deutschland 1998, 5.
2. *Archiv der Gegenwart* 1983, 272209.
3. *Archiv der Gegenwart* 1984, 27726. The accord itself is reprinted in Louet 1986.
4. Kessler 1988, 274; *Le Monde*, November 13, 1987, 4.
5. Carrez 2004 (October 13), 108.
6. *Les Echos*, March 25, 2002, 13; OCCAR-EA 2006, 16; *Wehrpolitik* 2002.
7. Fourgous 2009, 70.
8. Aerospaceweb.org 2008; Carrez 2004 (October 13), 108.
9. Leimbacher 1992, 100; Bundesrechnungshof der Bundesrepublik Deutschland 1998, 15.
10. Brühmann 1995; Heckmann 1993; *Soldat und Technik* 1991.
11. Brühmann 1995; Bundesrechnungshof der Bundesrepublik Deutschland 1998; Prämaßing 1996.

BIBLIOGRAPHY

Abdelal, Rawi. 2001. *National Purpose in the World Economy: Post-Soviet States in Comparative Perspective.* Ithaca, NY: Cornell University Press.

Abdelal, Rawi, and Jonathan Kirshner. 1999/2000. Strategy, Economic Relations and the Definition of National Interests. *Security Studies* 9(1–2):119–156.

Aerospaceweb.org, Aircraft Museum. 2008. Eurocopter Tiger, Tigre Attack Helicopter, accessible at <http://www.aerospaceweb.org/aircraft/helicopter-m/tiger/>; (accessed April 4, 2008).

Alich, Holger. 2007. Aschenputtel im Fliegerland, *Handelsblatt*, June 19, 2007, 10.

Archiv der Gegenwart. 1983. Bundesrepublik Deutschland, Frankreich: 42. Deutsch-Französische Konsultationen. *Archiv der Gegenwart* 53:27207–27209.

Archiv der Gegenwart. 1984. Die 43. Deutsch-Französischen Konsultationen in Rambouillet. *Archiv der Gegenwart* 54:27726–27727.

Aron, Raymond. 1983. *Mémoires: 50 Ans de Réflexion Politique.* Paris: Julliard.

Aubert, Vianney. 1996a. Coopération Franco-Allemande Renforcée, *Le Figaro*, October 3, 1996, 3.

Aubert, Vianney. 1996b. Turbulences autour du Tigre: Les Incertidues autour du Budget Allemand de la Défense Menacent l'Avenir de Plusiers Programmes Franco-Allemands, comme l'Hélicoptère Tigre, *Le Figaro*, July 9, 1996, 5.

Aubert, Vianney. 1999. Première Commande pour le Tigre, *Le Figaro*, June 18, 1999, 6.

Australian National Audit Office, The Auditor General. 2006. Management of the Tiger Armed Reconnaissance Helicopter—Air 87: Department of Defence, Defence Material Organisation (ANAO Audit Report No. 36 2005–06), edited by Australian National Audit Office: Commonwealth of Australia.

Ayson, Robert. 2007. *Australia-New Zealand.* In *Australia as an Asia Pacific Regional Power: Friendship in Flux?*, edited by Brendan Taylor. New York: Routledge.

Ball, Desmond. 1986. The Security Relationship between Australia and New Zealand. In *The ANZAC Connection*, edited by Desmond Ball. Sydney: Unwin Hyman.

Banchoff, Thomas. 1996. Historical Memory and German Foreign Policy: The Cases of Adenauer and Brandt. *German Politics and Society* 14(2):36–53.

Baring, Arnulf. 1997. Die Gartenlandschaft Europas: Außenpolitische Denkschulen in der Gegenwärtigen Debatte, *Frankfurter Allgemeine Zeitung*, February 14, 1997, 9.

Barnett, Michael, and Martha Finnemore. 2004. *Rules for the World: International Organizations in Global Politics.* Ithaca, NY: Cornell University Press.

Barrat, Jacques, and Claudia Moisei. 2004. *Géopolitique de la Francophonie: Un Nouveau Souffle?* Paris: Etudes de la Documentation Française.

Baums, Rainer. 1992. Die Deutsch-Französischen Beziehungen von 1969–1982 unter besonderer Berücksichtigung der Sicherheitspolitik. Ph.D. Thesis, Rheinische Friedrich-Wilhelm Universität Bonn.

Baylis, John. 1981. *Anglo-American Defence Relations 1939–1980.* New York: St. Martin's Press.

BBC. 2008. Israel Upgrades Ties with Germany," available at BBC Online News (March 17) <http://news.bbc.co.uk/2/hi/middle_east/7300691.stm>; (accessed June 8, 2008).

Beaulieu, Jean-Claude. 2005 (October 12). Assemblée Nationale, Avis Number 2572, edited by Assemblée Nationale. Paris: Assemblée Nationale.

Becker, Kurt. 1983. Eine Vernunftehe aus Neigung: Zwanzig Jahre Deutsch-Französischer Vertrag. Für beide Länder ist er inzwischen zum Kern ihrer Außenpolitik Geworden, *Die Zeit,* January 14, 1983, 3.

Bée, François, Olivier Legrand, and Jean Hamiot. 2004. Les Projets de Char Franco-Allemand. In *Histoire de la Coopération Européenne dans l'Armement,* edited by Jean-Paul Hébert, and Jean Hamiot, 57–66. Paris: CNRS.

Ben-Zvi, Abraham. 1993. *The United States and Israel: The Limits of the Special Relationship.* New York: Columbia University Press.

Bennett, Andrew, and Colin Elman. 2006. Qualitative Research: Recent Developments in Case Study Methods. *Annual Review of Political Science* 9:455–476.

Berger, Thomas. 1998. *Cultures of Antimilitarism: National Security in Germany and Japan.* Baltimore: Johns Hopkins University Press.

Berlioz, France. 1995. Les Britanniques Boycottent l'Europe, *L'Humanité,* July 17, 1995, 5.

Bigay, Jean-François. 1992. Deutsch-Französischer Schwebeflug, *Frankfurter Allgemeine Zeitung,* June 15. 1992, 34.

Bittner, Gustav A. 1986. Eine Positive Bilanz. In *Deutsch-Französische Sicherheitspolitik,* edited by Karl Kaiser and Pierre Lellouche, 113–128. Bonn: Europa Union Verlag.

Bock, Hans Manfred. 1989. Deutsch-Französischer Bilateralismus zwischen Begegnungsroutine und ungleicher Kooperation. *Lendemains* 54:158–166.

Brooks, Stephen G. 2005. *Producing Security: Multinational Corporations, Globalization, and the Changing Calculus of Conflict.* Princeton, NJ: Princeton University Press.

Brühmann, Wolfgang. 1995. Unterstützungshubschrauber Tiger/UHU. *Wehrtechnik* 27(7):20–25.

Brysk, Alison, Craig Parsons, and Wayne Sandholtz. 2002. After Empire: National Identity and Post-Colonial Families of Nations. *European Journal of International Relations* 8(2):267–305.

Bull, Hedley. 1977. *The Anarchical Society: A Study of Order in World Politics.* New York: Columbia University Press.

Bull, Hedley, and Adam Watson, eds. 1984. *The Expansion of International Society.* New York: Oxford University Press.

Bundesministerium der Verteidigung. 2003a. Deutsch-Französische Ausbildungseinrichtung hat Modellcharakter für Europa (Speech Given by Federal Minister of Defense, Peter Struck on September 26, 2003), accessible at <http://www.bmvg.de/archiv/reden/minister/030926_fassberg_rede.php>; (accessed September 29, 2003).

Bundesministerium der Verteidigung. 2003b. Deutsch-Französische Ausbildungseinrichtung ist eine große Chance für Faßberg, accessible at <http://www.bmvg.de/archiv/reden/minister/030926_fassberg.php>; (accessed September 29, 2003).

Bundesrechnungshof der Bundesrepublik Deutschland. 1998. Mitteilung an das Bundesministerium der Verteidigung über die Prüfung der Entwicklung und Beschaffung des Unterstützungshubschrauber Tiger (UH-Tiger) Az.: IV 6-1998-0006, 37pp. Bonn: Bundesrechnungshof der Bundesrepublik Deutschland.

Bundeswehr, Press Release (September 27, 2003). 2003. "Tiger"—Training in Faßberg und Le Luc. <http://www.bundeswehr.de/forces/heer/030927_tiger_fassberg.php>; (accessed September 29, 2003).

Burchill, Scott. 2005. *The National Interest in International Relations Theory.* New York: Palgrave Macmillan.

Buzan, Barry, and Eric Herring. 1998. *The Arms Dynamic in World Politics.* Boulder, CO: Lynne Rienner.

Cabirol, Michel. 2001. Eurocopter Peine à Vendre le Tigre aux Espagnols, *La Tribune,* December 18, 2001, 13.

Cabirol, Michel. 2002. L'Armée Espagnole devrait Choisir l'Hélicoptère Tigre, *La Tribune*, June 26, 2002, 13.

Cabirol, Michel. 2003a. L'Espagne Choisit l'Hélicoptère Tigre, *La Tribune*, September 8, 2003, 12.

Cabirol, Michel. 2003b. Madrid est prêt à Signer pour le Tigre, *La Tribune*, July 4, 2003, 14.

Cabirol, Michel. 2005a. Eurocopter Boucle une Année Historique, *La Tribune*, December 19, 2005, 10.

Cabirol, Michel. 2005b. Eurocopter sous Pression sur les Programmes Tigre et NH-90, *La Tribune*, November 8, 2005, 14.

Calleo, David P., and Eric R. Staal, eds. 1998. *Europe's Franco-German Engine*. Washington, DC: Brookings Institution Press.

Capoccia, Giovanni, and R. Daniel Kelemen. 2007. The Study of Critical Junctures: Theory, Narrative, and Counterfactuals in Historical Institutionalism. *World Politics* 59(3): 341–369.

Carrez, Gilles. 2004 (October 13). Rapport Number 1863, Annexe Number 39, Défense, edited by Assemblée Nationale. Paris: Assemblée Nationale.

Casamayou, Jean-Pierre. 1993. Hélicoptères de Combat: Les Atouts du Tigre. *Air and Cosmos/ Aviation Magazine* 1413:36–38.

Casdorff, Stephan-Andreas. 1987. Wörner und Giraud einig über Rüstungsprojekt: Der Entwicklung des Deutsch-Französischen Panzerabwehr-Hubschraubers PAH-2 steht Nichts Mehr im Wege, *Süddeutsche Zeitung*, July 17, 1987, 6.

Cerny, Philip G. 1986. *Une Politique de Grandeur: Aspects Idéologique de la Politique Extérieure de de Gaulle*. Paris: Flammarion.

Cerny, Philip G. 1994. Review of "A Certain Idea of France: French Security Policy and the Gaullist Legacy" by Philip H. Gordon. *French Politics and Society* 12(1):99–101.

Checkel, Jeffrey T. 1998. The Constructivist Turn in International Relations Theory. *World Politics* 50(2):324–348.

Checkel, Jeffrey T., ed. 2007. *International Institutions and Socialization in Europe*. New York: Cambridge University Press.

Checkel, Jeffrey T. 2008. Process Tracing. In *Qualitative Methods in International Relations: A Pluralist Guide*, edited by Audie Klotz and Deepa Prakash, 114–129. New York: Palgrave Macmillan.

Chirac, Jacques. 2005. Allocution du Président de la République à l'École Franco-Allemande "Tigre" au Luc en Provence (April 19, 2005). Press release of the Elysée Palace, <http:// www.elysee.fr/elysee/root/bank/print/29416.htm>; (accessed April 25, 2005).

Collier, David, and James Mahoney. 1996. Insights and Pitfalls: Selection Bias in Qualitative Work. *World Politics* 49(1):56–91.

Croizé, Jean-Paul, and Thierry d'Athis. 1991. Un Tigre au Salon: L'Hélicoptère Franco-Allemand en Vedette au Bourget, *Le Figaro*, June 18, 1991, 12.

Culpepper, Pepper D., Peter A. Hall, and Bruno Palier. 2006. *Changing France: The Politics That Markets Make*. New York: Palgrave Macmillan.

Danchev, Alex. 1998. *On Specialness: Essays in Anglo-American Relations*. New York: Palgrave Macmillan.

d'Athis, Thierry, and Jean-Paul Croizé. 1991. Bonn Renoncerait au Tigre, *Le Figaro*, November 5, 1991, 3.

Darcourt, Pierre. 1987a. Hélicoptère Franco-Allemand: L'Accord Paris-Bonn, *Le Figaro*, March 30, 1987, 3.

Darcourt, Pierre. 1987b. Une Étape Importante Vers le Marché Commun de l'Armement: Un Hélicoptère de Combat Franco-Allemand, *Le Figaro*, July 17, 1987, 5.

de Gaulle, Charles. 1954. *Mémoires de Guerre (Tome I): L'Appel 1940–1942*. Paris: Plon.

de Gaulle, Charles. 1970. *Mémoires d'Espoir (Tome I): Le Renouveau 1958–1962*. Paris: Plon.

De Grandi, Michel. 2003. Eurocopter bien Décidé à Relancer sa Coopération avec la Chine, *Les Echos*, September 30, 2003, 29.

de Montbrial, Thierry. 1989. Die Außenpolitik Frankreichs. *Europa Archiv* 44(10):283–290.

de Murville, Maurice Couve. 1983. Vortrag von Couve de Murville bei der Deutschen Gesellschaft für Auswärtige Politik am 25. Januar. Bonn: DGAP.

de Weck, Roger. 1997. Das Netz Fester Knüpfen!, *Die Zeit*, November 14, 1997, 3.

Défense et Sécurité Nationale: Le Livre Blanc (Volumes 1 and 2). 2008. Préface de Nicolas Sarkozy, Président de la République. Paris: Odile Jacob/La Doumentation Française.

Delattre, Lucas. 1997. Le Double Discours Franco-Allemand, *Le Monde*, December 11, 1997, 12.

Delmas, Philippe. 1999. *De la Prochaine Guerre avec l'Allemagne*. Paris: Éditions Odile Jacob.

Delors, Jacques, ed. 1998. *France-Allemagne: Le Bond en Avant*. Paris: Éditions Odile Jacob.

DePorte, Andrew. 1987. *Europe between the Superpowers*. Second Edition. New Haven, CT: Yale University Press.

DePorte, A.W. 1991. The Foreign Policy of the Fifth Republic: Between the Nation and the World. In *Searching for the New France*, edited by James F. Hollifield and George Ross, 221–274. New York: Routledge.

Deudney, Daniel and G. John Ikenberry. 1999. The Nature and Sources of Liberal International Order. *Review of International Studies* 25(2):179–196.

Deutsch, Karl W. 1953. *Nationalism and Social Communication: An Inquiry into the Foundations of Nationality*. Cambridge, MA: MIT Press.

Deutsch, Karl W. 1954. *Political Community at the International Level: Problems of Definition and Measurement*. Garden City, NY: Doubleday.

Deutsch, Karl W. 1963. *The Nerves of Government: Models of Political Communication and Control*. London: Collier-Macmillan.

Deutsch, Karl W. 1969. *Nationalism and Its Alternatives*. New York: Knopf.

Deutsch, Karl W., Sidney A. Burrell, Robert A. Kann, Jr. Maurice Lee, Martin Lichterman, Raymond E. Lindgren, Francis L. Loewenheim, and Richard W. Van Wagenen. 1957. *Political Community in the North Atlantic Area: International Organization in the Light of Historical Experience*. Princeton, NJ: Princeton University Press.

Deutsch-Französisches Institut, and Deutsche Frankreich-Bibliothek, eds. 1995 (and after). *Deutsch-Französische Konsultationsgespräche seit 1963 (Dokumentation)*. Ludwigsburg: DFI.

Doyle, Michael W. 1997. *Ways of War and Peace: Realism, Liberalism, and Socialism*. New York: Norton.

Drezner, Daniel W. 2007. *All Politics Is Global: Explaining International Regulatory Regimes*. Princeton, NJ: Princeton University Press.

Duffield, John S. 1999. *World Power Forsaken: Political Culture, International Institutions, and German Security Policy after Unification*. Stanford, CA: Stanford University Press.

Duhamel, Olivier. 2009. *Droit Constitutionnel et Institutions Politiques*. Paris: Éditions du Seuil.

Dumbrell, John. 2006. *A Special Relationship: Anglo-American Relations from the Cold War to Iraq*. Second Edition. New York: Palgrave Macmillan.

Dunn, James A. Jr. 1995. The French Highway Lobby: A Case Study in State-Society Relations and Policymaking. *Comparative Politics* 27(3):275–295.

Dunne, Timothy. 1998. *Inventing International Society: A History of the English School*. New York: St. Martin's Press.

Duverger, Maurice. 1974. *La Monarchie Républicaine*. Paris: Laffont.

EADS, Press Release. 2005 (December 5). Tiger HAD Contract for France and Spain Signed in Bonn. Available from <http://www.eads.net/web/printout/de/1024/content>; (accessed August 3, 2006).

EADS, Press Release. 2006 (August 10). Eurocopter Displays Combat Support Helicopter at ILA 2006. Available from <http://www.eads.com/web/printout/en/1024/content>; (accessed August 16, 2006).

EADS, Press Release. 2006 (January 18). Business Year 2005 Brings Considerably Expanded Order Book for Eurocopter. Available from <http://www.eads.net/web/printout/de/1024/content>; (accessed August 3, 2006).

Ellwein, Thomas, and Joachim Jens Hesse. 1987. *Das Regierungssystem der Bundesrepublik Deutschland*. Opladen: Westdeutscher Verlag.

Eurocopter, Press Release. 2005 (March 18). Eurocopter Salue l'Acceptation Officielle du Premier Tigre HAP par la Délégation Générale pour l'Armament. Mariagne: Eurocpoter.

Evangelista, Matthew. 1997. Domestic Structure and International Change. In *New Thinking in International Relations Theory*, edited by Michael W. Doyle and G. John Ikenberry, 202–228. Boulder, CO: Westview Press.

Evangelista, Matthew. 1999. *Unarmed Forces: The Transnational Movement to End the Cold War*. Ithaca, NY: Cornell University Press.

Evans, Peter B., Dietrich Rueschemeyer, and Theda Skocpol, eds. 1985. *Bringing the State Back In*. New York: Cambridge University Press.

Eyre, Dana P., and Mark C. Suchman. 1996. Status, Norms, and the Proliferation of Conventional Weapons: An Institutional Theory Approach. In *The Culture of National Security*, edited by Peter J. Katzenstein, 79–113. New York: Columbia University Press.

Fearon, James D. 1991. Counterfactuals and Hypothesis Testing in Political Science, *World Politics* 43(2):169–195.

Fearon, James D. 1998. Domestic Politics, Foreign Policy, and Theories of International Relations. *Annual Review of Political Science* 1(1):289–313.

Feldman, Lily Gardner. 1984. *The Special Relationship Between West Germany and Israel*. London: George Allen & Unwin.

Feldmeyer, Karl. 1996. Paris Kürzt, Bonn Spart: Neue Risiken für ein Gemeinsames Rüstungsvorhaben, *Frankfurter Allgemeine Zeitung*, May 11, 1996, 12.

Filser, Nicolas. 1996. *La Cooperation Militaire Franco-Allemande et le Couple Mitterrand-Kohl*. Mémoire. Saint-Cyr: Ecole Speciale Militaire de Saint-Cyr.

Finnemore, Martha. 1996a. *National Interests in International Society*. Ithaca, NY: Cornell University Press.

Finnemore, Martha. 1996b. Norms, Culture, and World Politics: Insights from Sociology's Institutionalism. *International Organization* 50(2):325–347.

Flynn, Gregory, ed. 1995. *Remaking the Hexagon: The New France in the New Europe*. Boulder, CO: Westview Press.

Fourgous, Jean-Michel. 2009. Projet de Loi des Finances pour 2009 (Défense: Préparation de l'Avenir). Paris: Assemblée Nationale, Rapport 1198, Annexe 10.

Franco, Alain. 1995. Les Pays-Bas Continuent d'Hésiter entre le Tigre et l'Apache, *Le Monde*, January 31, 1995, 3.

Frank, Birgit. 1991. Die Flexibilität der Französischen Sicherheits-und Verteidigungskonzeption am Ende des Kalten Krieges. Diplomarbeit, Friedrich-Alexander Universität Erlangen-Nürnberg.

Friend, Julius W. 1991. *The Linchpin: French-German Relations, 1950–1990*. New York: Praeger.

Gareis, Sven. 2008. Die Zusammenarbeit zwischen Deutschland und Frankreich—Ein Überblick. In *Vereint Marschieren—Marcher Uni: Die Deutsch-Französische Streitkräfteko-operation als Paradigma Europäischer Streitkräfte?*, edited by Nina Leonhard, and Sven Gareis. Wiesbaden: Verlag für Sozialwissenschaften.

Genscher, Hans-Dietrich. 1981. *Deutsche Aussenpolitik: Ausgewählte Grundsatzreden, 1975–1980*. Stuttgart: Bonn Aktuell.

Genscher, Hans-Dietrich. 1995. *Erinnerungen*. Berlin: Siedler.

George, Alexander L., and Andrew Bennett. 2005. *Case Studies and Theory Development in the Social Sciences*. Cambridge, MA: MIT Press.

George, Alexander L., and Robert O. Keohane. 1980. The Concept of National Interests: Uses and Limitations. In *Presidential Decisionmaking in Foreign Policy: The Effective Use of Information and Advice*, edited by Alexander L. George, 217–237. Boulder, CO: Westview Press.

Gerring, John. 2007. *Case Study Research: Principles and Practices*. New York: Cambridge University Press.

Gilpin, Robert. 1987. *The Political Economy of International Relations*. Princeton, NJ: Princeton University Press.

Gilpin, Robert. 2001. *Global Political Economy: Understanding the International Economic Order.* Princeton, NJ: Princeton University Press.

Gladstone, David. 1986. The Role of the Three Civil Services. In *Partners and Rivals in Western Europe: Britain, France and Germany,* edited by Roger Morgan and Caroline Bray, 102–119. Aldershot: Gower.

Goertz, Gary. 2006. *Social Science Concepts: A User's Guide.* Princeton, NJ: Princeton University Press.

Goertz, Gary, and Paul F. Diehl. 1993. Enduring Rivalries: Theoretical Constructs and Empirical Patterns. *International Studies Quarterly* 37(2):147–171.

Gordon, Philip H. 1993. *A Certain Idea of France: French Security Policy and the Gaullist Legacy.* Princeton, NJ: Princeton University Press.

Gordon, Philip H. 1995. *France, Germany, and the Western Alliance.* Boulder, CO: Westview Press.

Gourevitch, Peter. 2002. Domestic Politics and International Relations. In *Handbook of International Relations,* edited by Walter Carlsnaes, Thomas Risse, and Beth A. Simmons, 309–328. Thousand Oaks, CA: Sage.

Gouvernement de France. 2003. A l'École du Tigre: La Future Ecole Franco-Allemande. In *Dossier Defactu, No. 136,* <http://www.defense.gouv.fr/actualities/publications/defactu/n136/dossier.html>; (accessed February 11, 2003).

Grosser, Alfred. 1988. Die Grundsätzliche Klärung Steht Noch Aus: Deutsch-Französische Beziehung 25 Jahre nach dem Elysée-Vertrag, *Frankfurter Allgemeine Zeitung,* January 21, 1988, 9.

Guérin-Sendelbach, Valérie. 1993. *Ein Tandem für Europa? Die Deutsch-Französische Zusammenarbeit der Achtziger Jahre.* Bonn: Europa Union Verlag.

Guhl, Jean-Michel. 2009. French Tigers in Afghanistan. *Avionics Magazine* December 2009, accessible at <http://www.aviationtoday.com/av/issue/feature/French-Tigers-In-Afghanistan_36862.html>; (accessed May 10, 2010).

Guisnel, Jean. 1986a. Un Rapport au Bazooka Contre l'Hélicpotère Franco-Allemand, *Libération,* July 3, 1986, 9.

Guisnel, Jean. 1986b. L'Hélicoptère Franco-Allemand a du Mal à Décoller, *Libération,* May 12, 1986, 14.

Guisnel, Jean. 1987a. France et RFA font l'Hélico Ensemble, *Libération,* July 17, 1987, 8.

Guisnel, Jean. 1987b. Hélico Franco-Allemand: Le Coût de Retard, *Libération,* April 10, 1987, 3.

Guisnel, Jean. 1987c. L'Hélico Franco-Allemand se Porte Pâle, *Libération,* June 8, 1987, 6.

Guisnel, Jean. 1987d. Le Forcing de l'Aérospatiale pour Sauver l'Hélicoptère Franco-Allemand, *Libération,* June 18, 1987, 9.

Guisnel, Jean. 1989. Les Britanniques Veulent Monter dans l'Hélicoptère Franco-Allemand, *Libération,* January 6, 1989, 11.

Guzzini, Stefano. 2004. The Enduring Dilemmas of Realism in International Relations. *European Journal of International Relations* 10(4):533–568.

Hacke, Christian. 1996. Nationales Interesse als Handlungsmaxime für die Außenpolitik Deutschlands. In *Deutschlands Neue Außenpolitik. Band 3: Interessen und Strategien,* edited by Karl Kaiser, and Joachim Krause, 3–13. Munich: Oldenbourg.

Haftendorn, Helga. 1993. Führungsmacht Deutschland? Ein Rückblick auf die Rolle der Deutschen in Europa. In *Was Ändert die Einheit? Deutschlands Standort in Europa,* edited by Werner Weidenfeld, 31–43. Gütersloh: Verlag Bertelsmann Stiftung.

Haftendorn, Helga, Wolf-Dieter Karl, Joachim Krause, and Lothar Wilker, eds. 1978. *Verwaltete Außenpolitik: Sicherheits-und Entspannungspolitische Entscheidungsprozesse in Bonn.* Cologne: Verlag Wissenschaft und Politik.

Haftendorn, Helga, Robert O. Keohane, and Celeste A. Wallander, eds. 1999. *Imperfect Unions: Security Institutions over Time and Space.* New York: Oxford University Press.

Haglund, David G. 1991. *Alliance within the Alliance? Franco-German Military Cooperation and the European Pillar of Defense.* Boulder, CO: Westview Press.

Hall, Peter A. 1986. *Governing the Economy: The Politics of State Intervention in Britain and France.* New York: Oxford University Press.

Hall, Peter A. 2003. Aligning Ontology and Methodology in Comparative Research. In *Comparative Historical Analysis in the Social Sciences,* edited by James Mahoney and Dietrich Rueschemeyer, 373–404. New York: Cambridge University Press.

Hall, Peter A., and Rosemary C. R. Taylor. 1996. Political Science and the Three New Institutionalisms. *Political Studies* 44(5):936–957.

Harnisch, Sebastian, and Hanns W. Maull, eds. 2001. *Germany as a Civilian Power? The Foreign Policy of the Berlin Republic.* Manchester: Manchester University Press.

Heckmann, Erhard. 1993. Tiger als Mehrzweckkampfhubschrauber. *Wehrtechnik* 25(1):17–18.

Hellmann, Gunther. 1996. Goodbye Bismarck? The Foreign Policy of Contemporary Germany. *Mershon International Studies Review* 40:1–39.

Hellmann, Gunther. 1997. Jenseits von "Normalisierung" und "Militarisierung": Zur Standortdebatte über die Neue Deutsche Außenpolitik. *Aus Politik und Zeitgeschichte* (B 1–2/97):24–33.

Hellmann, Gunther, Christian Weber, and Frank Sauer, eds. 2008. *Die Semantik der Neuen Deutschen Aussenpolitik.* Wiesbaden: VS Verlag.

Hermann, Margaret G. 1987. Foreign Policy Role Orientations and the Quality of Foreign Policy Decisions. In *Role Theory and Foreign Policy Analysis,* edited by Stephen G. Walker, 123–140. Durham, NC: Duke University Press.

Hoffmann, Stanley, ed. 1963. *In Search of France.* New York: Harper and Row.

Hoffmann, Stanley. 1987. Liberalism and International Affairs. In *Janus and Minerva: Essays in the Theory and Practice of International Politics,* edited by Stanley Hoffmann, 394–417. Boulder, CO: Westview Press.

Hoffmann, Wolfgang. 1986. Krieg mit der Kasse: Der Deutsch-Französische Panzerhubschrauber wird zum Kostenskandal, *Die Zeit,* March 14, 1986, 40.

Hoffmann, Wolfgang. 1987. Start mit Hindernissen: Ist der Deutsch-Französische Kampfhubschrauber Veraltet? *Die Zeit,* March 27, 1987, 46.

Hollowell, Jonathan. 2001. *Twentieth-Century Anglo-American Relations.* New York: Palgrave Macmillan.

Holsti, Kal J. 1970. National Role Conceptions in the Study of Foreing Policy. *International Studies Quarterly* 14(3):233–309.

Hopf, Ted. 2002. *Social Construction and International Politics: Identities & Foreign Policies, Moscow, 1955 and 1999.* Ithaca, NY: Cornell University Press.

Howorth, Jolyon, and John T.S. Keeler, eds. 2003. *Defending Europe: The EU, NATO, and the Quest for European Autonomy.* New York: Palgrave.

Huebner, Bernd. 1989. The Importance of Arms Exports and Armament Cooperation for the West German Defence Industrial Base. In *The Defence Industrial Base and the West,* edited by David G. Haglund, 119–162. London: Routledge.

Huntington, Samuel P. 1968. *Political Order in Changing Societies.* New Haven, CT: Yale University Press.

Ikenberry, G. John. 2001. *After Victory: Institutions, Strategic Restraint, and the Rebuilding of Order after Major Wars.* Princeton, NJ: Princeton University Press.

Ikenberry, G. John. 2009. Liberal Internationalism 3.0: America and the Dilemmas of Liberal World Order. *Perspectives on Politics* 7(1):71–87.

Immergut, Ellen M. 1990. Institutions, Veto Points, and Policy Results: A Comparative Analysis of Health Care. *Journal of Public Policy* 10(4):391–416.

Immergut, Ellen M. 1992. The Rules of the Game: The Logic of Health Policy-Making in France, Switzerland, and Sweden. In *Structuring Politics: Historical Institutionalism in Comparative Analysis,* edited by Sven Steinmo, Kathleen Thelen, and Frank Longstreth, 57–89. New York: Cambridge University Press.

Isnard, Jacques. 1984. Relance Spectaculaire de la Coopération Militaire Franco-Allemande, *Le Monde,* May 30, 1984, 1, 3.

Isnard, Jacques. 1986. Très Couteux et trop Compliqué: Le Projet d'un Hélicoptère Franco-Allemand dans l'Impasse, *Le Monde*, June 5, 1986, 21.

Isnard, Jacques. 1987a. La Visite de M. Manfred Woerner en France: Paris et Bonn s'engagent à Construire en Commun un Hélicoptère de Combat, *Le Monde*, July 18, 1987, 10.

Isnard, Jacques. 1987b. Une Mise en Garde de M. Giraud aux Industriels: Le Prix de l'Hélicotère Franco-Allemand devra être Révisé à la Baisse, *Le Monde*, June 7–8, 1987, 16.

Isnard, Jacques. 1990a. La France et l'Allemagne Fédérale Réuniront Leurs Fabrications d'Hélicoptères, *Le Monde*, March 28, 1990, 16.

Isnard, Jacques. 1990b. Un Mariage de Raison, *Le Monde*, April 7, 1990, 33.

Isnard, Jacques. 1996a. Bonn Presse Paris de Maintenir Leurs Programmes d'Hélicoptères, *Le Monde*, February 13, 1996, 5.

Isnard, Jacques. 1996b. L'Allemagne et la France Cherchent à Harmoniser Leurs Besoins en Matière d'Armement, *Le Monde*, December 10, 1996, 2.

Isnard, Jacques. 1996c. L'Armée Française Réduirait de Moitié des Commandes d'Hélicoptères, *Le Monde*, June 16–17, 1996, 24.

Isnard, Jacques. 1996d. Malaise autour de la Coopération Franco-Allemande dans l'Armement, *Le Monde*, May 4, 1996, 3.

Isnard, Jacques. 1996e. Relancer la Copération en Matière d'Armement, *Le Monde*, June 6, 1996, 2.

Isnard, Jacques. 1997. Paris et Bonn Lancent l'Indutrialisation de Leur Hélicoptère d'Attaque Tigre, *Le Monde*, June 21, 1997, 22.

Isnard, Jacques. 1999. La Turquie Écarte une Offre d'Hélicoptères Franco-Allemands, *Le Monde*, February 11, 1999, 3.

Isnard, Jacques. 2001. Paris-Berlin et Madrid Préparent un Hélicoptère de Combat Polyvalent, *Le Monde*, July 26, 2001, 3.

Isnard, Jacques. 2003a. L'Hélicoptère Tigre au Cœur de la Coopération Franco-Allemande, *Le Monde*, June 19, 2003, 20.

Isnard, Jacques. 2003b. Paris et Berlin Vont Former en Commun Leurs Équipages d'Hélicoptères Tigre, *Le Monde*, July 12, 2003, 7.

Jepperson, Ronald L. 1991. Institutions, Institutional Effects, and Institutionalism. In *The New Institutionalism in Organizational Analysis*, edited by Walter W. Powell, and Paul J. DiMaggio. Chicago: University of Chicago Press.

Jervis, Robert. 1998. Realism in the Study of World Politics. *International Organization* 52(4):971–991.

Johnston, Alastair Iain. 1995. *Cultural Realism: Strategic Culture and Grand Strategy in Chinese History*. Princeton, NJ: Princeton University Press.

Johnston, Alastair Iain. 2008. *Social States: China in International Institutions, 1980–2000*. Princeton, NJ: Princeton University Press.

Jones, Seth G. 2007. *The Rise of European Security Cooperation*. New York: Cambridge University Press.

Juppé, Alain, and Louis Schweitzer, eds. 2008. *La France et l'Europe dans le Monde: Livre Blanc sur la Politique Étrangère et Européenne de la France 2008–2020*. Paris: Ministry of Foreign Affairs.

Kageneck, A. Graf. 1984. Einigung in Paris über Hubschrauberprojekt. Gipfel: Hernu und Wörner Unterzeichnen Abkommen, *Die Welt*, May 29, 1984, 6.

Kanalmüller, Rudi. 1991. Mit Argwohn den Weg des Tigers Verfolgen: Der Mögliche Export eines Deutsch-Französischen Kampfhubschraubers wirft Fragen auf, *Süddeutsche Zeitung*, March 20, 1991, 3.

Kapstein, Ethan B., and Michael Mastanduno, eds. 1999. *Unipolar Politics: Realism and State Strategies after the Cold War*. New York: Columbia University Press.

Katzenstein, Peter J., ed. 1978. *Between Power and Plenty: Foreign Economic Policies of Advanced Industrial States*. Madison: University of Wisconsin Press.

Katzenstein, Peter J. 1985. *Small States in World Markets: Industrial Policy in Europe*. Ithaca, NY: Cornell University Press.

Katzenstein, Peter J. 1987. *Policy and Politics in West Germany: The Growth of a Semisovereign State*. Philadelphia: Temple University Press.

Katzenstein, Peter J., ed. 1996a. *The Culture of National Security: Norms and Identity in World Politics*. New York: Columbia University Press.

Katzenstein, Peter J. 1996b. *Cultural Norms and National Security*. Ithaca, NY: Cornell University Press.

Katzenstein, Peter J., ed. 1997. *Tamed Power: Germany in Europe*. Ithaca, NY: Cornell University Press.

Katzenstein, Peter J. 2005. *A World of Regions: Asia and Europe in the American Imperium*. Ithaca, NY: Cornell University Press.

Katznelson, Ira, and Barry R. Weingast, eds. 2005. *Preferences and Situations: Points of Intersection between Historical and Rational Choice Institutionalism*. New York: Russell Sage.

Keohane, Robert O. 1983. The Demand for International Regimes. In *International Regimes*, edited by Stephen D. Krasner, 141–171. Ithaca, NY: Cornell University Press.

Keohane, Robert O. 1984. *After Hegemony: Cooperation and Discord in the World Political Economy*. Princeton, NJ: Princeton University Press.

Keohane, Robert O. 1989a. *International Institutions and State Power: Essays in International Relations Theory*. Boulder, CO: Westview Press.

Keohane, Robert O. 1989b. International Institutions: Two Approaches. In *International Institutions and State Power. Essays in International Relations Theory*, edited by Robert O. Keohane, 158–179. Boulder, CO: Westview Press.

Keohane, Robert O. 1989c. Neoliberal Institutionalism: A Perspective on World Politics. In *International Institutions and State Power. Essays in International Relations Theory*, edited by Robert O. Keohane, 1–20. Boulder, CO: Westview Press.

Kerdraon, Jean-Noël. 1999 (December 7). Assemblée Nationale, Avis No. 260, Présenté au Nom de la Commission de la Défense Nationale et des Forces Armée Portent Creation de l'Organisation Conjointe de Coopération en Matiére d'Armament (Occar), edited by Assemblée Nationale. Paris: Assemblée Nationale.

Kessler, Michael. 1988. Die Zusammenarbeit in der Rüstung. *Dokumente: Zeitschrift für den deutsch-französischen Dialog* 44(4):272–276.

Kier, Elizabeth. 1997. *Imagining War: French and British Military Doctrine between the Wars*. Princeton, NJ: Princeton University Press.

King, Gary, Robert O. Keohane, and Sidney Verba. 1994. *Designing Social Inquiry: Scientific Inference in Qualitative Research*. Princeton, NJ: Princeton University Press.

Kinkel, Klaus. 1998. Urlaub von der Geschichte gibt es Nicht: An die Stelle des Kalten Krieges ist die Herausforderung der Globalisierung Getreten, *Frankfurter Allgemeine Zeitung*, August 26, 1998, 13.

Kirshner, Jonathan. 1999. The Political Economy of Realism. In *Unipolar Politics: Realism and State Strategies after the Cold War*, edited by Ethan B. Kapstein, and Michael Mastanduno, 69–102. New York: Columbia University Press.

Kocs, Stephen A. 1995. *Autonomy or Power? The Franco-German Relationship and Europe's Strategic Choices, 1955–1995*. Westport, CT: Praeger.

Kohl, Helmut. 1984 (1983)-a. Erklärung (des Deutschen Bundeskanzlers Helmut Kohl) zum Abschluß der 42. Deutsch-Französischen Konsultationen in Bonn am 25. November 1983. *Europa Archiv* 39(2):D48-D49.

Kohl, Helmut. 1984 (1983)-b. Tischrede (des Deutschen Bundeskanzlers Helmut Kohl) aus Anlaß der 42. Deutsch-Französischen Konsultationen in Bonn am 24. November 1983. *Europa Archiv* 39(2):D43-D46.

Kohl, Helmut. 1988. Ansprache des Bundeskanzlers Helmut Kohl zum 25. Jahrestag des Deutsch-Französischen Vertrages am 22. Januar in Paris. *Bulletin: Presse-und Informationsamt der Bundesregierung* 1988 (11):77–81.

Kohl, Helmut, and François Mitterrand. 1982. Gemeinsame Pressekonferenz des Bundeskanzlers der Bundesrepublik Deutschland, Helmut Kohl, und des Französischen Staatspräsidenten,

François Mitterrand, in Bonn zm 22. Oktober 1982 nach Zweitägigen Bilateralen Konsultationen. *Europa Archiv* 37(24):D627-D630.

Koremenos, Barbara, Charles Lipson, and Duncan Snidal, eds. 2004. *The Rational Design of International Institutions.* New York: Cambridge University Press.

Kramer, Steven Philip. 1991. La Question Française. *Politique Étrangère* 56(4):959–974.

Krasner, Stephen D. 1978. *Defending the National Interest: Raw Materials Investment and U.S. Foreign Policy.* Princeton, NJ: Princeton University Press.

Krasner, Stephen D. 1999. *Sovereignty: Organized Hypocrisy.* Princeton, NJ: Princeton University Press.

Krasner, Stephen D. 2009. Defending the National Interest. In *Power, the State, and Sovereignty: Essays on International Relations,* edited by Stephen D. Krasner, 25–35. New York: Routledge.

Kratochwil, Friedrich V. 1989. *Rules, Norms, and Decisions: On the Conditions of Practical and Legal Reasoning in International Relations and Domestic Affairs.* New York: Cambridge University Press.

Krause, Keith. 1995. *Arms and the State: Patterns of Military Production and Trade.* New York: Cambridge University Press.

Kriesi, Hanspeter. 1994. *Les Démocraties Occidentales: Une Approche Comparée.* Paris: Economica.

Kriesi, Hanspeter, and Alexander Trechsel. 2008. *The Politics of Switzerland: Continuity and Change in a Consensus Democracy.* New York: Cambridge University Press.

Krotz, Ulrich. 2002a. Social Content of the International Sphere: Symbols and Meaning in Franco-German Relations. Cambridge, MA: Program for the Study of Germany and Europe Working Paper 02.2. Minda de Gunzburg Center for European Studies, Harvard University.

Krotz, Ulrich. 2002b. National Role Conceptions and Foreign Policies: France and Germany Compared. Cambridge, MA: Program for the Study of Germany and Europe Working Paper 02.1. Minda de Gunzburg Center for European Studies, Harvard University.

Krotz, Ulrich. 2007. Parapublic Underpinnings of International Relations: The Franco-German Construction of Europeanization of a Particular Kind. *European Journal of International Relations* 13(3):385–417.

Krotz, Ulrich. 2009. Momentum and Impediments: Why Europe Won't Emerge as a Full Political Actor on World Stage Soon. *Journal of Common Market Studies* 47(3):555–578.

Krotz, Ulrich. 2010. Regularized Intergovernmentalism: France-Germany and Beyond (1963–2009). *Foreign Policy Analysis* 6(2):147–185.

Krotz, Ulrich. Forthcoming. *History and Foreign Policy in France and Germany.* Basingstoke and New York: Palgrave Macmillan.

Krotz, Ulrich, and Richard Maher. 2011a. International Relations Theory and the Rise of European Foreign and Security Policy. *World Politics* 63(3).

Krotz, Ulrich, and Richard Maher. 2011b. Power Shifts and Global Governance: Europe in the Post-Post-Cold War World. Unpublished manuscript, Brown University.

Krotz, Ulrich, and James Sperling. 2011. Discord and Collaboration in Franco-American Relations: What Can RoleTheory Tell Us? In *Role Theory in International Relations: Contemporary Approaches and Analyses,* edited by Sebastian Harnisch, Cornelia Frank, and Hanns W. Maull. New York: Routledge.

Kurth, James R. 1973. Why We Buy the Weapons We Do. *Foreign Policy* 11 (Summer):33–56.

Kurth, James R. 1995. A Widening Gyre: The Logic of American Weapons Procurement. In *American Foreign Policy: Theoretical Essays,* edited by G. John Ikenberry, 15–38. New York: HarperCollins.

Lane, Jan-Erik. 2001. *The Swiss Labyrinth: Institutions, Outcomes, and Redesign.* New York: Routledge.

Lavy, George. 1996. *Germany and Israel: Moral Debt and National Interest.* London: Frank Cass.

Leblond, Laurent. 1997. *Le Couple Franco-Allemand depuis 1945: Chronique d'une Relation Exemplaire.* Paris: LeMonde Editions/Marabout.

Lecacheleux, Julien. 2003. *Elaboration et Réalisation d'une Base de Données des Outillages Tigre et NH90* (Eurocopter Document). Eurocopter and EADS Company.

Le Drian, Jean-Yves. 2002 (October 10). Assemblée Nationale, Avis No. 260, Présenté au Nom de la Commission de la Défense Nationale et des Forces Armée sur le Projet de Loi de Finances pour 2003 (No. 230), edited by Assemblée Nationale. Paris: Assemblée Nationale.

Lehmbruch, Gerhard. 1987. Administrative Interesenvermittlung. In *Verwaltung und Ihre Umwelt*, edited by Adrienne Windhoff-Héritier. Opladen: Westdeutscher Verlag.

Leimbacher, Urs. 1992. *Die Unverzichtbare Allianz: Deutsch-Französische Sicherheitspolitische Zusammenarbeit 1982–1989.* Baden-Baden: Nomos.

Lignières-Cassou, Martine. 2000 (December 12). Assemblée Nationale, Rapport No. 2793: La Commission de la Défense Nationale et des Forces Armée sur les Etudes en Amont des Programme d'Armament dans les Domains de la Defense et de l'Aeronautique, edited by Assemblée Nationale. Paris: Assemblée Nationale.

Lindley, Dan. 2007. *Promoting Peace with Information: Transparency as a Tool of Security Regimes.* Princeton, NJ: Princeton University Press.

Lobell, Steven E., Norrin M. Ripsman, and Jeffrey W. Taliaferro, eds. 2009. *Neoclassical Realism, the State, and Foreign Policy.* New York: Cambridge University Press.

Louet, Henri. 1986. Rapport d'Information déposé en Application de l'Article 145 du Régle-ment par la Commission de la Défense Nationale et des Forces Armées sur la Coopération Industrielle Franco-Allemande en Matière d'Hélicoptères de Combat. Paris: Assemblée Nationale, Commission de la Défense Nationale et des Forces Armées.

Louis, William Roger, and Hedley Bull, eds. 1986. *The "Special Relationship": Anglo-American Relations since 1945.* New York: Clarendon/Oxford University Press.

Lüger, Heinz-Helmut. 1996. Zentralistische Staatsgewalt und Monarchisches Präsidialsystem? In *Frankreich Verstehen*, edited by Ernst Ulrich Große, and Heinz-Helmut Lüger. Darm-stadt: Wissenschaftliche Buchgesellschaft.

Lustick, Ian S. 1996. History, Historiography, and Political Science: Multiple Historical Records and the Problem of Selection Bias. *American Political Science Review* 90(3):605–618.

MacKenzie, Christina. 2009. On the Front Lines, Choppers Supplement Ground Convoys. *The New York Times* Online edition, June 14, 2009 (accessed May 11, 2010).

Mahoney, James, and Dietrich Rueschemeyer, eds. 2003. *Comparative Historical Analysis in the Social Sciences.* New York: Cambridge University Press.

Majza, Béatrice. 2005. *La Francophonie, Acteur des Relations Internationales.* In *Annuaire Français de Relations Internationales 2005*, Vol. 6, 539–553. Bruxelles: Bruylant.

Malraux, André. 1971. *Les Chênes Qu'on Abat.* Paris: Gallimard.

March, James G., and Johan P. Olsen. 1984. The New Institutionalism: Organizational Factors in Social Life. *American Political Science Review* 78:734–749.

March, James G., and Johan P. Olsen. 1989. *Rediscovering Institutions: The Organizational Basis of Politics.* New York: Free Press.

March, James G., and Johan P. Olsen. 1998. The Institutional Dynamics of International Politi-cal Orders. *International Organization* 52(4):943–969.

Martin, Lisa L., and Beth A. Simmons, eds. 2001. *International Institutions: An International Organization Reader.* Cambridge, MA: MIT Press.

Martini, André. 1997. L'Hélicoptère d'Attaque dans les Armées Modernes: Le Tigre Franco-Allemand. *Défense Nationale: Études Politiques-Stratégiques-Militaires-Économiques-Scientifiques* 53(February):41–54.

Marx, Patrick. 1998. Après le NH-90, Paris et Bonn Passent Commande de l'Hélicoptère de Combat Tigre, *La Tribune*, May 22, 1998, 28.

Mastanduno, Michael. 2008. Economic Statecraft Revisited. In *Foreign Policy: Theories, Actors, and Cases,* edited by Steve Smith, Amelia Hadfield, and Tim Dunne, 171–187. New York: Oxford University Press.

Mathieu, Jean-Luc. 1996. *La Défense Nationale.* Paris: Presses Universitaires de France.

Maull, Hanns W. 1990. Germany and Japan: The New Civilian Powers. *Foreign Affairs* 69(5): 91–106.

Maull, Hanns W. 1992a. Zivilmacht Bundesrepublik Deutschland: Vierzehn Thesen für eine Neue Deutsche Außenpolitik. *Europa Archiv* 47(10):269–278.

Maull, Hanns W. 1992b. Zivilmacht: Die Konzeption und ihre Sicherheitspolitische Relevanz. In *Sicherheitspolitik Deutschlands: Neue Konstellationen, Risiken, Instrumente*, edited by Wolfgang Heydrich, Joachim Krause, Uwe Nerlich, Jürgen Nötzold, and Reinhardt Rummel, 771–786. Baden-Baden: Nomos.

McIntyre, W. David. 1978. *The Commonwealth of Nations: Origins and Impact, 1869–1971*. Minneapolis: University of Minnesota Press.

McIntyre, W. David. 2009. *The Britannic Vision: Historians and the Making of the British Commonwealth of Nations, 1907–48*. New York: Palgrave Macmillan.

McKeown, Timothy. 2004. Case Studies and the Limits of the Quantitative World View. In *Rethinking Social Inquiry: Diverse Tools, Shared Standards*, edited by Henry E. Brady and David Collier, 139–167. Lanham, MD: Rowman and Littlefield.

McNamara, Kathleen. 1999. *The Currency of Ideas: Monetary Politics in the European Union*. Ithaca, NY: Cornell University Press.

Mearsheimer, John J. 1994/1995. The False Promise of International Institutions. *International Security* 19(3):5–49.

Mearsheimer, John J. 1995. A Realist Reply. *International Security* 20(1):82–93.

Mearsheimer, John J. 2001. *The Tragedy of Great Power Politics*. New York: Norton.

Metzler, Rudolf. 1983. Paris will Pilot beim Panzerkiller sein: Vor dem Bau eines Deutsch-Französischen Kampfhubschraubers sind noch viele Hürden zu Überwinden, *Süddeutsche Zeitung*, May 19,1983, 4.

Metzler, Rudolf. 1984. Bonn und Paris im Gleichschritt: Vor allem Franzosen Dringen auf Weitere Militärische Zusammenarbeit, *Süddeutsche Zeitung*, May 28, 1984, 4.

Mény, Yves. 1996. France: The Institutionalization of Leadership. In *Political Institutions in Europe*, edited by Josep M. Colomer, 99–137. New York: Routledge.

Mény, Yves. 1998. *The French Political System*. Paris: Documentation Française.

Mény, Yves. 2008. *Le Système Politique Français*. Sixth Edition. Paris: Montchrestien-Lextenso.

Meyer, John W., John Boli, George M. Thomas, and Francisco O. Ramirez. 1997. World Society and the Nation-State. *American Journal of Sociology* 103(1):144–181.

Migault, Philippe. 2002. Eurocopter Produit le Tigre en Série, *Le Figaro*, March 25, 2002, 5.

Migault, Philippe. 2003. Eurocopter Multiplie les Contrats à l'International, *Le Figaro*, September 17, 2003, 4.

Millot, Lorraine. 1996. Un Budget Allemand Dur pour la France, *Libération*, July 11, 1996, 15.

Ministère de Défense (France). 2010. L'Hélicoptère de Combat Tigre en Afghanistan. <http://www.defense.gouv.fr/terre/actualite_et_dossiers/l_helicoptere_de_combat_tigre_en_afghanistan>; (accessed May 11, 2010).

Moniac, Rüdiger. 1983a. Deutsch-Französischer Kampfhubschrauber? Verbesserte Zusammenarbeit in der Sicherheitspolitik, *Die Welt*, April 21, 1983, 8.

Moniac, Rüdiger. 1983b. Konkrete Projekte und Zukunftsmusik: Die Sicherheitspolitischen Themen des Deutsch-Französischen Gipfels in Bonn, *Die Welt*, November 24, 1983, 6.

Moniac, Rüdiger. 1987a. Bonn und Paris Bauen Gemeinsamen Hubschrauber, *Die Welt*, July 17, 1987, 8.

Moniac, Rüdiger. 1987b. Bonn und Paris setzen die Helikopter-Serie Fort, *Die Welt*, July 15, 1987, 5.

Moniac, Rüdiger. 1995. Tiger und Apache, *Die Welt*, July 15, 1995, 4.

Moravcsik, Andrew. 1991. Arms and Autarky in Modern European History. *Daedalus* 120(4):23–45.

Moravcsik, Andrew. 1993. Preferences and Power in the European Community: A Liberal Intergovernmentalist Approach. *Journal of Common Market Studies* 31(4):473–524.

Moravcsik, Andrew. 1997. Taking Preferences Seriously: A Liberal Theory of International Politics. *International Organization* 51(4):513–553.

Moravcsik, Andrew. 1998. *The Choice for Europe: Social Purpose and State Power from Messina to Maastricht.* Ithaca, NY: Cornell University Press.

Moravcsik, Andrew. 2001. Why Is U.S. Human Rights Policy So Unilateralist? In *Multilateralism and U.S. Foreign Policy: Ambivalent Engagement,* edited by Stewart Patrick and Shepard Forman, 345–376. Boulder, CO: Lynne Rienner.

Moravcsik, Andrew. 2003. Liberal International Relations Theory: A Scientific Assessment. In *Progress in International Relations Theory: Appraising the Field,* edited by Colin Elman and Miriam Fendius Elman, 159–204. Cambridge, MA: MIT Press.

Moravcsik, Andrew. 2005. The Paradox of U.S. Human Rights Policy. In *American Exceptionalism and Human Rights,* edited by Michael Ignatieff, 147–197. Princeton, NJ: Princeton University Press.

Moravcsik, Andrew. 2008. The New Liberalism. In *The Oxford Handbook of International Relations,* edited by Christian Reus-Smit and Duncan Snidal, 234–254. New York: Oxford University Press.

Nesshöver, C. and A. Rinke. 2003. Zu viel Konkurrenz statt Partnerschaft, *Handelsblatt,* December 9, 2003, 6.

Neu, Jean-Pierre. 2001. Jean-François Bigay: "Le Tigre Entame sa Carrière à l'Export," *Les Echos,* August 13, 2001, 10.

Neustadt, Richard E. 1999. *Report to JFK: The Skybolt Crisis in Perspective.* Ithaca, NY: Cornell University Press.

Niclauss, Karlheinz. 1988. *Kanzlerdemokratie.* Stuttgart: Kohlhammer.

Nonnenmacher, Günther. 1986. Jenseits der Manöver-Routine, *Frankfurter Allgemeine Zeitung,* October 6, 1986, 1.

Nonnenmacher, Günther. 1999. De Gaulles Erbe, *Frankfurter Allgemeine Zeitung,* August 12, 1999, 1.

OCCAR-EA, Central Office. 2006. *Occar-EA Business Plan 2006.* Bonn: OCCAR-EA.

Officers of the Führungsstab des Heeres im Bundesministerium der Verteidigung. 1986. Der PAH im Kampf gegen Gepanzerte Angriffstruppen. *Soldat und Technik* 29(4):210–212.

Owen, David. 1998a. France, Germany Delay Signing, *Financial Times,* December 22, 1998, 2.

Owen, David. 1998b. Tiger Order "on Time," *Financial Times,* December 26, 1998, 2.

Owen, David. 1999. France and Germany Sign Deal, *Financial Times,* June 20, 1999, 4.

Pajon, Christophe. 2006. La Coopération Militaire Franco-Allemande au Concret: Cultures, Structures et Acteurs. Paris: Centre d'Études en Sciences Sociales de la Défense. Les Documents du C2SD-No. 82 (accessible at <www.c2sd.sga.defense.gouv.fr>;).

Pallade, Yves. 2005. *Germany and Israel in the 1990s and Beyond: Still a Special Relationship?* New York: Peter Lang.

Parsons, Craig. 2006. *A Certain Idea of Europe.* Ithaca, NY: Cornell University Press.

Peiron, Denis. 2003. L'École du Tigre, "Laboratoire d'Intégration," *La Croix,* July 11, 2003, 5.

Picaper, Jean-Paul. 1987. Oui à l'Hélicoptère Franco-Allemand: Accord de Principe Franco-Allemand sur la Construction de l'Hélicoptère de Combat Commun, *Le Figaro,* March 21–22, 1987, 3.

Pierson, Paul. 2004. *Politics in Time: History, Institutions, and Social Analysis.* Princeton, NJ: Princeton University Press.

Pierson, Paul, and Theda Skocpol. 2002. Historical Institutionalism in Contemporary Political Science. In *Political Science: State of the Discipline,* edited by Ira Katznelson and Milner Helen V., 1–28. New York: Norton.

Pivet, Henry. 2001. Eurocopter Veut Équiper l'Armée de l'Air Australienne, *La Tribune,* January 4, 2001, 13.

Posen, Barry. 1984. *The Sources of Military Doctrine: France, Britain, and Germany between the World Wars.* Ithaca, NY: Cornell University Press.

Prämaßing, Stefan. 1996. Deutsch-Französische Hubschrauberentwicklung: Ein Aktueller Sachstand. *Soldat und Technik* 39(5):297–301.

Presse-und Informationsamt der Bundesregierung (Bulletin). 1987. 50. Deutsch-Französische Konsultationen in Karlsruhe am 12. und 13. November 1987. *Bulletin: Presse-und Informationsamt der Bundesregierung* (issue 126, 1987).

Presse-und Informationsamt der Bundesregierung (Bulletin). 1997. Gemeinsames Deutsch-Französisches Sicherheits-und Verteidigungskonzept: Gebilligt bei der 16. Sitzung des Deutsch-Französischen Verteidigungs-und Sicherheitsrates am 9. Dezember 1996 in Nürnberg. *Bulletin: Presse-und Informationsamt der Bundesregierung* (12/1997) (February 5, 1997):117–120.

Provost, Olivier. 1997. Après l'Industrialisation du Tigre, Eurocopter Attend pour 1998 celle du NH90, *La Tribune Desfossés,* June 23, 1997, 8.

Puhl, Detlef. 1987. Wörner und die Wünsche des Heeres, *Stuttgarter Zeitung,* July 18, 1987, 2.

Puhl, Detlef. 1996. Und die Rüstungkooperation Geht Weiter Voran, *Stuttgarter Zeitung,* November 14, 1996, 4.

Puhl, Detlef. 1997. Zugleich Partner und Konkurrenten: Vor Allem aus Geldmangel Kommen die Deutsch-Französischen Rüstungsprojekte Nicht Voran, *Stuttgarter Zeitung,* March 3, 1997, 4.

Puhl, Detlef. 1998. Türkei Kauft Hubschrauber zum "Kampf Gegen die Guerilla", *Stuttgarter Zeitung,* March 21, 1998, 1.

Ragin, Charles C. 1992. "Casing" and the Process of Social Inquiry. In *What Is a Case? Exploring the Foundations of Social Inquiry,* edited by Charles C. Ragin, and Becker Howard S., 217–226. New York: Cambridge University Press.

Ragin, Charles C., and Howard S. Becker, eds. 1992. *What Is a Case? Exploring the Foundations of Social Inquiry.* New York: Cambridge University Press.

Ravery, Jean-Pierre. 1984. Hélicoptère Franco-Allemand: Un Marché de Dupe pour la France: La RFA Risque d'être la Seule Bénéficiaire du Projet, *L'Humanité,* June 6, 1984, 8.

Ravery, Jean-Pierre. 1987. Vol de Faucons: Nouvel Accord pour un Hélicoptère Franco-Allemand, *L'Humanité,* July 18, 1987, 6.

Rémond, René. 1982. Die Verweigerte Integration: Nationalstaatliche Autonomie als Prinzip der Französischen Geschichte. In *Das Bündnis Im Bündnis: Deutsch-Französische Beziehungen Im Internationalen Spannungsfeld,* edited by Robert Picht, 21–39. Berlin: Severin und Siedler.

Reus-Smit, Christian. 1999. *The Moral Purpose of the State.* Princeton, NJ: Princeton University Press.

Risse-Kappen, Thomas. 1995. *Cooperation among Democracies: The European Influence on U.S. Foreign Policy.* Princeton, NJ: Princeton University Press.

Roland, Michel. 1995. Londres Préfère l'Apache Américain au Tigre, *La Tribune Desfossés,* July 17, 1995, 12.

Rose, Gideon. 1998. Neoclassical Realism and Theories of Foreign Policy. *World Politics* 51(1):144–172.

Rouget, Werner. 1989. Grundpositionen Französischer Außenpolitik Unter Mitterrand. In *Frankreich-Jahrbuch 1989,* edited by Deutsch-Französisches Institut et al., 67–80. Opladen: Leske and Budrich.

Roy, Joaquin and Albert Galinsoga, eds. 1997. *The Ibero-American Space.* Miami: University of Florida Press.

Rudzio, Wolfgang. 1991. *Das Politische System Der Bundesrepublik Deutschland.* Opladen: Leske and Budrich.

Ruge, Peter. 1986. Das Deutsch-Französische Projekt eines Gemeinsamen Kampfhubschraubers Steht vor dem Abbruch: Paris sieht Schwarzen Peter bei den Deutschen, *Die Welt,* June 7, 1986, 5.

Ruge, Peter. 1990. "Tiger" Setzt Maßstäbe für Kampfhubschrauber: Deutsch-Französisches Projekt übertrifft US-Konkurrenz, *Die Welt,* March 28, 1990, 7.

Ruggie, John Gerard. 1983. International Regimes, Transactions, and Change: Embedded Liberalism in the Postwar Economic Order. In *International Regimes*, edited by Stephen D. Krasner, 195–231. Ithaca, NY: Cornell University Press.

Ruggie, John Gerard, ed. 1993. *Multilateralism Matters: The Theory and Praxis of an Institutional Form*. New York: Columbia University Press.

Ruggie, John Gerard. 1997. The Past as Prologue? Interests, Identity, and American Foreign Policy. *International Security* 21(4):89–125.

Ruggie, John Gerard, ed. 1998a. *Constructing the World Polity: Essays on International Institutionalization*. New York: Routledge.

Ruggie, John Gerard. 1998b. What Makes the World Hang Together? Neo-Utilitarianism and the Social Constructivist Challenge. *International Organization* 52(4):855–885.

Ruggie, John Gerard. 1998c. Introduction: What Makes the World Hang Together? Neo-Utilitarianism and the Social Constructivist Challenge. In *Constructing the World Polity: Essays on International Institutionalization*, edited by John Gerard Ruggie, 1–39. London: Routledge.

Sabatier, Thierry. 2001a. Eurocopter Espère Vendre des Hélicoptères Militaries à l'Australie, *Le Monde*, January 11, 2001, 17.

Sabatier, Thierry. 2001b. Premier Contrat à l'Export pour le Tigre d'Eurocoper, *La Tribune*, August 13, 2001, 9.

Sagan, Scott D. 1996/97. Why Do States Build Nuclear Weapons? Three Models in Search of a Bomb. *International Security* 21(3):54–86.

Salendre, Alain. 2007. École Commune Franco-Allemande Tigre. In *Les Armées Françaises à l'Heure de l'Interamisation et de la Multinationalisation (Tome V)*, edited by Pierre Pascallon, 413–420. Paris: Harmattan.

SALSS, Sozialwissenschaftliche Forschungsgruppe GmbH. 1985. Die Zukunft der Bundeswehr: Eine Durchleuchtung der amtlichen Planung. Bonn: Report to the Board of the German Social Democratic Party (Vorstand der Sozialdemokratischen Partei Deutschlands).

Sampson, Martin W. III., and Stephen G. Walker. 1987. Cultural Norms and National Roles: A Comparison of Japan and France. In *Role Theory and Foreign Policy Analysis*, edited by Stephen G. Walker, 105–122. Durham, NC: Duke University Press.

Sauder, Axel. 1995. *Souveränität und Integration: Französische und Deutsche Konzeptionen Europäischer Sicherheit nach dem Ende des Kalten Krieges (1990–1993)*. Baden-Baden: Nomos.

Sauvaget, Jacques. 2007. L'Occar a Dix Ans. *Défense Nationale et Sécurité Collective* 64 (February):31–41.

Savignac, Jean-Charles. 1995. *Les Administrations de la France*. Paris: Masson.

Schmalz, Peter. 1997. Eurocopter Schwebt mit dem Tiger aus dem Finanzloch: Gemeinschaftsunternehmen Wächst gegen den Trend, *Die Welt*, June 14, 1997, 17.

Schmidt, Helmut. 1990. *Die Deutschen und Ihre Nachbarn*. Berlin: Siedler.

Schmidt, Manfred G. 1992. *Regieren in der Bundesrepublik Deutschland*. Opladen: Leske and Budrich.

Schmidt, Manfred G. 1996. Germany: The Grand Coalition State. In *Political Institutions in Europe*, edited by Josep M. Colomer, 62–98. New York: Routledge.

Schmidt, Max. 1994. Elemente eines Konzepts Ziviler Deutscher Außenpolitik. In *Die Zukunft der Außenpolitik: Deutsche Interessen in den Internationalen Beziehungen*, edited by Jörg Calließ and Bernhard Moltmann, 314–329. Rehburg-Loccum: Evangelische Akademie Loccum.

Schoenbaum, David. 1993. *The United States and the State of Israel*. New York: Oxford University Press.

Scholl-Latour, Peter. 1988. *Leben mit Frankreich: Stationen eines halben Jahrhunderts*. Stuttgart: Deutsche Verlags-Anstalt.

Schubert, Christian. 2010. EADS kommt auch mit dem Tiger zu spät. *Frankfurter Allgemeine Zeitung*, May 25, 2010, 16.

Schwartzbrod, Alexandra. 1998. Le Juteux Marché Turc d'Eurocopter, *Libération*, February 3, 1998, 8.

Schweigler, Gebhard. 1985. *Grundlagen der Außenpolitischen Orientierung der Bundesrepublik Deutschland: Rahmenbedingungen, Motive, Einstellungen*. Baden-Baden: Nomos.

Schweigler, Gebhard. 1996. The Legacy of History and Germany's Future Role in Internatioal Politics. Ebenhausen: Stiftung Wissenschaft und Politik.

Scott, W. Richard, and John W. Meyer, eds. 1994. *Institutional Environments and Organizations: Structural Complexity and Individualism*. Thousand Oaks, CA: Sage.

Searle, John R. 1995. *The Construction of Social Reality*. New York: Free Press.

Seibert, Thomas. 2000. Der Tiger Bleibt in Ankara auf der Strecke, *Stuttgarter Nachrichten*, March 7, 2000, 2.

Seiffert, Marc-Daniel. 2004. Les Facteur de Contingence dans les Coopérations: L'Exemple de l'Inudstrie des Hélicoptères. In *Histoire de la Coopération Européenne dans l'Armement*, edited by Jean-Paul Hébert and Jean Hamiot, 81–98. Paris: CNRS.

Sicherheitspolitik. 1986. Eine Späte Entdeckung: Die Unmögliche Einhaltung des Abkommens vom 29. Mai 1984. *Sicherheitspolitik* (2):11–14.

Simonian, Haig. 1985. *The Privileged Partnership: Franco-German Relations in the European Community 1969–1984*. New York: Oxford University Press.

Singer, J. David. 1961. The Level-of-Analysis Problem in International Relations. *World Politics* 14(October):77–93.

Smith, Michael E. 2004. *Europe's Foreign and Security Policy: The Institutionalization of Cooperation*. New York: Cambridge University Press.

Smith, Michael Joseph. 1986. *Realist Thought from Weber to Kissinger*. Baton Rouge: Louisiana State University Press.

Snyder, Glenn H. 1997. *Alliance Politics*. Ithaca, NY: Cornell University Press.

Soldat und Technik. 1991. Der Panzerabwehrhubschrauber Tiger: Programmstand und Technik. *Soldat und Technik* 34(2):100–103.

Soldat und Technik. 1995. Deutsch-Französische Rüstungskooperation: Ein Wichtiger Beitrag zur Einigung Europas. *Soldat und Technik* 38(6):327–338.

Soutou, Georges-Henri. 1996. *L'Alliance Incertaine: Les Rapports Politico-Stratégiques Franco-Allemands, 1954–1996*. Paris: Arthème Fayard.

Spain-France Forum. (2008), <http://www.thespainforum.com/f188/franco-spanish-summit-focus-illegal-immigration-rail-links-56538/>; (accessed March 3, 2009).

Srinivasan, Krishnan. 2008. *The Rise, Decline, and Future of the British Commonwealth*. New York: Palgrave Macmillan.

Stein, George. 1990. *Benelux Security Cooperation: A New European Defence Community*. Boulder, CO: Westview Press.

Steinmo, Sven. 2008. Historical Institutionalism. In *Approaches and Methodologies in the Social Sciences*, edited by Donatella Della Porta and Michael Keating, 113–138. New York: Cambridge University Press.

Steinmo, Sven, Kathleen Thelen, and Frank Longstreth, eds. 1992. *Structuring Politics: Historical Institutionalism in Comparative Politics*. New York: Cambridge University Press.

Stephens, Elizabeth. 2006. *US Policy towards Israel: The Role of Political Culture in Defining the "Special Relationship."* Portland: Sussex Academic Press.

Stützle, Walther. 1983. Ein Hubschrauber soll die Beziehungen neu Beflügeln. *Stuttgarter Zeitung*, May 21, 1983, 2.

Svendsen, Adam. 2010. *Intelligence Cooperation and the War on Terror: Anglo-American Security Relations after 9/11*. New York: Routledge.

Sverdrup, Bjørn Otto. 1994. Institutionalising Co-Operation. A Study of the Elysée Treaty and Franco-German Co-Operation 1963–1993. M.A., Department of Political Science, University of Oslo.

Szandar, Alexander. 1986. Beim Hubschrauber Steigen Nur die Kosten: Eine Deutsch-Französische Gemeinschaftsproduktion wird Nicht Abheben, *Süddeutsche Zeitung*, February 19, 1986, 4.

Taverna, Michael A. 1997. Tiger Production Award Signed, but NH-90 Proposal Delayed. *Aviation Week and Space Technology* 146(27):60–61.

Tetlock, Philip E., and Aaron Belkin, eds. 1996. *Counterfactual Thought Experiments in World Politics.* Princeton, NJ: Princeton University Press.

Thelen, Kathleen, and Sven Steinmo. 1992. Historical Institutionalism in Comparative Politics. In *Structuring Politics: Historical Institutionaism in Comparative Analysis,* edited by Sven Steinmo, Kathleen Thelen, and Frank Longstreth, 1–32. New York: Cambridge University Press.

Thies, Cameron G. 2002. A Pragmatic Guide to Qualitative Historical Analysis in the Study of International Relations. *International Studies Perspectives* 3(4):351–372.

Thomas, George M., John W. Meyer, Francisco O. Ramirez, and John Boli, eds. 1987. *Institutional Structure: Constituting State, Society, and the Individual.* Newbury Park, CA: Sage.

Thompson, William R. 2001. Identifying Rivals and Rivalries in World Politics. *International Studies Quarterly* 45(4):557–586.

Trachtenberg, Marc. 1999. *A Constructed Peace: The Making of the European Settlement, 1945– 1963.* Princeton, NJ: Princeton University Press.

Trachtenberg, Marc. 2006. *The Craft of International History: A Guide to Method.* Princeton, NJ: Princeton University Press.

Tran, Pierre (2010). France Sends 3 Tigers to Afghanistan. *Defense News* 2010, accessible at <http://www.defensenews.com/story.php?i=4210200>; (accessed May 10, 2010).

Trefz, Dagmar. 1989. Deutsch-Französische Verteidigungskooperation: Chancen und Handlungsspielräume. Unpublished manuscript, University of Heidelberg.

Tsebelis, George. 2002. *Veto Players: How Political Institutions Work.* Princeton, NJ: Princeton University Press.

U.S. Department of State. 2007. Diplomacy in Action, Bureau of Near Eastern Affairs (October), "Background Note: Israel," available at <http://www.state.gov/r/pa/ei/bgn/3581.htm>; (accessed January 12, 2009).

Vaïsse, Maurice. 1998. *La Grandeur: Politique Etrangère du Général de Gaulle 1958–1969.* Paris: Fayard.

Van Evera, Stephen. 1999. *Causes of War: Power and the Roots of Conflict.* Ithaca, NY: Cornell University Press.

Védrine, Hubert. 1996. *Les Mondes de François Mitterrand: À l'Élysée 1981–1995.* Paris: Fayard.

Vernet, Daniel. 1997. Außen-und Sicherheitspolitik. In *Les Relations Franco-Allemandes: Scène de Ménage ou Divorce?,* edited by Friedrich-Ebert-Stiftung (Bureau de Paris). Paris: Plump.

Vernet, Daniel. 1998a. Joschka Fischer, l'Européen, dans les Pas d'Helmut Kohl, *Le Monde,* October 17, 1998, 15.

Vernet, Daniel. 1998b. Une Certaine Idée de la France, *Le Monde des Livres,* February 13, 1998, 12.

von Weizsäcker, Richard. 1992. *Richard von Weizsäcker im Gespräch mit Gunter Hofmann und Werner A. Perger.* Frankfurt/M.: Eichborn.

von Weizsäcker, Richard. 1998. Un Utile Miroir Franco-Allemand, *Le Monde,* April 3, 1998, 22.

Walker, Stephen G., ed. 1987. *Role Theory and Foreign Policy Analysis.* Durham, NC: Duke University Press.

Walker, Stephen G. 2004. Role Identities and the Operational Codes of Political Leaders. In *Advances in Political Psychology,* edited by Margaret G. Hermann, 71–106. Amsterdam: Elsevier.

Wallace, William. 2005 Foreign and Security Policy: The Painful Path from Shadow to Substance. In *Policy-Making in the European Union.* Fifth Edition. Edited by Helen Wallace, William Wallace, and Mark A. Pollack, 429–456. New York: Oxford University Press.

Wallander, Celeste A. 1999. *Mortal Friends, Best Enemies: German-Russian Cooperation after the Cold War.* Ithaca, NY: Cornell University Press.

Walt, Stephen M. 1987. *The Origins of Alliances.* Ithaca, NY: Cornell University Press.

Waltz, Kenneth N. 1959. *Man, the State, and War: A Theoretical Analysis.* New York: Columbia University Press.

Waltz, Kenneth N. 1979. *Theory of International Politics.* New York: McGraw-Hill.

Weaver, Ole. 1998. Insecurity, Security, and Asecurity in the West European Non-War Community. In *Security Communities,* edited by Emanuel Adler and Michael Barnett, 69–118. New York: Cambridge University Press.

Weber, Max. 1949. "Objectivity" in Social Science and Social Policy. In *The Methodology of the Social Sciences,* edited by Max Weber, translated by Edward A. Shils and Henry A. Finch, 50–112. New York: Free Press.

Weber, Max. 1972 (1921). *Wirtschaft und Gesellschaft.* Tübingen: J.C.B. Mohr (Paul Siebeck).

Weber, Max. 1988 (1922). Die "Objektivität" Sozialwissenschaftlicher und Sozialpolitischer Erkenntnis. In *Gesammelte Aufsätze zur Wissenschaftslehre,* edited by Max Weber, 146–214. Tübingen: J.C.B. Mohr.

Wehrpolitik. 2002. Herausgegeben vom Wehr-und Sicherheitspolitischen Arbeitskreis (WPA). Roll-out des UH-Tiger, accessible at <http://www.wehrpolitik.com/noframe/april_2002/roll_out-uht_tiger.html>; (accessed March 21, 2003).

Wehrtechnik. 2003. Der Tiger: Vielseitig, Schnell und Gut Bewaffnet. *Wehrtechnik* March 2003, accessible at <http://www.wehrtechnik.net/wehrtechnik/der_tiger-helikopter.html>; (accessed June 11, 2004).

Weiand, Michael, and José d'Antin. 1995. Deutsch-Französisches Hubschrauberbüro—DFHB. *Wehrtechnik* 27(10):33–34.

Weidemann, Siggi. 1995. Luftkampf über Holland: Amerika oder Europa im Hubschrauber-Geschäft, *Süddeutsche Zeitung,* March 24, 1995, 13.

Wendt, Alexander. 1994. Collective Identity Formation and the International State. *American Political Science Review* 88(2):384–396.

Wendt, Alexander. 1999. *Social Theory of International Politics.* New York: Cambridge University Press.

Wennekers, Roland. 2001. Unterstützungshubscharuber Tiger—Neue Fähigkeiten für das Heer, accessible at <http://www.wehrpolitik.com/noframe/dezember_2001/unterstuetzungshubschrauber_tiger.ht>; (accessed March 21, 2003).

Wilsford, David. 1988. Tactical Advantages versus Administrative Heterogeneity: The Strengths and Limits of the French State. *Comparative Political Studies* 21(1):126–168.

Wohlforth, William C. 2008. Realism. In *The Oxford Handbook of International Relations,* edited by Christian Reus-Smit and Duncan Snidal, 131–149. New York: Oxford University Press.

Wolffsohn, Michael. 1993. *Eternal Guilt? Forty Years of German-Jewish-Israeli Relations.* New York: Columbia University Press.

Wouters, Jan and Maarten Vidal. 2008. Towards a Rebirth of Benelux? Working Paper No. 2 (January), Leuven Centre for Global Governance Studies, Katholieke Universiteit Leuven.

X.X.X. (Anonymous). 1990. Le Programme "Tigre." *Défense Nationale: Problèmes Politiques, Économiques, Scientifiques, Militaires* 46(May):43–47.

Zacher, Mark W., and Richard A. Matthew. 1995. Liberal International Theory: Common Threads, Divergent Strands. In *Controversies in International Relations Theory: Realism and the Neoliberal Challenge,* edited by Charles W. Kegley, 107–150. New York: St. Martin's Press.

Zakaria, Fareed. 1998. *From Wealth to Power: The Unusual Origins of America's World Role.* Princeton, NJ: Princeton University Press.

Ziebura, Gilbert. 1997. *Die Deutsch-Französischen Beziehungen seit 1945: Mythen und Realitäten.* Stuttgart: Neske.

INDEX

A-129 Mangusta helicopter, 64, 68, 151
activism, 42
Adenauer, Konrad, 9, 15, 33, 86, 200
Aérospatiale (French defense company), 130,
    218n52
    development of helicopter cell, 114
    development program with MBB, 66, 67, 71, 78,
        81, 82, 88, 89, 94, 99, 109
    production of Tiger helicopter, 134–135,
        155–156, 157
Aérospatiale S.A., 135
Afghanistan, 5, 147, 154, 174
Agusta (Italian defense company), 64, 68
Air-to-Ground Missile (AGM), 152–153
alliances, 52
Alliot-Marie, Michèle, 152
Alpha-Jet, 173
anti-tank helicopters. See combat helicopters
Apache AH 64 helicopter, 64, 68, 70, 73, 112, 116,
    122, 138, 139–140, 151, 152
Apel, Hans, 66
ARH Tigers, 151–152, 154
arms development, weapons production and, 4
arms exports, German, 104, 106, 149, 160, 161
Aron, Raymond, 28, 80, 197
ARTE (television station), 15, 34
Atlas Denel, 139
Australia, 147, 151–153, 154, 159–160, 196
authority centralization, state autonomy and,
    47–48, 49–50
autonomy
    independence and, 42
    state, 47–48, 49–50

Baden-Baden declaration, 137, 166, 202
Berlin Wall, 6, 133
Bigay, Jean-François, 138, 141, 147, 151, 155,
    157

bilateral interstate institutionalization and
    construction, 117, 124, 156, 158, 182,
    225n123
bilateral will, 84–90, 97–100
Bischoff, Manfred, 142
Blaesheim process, 31
BO 105 anti-tank helicopter, 60
Bourges, Yvon, 64, 66
British export episode, 137–140, 159–160
British Financial Times, 165
BWB (German armament acquistion office), 109,
    133–134, 148–149

China, 155
Chirac, Jacques, 33, 111, 114, 115, 124, 137, 140,
    141–143, 146, 156
Clinton, William Jefferson, 138
coalition governments, 47, 49, 123
cohabitation, 31, 47, 48, 124, 213–214n5
Cold War, 4, 5, 8, 26, 31, 53, 76, 84, 167, 174, 184,
    199
combat helicopters, 23–25
    as anti-tank weapons, 19
    first-generation, 60, 116
    how to obtain, 64–65
    as "tank killers", 18
Common Organization for Armament Cooperation
    (OCCAR), 132, 133, 137, 148, 152, 153, 155,
    157, 158, 202
constructivist-institutionalist model/perspectives,
    11, 13, 16, 28–56, 75, 99–100, 104, 120, 121,
    160, 176–177, 180–181
Conzé, Henri, 139
Croize, Jean-Paul, 165

Daimler-Benz, 135, 142, 157, 160, 164, 201
Darcourt, Pierre, 115

d'Athis, Thierry, 165
Debré-Schmidt accord, 92, 104, 150
decentralization, 49, 50, 187–188
de Gaulle, Charles, 9, 15, 33, 42, 44, 86, 144, 200
de la Mettrie, Philippe, 144
de Murville, Maurice Couve, 32
Deutsche Aerospace (DASA), 135, 142, 157, 164,
     165, 168, 201
de Villepin, Xavier, 144
domestic construction, 8, 16–17, 39–40, 214n15
   France and Germany, 40–43
   helicopter politics and French and German, 71,
     73, 74–75, 79–80, 104, 105, 120, 126–127,
     160, 162, 167, 177, 180–181, 218n42
   historical forces and, 193–194, 227nn26–27
   historical reference points, 43–44
   hypotheses, 44–46, 215–216n41
domestic institutional structures, 46
   authority centralization and state autonomy,
     47–48
   France and Germany, 48–49, 214n18
   hypotheses, 49–51
domestic politics
   interstate institutionalization and, 187–188
   liberalism and, 54–55
Dutch export episode, 137–140, 159–160

EADS (European Aeronautic Defense and Space
     Company), 152, 157, 199, 201, 202
EC/EU-centered integration, 27, 198–200
Economic and Monetary Union (EMU), 164
Eltro, 114, 130
Elysée Treaty on Franco-German Cooperation and
     Friendship, 1963, 7, 9, 14, 15, 30–31, 32, 33,
     85, 86, 90, 116, 133, 153, 158, 200
enmity, 7, 197
Eurocopter, 132, 133, 135, 138, 139, 140, 141, 142,
     143, 147, 149, 150, 153, 154, 155, 157, 162,
     199, 201–202
Eurocopter France S.A., 147
Eurocopter GmbH, 94, 110, 133, 134, 147
Eurocopter International GIE, 135, 147
Eurocopter S.A., 135, 137, 147
European Aeronautic Defense and Space Company
     (EADS), 152, 157, 199, 201, 202
European arms agency, 137
European politics and history, 198
   European integration, 198–200
   Franco-German relations, 200–201
European Union (EU), 20, 26, 150, 160, 161, 196
export episodes, Tiger, 133, 137–140, 159–163, 181
exports, arms, German, 104, 106, 149, 160, 161

"fire and forget" missiles, 3, 25, 136
Force d'Action Rapide (FAR), 89, 219n21

foreign policies, 13
Franco-German armament cooperation, 69–72,
     78–82, 95
Franco-German armament politics, 3, 4, 8, 13, 94,
     137, 158, 165–166
Franco-German Baden-Baden initiative, 137, 166,
     202
Franco-German bilateralism, 30–32
Franco-German Council for Economics and
     Finance, 182
Franco-German Defense and Security Council,
     30, 182
Franco-German Defense Council, 86
Franco-German Eurocopter S.A., 147, 160
Franco-German Helicopter Office, 133, 155, 202
Franco-German intergovernmentalism, 14–15,
     29–32, 94
"Francogermanization", 128, 207
Franco-German relations
   domestic political factors, 11, 14
   early development of anti-tank helicopters,
     59–65
   early rivalries between France and Germany, 6–7
   Elysée Treaty and, 9, 14, 30–31, 32, 33
   European politics and, 200–201
   institutionalized interstate relationship, 7–8,
     10–11, 13, 14–16, 17, 29–39
   parapublic underpinnings of, 15, 34–35
   symbolic acts, 15, 32–33
Franco-German Security and Defense
     Commission, 30, 86, 87
Franco-German summit meetings, 14, 30, 85, 86,
     87, 89–90, 94–95, 97, 116–117, 143–144,
     146, 165–166
Franco-German Youth Office, 15
Franco-Prussian War, 6
Frankfurter Allgemeine Zeitung, 145
French Defense Ministry, 150
French General Armament Delegation, 137
French Technical Direction of Aeronautic
     Constructions, 64–65

Gazelle SA 342 helicopter, 63
GEC-Bell-Textron, 139
German Budgetary Commission, 101–102
German-French Society, 68–69
German Ministry of Defense, 19, 60, 61, 100
GIE Eurocopter, Paris, 94, 109, 110
Giraud, André, 111, 112, 113, 114, 115, 117–118,
     124, 127, 128, 129, 130
Giscard d'Estaing, Valéry, 85, 86, 115
Golden Eye (movie), 3, 140

HAD version, Tiger, 152, 153, 154
Handelsblatt, 156

HAP and HAC 3G anti-tank helicopters, 92, 93,
  114, 128, 137, 144, 148, 152, 154
Heinzmann, Werner, 142
helicopters. *See* combat helicopters; Tiger combat
  helicopter program
Helmer, Jean-Yves, 146, 148, 149
hereditary enmity, 7, 197
Hernu, Charles, 87, 88, 90, 118, 173
Heseltine, Michael, 140
Hoffman, Wolfgang, 74, 111, 218n46
Holocaust, 43–44

independence and autonomy, 42
institutionalization and construction, between
  states, 29–39
institutionalized relations
  conceptualization of, 10, 11, 14–16
  between France and Germany, 7–8, 10–11, 13,
    16–17, 39–40, 174–201, 214n15
International Aeronautic Fair (ILA), 148
international institutionalization
  domestic politics and, 39–51, 187–188
  liberalism and, 55
  neoliberalism and, 53–54
  realism and, 52
international relations, national interest and,
    28–56
international relations theory, 4, 25–26, 28–56,
    187–198
interstate institutionalization, 10–11, 13, 28–39
  bilateral, 117
  construction and, 6, 28–29, 55, 117, 175, 180
  institutional logics, 38–39
  parapublic underpinnings, 15, 34–35
  realism and, 52
  regularized intergovernmentalism, 29–32
  between states, 29–39
  symbolic acts, 15, 32–33
interstate relations
  domestic construction and, 39–43
  domestic institutional structures and, 46–51
Iron Curtain, 5, 6, 26, 59, 111, 174
Israel, 196
Italian-German helicopter program, 74, 124–125,
    218n46

joint Ministerial Councils, 31
Joint Political Military Group, 196
Joxe, Pierre, 136
Juppé, Alain, 138

Kinkel, Klaus, 41
Kocs, Stephen, 68, 95
Koerner, Peter, 148

Kohl, Helmut, 15, 33, 85–86, 88, 89–90, 95, 97–98,
  102, 111, 113, 114, 116–117, 123, 130, 137,
  138, 142, 145, 146, 153, 166
Kok, Wim, 139

Länder governments, 47, 49, 144
La Tribune Desfossés, 149
League of Nations, 183, 188
Leber, Georg, 64, 66
Le Figaro, 113, 128, 141
Leimbacher, Urs, 123, 130
Le Monde, 9, 88, 118, 124
Léotard, François, 136, 137
liberalism, 51, 54–55, 127, 186–187
Libération, 114
Louet, Henri, 73–74, 79, 86, 98, 110, 118, 126,
  129, 130

Maastricht Treaty, 137, 141, 145, 163–164
Major, John, 140
Mangusta helicopters, 64, 68, 151
Martin-Marietta, 64, 65, 68, 96, 100, 123
Martre, Henri, 134–135, 155–156, 157
MBB, (German defense company), 201, 218n31
  development of helicopter cell, 114
  development program with Aérospatiale, 66, 67,
    71, 78, 81, 82, 88, 89, 94, 99, 109
  (potential) German-Italian helicopter program,
    64, 68, 69, 74
  helicopter program difficulties, 111, 125, 130
  production of Tiger helicopter, 134–135, 157,
    160, 164
Memorandum of Understanding, 1984 (MoU), 84,
    90–91, 108, 157, 180
  execution of helicopter program, 93–94
  stipulations and specifications, 91–92, 101, 109,
    110, 111, 114, 119, 219n34
  unresolved vision and targeting issue, 93
Mendès-France, Pierre, 128
Metzler, Rudolf, 87–88
military force, 41
Millon, Charles, 139, 140, 143, 147–148, 153, 165
missiles
  air-to-air and air-to-surface, 61, 64, 136, 153
  air-to-ground, 152–153
  anti-tank, 60–61, 63
  "fire and forget", 3, 25, 136
  first-generation, 25
  HOT, 60, 63, 78, 92, 136, 147
  second-generation, 25, 60–61
  third-generation, 25, 60–61, 63, 116, 147
  Trigat AC3G-LP, 147, 152
Mitterrand, François, 15, 33, 42, 44, 68, 85, 86, 88,
    97–98, 111, 113, 114, 134, 153
Mitterrand, Jacques, 68–69

Moniac, Rüdiger, 87
Motoren Turbinen Union, German (MTU), 92, 94
MTU, 114
multilateral EC/EU-centered integration, 198–200

National Aircraft and Aerospace Company
    (SNIAS). *See* Aérospatiale (French defense
    company)
national interest, 12, 13
    international relations and, 28–56
national security issue, Tiger as, 19
neoliberal institutionalism, 51, 53–54, 72, 99, 125,
    127, 160, 185–186
    rationalist institutionalists and, 53–54, 72, 81
Neue Züricher Zeitung, 128–129
New Zealand, 196
night vision system. *See* targeting and night vision
    system (TADS/PNVS)
North Atlantic Treaty Organization (NATO), 19,
    20
    forward defense doctrine, 59, 60, 61, 76
    French nonparticipation in, 80
    German domestic construction and, 104, 177
    member states in, 160, 161, 162
    Turkey and, 150

OCCAR (Common Organization for Armament
    Cooperation), 132, 133, 137, 148, 152, 153,
    155, 157, 158, 202

PAH-1 anti-tank helicopter, 60, 116
PAH-2 anti-tank helicopter, 92, 96, 114, 116, 128,
    167
PAH-2 Tiger, 136–137, 167
parapublic underpinnings, of international
    relations, 15, 28, 34–35
particularistic interests, 50
Plückthun, Heinz, 135
policies, 12–13
political authority centralization, 47–48, 49–50
political parties, German, 74, 116, 123, 183
political realism, 51, 52–53
polyvalent combat helicopter, 60, 62, 63, 104, 148,
    152, 176–177
Portillio, Michael, 139
Puhl, Detlef, 166

Quilès, Paul, 111

rapprochement, 7
rationalist institutionalists, 106
    neoliberalism and, 53–54, 72, 81

Ravery, Jean-Pierre, 95, 220n52
realism, 51, 52–53, 76, 120–121, 124, 159–160,
    163, 184–185
regularized intergovernmentalism, 28, 29–32
Reith, Peter, 151
Richard, Alain, 148, 149, 158
Rifkind, Malcolm, 139
Rühe, Volker, 136, 137, 142, 143, 145, 147–148,
    153, 158, 164–165

Scharping, Rudolf, 149
Schmidt-Debré Accord, 1972, 92, 104, 150
Schmidt, Helmut, 85, 86, 102, 183
Schöhnbohm, Jörg, 136, 139
Schröder, Gerhard, 149
Siemens, 100, 123, 127
Simon, Gunnar, 148
SNIAS (National Aircraft and Aerospace Company).
    See Aérospatiale (French defense company)
Sobotta, Siegfried, 138, 139
social constructivism, 5, 29–46, 211n5
Social Scientific Study Group (SALSS), 74
Société National Industrielle Aérospatiale
    (SNIAS). *See* Aérospatiale (French defense
    company)
society-rooted inside-out liberalism, 51, 54–55,
    106, 160
sociological institutionalism, 192–193, 227n21
Spain, 147, 151–153, 157, 158, 159–160, 196
Speidel, Hans, 144
state arming, 189–190
state autonomy, 47–48, 49–50, 187–188
state strength, 48, 49, 50, 101, 121, 127, 182, 183,
    190–191
Switzerland, 188, 194–195
symbolic acts and practices, 15, 32–33
Szandar, Alexander, 111, 122

targeting and night vision system (TADS/PNVS),
    24, 25, 62–63, 64, 65, 67, 68, 73, 80
    European components for, 114
    French production of its own, 62, 114,
        125–126
    as issue in MoU, 93, 96, 100–101, 102, 103, 104,
        105, 106, 107
    outcome of 1987, 125–126, 127
Thomson CSF, 107, 114, 130
Tiger combat helicopter program, 3–4, 5, 8, 13,
    132–133, 201–203
    A-129 Mangusta helicopter, 64, 68, 151
    Apache AH 64 helicopter, 64, 68, 70, 73, 112,
        116, 122, 138, 139–140, 151, 152
    ARH Tigers, 151–152, 154
    armament and missions of, 25
    armament cooperation, 69–72, 78–82

becoming reality, 147–155
bilateral will, 84–90, 97–100
BO 105 helicopter, 60
budgetary pressures, 140–146
costs and delays, 19, 111–112, 120, 121–122, 125–127, 135–136, 205–207
deadlock and near cancellation of, 109–112, 119–125
definition phase failure, 66–69, 79, 218n31
difficulties with, 108–131
early development of new-generation anti-tank helicopters, 59–65, 72–78
export episodes, 133, 137–140, 159–163
first combat missions, 5, 147, 154, 174
fixed-price contracts, 117–118, 130, 145
Gazelle SA 342 helicopter, 63
HAP and HAC 3G helicopters, 92, 93, 114, 128, 137, 144, 148, 152, 154
HAP and HAD versions, 152, 153, 154
history and cases, 20–22
how to obtain combat helicopters, 64–65
hypotheses, 176–185
implementation and export skirmishes, 133–137
Memorandum of Understanding, 84, 90–94, 108
names, 207–209
national security and, 19
outcomes between 1974 and 1982, 72–82
outcomes between 1982 and 1984, 97–107
outcomes between 1984 and 1987, 119–130
outcomes between 1988 and 2009, 159–168, 177–180
PAH-1 helicopter, 60, 116
PAH-2 helicopter, 92, 96, 114, 116, 128, 136–137, 167
phases of development and production, 207–209
pilots training and mechanics schools, 153–154, 155, 156, 157, 158–159, 202
political processes between 1984 and 1987, 117–119
polyvalent helicopter, 60, 62, 63, 104, 148, 152, 176–177
processes and implications of, 155–159
processes and outcomes of, 172–176
production, 147–149, 154–155, 156, 207–209
re-inauguration of program, 84–107
revival and revamping of, 112–117, 121–125
second-generation, 23–25, 63, 65
survivability, 24, 25, 60, 61
tandem seating issue, 62, 91, 101, 114, 116

Tigers for Australia and Spain, 151–153, 159–160
Tigers for Turkey, 149–151, 161–163
"two battles" concept and, 80, 218n51
UH-Tiger, 136–137, 148, 154, 167
Treaty on Franco-German Cooperation and Friendship, 1963, 7, 9, 14, 15, 30–31, 32, 33, 85, 86, 90, 116, 133, 153, 158, 200
Trefz, Dagmar, 79
Trillo, Federico, 152
Turboméca, French (engine design company), 92, 94, 114
Turkey, 147, 149–151, 161–163, 181
"two battles" concept, French military and, 80, 218n51

UH-Tiger, 136–137, 148, 154, 167
unilateralism, 41
unionists, French, 142, 144
United Nations (UN), 188
United States
    American Apache helicopters, 64, 68, 70, 73, 112, 116, 122, 138, 139–140, 151, 152
    political system, 183, 187–188, 194–195

Védrine, Hubert, 42
Vogler, Willi, 138
von Weizsäcker, Richard, 41

Waigel, Theo, 141, 145
Warsaw Pact, 19, 26, 122, 124, 127, 133, 167, 199
Warsaw Pact tanks, 5, 18, 19, 59, 76, 104, 122, 167
weapons production, arms development and, 4
Weber, Max, 28
Wendt, Alexander, 193
Wilson, Woodrow, 183, 188
world politics and international relations theory, 187
    historical forces, 190–196
    interstate institutionalization and domestic politics, 187–188
    loose coupling of different historical forces, 188–189
    state arming, 189–190
    view of history, 196–198
World War I, 183, 188
World War II, 7, 43–44
Wörner, Manfred, 87, 88, 90, 111, 112, 113, 114, 115–116, 117, 118, 128, 129, 130, 173